QuickBooks®
Fundamentals Learning
Guide 2012

For QuickBooks Pro and Premier Version 2012

Copyright © 2011

Product Name	QuickBooks Fundamentals Learning Guide 2012
	ISBN# 978-1-57338-114-7

Developed and Written By

Douglas Sleeter

Contributing Authors, Testers, and Reviewers

Deborah Pembrook
Pat Carson
David Horwitz
Joy Prado

Table of Contents

Preface

This guide introduces you to QuickBooks—Intuit's easy-to-use, powerful accounting systems for small businesses. The guide contains 14 lessons including a final business scenario.

This guide is designed to teach you how to use many of the features available in QuickBooks Financial Software for Windows. The main focus of this guide is on how to use the features in QuickBooks Premier, but most exercises can be completed using QuickBooks Pro. This guide does not cover how to use the features in QuickBooks Online Edition or QuickBooks Pro for Mac.

While this guide does not specifically address how to use QuickBooks Enterprise Solutions, many of the procedures described in the guide will work with Enterprise Solutions editions. If you restore the exercise file using a QuickBooks Enterprise Solutions product, QuickBooks walks you through the file update process that is necessary for Enterprise Solutions to be able to read the file.

The step-by-step instructions and screen captures in this guide were created with QuickBooks Premier General Business 2012. Your screens may differ, and some instructions may vary slightly, if you are using a different edition.

Using This Book

Throughout this book, you will find tips on how to set up and use QuickBooks so that you and your company have the information you need to make business decisions.

Each chapter covers how to manage a general part of your business. To allow you to learn the chapters in any order, each chapter uses a separate QuickBooks data file that you can use with QuickBooks to complete the practice lessons in the chapter.

Academy Photography, Inc. is the model company used throughout the chapters. By performing the in-chapter practices, students gain a hands-on experience with the topics discussed in the chapter, which are based on the day-to-day operations of this small corporation.

Each chapter is designed to aid understanding by providing a list of objectives, numerous hands-on tutorial practices, key terms, the "accounting behind the scenes," and many extra notes. The illustrated text includes step-by-step instructions with hands-on computer exercises to provide you with practical experience.

The end-of-chapter applications include multiple choice questions and real-world problems that require you to perform tasks with the software. In the final chapter, the Horizon Business Scenario is a summary problem covering topics from all the chapters in this book.

Integrating QuickBooks with other products

If you plan to use the Microsoft Office integration features available in QuickBooks, such as exporting to Excel, you will need to have Microsoft® Office 2000, 2002, 2003, 2007, or 2010 installed on your system. QuickBooks Statement Writer (not used in this book) integrates QuickBooks Premier Accountant with Microsoft Excel 2003, 2007, and 2010.

Using QuickBooks Premier Student Trial

QuickBooks Premier Accountant 2012 Student Trial is a full-featured version of QuickBooks that is included with this guide. You can install it on your computer and use it to complete the exercises in this guide and to practice using QuickBooks.

To install QuickBooks Premier Accountant 2012, insert the software CD into your computer and follow the on-screen instructions. You will be required to register this copy of QuickBooks using the Product Number and License Number printed on the yellow sticker that is adhered to the software sleeve.

You can use this product for 140 days after installation.

Toggling between QuickBooks editions

We've provided you with QuickBooks Premier Accountant because this software gives you the ability to toggle among different QuickBooks editions. QuickBooks Premier Accountant allows you to switch to each of the QuickBooks Premier industry-specific editions—as well as to QuickBooks Pro. This offers you the ability to experience the full spectrum of features available to support different industries, such as construction, non-profit, or retail.

However, the exercises are designed for QuickBooks Premier General Business, and some screenshots will not match your screen unless you switch to the General Business edition.

> Note:
> QuickBooks does not support integrated applications while in toggle mode.
> Close any applications that share data with QuickBooks before toggling.

To switch to a General Business Edition:

Step 1.   From the *File* menu, choose **Toggle to Another Edition**.

Step 2.   When prompted, choose the **Premier Edition (General Business)** and then click **Next**.

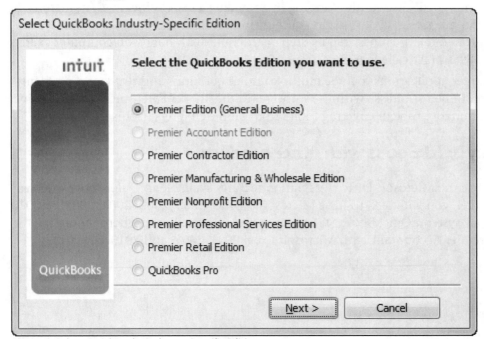

Figure 1 Select QuickBooks Industry-Specific Edition

Step 3.   Confirm the edition of QuickBooks to switch to and click **Toggle**.

Step 4.   Read any messages and click **OK**. QuickBooks closes and reopens as the edition you selected. Once reopened, the application title bar shows that you are running QuickBooks Accountant configured as the current open edition, for example *QuickBooks Premier 2012 (via Accountant Edition)*.

Step 5.   When you are done, go to the *File* menu and choose **Toggle to Another Edition** to return to QuickBooks Premier Accountant Edition.

About the exercise file

Exercise file are used with the chapters and problems throughout this book. For each lesson and problem in this guide, you'll restore a copy of the exercise file named in the beginning of the section, and use that file to complete the lesson. This means that at the start of each lesson, you'll be restoring a new file. It is very important to be in the correct file to ensure that your screen will match the book's screenshots.

Installing the exercise file

The exercise files for the chapters and problems have been provided on the CD that accompanied this book. To install the files on your hard drive, follow these steps:

Step 1.   Insert the CD and navigate to the exercise file location.

Step 2.   Copy the files to the desired location on your local system.

                  If you are using a computer in a classroom or lab environment, ask your instructor for the proper location to store your exercise files.

Step 3.   Eject and retain the CD containing the exercise files.

> **Important:**
> The Classroom Files are in QuickBooks Portable File Format. You cannot open these files by double-clicking them. For more on how to begin using these files, see page 8.

Restoring exercise files

Each chapter uses a separate practice file (e.g., Intro-12.QBW) for performing the in-chapter practices. In order to open this file, you must "restore" it as described in the first chapter (see page 8).

In the beginning of each chapter, the *Restore This File* instruction (see example below) instructs you to restore the practice file for that chapter to use with the computer practice lessons.

Example *Restore this file* instruction:

> **Restore this File**
>
> This chapter uses XXXXXXXXXXX-12.QBW. To open this file, restore the XXXXXXXXXXX -12.QBM file to your hard disk. See page 10 for instructions on restoring files.

The lessons are identified throughout the book with the words **COMPUTER PRACTICE**.

In some cases, concepts are presented in step form, but are not intended to be performed in your data file. In this case, you'll see a note at the top of the section that says:

> **DO NOT PERFORM THESE STEPS NOW. THEY ARE FOR REFERENCE ONLY.**

For these sections, you should look through and understand the material, but you should not enter any of the data in your practice file.

Certification

This book is excellent preparation for the QuickBooks User Certification Exam. This certification validates your QuickBooks knowledge. After successfully completing the exam, you will become an Intuit QuickBooks Certified User. For more information and for locations of testing centers, visit http://www.certiport.com/quickbooks.

Acknowledgements

I'd like to extend my heartfelt thanks to the co-authors, consultants, copy editors and contributors who have worked on all of our college textbooks over the years. Many people have put their head and their heart into each edition. All of you have improved and enhanced this textbook and I offer my gratitude.

This year's update was managed by The Sleeter Group's Manager of Educational Products, Deborah Pembrook. Updating this textbook is a labor of love for Deborah and I hope you see this reflected on the following pages.

My sincere thanks also goes to Pat Carson, David Horwitz, Joy Prado and Sheetal Reddy who all contributed to this book. Thank you for being such valued part of bringing this book into being.

I also want to thank everyone on the Intuit Team, including Donna Ohman, Trae Harris and Lisa Schwartz.

We all hope you enjoy *QuickBooks Fundamentals Learning Guide 2012*.

Doug Sleeter
Pleasanton, CA
November, 2011

Chapter 1
Introducing
QuickBooks

Objectives

In this chapter, you will learn about the following:

- An overview of the QuickBooks product line (page 1)
- Some of the basic principles of accounting (page 2)
- The accounting behind the scenes in QuickBooks (page 4)
- An overview of QuickBooks data files and types (page 6)
- Opening portable files (page 8)
- How to restore backup files (page 10)
- Entering transactions in QuickBooks (page 16)
- QuickBooks user interface features (page 22)
- About QuickBooks help and support (page 26)

QuickBooks is one of the most powerful tools you will use in managing your business. In addition to being a robust bookkeeping program, QuickBooks is a *management tool*. When set up and used properly, QuickBooks allows you to track and manage income, expenses, bank accounts, receivables, inventory, fixed assets, payables, loans, payroll, billable time, and equity in your company. It also provides you with detailed reports that are essential to making good business decisions. Throughout this book, you will learn in detail about most of the features in QuickBooks.

QuickBooks helps small business owners run their businesses efficiently without worrying about the debits and credits of accounting entries. However, to use QuickBooks effectively, you still need to understand how QuickBooks is structured, how its files work, how to navigate in the system to do tasks, and how to retrieve information about your business. In this chapter you will explore the world of accounting and then you'll learn some of the basics of the QuickBooks program.

The QuickBooks Product Line

The QuickBooks family of products is designed to be easy to use, while providing a comprehensive set of accounting tools including general ledger, inventory, accounts receivable, accounts payable, sales tax, and financial reporting. In addition, a variety of optional, fee-based payroll services, merchant account services, and other add-on products integrate with the QuickBooks software.

QuickBooks Editions

The QuickBooks product line includes four separate product editions: *QuickBooks Online, QuickBooks Pro, QuickBooks Premier,* and *QuickBooks Enterprise Solutions.* The *Premier* and *Enterprise Solutions* editions are further broken down into six industry-specific editions for *Accounting Professionals, Contractors, Manufacturers/Wholesalers, Nonprofit Organizations, Professional Services,* and *Retailers.* All editions of QuickBooks support multiple users, however, each user must have the same version of QuickBooks to access the file.

This book covers the features and usage of *QuickBooks Pro* and *Premier (non-industry specific),* since most small businesses will use one of these editions. Also, once you learn how to use one of these editions, you'll be prepared to use *any* of the other editions, with the exception of the online edition. The online edition is a web-based software product, with different, yet similar features to the editions covered in this book. For a comparison of all editions and options, see www.quickbooks.com.

QuickBooks Releases

Occasionally, errors are found in the QuickBooks software after the product is released for sale. As errors are discovered, Intuit fixes the problem and provides program "patches" via the Internet. Each patch increases the **Release Level** of the QuickBooks application. To see what release level of the software you have, press **Ctrl+1** (or **F2**) while QuickBooks is running. At the top of the window, you will see the QuickBooks product information including the release level.

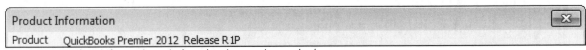

Figure 1-1 *Product information window showing version and release*

This book is based on QuickBooks Premier 2012 release R6P. If you have a newer (higher) release, you may see some slight differences compared to the screens in this book, but most likely you won't see any differences.

To patch your software with the latest maintenance release, download this release by selecting the *Help* menu and then selecting **Update QuickBooks.** Follow the instructions on these screens to download and install maintenance releases in QuickBooks via the Internet.

Accounting 101

Before we begin learning how to use QuickBooks, let's look at some of the background and key concepts of the accounting process.

Accounting's Focus

Accounting's primary concern is the accurate recording and categorizing of transactions so that you can produce reports that accurately portray the financial health of your organization. Put another way, accounting's focus is on whether your organization is succeeding and how well it is succeeding.

The examples in this book are about a *for-profit* company called Academy Photography, but similar needs for information and tracking rules apply to *not-for-profit organizations.*

The purpose of accounting is to serve management, investors, creditors, and government agencies. Accounting reports allow any of these groups to assess the financial position of the organization relative to its debts (liabilities), its capabilities to satisfy those debts and continue operations (assets), and the difference between them (net worth or equity).

The fundamental equation (called the *Accounting Equation*) that governs all accounting is:

Assets = Liabilities + Equity, or Equity = Assets - Liabilities.

Accounts, Accounts, Everywhere Accounts

Many factors go into making an organization work. Money and value are attached to everything that is associated with operating a company — cash, equipment, rent, utilities, wages, raw materials, merchandise, and so on. For an organization to understand its financial position, business transactions need to be recorded, summarized, balanced, and presented in reports according to the rules of accounting.

Business transactions (e.g., sales, purchases, operating expense payments) are recorded in several types of *ledgers*, called accounts. The summary of all transactions in all ledgers for a company is called the *General Ledger*. A listing of every account in the General Ledger is called the *Chart of Accounts*.

Each account summarizes transactions that increase or decrease the *equity* in your organization. The figure below shows a general picture of the effect your accounts have on the equity of your organization. Some accounts (those on the left) increase equity when they are increased, while others (those on the right) decrease equity when they are increased.

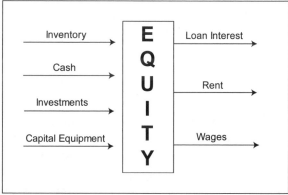

So let's return to the Accounting Equation. To understand the accounting equation, consider the following statement. **Everything a company owns was purchased by funds from creditors or by the owner's stake in the company.**

Account Types and Financial Reports

Each account in the general ledger has a type, which describes what kind of business transaction is stored in that account. There are primarily five types of accounts: asset, liability, equity, income, and expense. Assets, liabilities, and equity accounts are associated with the **Balance Sheet** report which is used to analyze the net worth of a business. The income and expense accounts are associated with the **Profit and Loss** report (also called Income Statement) which is used to analyze the operating profit or loss for a business over a specific time range (month, quarter, year, etc.).

The Balance Sheet report preserves the fundamental accounting equation - **Total assets always equal the total liabilities plus equity**, between the accounts. This means that the total of the assets (which represent what the company "owns") is always equal to the sum of the liabilities (representing what the company owes) plus the equity (representing the owner's interest in the company). Although income and expense accounts are not directly shown in the accounting equation, they do affect this equation via the equity account as shown below.

The income and expenses are tracked throughout the year as business transactions occur and are totaled at the end of the year to calculate Net Income (or Loss). **Net income (total revenues minus total expenses) increases the owner's equity in the business, and net loss (when expenses exceed revenues) decreases the owner's equity in the business.** Thus the Income and Expense accounts indirectly affect the Equity component of the Accounting Equation of Assets = Liabilities + Equity, where **Equity increases or decreases each year depending on whether the year's income exceeds expenses or not.**

At the end of the year, the balance of each income and expense account is reset to zero so these accounts can track the next year's transactions.

Double-Entry Accounting

Double-entry accounting is the technique that makes the Accounting Equation work. It divides each account into two sides. One side is a record of transactions that increase the account and the other side is a record of all transactions that decrease the account. One side (the left side) is for debits, and the other (the right side) is for credits. Depending on the type of account, a debit might increase the account or decrease it. The same is true of credits. Therefore, debits are not always bad and credits are not always good. They are just part of the system of accounting. However, the rule of double-entry accounting is that **total debits must always equal total credits.** Every transaction creates a debit in one or more accounts and a credit in one or more accounts. If the debits and credits for any transaction are not equal, the transaction has an error or is incomplete.

Accounting Behind the Scenes

Recording and categorizing all of your business transactions into the proper accounts, summarizing and adjusting them, and then preparing financial statements can be an enormous, labor-intensive task without the help of a computer and software. This is where QuickBooks comes in. QuickBooks focuses on ease of use and hiding accounting details. To make all this possible, QuickBooks uses components like accounts, items, forms, registers, and lists, which are discussed later in the chapter. Familiar-looking forms such as invoices, checks, and bills are used for data entry. As you enter data in forms, QuickBooks handles the accounting entries for you. Thus business owners can use QuickBooks to efficiently run a business without getting bogged down with the debits and credits of accounting entries.

QuickBooks also handles double-entry for you. Every transaction you enter in the program automatically becomes a debit to one or more accounts and a credit to one or more other accounts, and QuickBooks won't let you record the transaction until the total of the debits equals the total of the credits. This means you can create reports that show the transactions in the full double-entry accounting format whenever you need them, allowing you to focus on the business transaction rather than the debits and credits in the General Ledger.

Cash or accrual method, as discussed in the next section, is handled in QuickBooks as a simple reporting option. You can create reports for either cash or accrual basis regardless of the method you use for taxes.

As the book introduces new transactions types (e.g., Invoices, Bills, or Checks), the text will include a section called "The accounting behind the scenes." For example, when you first learn about invoices you will see the following message:

> **The accounting behind the scenes:**
> When you create an **Invoice**, QuickBooks increases (with a debit) **Accounts Receivable** and increases (with a credit) the appropriate **income** account. If applicable, **Invoices** and **Sales Receipts** also increase (with a credit) the sales tax liability account.

Letting QuickBooks handle the accounting behind the scenes means you can focus on your organization and identify the important factors that will help you succeed. Once you identify these factors, you can use QuickBooks to monitor them and provide information that will guide you in managing your operations.

Accounting for the Future: Cash or Accrual?

Another critical aspect of accounting is managing for the future. Many times, your organization will have assets and liabilities that represent money owed to the company, or owed to others by the company, but are not yet due. For example, you may have sold something to a customer and sent an invoice, but the payment has not been received. In this case, you have an outstanding *receivable*. Similarly, you may have a bill for insurance that is not yet due. In this case, you have an outstanding *payable*.

An accounting system that uses the *accrual basis* method of accounting tracks these receivables and payables and uses them to evaluate a company's financial position. The *accrual basis* method specifies that revenues and expenses are *recognized* in the period in which the transactions occur, rather than in the period in which cash changes hands. So to help you manage the future and to more accurately reflect the true profitability of the business in each period, assets, liabilities, income, and expenses are entered when you know about them, and they are used to identify what you need on hand to meet both current, and known, future obligations.

In the *cash basis* method, revenues and expenses are not *recognized* until cash changes hands. So revenue is recognized when the customer pays, and an expense is recognized when you pay the bill for the expense. In most cash basis systems, you must use an outside system to track open invoices and unpaid bills, which means you cannot view both cash and accrual reports without going to several places to find information. However, in QuickBooks, you can record transactions such as invoices and bills to facilitate *accrual basis* reporting, and you can create *cash basis* reports that remove the receivables and payables with the same system.

Although certain types of organizations can use the cash basis method of accounting (many are not allowed to do so under IRS regulations), the accrual method provides the most accurate picture for managing your organization. You should check with your tax accountant to determine which accounting method — cash or accrual — is best for you.

Academy Photography Sample Company

Throughout this book, you will see references to a fictitious company called Academy Photography. Academy Photography is a photography studio that also sells camera equipment. This company uses QuickBooks for its accounting and business management. Academy Photography may not be exactly like your business; however, the examples in this text that focus on Academy Photography are generic enough to guide you on your own use of QuickBooks.

Academy Photography has two locations, one in San Jose and another in Walnut Creek. In order for management to separately track revenue and expenses for each store, Academy Photography uses **Classes** in QuickBooks. As you proceed through the book, you'll see how each transaction (bill, check, invoice, etc.) is tagged with what *Class* it belongs to, so that later you can create reports like Profit & Loss by Class. Classes can be used to separately track departments, profit centers, store locations, or funds in any business.

Academy Photography also needs to separately track revenue and expenses for each job it performs. When a customer orders a photo shoot, Academy Photography needs to track all of the revenue and expenses specifically related to that job so it can look back and see how profitable the job was. This concept is called *job costing*, and many different businesses need to track jobs in similar ways.

As you think through the examples with Academy Photography, ask yourself what parallels you see to your own organization. Certainly, areas such as salaries, supplies, equipment, and others will be appropriate for your setup, but the names and specifics of the accounts, items, lists, and forms will probably be different.

About QuickBooks Files

Before using QuickBooks, it is important for you to understand how QuickBooks files are structured and used. QuickBooks has three primary types of files described below. In the filename the letters after the dot (.) are referred to as the file extension and are used by Microsoft Windows to associate files with the appropriate application program. All file types can be opened using the *Open or Restore Company* option from the *File* menu.

1. *Working Data Files* – These files are used to enter transactions and create reports. The file extension for these files is **.QBW**.
2. *Portable Company Files* –These files are a compact version of the company data files and are used to transport the file between computers or send as an email attachment. The file extension for these files is **.QBM**. These files should never be used to back up your QuickBooks data. These files must be "Restored" to a working data file to be used.
3. *Backup Files* –These files are a compressed version of the company data files and are used as backup to safeguard the information. The file extension for these files is **.QBB**. These files cannot be used directly within QuickBooks and must be "Restored" to working data file format.

This means, if you name your company file ABC, QuickBooks will store the working data file on disk as "ABC.QBW." When you back up your company file using the QuickBooks Backup function, QuickBooks will store your backup file with the name "ABC.QBB." If you create a portable data file using the QuickBooks Portable file creation function, the portable file "ABC.QBM" will be created and stored on the disk.

> **Important:**
> Each file type has a specific purpose and should be used accordingly. Working data files are used to enter data and run reports, backup files are used to safeguard the data, and portable files are compressed files used to transport data via the Internet where smaller files transfer faster.

Creating a New File

There are two ways to create a new QuickBooks file, *Express Start* and *Advanced Setup*. Although it is possible to create a QuickBooks file relatively quickly using *Express Start*, we recommend utilizing a 12-Step process for creating a file to properly set up accounts and account balances. We have placed the chapter that explains file setup later in the book so you will be able to utilize knowledge gained in earlier chapters. You can learn more about file setup in our File Setup chapter starting on page 365.

Opening a QuickBooks Sample File

For learning purposes, QuickBooks provides sample data files that allow you to explore the program. To open a sample data file, follow these steps:

COMPUTER PRACTICE

Step 1.   Launch the QuickBooks program by double-clicking the icon on your desktop or selecting it from the Windows Start menu.

Step 2.   When QuickBooks opens, you will either see the *No Company Open* window (Figure 1-2) or the *last working data file* used.

No Company Open window is displayed if you are opening QuickBooks for the first time or if you closed the working data file *before* exiting in your last session. By default, the last working data file used will open, if you closed the QuickBooks *program* before closing the *file*.

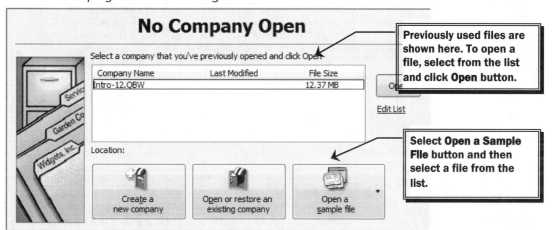

Figure 1-2 No Company Open window

Step 3.   If you don't see the *No Company Open* window (Figure 1-2), select the **File** menu, and then select **Close Company**. Click **No** if you are prompted to back up your file.

Step 4.   Click **Open a Sample file** button (Figure 1-2) and select one of the files from the list. The selected sample file will open with the *QuickBooks Information* screen (Figure 1-3).

Step 5.   Click **OK** to continue.

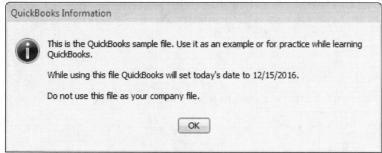

Figure 1-3 Sample File Information Screen

Step 6.   The sample file you selected will open and then the Overview & Setup screen (Figure 1-4) may be displayed. This appears by default when you open a file; however, if you do not want to see it appear next time you open *this* file, you can uncheck the *Show this window at startup* box.

You can work with the tutorials available on this window to become familiar with the QuickBooks program. After you are done, close this window by clicking the *Go to QuickBooks* button at the bottom right corner of the window.

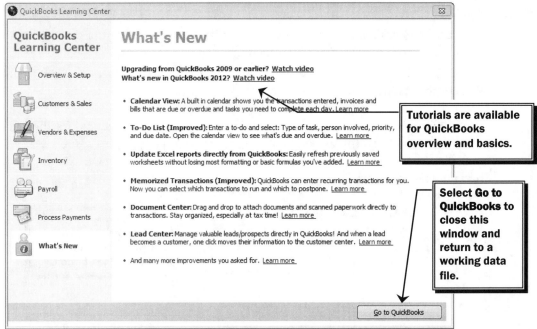

Figure 1-4 Welcome to QuickBooks Screen

Opening Portable Company Files

Portable Company Files are compact company data files that can be easily transported. The exercise files that accompany this book are Portable Company Files. You will need to open these exercise files at the start of each chapter and each problem.

> When you move a data file from one computer (computer A) to another (computer B), any data you enter on computer B will cause the file on the computer A to become "obsolete." That is, the file on computer B has new data and there is no way to transfer that new data into the file on computer A, except by manually entering the data or by replacing the whole file on computer A with the new file. Therefore, when you copy data files from one computer to another, you cannot continue to work on the file in both places.

COMPUTER PRACTICE

To open portable files follow the steps below.

Step 1.   Select the **Open or Restore Company** option from the *File* menu (see Figure 1-5).

Figure 1-5 Open or Restore Company

Step 2.   QuickBooks displays the *Open or Restore Company* window. Select **Restore a portable file (.QBM)** and click **Next**.

Figure 1-6 Open or Restore Company window

Step 3.   QuickBooks displays the *Open Portable Company File* window (see Figure 1-7). Navigate to the location of your exercise files. You may need to ask your instructor if you do not know this location. Once you are viewing the contents of correct folder, select **Intro-12.QBM** and click **Open**.

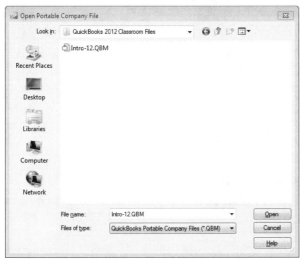

Figure 1-7 Open Portable Company File window

Step 4.   Next you will need to tell QuickBooks where to save the working file that will be created from the portable file (see Figure 1-8). Click **Next** in the *Open or Restore Company* window to continue.

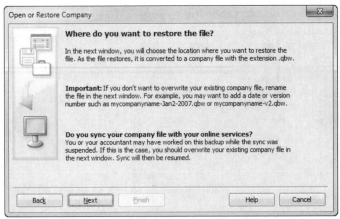

Figure 1-8 Open or Restore Company Location

Step 5.   The *Save Company File as* window displays (see Figure 1-9). Ask your instructor or choose a location to save the file. When you have navigated to the appropriate folder, click **Save**.

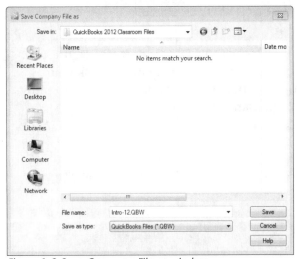

Figure 1-9 Save Company File as window

Step 6.   If asked to update your company files, click **Yes**.

Step 7.   Once the Intro-12.QBW company file finishes opening, you will see the Home page.

Restoring Backup Files

When working with important financial information, creating backup files is a crucial safeguard against data loss. Every business should conduct regular backups of company information. QuickBooks has useful tools to automate this process.

In the event of an emergency, you may need to restore lost or damaged data. For example, if your computer's hard drive fails, you can restore your backup onto another computer and continue to work.

> **Important:**
> Restoring **does not add information** to your file, but **replaces your data** with a new file that has all of the data you had when you created the backup.
> Consequently, you should only restore a file when you are certain it is necessary.

Portable files should never be used as a substitute for backup files. Backup files are larger than portable files and hold more information about the company. When you create a backup file, QuickBooks resets a log file that tracks all the changes made to the file between backups. Intuit Customer Support can use this file to troubleshoot and help restore information in case you need to recreate your current company information from a restored backup.

In general, there are two main uses for QuickBooks backup files.

1. When you transfer files between computers and need more information than is contained within the portable file (for example, between accountant and client).
2. To recover damaged or lost data files.

> **Note:**
> In addition to the Backup and Restore process which moves the complete QuickBooks file between computers, QuickBooks also has a feature called the Accountant's Copy. This feature enables an accountant to review and make corrections to a special copy of the client's company file while the client continues to work. Then the client can *merge* the accountant's changes back into the original file. See the QuickBooks Help Index for information on this feature.

Backing up Your Data File

Backing up your data is one of the most important safeguards you have to ensure the safety of your data.

> **DO NOT PERFORM THESE STEPS. THEY ARE FOR REFERENCE ONLY.**

1. To back up your company file, select **Create Copy** from the *File* menu.

2. Choose **Backup copy** from the *Save Copy or Backup* window. Click **Next**.

3. You are given the option to save the backup to a local area, such as a removable hard disk, or an online backup using a fee-based service available from Intuit (see Figure 1-10). Online backup is a good option for many companies.

   Choose **Local backup** and click **Next**.

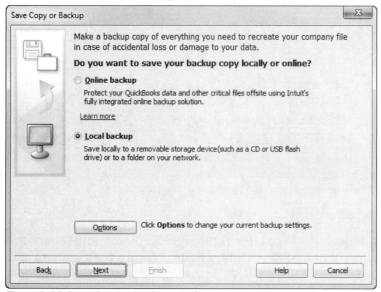

Figure 1-10 Save Copy or Backup window

4. The *Backup Options* window is displayed (see Figure 1-11). Under the *Local backup only* section, click the Browse button.

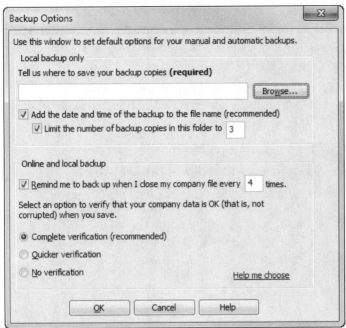

Figure 1-11 Backup Options window

5. Select the folder where you want to store your backup file (see Figure 1-12). You should store the backup files on a safe location, preferably on a different drive than your working data file. That way, if the drive with the working file is damaged, the backup will still be available.

Figure 1-12 Backup options Browse for Folder window

6. When finished, click OK.

7. The *Save Copy or Backup* window is displayed (see Figure 1-13). You can save a backup now, schedule future backups, or both. Select **Only schedule future backups** and click **Next**.

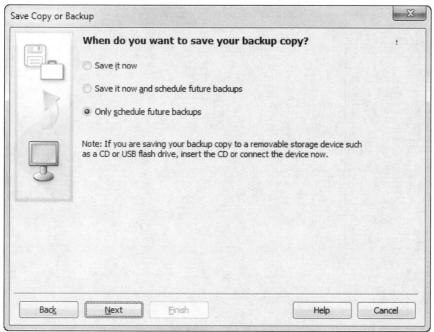

Figure 1-13 Save Copy or Backup window

8. In the *Save Copy or Backup* window, select **New** under the *Schedule Backup* area.

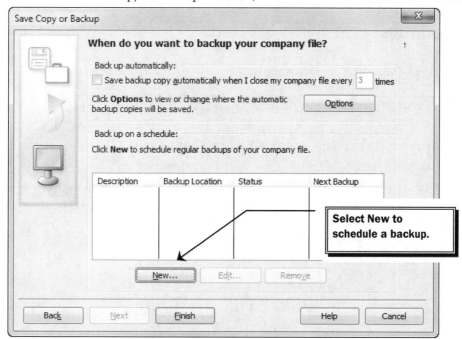

Figure 1-14 Save Copy or Backup window

9. The Schedule Backup window appears (see Figure 1-15). Enter a descriptive name for the backup, the location of the folder to contain the backups, and the time when the backup file will be created.

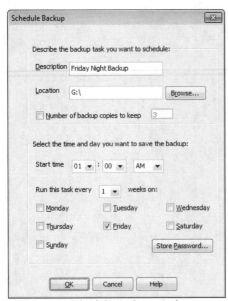

Figure 1-15 Schedule Backup window

10.   When finished, click **OK** to close the *Schedule Backup* window

11.   Click **Finish** to close the *Schedule Backup* window.

12.   If necessary, click **No, Thanks** for the offer to try Online Backup.

Restoring a Backup File

To restore a QuickBooks backup file, follow these steps.

> **DO NOT PERFORM THESE STEPS. THEY ARE FOR REFERENCE ONLY.**

1.   Select the **File** menu and then select **Open or Restore Company**.

2.   Choose **Restore a backup copy** from the *Open or Restore Company* window.

3.   In the *Open or Restore Company* window (see Figure 1-16) you can specify whether the file is stored locally or through Intuit's fee-based *Online Backup* service. Choose **Local backup** and click **Next**.

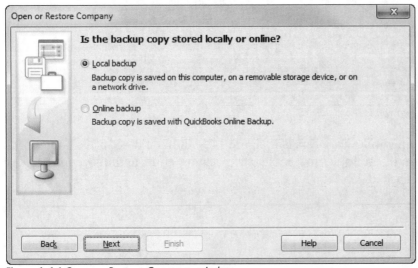

Figure 1-16 Open or Restore Company window

4.   The *Open Backup Copy* window allows you to specify where the backup file is located (see Figure 1-17). Navigate to the folder that contains the file, select it and click **Open**.

Figure 1-17 Open Backup Copy window

5.   The *Open or Restore Company* window displays. Click **Next**.

6.   The *Save Company File as* window allows you to specify where to restore the working files (see Figure 1-18). Navigate to the appropriate folder and click **Save**.

QuickBooks will then restore your backup file in the folder you specified. When QuickBooks restores the file, it creates a **.QBW** file.

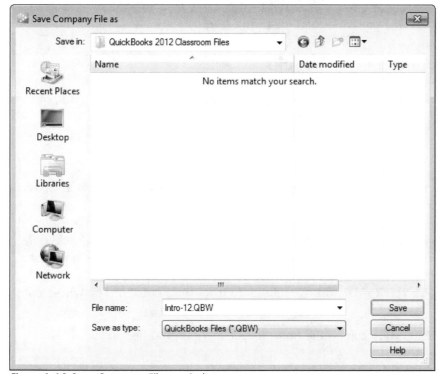

Figure 1-18 Save Company File as window

7.   If you receive the warning message shown in Figure 1-19, it means that QuickBooks is attempting to overwrite an existing file on your computer. If this is your intention, click **Yes**. If you do not intend to replace an existing file, click **No** and change the name of the restored file. You will be asked again to key in the word "Yes" so you don't accidentally overwrite a needed file.

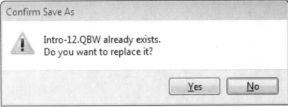

Figure 1-19 Restore To warning

> **Tip:** If you are not sure if you should replace a file, change the name of the restoring file slightly. For example *Intro-12 (version 2).QBW* would keep the file from being overwritten and indicate to users the most recent version.

8.   After completion, a window displays that the new file has been successfully restored (see Figure 1-20).

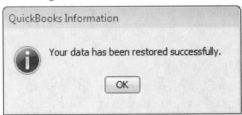

Figure 1-20 After restoring backup file

> **Note:** When you restore a data file, depending on today's date, you may see one or more "Alerts" for learning to process credit cards, pay taxes, or similar activities. Click *Mark as Done* when you see these alerts.

Entering Transactions in QuickBooks

Whenever you buy or sell products or services, pay a bill, make a deposit at the bank, or transfer money, you need to enter a transaction into QuickBooks.

Forms

In QuickBooks, transactions are created by filling out familiar-looking forms such as invoices, bills, and checks. As you fill out forms, you choose names from *lists* such as the customer list, the item list, and the account list. When you finish filling out a form, QuickBooks automatically records the accounting entries behind the scenes. Most forms in QuickBooks have drop-down lists to allow you to pick items from lists instead of spelling the name of a customer, vendor, item, or account. The Pop-up calendar is another feature available on forms, which allows you to pick a date on the calendar rather than entering the whole date.

COMPUTER PRACTICE

Step 1.   Click the **Enter Bills** icon on the *Home* page (see Figure 1-21).

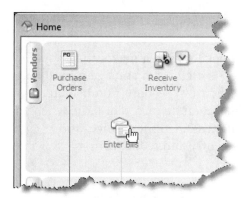

Figure 1-21 Enter Bills on the Home page

Step 2.   Click the **Previous** button on the *Enter Bills* window until you see the previously entered bills in Figure 1-22.

Step 3.   Click the down arrow next to the vendor field to see the dropdown list for vendors.

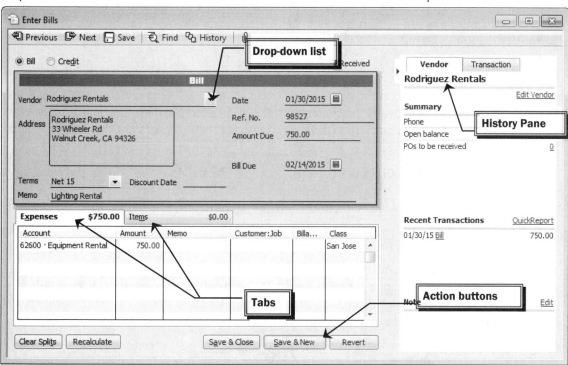

Figure 1-22 Bill form

Step 4.   Click the calendar icon next to the date to see the calendar pop-up menu.

Step 5.   When finished exploring, click the **Revert** button which will return the transaction to the last saved state.

Step 6.   Close the Enter Bills window.

By using forms to enter transactions, you provide QuickBooks with *all of the details* of each transaction. For example, by using the Enter Bills form in Figure 1-22, QuickBooks will track the vendor balance, the due date of the bill, the discount terms, and the debits and credits in the General Ledger. This is a good example of how QuickBooks handles the accounting behind the scenes, and also provides management information beyond just the accounting entries.

Lists

Lists are one of the most important building blocks of QuickBooks that makes the program very powerful and efficient. Lists store information which is used again and again to fill out forms. For example, when you set up a customer's name, address, account number, etc. QuickBooks can use the information to automatically fill out an invoice. Similarly, when an Item is set up, QuickBooks can automatically fill in the Item's description, price, and associated account information. This helps speed up data entry and reduces errors.

> **Note:**
> There are two kinds of lists — **menu-based** and **center-based**. Menu-based lists are accessible through the *List* menu and include the *Item* list and *Terms* lists. Center-based lists include the *Customer Center* and *Vendor Center*, discussed on page 23.

Lists can be viewed by selecting an icon from the *Home* page (for example, the *Items & Services* button), choosing a menu option from the *Lists* menu, or viewing a list through one of the various QuickBooks Centers.

Accounts

QuickBooks provides the means to efficiently track all of your business transactions by categorizing them into *accounts*. The **Chart of Accounts** is the list of these accounts.

COMPUTER PRACTICE

Step 1.   To display the Chart of Accounts, click the *Chart of Accounts* icon on the *Home* page.

             Alternatively, you could select **Chart of Accounts** from the *List* menu, or press **Ctrl+A**.

Step 2.   Scroll through the list. Leave the *Chart of Accounts* open for the next exercise.

By default, the Chart of Accounts is sorted *by account number* within each account type (see Figure 1-23). The *Name* column shows the account names that you assign; the *Type* column shows their account type; the *Balance Total* column shows the balance for asset, liability, and equity accounts (except Retained Earnings), and the *Attach* column shows if there are attached documents.

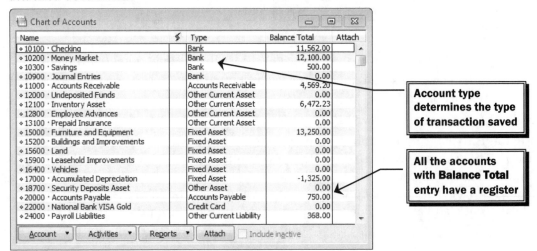

Figure 1-23 Chart of Accounts List

Registers

Each asset, liability, and equity account (except Retained Earnings) has a *register*. Registers allow you to view and edit transactions in a single window. Income and expense accounts do not have registers; rather, their transactions must be viewed in a report.

COMPUTER PRACTICE

Step 1.   To open the *Checking* account register, double-click on **10100 Checking** in the *Chart of Accounts* list.

Step 2.   The **Checking** register opens (see Figure 1-24). Scroll through the register.

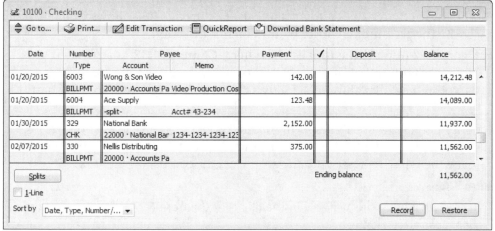

Figure 1-24 Checking account register

Step 3.   Close the Checking account register by clicking the close button in the upper right corner.

Step 4.   Double click the **40000 Services** account. This is an *Income* account.

Step 5.   Instead of opening a register, QuickBooks opens a report (see Figure 1-25).

Step 6.   If necessary, change the *Date* field to **All**.

Step 7.   Close the report.

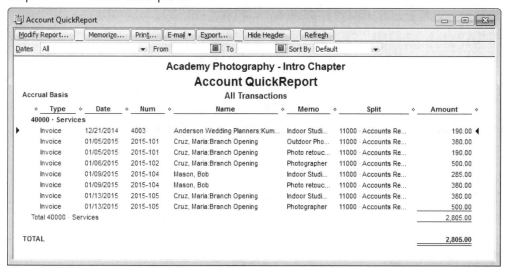

Figure 1-25 Services Account QuickReport – your screen may vary

Step 8.   Close the *Chart of Accounts*.

Items

Items are used to track the detail behind QuickBooks transactions. Since every business has its own unique set of products and services, QuickBooks can be customized to your business by creating Items for each service or product your company buys or sells.

QuickBooks allows twelve Item types for Items associated with buying and selling: *Service, Inventory Part, Inventory Assembly* (Premier and Enterprise Solutions only), *Non-inventory Part, Fixed Asset, Other Charge, Subtotal, Group, Discount, Payment, Sales Tax Item,* and *Sales Tax Group*.

When you define Items, you associate Item names with Accounts in the Chart of Accounts. This association between Item names and Accounts is the "magic" that allows QuickBooks to automatically create the accounting entries behind each transaction.

For example, Figure 1-27 displays the *Item* list. The Item, **Camera SR32**, is associated, or linked, to the **Sales** account in the Chart of Accounts. Every time the **Camera SR32** Item is entered on an invoice, the dollar amount actually affects the **Sales** account in the Chart of Accounts.

Items are necessary because to use a sales form in QuickBooks (e.g., invoices and sales receipts), you must use Items. On an invoice, for example, every line item will have a QuickBooks Item which may represent products, services, discounts, or sales tax.

COMPUTER PRACTICE

Step 1.   To see what Items are available in the file, click the **Item & Services** icon on the *Home page* (see Figure 1-26).

Alternatively, you could select **Item List** from the *Lists* menu.

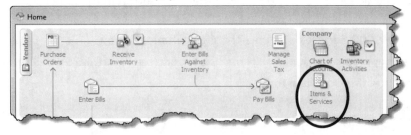

Figure 1-26 Items & Services button on Home page

Step 2.   Figure 1-27 shows the *Item* list. Double click the **Camera SR32** item.

Name	Description	Type	Account	Total Quantity On Hand	On Sales Order	Price	Attach
◇ Indoor Photo Session	Indoor Studio Session	Service	40000 · Services			95.00	
◇ Outdoor Photo Session	Outdoor Photo Session	Service	40000 · Services			95.00	
◇ Photographer	Photographer	Service	40000 · Services			125.00	
◇ Retouching	Photo retouching services	Service	40000 · Services			95.00	
◇ Camera SR32	Supra Digital Camera SR32	Inventory Part	45000 · Sales	9	0	695.99	
◇ Case	Camera and Lens High Impact Case	Inventory Part	45000 · Sales	24	0	79.99	
◇ Frame 5x7	Picture Frame - 5' x 7' Metal Frame	Inventory Part	45000 · Sales	22	0	5.99	
◇ Lens	Supra Zoom Lens	Inventory Part	45000 · Sales	7	0	324.99	
◇ Film 36C	200 ASA, 36 Color Film	Non-inventory Part	45000 · Sales			12.36	
◇ Premium Photo Package	Premium Package of Photography from Session	Non-inventory Part	45000 · Sales			85.00	
◇ Standard Photo Package	Standard Package of Photography from Session	Non-inventory Part	45000 · Sales			55.00	
◇ Bad Debt	Bad Debt - Write off	Other Charge	60300 · Bad Debts			0.00	
◇ Bounce Chg	Return Check Fee	Other Charge	45000 · Sales			0.00	
◇ Contra Costa	Contra Costa County Sales Tax	Sales Tax Item	25500 · Sales Tax Payable			8.25%	
◇ Out of State	Out-of-state sale, exempt from sales tax	Sales Tax Item	25500 · Sales Tax Payable			0.0%	
◇ Santa Clara	Santa Clara County Sales Tax	Sales Tax Item	25500 · Sales Tax Payable			8.25%	

Figure 1-27 Item List

Step 3.   If the New Feature window opens, click **OK**.

Step 4.   The *Edit Item* window opens (see Figure 1-28). Notice this item is linked to the Sales account. Every time this item is entered on an invoice, it changes the **Sales** account.

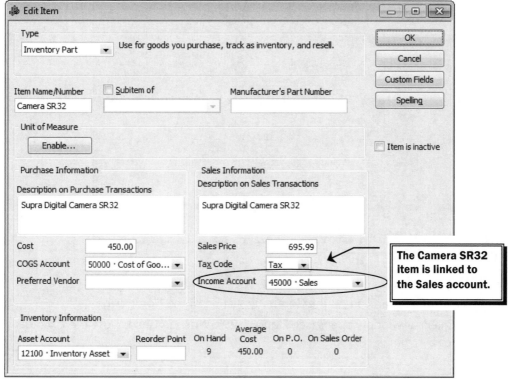

Figure 1-28 Camera SR32 Edit Item window – your screen may vary

Step 5.   Close the *Edit Item* and *Item List* windows.

Calendar

New with QuickBooks 2012, you can view transactions on a *Calendar*. The calendar displays transaction on the *Entered* date and the *Due* date.

> **Note:**
> The *Entered* date is not literally the date when the transaction is entered into QuickBooks. It is the transaction date that is input on the transaction form. If you create an invoice on January 5th, 2015 and enter the date 01/06/2015 in the date field, the invoice will show on January 6th, 2015 on the Calendar.

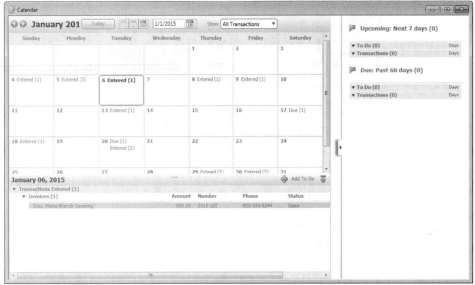

Figure 1-29 QuickBooks Calendar

COMPUTER PRACTICE

Step 1.   Click the Calendar icon on the Company section of the Home page.

Step 2.   The Calendar window opens (see Figure 1-29). When finished, close the Calendar window.

QuickBooks User Interface Features

QuickBooks provides a number of shortcuts and aids that assist the user in entering information and transactions. You should become familiar with these features so you can get to a task quickly.

There are various methods of accessing the data entry windows: the **Home** page, **Snapshots**, **Menus**, **QuickBooks Centers**, **Icon Bar**, and **Shortcut Keys**.

Home Page

As soon as you open a company file, QuickBooks displays the *Home* page (Figure 1-30). The *Home* page is broken into five sections – each dealing with a separate functional area of a business. These areas are: Vendors, Customers, Employees, Company, and Banking. Each area has icons to facilitate easy access to QuickBooks tasks. The *Home* page also displays a flow diagram showing the interdependency between tasks.

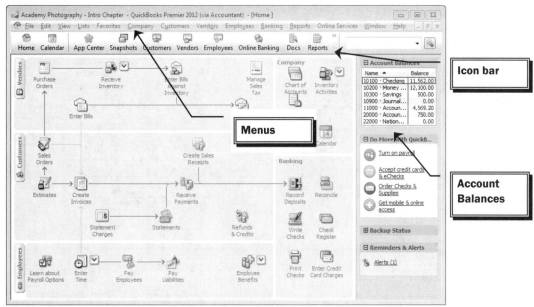

Figure 1-30 QuickBooks Premier 2012 Home page

To start a task, just click on its related icon on the *Home* page. The *Home* page displays the account balance information, which can be closed or even hidden based upon the user's access privileges (see Figure 1-31). If you close the *Home* page, it can be opened by clicking on the **Home** icon on the Icon bar.

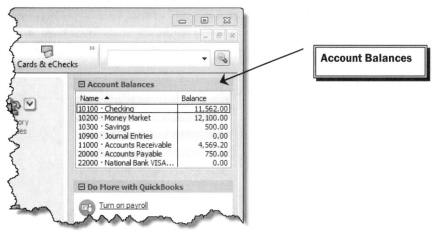

Figure 1-31 Account Balances on Home page

Centers

There are several Centers in QuickBooks, such as the Customer Center and Vendor Center, as well as many others. Centers are organized to give pertinent information in one place.

Customer, Vendor, and Employee Centers are very important since they provide the only way to access the Customer list, Vendor list, and Employee list. These three lists are referred to as the *Center-based Lists*. These Centers summarize general information and transactions in the same area. For example, the Customer Center shows the customer balance, their general information, and all transactions for each customer (see Figure 1-32).

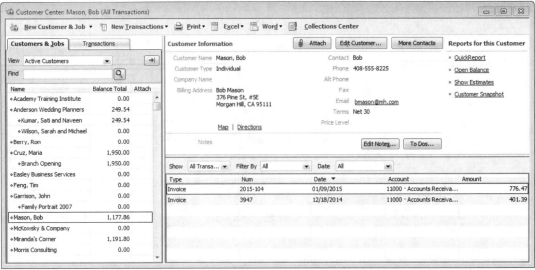

Figure 1-32 Customer Center

Other Centers include the *Application Center, Online Banking Center, Report Center,* and *Document Management Center.* These Centers will be addressed later in this book.

Snapshots

The *Snapshots* is a single screen summary of different aspects of a company. Charts such as *Income and Expense Trends, Previous Year Income Comparison,* and *Expense Breakdown* are displayed along with important lists such as *Account Balances* and *Customers Who Owe Money.* The Snapshots can be easily customized to show the information that is of most interest to you and your company.

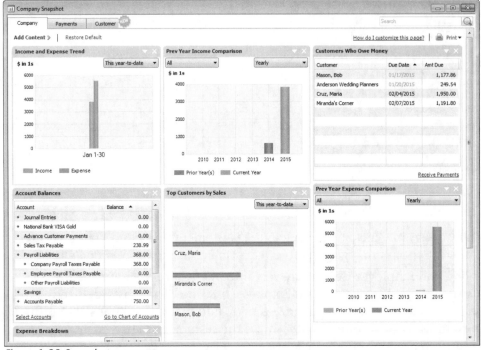

Figure 1-33 Snapshots - your screen may vary

Icon Bar

Figure 1-34 Icon Bar

The QuickBooks Icon Bar allows you to select activities and available services by clicking icons on the bar (see Figure 1-34). For example, you can open the Home page by clicking **Home** on the Icon Bar. To modify the contents or position of the icons on the Icon Bar, select the *View* menu, and then choose **Customize Icon Bar** (see Figure 1-35).

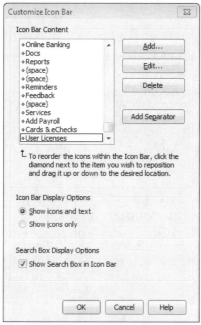

Figure 1-35 Customize Icon Bar

QuickBooks Mobile

You can download a free mobile app for a smartphone that enables you to use several QuickBooks features when you are not at your desktop computer. Features include accessing your customers' contact information as well as creating *Estimates*, *Invoices* and *Sales Receipts*. As of this printing, QuickBooks Mobile is available for the iPhone, iPad, and Android devices.

Figure 1-36 Example Main Menu screen for QuickBooks Mobile

QuickBooks Help

Support Resources

QuickBooks provides a variety of support resources that assist in using the program. Some of these resources are on the Internet and others are stored in help files locally along with the QuickBooks software on your computer. To access the support resources, select the *Help* menu and then select **QuickBooks Help.** QuickBooks will display answers to problems you might be having based on your recent activilty. You can also enter a question and QuickBooks will search its Help Content and the Online Community for related answers.

QuickBooks Learning Center

As you begin using QuickBooks, the first thing you see is the QuickBooks Learning Center (see Figure 1-4). This center provides interactive tutorials to help users learn how to use QuickBooks in common business scenarios. If you have deactivated the Learning Center so that it does not start once the program is launched, you can always access it by selecting **Learning Center Tutorials** from the *Help* menu.

Certified QuickBooks ProAdvisors

Certified QuickBooks ProAdvisors are independent consultants, accountants, bookkeepers, and educators who are proficient in QuickBooks and who can offer guidance to small businesses in various areas of business accounting. To find a Certified ProAdvisor, select **Find a Local QuickBooks Expert** from the *Help* menu.

Review Questions

Select the best answer(s) for each of the following:

1. The fundamental accounting equation that governs all accounting is:
    a)   Net income = Revenue - expenses.
    b)   Assets + Liabilities = Equity.
    c)   Assets = Liabilities + Equity.
    d)   Assets = Liabilities - Equity.

2. Which of the following statements is true?
    a)   Debits are bad because they reduce income.
    b)   Equity is increased by a net loss.
    c)   Debits - credits = 0.
    d)   Assets are increased with a credit entry.

3. Under accrual accounting:
    a)   A sale is not recorded until the customer pays the bill.
    b)   Income and expenses are recognized when transactions occur.
    c)   An expense is not recorded until you write the check.
    d)   You must maintain two separate accounting systems.

4. QuickBooks is:
    a)   A job costing system.
    b)   A payroll system.
    c)   A double-entry accounting system.
    d)   All of the above.

5. Which is not a method of accessing the data entry screens?

    a) Menus
    b) Home page
    c) Icon bar
    d) Data entry button

Introduction-Problem 1

> Restore the **Intro-12Problem1.QBM** file.

1. Select **Customers** from the QuickBooks *Icon* Bar. This will display the *Customer Center*.

    a) What is the first customer listed on the left of the Customer Center?

> **Note:**
> The answer to this first question **AAA Services**. If you don't see AAA Services in the *Customer Center*, make sure to restore *Intro-12Problem1.QBM* as directed in the box above. This book uses specific files for each chapter and each problem. If you don't restore the correct file, you will have trouble completing the exercises.

    b) In the Customers & Jobs list, single click on **Miranda's Corner**. What is Miranda's Corner's balance? *3,575.40*

    c) Click the *Date* dropdown list above the transaction listing in the right-hand panel and scroll up to the top of the list to select **All**. How many transactions do you see and of what type? *1 - Invoice   - Acc Recered.*

    d) Close the Customer Center.

2. Select **Vendors** from the QuickBooks *Icon* Bar. This displays the *Vendor Center*.

    a) Double-click *Sinclair Insurance*. This opens the *Edit Vendor* window. What is the Phone Number? Close the *Edit Vendor* window. *831 - 555 - 2800*

    b) What is the amount of Bill number 5055 to *Sinclair Insurance*? (You may need to set the *Date* to **All** as in Step 1.) *400.00*

    c) Close the Vendor Center.

3. From the *Home* page, click the **Chart of Accounts** icon to display the Chart of Accounts.

    a) What type of account is the **Checking** Account? *Bank*

    b) How many accounts of type **Bank** are in the Chart of Accounts? *4*

    c) How many accounts of type **Income** are in the Chart of Accounts? *3*

4. While still in the **Chart of Accounts**, Double-click the **Checking** account on the Chart of Accounts list. This will open the register for Checking account.

    a) Who was the payee for the check on 2/11/2015? *National Bank*

    b) What was the amount of the check? *1542.00*

    c) Close the checking account register and Chart of Accounts list.

5. Click the **Create Invoices** icon on the *Home page*, and then click **Previous** (top left).

    a) What is the Invoice #? *2015-106.*

    b) What is the first Item listed in this invoice? *Camera SR32*

    c) Close the invoice.

6. Select the **Chart of Accounts** option from the *Lists* menu. Double-click on the **Checking** account.

    a) Which vendor was paid by the last bill payment in the register? *Wong & Son*

    b) What is the amount of the last bill payment in the register? *142.00*

    c)   Close the **Checking** register and close the **Chart of Accounts** list.

7.   Click the **Write Checks** icon on the *Home* page and follow these steps:

    a)   Click on the *Calendar* icon immediately to the right of the *Date* field. Select **tomorrow's date** in the *Date* field and press **Tab**.

    b)   In the Pay to the Order of field, enter *Boswell Consulting*. Press **Tab**.

    c)   Enter *80.00* in the *Amount* field and press **Tab**.

    d)   Click in the **To be printed** check box.

    e)   What is the city displayed in the Address field on the check for *Boswell Consulting*? *Oakland*

    f)   Click **Clear** and then close the check window.

8.   Select the **Chart of Accounts** option from the *Lists* menu and double-click on **Accounts Receivable**.

    a)   What is the ending balance in the account? *2228.78*

    b)   What is the date of the last transaction in the register? *2/2/2013*

    c)   Close the register and the Chart of Accounts.

9.   Click the **Check Register** button on the Home page.

    a)   Select **10100 – Checking** from the *Use Register* dialog box.

    b)   What is the ending balance in the checking register? *12.617 48*

    c)   Close the **Checking Register**.

10. Close the working data file Intro-12Problem1.QBW.

Chapter 2
The Sales Process

Objectives

After completing this chapter, you should be able to:

- Track company sales(page 29)
- Set up customer records in the Customer Center (page 34)
- Track income and expenses by Job (page 41)
- Record Sales Receipts (page 42)
- Use the Undeposited Funds account to track your cash receipts (page 46)
- Record Invoices and Payments from customers (page 49)
- Record bank deposits of cash, check, and credit card receipts (page 63)

Restore this File

This chapter uses Sales-12.QBW. To open this file, restore the Sales-12.QBM file
to your hard disk. See page 8 for instructions on restoring files. If you are using
QuickBooks Premier Accountant, we recommend that you toggle to QuickBooks
Premier General Business as described on page x.

Note: When you restore a data file, depending on today's date, you may see one
or more "Alerts" for learning to process credit cards, pay taxes, or similar
activities. Click Mark as Done when you see these alerts.

In this chapter, you will learn how QuickBooks can help you record and track revenues in
your business.

Each time you sell products or services, you will record the transaction using one of
QuickBooks' forms. When you fill out a QuickBooks **Invoice** or **Sales Receipt**, QuickBooks
tracks the detail of each sale, allowing you to create reports about your sales.

Tracking Company Sales

Academy Photography tracks each sale individually on either an **Invoice** form (for sales to
credit customers) or a **Sales Receipt** form (for customers who pay immediately using cash,
checks, or credit cards).

The *Customers* section of the *Home* page window provides you with a graphical flow of the
steps involved in the sales process.

When you open the sample file, the *Home* page is displayed. Academy Photography is a
service and merchandising photo studio which sells products and provides services, so the
home page displays activities likely to be used in this type of business (see Figure 2-1). The
Home page is customized for each business type based on answers to questions in the setup
interview. You'll learn about the company setup process later in this book.

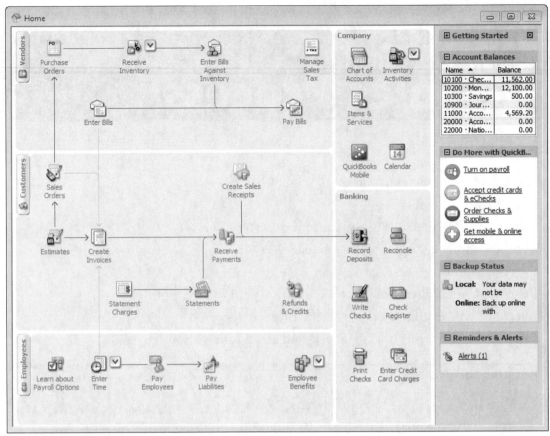

Figure 2-1 QuickBooks Home page

Sales are recorded two different ways, depending on whether the customer pays at the time of sale or service (called *cash customers*), or if the customer pays after the sale or service (*credit customers*). Transactions with cash customers follow a specific process. At the time of sale, a Sales Receipt is issued, and then a deposit is recorded. This process is displayed in Figure 2-2.

> **Note:**
> Payment with a credit card is received immediately, therefore a customer who pays at the time of sale with a credit card is a cash customer.

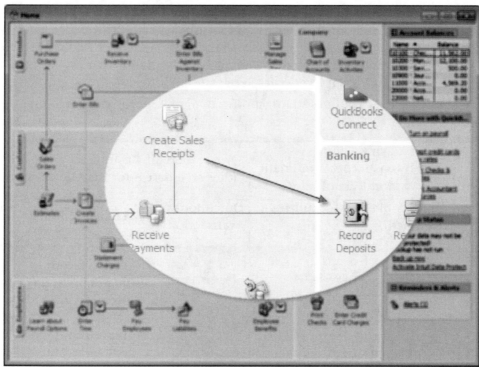

Figure 2-2 Payment with Cash Sale Workflow

When working with a credit customer, who pays after the sale or service, the sales process is different. Often, the first step is to create an Invoice. Once payment is received, the amount is applied to the Invoice and the deposit is recorded. This process is displayed in Figure 2-3. This process can also begin with creating an Estimate.

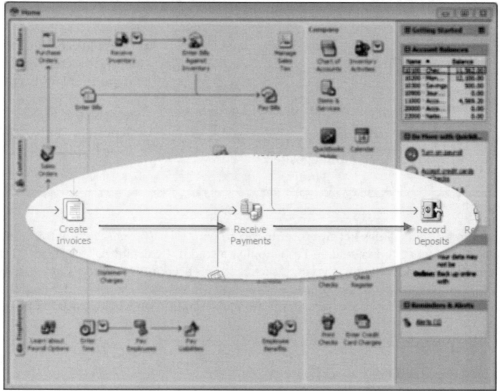

Figure 2-3 Invoicing Workflow

Table 2-1 provides more details about the cash and credit customer sales processes. In this table, you can see how to record business transactions for cash and credit customers. In addition, the table shows the *accounting behind the scenes* of each transaction. As discussed on page 4, the accounting behind the scenes is critical to your understanding of how QuickBooks converts the information on forms (Invoices, Sales Receipts, etc.) into accounting entries.

Each row in the table represents a business transaction you might enter as you proceed through the sales process.

Business Transaction	Cash Customers (Pay by cash, check, or credit card at time of sale)		Credit Customers (Pay on a date after the sale date)	
	QuickBooks Transaction	Accounting Entry	QuickBooks Transaction	Accounting Entry
Customer Estimate (Optional)	Not Usually Used		Estimates	Non-posting entry used to record estimates (bids) for Customers or Jobs
Customer Sales Order (Optional)	Not Usually Used		Sales Orders	Non-posting entry used to record customer orders
Recording a Sale	Create Sales Receipts	Increase (debit) **Undeposited Funds**, increase (credit) *income* account.	Create Invoices	Increase (debit) **Accounts Receivable**, increase (credit) *income* account
Receiving Money in Payment of an Invoice	No additional action is required on the sales form.		Receive Payments	Decrease (credit) **Accounts Receivable**, increase (debit) **Undeposited Funds**
Depositing Money in the Bank	Record Deposits	Increase (debit) *bank* Account, decrease (credit) **Undeposited Funds**.	Record Deposits	Decrease (credit) **Undeposited Funds**, increase (debit) *bank* Account

Table 2-1 Steps in the sales process

For cash customers, use the **Sales Receipt** form to record your sale. The *Sales Receipt* form records the details of what you've sold and to whom you sold it. By default, a special account called **Undeposited Funds** is used in these transactions. This account is an *Other Current Asset* account, and it can be thought of as a drawer where you keep your checks and other deposits before making a trip to the bank. See page 46 for more information on **Undeposited Funds**.

> **The accounting behind the scenes:**
> When you create a **Sales Receipt**, QuickBooks increases (with a debit) **a bank account or Undeposited Funds** (i.e., funds you have received from customers but have not yet deposited at your bank), and increases (with a credit) the appropriate *income* account. If applicable, **Sales Receipts** also increase (with a credit) the sales tax liability account. If the sale includes an Inventory Item, it also decreases (credits) the Inventory asset and increases (debits) the Cost of Goods Sold account.

For credit customers, create an **Invoice** for each sale. The **Invoice** form records the details of what you've sold and to whom you sold it.

> **The accounting behind the scenes:**
> When you create an **Invoice**, QuickBooks increases (with a debit) **Accounts Receivable** and increases (with a credit) the appropriate *income* account. If applicable, **Invoices** also increase (with a credit) the sales tax liability account. If the sale includes an Inventory Item, it also decreases (credits) the Inventory asset and increases (debits) the Cost of Goods Sold account.

As shown in Table 2-1, when you receive money from your credit customers, use the **Receive Payments** function to record the receipt.

> **The accounting behind the scenes:**
> When you record a received **Payment**, QuickBooks increases (with a debit) **Undeposited Funds** or a bank account, and decreases (with a credit) **Accounts Receivable**.

If you post a **Sales Receipt** or a **Payment** to **Undeposited Funds**, which is the default option, the last step in the process is to make a **Deposit** to your bank account. This step is the same for both cash and credit customers. Use the **Make Deposits** function to record the deposit to your bank account. This is the only way to ensure that the amount in **Undeposited Funds** gets applied to the correct bank account.

If you prepare estimates (sometimes called bids) for Customers or Jobs, you can create an **Estimate** to track the details of what the sale will include. QuickBooks does not post **Estimates** to the **General Ledger**, but it helps you track the estimate until the job is complete. QuickBooks also provides reports that help you compare estimated vs. actual revenues and costs.

> **The accounting behind the scenes:**
> When you create an **Estimate**, QuickBooks records the estimate, but there is no accounting entry made. **Estimates** are "non-posting" entries.

If you use sales orders in your business, you can use a **Sales Order** form to track the details of what the sale will include. QuickBooks does not post **Sales Orders** to the **General Ledger**, but it helps you track your orders until they are shipped to the customer. **Sales Orders** are very similar to **Estimates** because they are both non-posting entries, and they both help you track future sales. **Sales Orders** are more appropriate for product businesses, and **Estimates** are more appropriate for service businesses. **Sales Orders** are only available in QuickBooks Premier and Enterprise Solutions.

> **The accounting behind the scenes:**
> When you create a **Sales Order**, QuickBooks records the sales order, but there is no accounting entry made. **Sales Orders** are "non-posting" entries.

In the following sections, you will learn about each step of the payment at the time of sale and invoicing workflows.

Setting Up Customers

For each of your customers, create a record in the **Customers & Jobs** list of the *Customer Center*. Academy Photography has a new credit customer – Dr. Tim Feng. To add this new customer, follow these steps:

COMPUTER PRACTICE

Step 1.   Select the **Customers** icon from the *Icon bar*

Step 2.   To add a new customer, select **New Customer** from the **New Customer & Job** drop-down menu (see Figure 2-4).

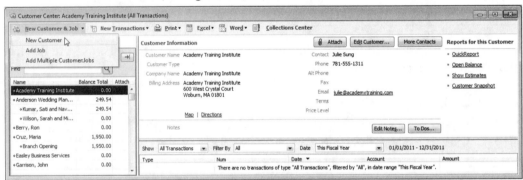

Figure 2-4 Adding a new customer record

Step 3.   Enter *Feng, Tim* in the *Customer Name* field (see Figure 2-5) and then press **Tab**.

Step 4.   Press **Tab** twice to skip the *Opening Balance* and *as of* fields.

The date in the *as of* field defaults to the current date. Since you will not enter an amount in the *Opening Balance* field, there is no need to change this date.

Do not enter anything in the *Opening Balance* field. It shows on the *New Customer* window so that you *could* enter the balance due from this customer, but it is much better to enter each open Invoice for each customer. See the following important tip for a more thorough explanation.

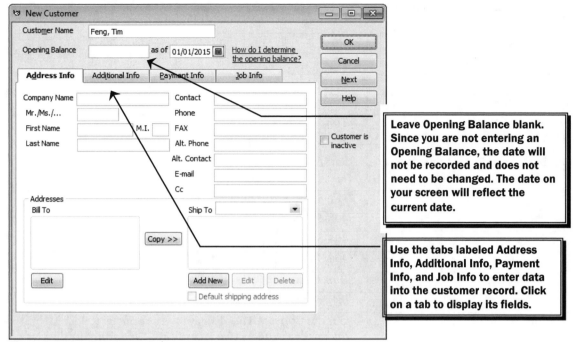

Figure 2-5 New Customer window

> **Important Tip:**
> It is best NOT to use the *Opening Balance* field in the customer record. When you enter an opening balance for a customer in the *Opening Balance* field, QuickBooks creates a new account in your Chart of Accounts called Uncategorized Income. Then, it creates an **Invoice** that increases (debits) **Accounts Receivable** and increases (credits) **Uncategorized Income**.
>
> It is preferable to enter the actual open Invoices for each customer when you set up your company file. That way, you will have all of the details of which Invoice is open, and what items were sold on the open Invoices. When you use Invoices, the actual income accounts will be used instead of **Uncategorized Income**.

Step 5.   Because this customer is an individual (i.e., not a company), press **Tab** to skip the *Company Name* field.

Step 6.   Continue entering information in the rest of the fields using the data in Table 2-2. Press **Tab** after each entry.

Field	Data
Mr./Mrs.	*Dr.*
First Name	*Tim*
M.I.	*S.*
Last Name	*Feng*
Bill To Address **Hint**: Press **Enter** to move to a new line in this field.	*Tim S. Feng* *300 Main St., Suite 3* *San Jose, CA 95111*
Contact	Tim S. Feng (this field will auto-populate)
Phone	*408-555-8297*
FAX	*408-555-8298*
Alt. Ph.	*408-555-6711*
Alt. Contact	*Don Brewer*
E-Mail	*drf@df.com*
Ship To	Click >>**Copy**>>. This displays the *Add Shipping Address Information* window (see Figure 2-6). Type *Office* in the Address Name field and click **OK**. In QuickBooks, you can select multiple Ship To addresses for your customers.

Table 2-2 Data to complete the Address Info tab

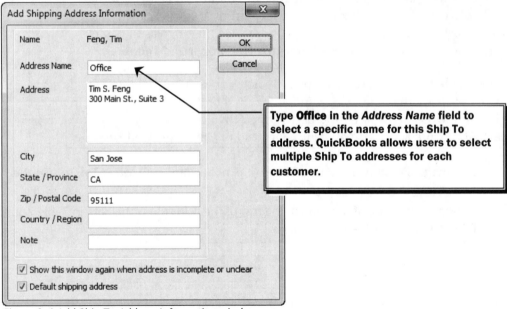

Figure 2-6 Add Ship To Address Information window

Figure 2-7 shows the finished Address Info section of the customer record. Verify that your screen matches Figure 2-7.

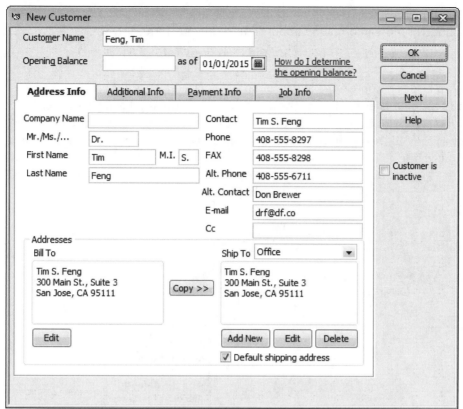

Figure 2-7 Completed Address Info tab

> **Tip:**
> There are four name lists in QuickBooks: **Vendor**, **Customer:Job**, **Employee**, and **Other Names**. After you enter a name in the *Customer Name* field of the *New Customer* window, you cannot use that name in any of the other three lists in QuickBooks.
>
> **When Customers are Vendors:**
> When you sell to and purchase from the same company, you'll need to create two records – one in the Vendor List and one in the Customer:Job list. Make the two names slightly different. For example, you could enter Feng, Tim-C in the *New Customer* window and Feng, Tim-V in the *New Vendor* window. The vendor and customer records for Tim Feng can contain the same contact information.

Step 7.   Click the **Additional Info** tab to continue entering information about this customer as shown in Figure 2-8.

Step 8.   Select **Business** from the *Type* drop-down list and then press **Tab**.

QuickBooks allows you to group your customers into common types. By grouping your customers into types, you'll be able to create reports that focus on one or more types. For example, if you create two types of customers, Residential and Business, you are able to tag each customer with a type. Then you can create reports, statements, or mailing labels for all customers of a certain type.

Step 9.   Select **Net 30** from the *Terms* drop-down list as the terms for this customer and then press **Tab**.

QuickBooks is *terms smart*. For example, if you enter terms of 2% 10 Net 30 and a customer pays within 10 days, QuickBooks will automatically calculate a 2% discount. For more information about setting up your Terms list, see page 218.

Step 10.   Select **MM** in the *Rep* drop-down list and then press **Tab**.

The *Rep* field can contain the initials of one of your employees or vendors. Use this field to assign a sales rep to this customer. If you use the *Rep* field, you can create reports (e.g., Sales by Rep report) that provide the sales information you need to pay commissions. Each sales form (**Invoice** or **Sales Receipt**) can have a different name in the *Rep* field.

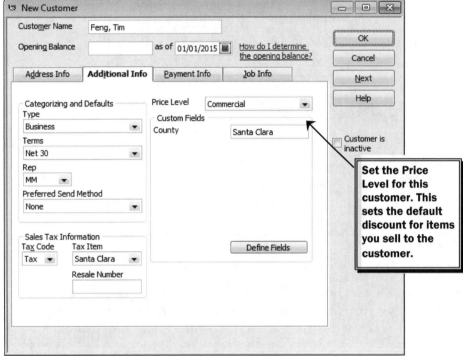

Figure 2-8 Completed Additional Info tab

Step 11.   Press **Tab** to leave the default setting of **None** in the *Preferred Send Method* field.

You would use the *Preferred Send Method* field if you plan to email Invoices to a customer on a regular basis or if you plan to use QuickBooks' Invoice printing and mailing service.

> **Note:**
> For more information on the QuickBooks invoice payment and mailing service, select the **Help** menu and then select **Add QuickBooks Services**. You will then be directed online to the Intuit website. Scroll down and click on the **QuickBooks Billing Solutions** link under the *Financial Services* section. Additional transaction fees apply for this service.

Step 12.   Press **Tab** to accept the **Tax** default **Sales Tax Code** in the *Tax Code* field.

Sales Tax Codes serve two purposes. First, they determine the default taxable status of a customer, item, or sale. Second, they are used to identify the type of tax exemption. For complete information on sales tax codes, see page 81.

Step 13.   Set the *Tax Item* field to **Santa Clara**. This indicates which sales tax rate to charge and which agency collects the tax. Press **Tab** when finished.

> **Tip:**
> In most states, you charge sales tax based on the delivery point of the shipment. Therefore, the **Sales Tax Item** should be chosen to match the tax charged in the county (or tax location) of the *Ship To* address on the *Address Info* tab.

Step 14.   Press **Tab** to leave the *Resale Number* field blank.

If the customer is a reseller, you would enter his or her reseller number.

Step 15.   Select **Commercial** from the *Price Level* drop-down list. See page 220 for information on setting up and using price levels. Press **Tab**.

Step 16.   Enter *Santa Clara* in the *County* field.

The **Define Fields** button on the **Additional Information** tab allows you to define **Custom Fields** to track more information about your customers. For more information on setting up and using custom fields, see page 223.

Step 17.   Verify that your screen matches Figure 2-8 and then click the **Payment Info** tab to continue entering information about this customer as shown in Figure 2-9.

Step 18.   Enter *3543* in the *Account No.* field to assign a customer number by which you can sort or filter reports. Press **Tab**.

Step 19.   Enter *3,000.00* in the *Credit Limit* field and press **Tab**.

QuickBooks will warn you if you record an Invoice to this customer when the balance due (plus the current sale) exceeds the credit limit. Even though QuickBooks warns you, you'll still be able to record the Invoice.

Step 20.   Select *Visa* from the *Preferred Payment Method* drop-down list and then press **Tab**. When you set the fields on this window, you won't have to enter the credit card information each time you receive money from the customer.

> **Tip:**
> If more than one person accesses your QuickBooks file, set up a separate user name and password for each additional user. When you set up a user, you can restrict him or her from accessing *Sensitive Accounting Activities*. This will prevent the additional user from seeing the customer's credit card number. See page 405 for more information about setting up user names and passwords.

Step 21.   Enter the remaining data as shown in Figure 2-9 in the *Preferred Payment Method* section. Some of the fields will auto-populate as you tab into those fields. You may overwrite the auto-populated values if needed.

> **Note:**
> If you track multiple jobs for each customer, it is best NOT to enter job information on the *Job Info* tab of the main customer record. If you want to track jobs for this customer, you can create separate job records in the **Customers & Jobs** list.

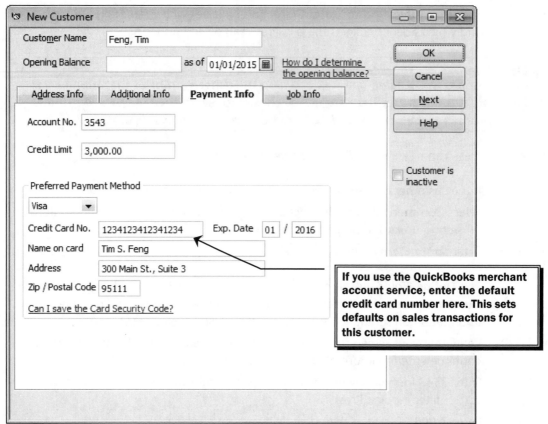

Figure 2-9 Completed Payment Info tab

Step 22.   If you were adding several customers at a time, you would click **Next** to begin
            adding another customer. In this case, click **OK** to save and close the *New Customer*
            window.

> **Note:**
> If you see an error message when saving the Feng, Tim customer (see
> Figure 2-10), you may not be in the correct exercise file. Make sure you
> restore the correct file at the start of each chapter and problem,
> otherwise your exercises may not match the activities in this book. For
> this chapter, you should be using Sales-12.QBW. For instructions on
> restoring portable files, please see page 8.

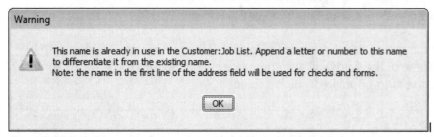

Figure 2-10 Error Message when saving a Name that already exists

Step 23.   Close the Customer Center by clicking the close button (☒) on the *Customer Center*
            window or by pressing the **Esc** key.

Job Costing

QuickBooks tracks jobs in addition to customers. For each customer in the **Customers & Jobs** list, you can create one or more jobs. This helps you track income and expenses on each *Job*, so that you can create reports showing detailed or summarized information about each *Job*.

To create a job for an existing customer record, open the *Customer Center*, then select the customer, and then select **Add Job** from the **New Customer & Job** drop down menu. You don't need to do this now, because the sample data file already has Jobs set up.

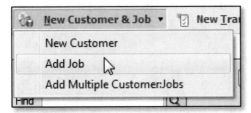

Figure 2-11 Adding a Job to an existing customer record

> **Key Term:**
> Tracking income and expenses separately for each Job is known as *Job Costing*. If your company needs to track job costs, make sure you include the Job name on each income and expense transaction as these transactions are entered.

In the **Name** column of the *Customers & Jobs* list, Jobs are slightly indented under the Customer name.

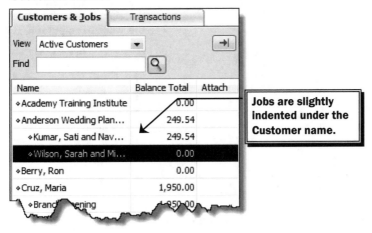

Figure 2-12 Customers & Jobs list

> **Did You Know?**
> To *Quick Add* a **Job** for a **Customer** on an Invoice or Sales Receipt, enter the Customer's name followed by a colon (the Customer name must already exist in the Customer list first). After the colon, enter the name of the job. QuickBooks will then prompt you to either *Quick Add* or *Set Up* the Job. If the *Customer* record already includes job information on its Job tab, you won't be able to use *Quick Add* to create a Job for the customer. In this case, you will need to create the job in the **Customers & Jobs** list before you begin entering sales.

Recording Sales

Now that you've set up your **Customers,** you're ready to begin entering sales. You don't have to have all your customers set up before you begin entering sales transactions. As you'll see, it's also possible to create a new Customer record when you record the first sale to a customer. However, creating the Customer records beforehand will significantly reduce the amount of time needed to record each sale.

There are two QuickBooks forms for recording sales transactions. The first is the **Sales Receipts** form. Use this form when you receive a cash, check, or credit card payment at the time of the sale. The other sales form is the **Invoice.** Use this form when you record credit sales to customers.

Entering Sales Receipts

When customers pay at the time of the sale by cash, check, or credit card, create a **Sales Receipt** transaction.

COMPUTER PRACTICE

Step 1.   Click the **Create Sales Receipts** icon in the *Customers* section on the *Home* page (see Figure 2-13). This opens the *Enter Sales Receipts* window (see Figure 2-14).

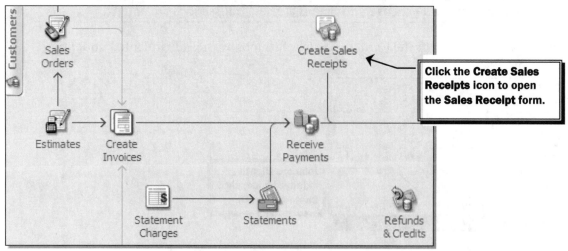

Figure 2-13 Selecting Sales Receipts icon on the Home page

Step 2.   Enter *Perez, Jerry* in the *Customer:Job* field and press **Tab.**

> **Note:**
> Many forms display Customer Summary information in the *History Pane* on the right side of the form, which includes two tabs – one for *Customer* (also called *Name*) information and the other for *Transaction* information. Jerry Perez is a new Customer and therefore does not have any information or history to display.

Step 3.   When the *Customer:Job Not Found* warning window appears (see Figure 2-15), click **Quick Add** to add this new customer to the *Customer:Job* list. If you choose this option, you can edit the customer record later to add more details.

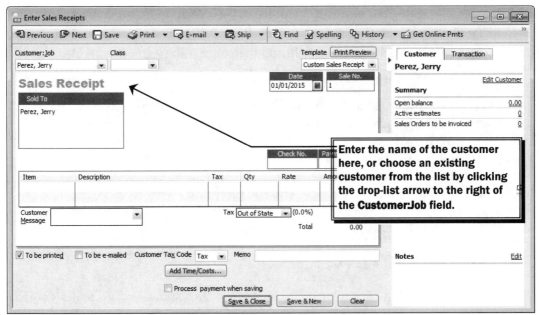

Figure 2-14 Sales Receipt form

> **Note:**
> **Quick Add** works on all your lists. Whenever you type a new name into any field on any form, QuickBooks prompts you to **Quick Add**, **Set Up**, or **Cancel** the name.
>
> **Tip:**
> If your customer is an individual (i.e., not a business), it's a good idea to enter the customer's last name first. This way, your **Customer:Job** list sorts by last name so it will be easier to find names in the list.

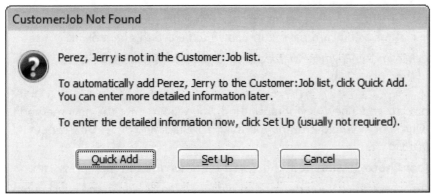

Figure 2-15 Use Quick Add to add new customers

Step 4. Enter *San Jose* in the *Class* field and then press **Tab** twice.

QuickBooks uses classes to separately track income and expenses for departments, functions, activities, locations, or profit centers. For more information on classes, see page 103. Note that if the Class has already been set up, it will appear in that field as you type it or in the drop-down menu.

Step 5. In the *Template* field, **Custom Sales Receipt** is already selected. Press **Tab**.

You can create your own custom forms, as you'll learn in the section beginning on page 224.

Step 6.   Enter *01/25/2015* in the *Date* field and then press **Tab** (see Figure 2-16).

Did You Know?

Whenever you enter a date in QuickBooks, you can use any of several shortcut keys to quickly change the date. For example, if you want to change the date to the first day of the year, press **y**. "Y" is the first letter of the word "year," so it's easy to remember this shortcut. The same works for the end of the year. Press **r** since that's the last letter of the word "year." The same works for "month" (**m** and **h**) and "week" (**w** and **k**). You can also use the + and - keys to move the date one day forward or back. All of these shortcuts will be relative to the date already entered in the date field. Finally, press **t** for "today" or the system date.

Step 7.   Enter *2015-1* in the *Sale No.* field.

The first time you enter a *Sales Receipt*, enter any number you want in the *SALE NO.* field. QuickBooks will automatically number future Sales Receipts incrementally. You can change or reset the numbering at any time by overriding the *SALE NO.* on a Sales Receipt.

Step 8.   Press **Tab** to skip the *Sold To* field.

QuickBooks automatically fills in this field, using the information in the *Bill To* field of the customer record. Since you used *Quick Add* to add this customer, there is no address information. You could enter an address in the *Sold To* field by entering it directly on the sales form. When you record the Sales Receipt, QuickBooks will give you the option of adding the address in the *Bill To* field of the customer record.

Step 9.   Enter *3612* in the *Check No.* field and then press **Tab**.

The number you enter here shows up on your printed deposit slips. If you were receiving a cash or credit card payment, you would leave this field blank.

Step 10.   Select **Check** from the *Payment Method* drop-down list (or start typing the word **Check**) and then press **Tab**.

If you wanted to add a new payment method, you would enter the new method in this field. QuickBooks would prompt you to either *Quick Add* or *Set Up* the new *Payment Method*.

Step 11.   Select **Indoor Photo Session** from the *Item* drop-down list and then press **Tab**.

Step 12.   Press **Tab** to accept the default description *Indoor Studio Session* in the *Description* column.

As soon as you enter an Item, QuickBooks enters the description, rate, and sales tax code using data from the Item that has already been set up.

Step 13.   In the *Tax* column, the *Non* sales tax code is already selected. Press **Tab**.

Step 14.   Enter *1* in the *Qty.* (quantity) column and then press **Tab**.

Step 15.   Leave the default rate at *95.00* in the *Rate* column and then press **Tab**.

Step 16.   Press **Tab** to accept the calculated amount in the *Amount* column.

After you enter the rate and press **Tab**, QuickBooks calculates the amount by multiplying the quantity by the rate. If you override the *Amount* field, QuickBooks calculates a new rate by dividing the amount by the quantity.

Step 17.   Select **Premium Photo Package** from the *Item* drop-down list and then press **Tab** three times.

Step 18.   Enter *2* in the *Quantity* column and press **Tab**.

Step 19.   Press **Tab** to accept the default rate of *85.00*.

You can override this amount directly on the Sales Receipt if necessary. As with the line above, QuickBooks calculates the total in the *Amount* column and QuickBooks uses the default sales tax code *Tax,* which is set up for the *Premium Photo Package* Item.

Step 20.   Select **Thank you for your business.** from the *Customer Message* drop-down list.

You can enter a message in the *Customer Message* field that will show on the printed *Sales Receipt.* This is typically a thank you message, but it can be whatever you want. If you type in a new message, *Quick Add* will prompt you to add your new message to the *Customer Message* list. If you want to edit an existing Customer Message, or if you want to remove a Customer Message from the list, select the *Lists* menu, then select *Customer & Vendor Profile Lists*, and then select *Customer Message List.*

Step 21.   Press **Tab** and enter *Santa Clara* in the *Tax* field, then **Tab** again to advance to the *Memo* field.

The Sales Tax item shown in the *Tax* field determines the rate of tax to be charged on all *Taxable* Items shown on the form. Each line in the body of the Invoice is marked with a Sales Tax Code that determines the taxability or non-taxability of the item on that line (see Figure 2-16).

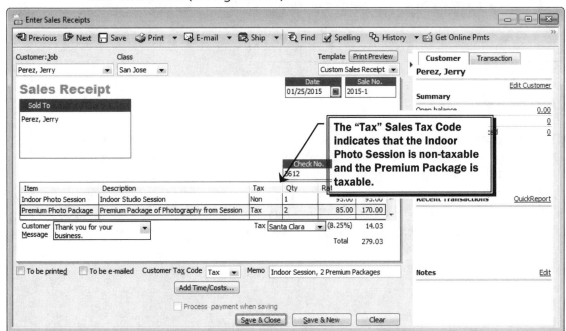

Figure 2-16 Completed Sales Receipt

Step 22.   Enter *Indoor Session, 2 Premium Packages* in the *Memo* field.

Step 23.   Press **Tab** so that the *To be printed* checkbox is selected. Enter the **Spacebar** on the keyboard to uncheck this box.

> **Note:**
> Entering the spacebar on the keyboard when a checkbox is selected will either check or uncheck that checkbox.

Step 24.   Click **Save & Close** to record the sale.

                     QuickBooks does not record any of the information on any form until you save the transaction by clicking *Save & Close, Save & New, Previous,* or *Next.*

> **Note:**
> If you prefer to use your keyboard over the mouse, you can use the *Alt* key on in combination with other keys to execute commands. QuickBooks will tell you which key can be used in connection with the *Alt* key by underlining the letter in the command. For example, in the Sales Receipt window, the *S* is underlined on the *Save & New* button. You can save the receipt and move to a new Sales Receipt window by pressing the **Alt** key with the **S**.

Step 25.   QuickBooks displays the *Name Information Changed* dialog box. This dialog box appears because you set the *Tax Item* field to *Santa Clara.* Click the **Yes** button.

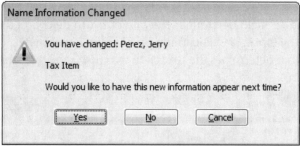

Figure 2-17 Name Information Changed dialog box

Undeposited Funds

The **Undeposited Funds** account is a special account that is automatically created by QuickBooks. The account works as a temporary holding account where QuickBooks tracks checks and other receipts before the money is deposited in a bank account.

As illustrated in Figure 2-18, as you record Payments and Sales Receipts, QuickBooks gives you a choice between (Option 1) grouping all receipts into the **Undeposited Funds** account or (Option 2) immediately depositing the funds to one of your bank accounts.

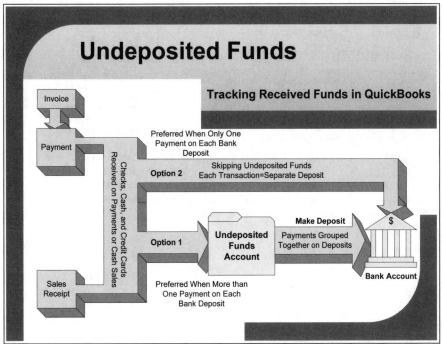

*Figure 2-18 All funds from sales transactions go through **Undeposited Funds** or directly to a bank account.*

There is a tradeoff here. When you use the **Undeposited Funds** account, you have to create a separate transaction (an additional step) to actually deposit money into a bank account. At first that might seem like extra work. However, when you skip the **Undeposited Funds** account, each sales transaction creates a separate deposit in your bank account.

Since it is most common to have multiple sales transactions per bank deposit, QuickBooks has a default preference setting that makes all Payments and Sales Receipts affect the balance in the **Undeposited Funds** account. Then when you actually make a deposit at the bank, you record a single deposit transaction in QuickBooks that empties the **Undeposited Funds** account into the bank account. This method makes it much easier to reconcile the bank account at the end of each month because the deposits on the bank statement will match the deposits in your QuickBooks bank account. Unless you only make one sale each day and your deposits include only the funds from that single sale, you will want to keep this default preference.

COMPUTER PRACTICE

You can modify the **Undeposited Funds** preference by following these steps:

Step 1.   Select the *Edit* menu and then select **Preferences**.

Step 2.   Select **Payments** on the left side of the *Preferences* window.

Step 3.   In the **Company Preferences** tab, the box next to **Use Undeposited Funds as a default deposit to account** is checked (see Figure 2-19).

Step 4.   If you prefer to deposit payments individually, uncheck the box next to **Use Undeposited Funds as a default deposit to account**. You will then have the option to select an account to deposit to in the *Sales Receipt* and *Receive Payment* windows.

Step 5.   Click **Cancel** to leave default setting for the use of **Undeposited Funds**.

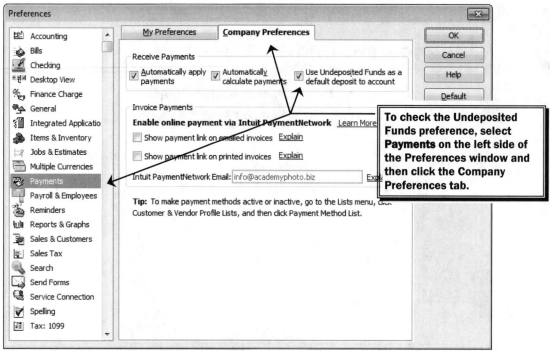

*Figure 2-19 Preference for Payments to go to **Undeposited Funds** or another account*

When this preference is off (see Figure 2-20), QuickBooks displays the **Deposit To** field on the **Receive Payments** and **Enter Sales Receipt** windows (see Figure 2-21).

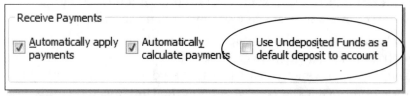

*Figure 2-20 Setting for **Undeposited Funds** on Company Preferences for Payments*

You must choose a destination account for the transaction from the *Deposit to* drop-down list.

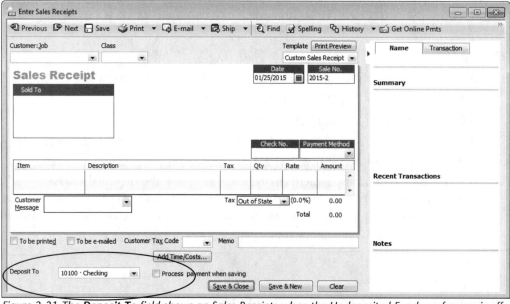

*Figure 2-21 The **Deposit To** field shows on Sales Receipts when the Undeposited Funds preference is off.*

Creating Invoices

Invoices are very similar to **Sales Receipts**. The only difference is that **Invoices** increase **Accounts Receivable** while **Sales Receipts** increase **Undeposited Funds** (or the specified bank account). You should use **Invoices** to record sales to your credit customers.

COMPUTER PRACTICE

To create an Invoice, follow these steps:

Step 1.   From the *Customer Center* select **Mason, Bob** from the *Customers & Jobs* list. Then select **Invoices** from the *New Transactions* drop-down list.

Alternatively, click the **Create Invoices** icon on the *Home page* and select **Mason, Bob** from the *Customer:Job* drop-down list. Press **Tab** (see Figure 2-22).

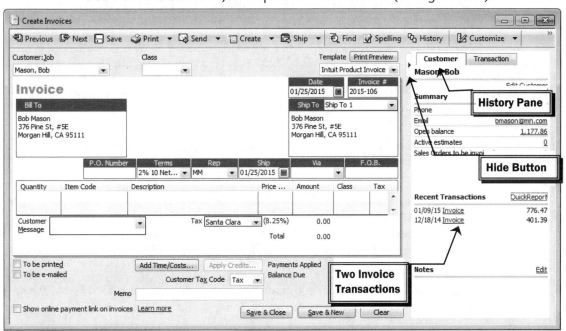

Figure 2-22 Invoice with Bob Mason selected

> **Did You Know?**
> When you type the first few characters of any field that has a list behind it, QuickBooks completes the field using a feature called *QuickFill*. QuickFill uses the first few characters you type to find the name in the list. If the name does not come up right away, keep typing until the correct name appears.

Step 2.   Notice that Bob Mason has two open invoices listed in the *History Pane*.

The *History Pane* displays recent transactions and notes about a customer or a transaction on *Invoices* and *Sales Receipts*.

Step 3.   Click the **Hide** button to hide the *History Pane*. The Hide button is a right facing triangle on the top left edge of the *History Pane* (see Figure 2-22).

Step 4.   Click in the **Class** field. Enter an *s* in the *Class* field. QuickBooks will QuickFill the field with the full word *San Jose*. Then press **Tab** twice.

Step 5.   In the *Template* field, select **Academy Photo Service Invoice**. Press **Tab**.

Step 6.   Enter *01/26/2015* in the *Date* field and then press **Tab**.

Step 7.   Leave *2015-106* in the *Invoice #* field and then press **Tab**.

               The first time you enter an Invoice, enter any number you want in the *Invoice #* field. QuickBooks will automatically number future Invoices incrementally. You can change or reset the numbering at any time by overriding the number on a future Invoice.

Step 8.   Press **Tab** to accept the default information in the *Bill To* field.

               QuickBooks automatically enters the address in this field, using the information in the *Bill To* field of the customer record. If necessary, change the *Bill To* address by typing over the existing data.

Step 9.   Leave the *P.O. No.* field blank and then press **Tab**.

               The P.O. (purchase order) number helps the customer identify your Invoice. When your customers use purchase orders, make sure you enter their P.O. numbers on Invoices you create for them.

> **Warning:**
> Make sure you enter the P.O. number if your customer uses purchase orders. Some customers may reject Invoices that do not reference a P.O. number.

Step 10.   In the *TERMS* field, *2% 10 Net 30* is already selected. Press **Tab** to proceed to the next field.

               The *TERMS* field on the *Invoice* indicates the due date for the *Invoice* and how long your customer can take to pay you. The entry in this field determines how this Invoice is reported on Customers & Receivables reports such as the *A/R Aging Summary* and the *Collections Report*. To learn more about the *Terms List*, and how to set up terms, see page 218.

Step 11.   Enter the sale of 2 Hours for an Indoor Photo Session and 1 Standard Photo Package into the body of the *Invoice* as shown in Figure 2-23.

Step 12.   Select **Thank you for your business** from the *Customer Message* drop-down list and then press **Tab**.

Step 13.   **Santa Clara** in the *Tax* field is already selected. Press **Tab**.

               As with Sales Receipts, QuickBooks selects the *Sales Tax Item* based on the defaults in *Sales Tax Preferences* or in the Customer's record.

Step 14.   Enter *2 Hr Indoor Session, 1 Standard Package* in the *Memo* field at the bottom of the form.

> **Tip:**
> If you intend to send statements to your customers, the *Memo* field is extremely important. QuickBooks allows you to show line item detail from your customer's Invoices. However, if you want your statements to be more concise, you can choose not to show the line item detail and show the text from the *Memo* field instead. The text from the *Memo* field will show along with the information in the *INVOICE #*, and *DATE* fields. The customer's statement will also show a three-letter code "INV" representing the Invoice transaction. Therefore, it is best to include information about the products or services you sold to the customer in the *Memo* field.

Step 15.   Make sure *Show online payment link of invoices* is unchecked.

If you check *Show online payment link on invoices,* your customers can pay you through the *Intuit PaymentNetwork.* These transactions include a fee and will not be used in the classroom environment. You can learn more about the *Intuit PaymentNetwork* at the Intuit website or by clicking the Learn More link next to the checkbox.

Step 16.   Compare your screen with the Invoice shown in Figure 2-23. If you see any errors, correct them. Otherwise, click **Save & Close** to record the Invoice.

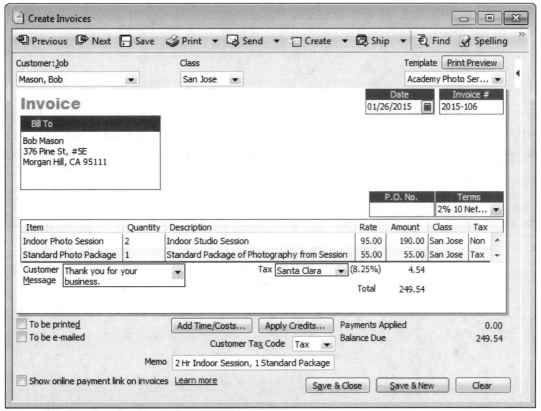

Figure 2-23 Completed Invoice

QuickBooks automatically tracks all of the accounting details behind this transaction so that all of your reports will immediately reflect the sale. For example, the Open Invoices report, the Profit & Loss Standard report, and the Balance Sheet Standard report will all change when you record this Invoice.

Adding Calculating Items to an Invoice

On the next Invoice, you'll learn how to include discounts and subtotals on an **Invoice**. Discounts and subtotals are called *Calculating Items.*

> **Key Term:**
> *Calculating Items* use the amount of the preceding line to calculate their amount. For example, if you enter 10% in the Discount item setup window and then enter the Discount item on an Invoice, QuickBooks will multiply the line just above the Discount item by 10% and enter that number, as a negative, in the **Amount** column for the discount line.

COMPUTER PRACTICE

To create an Invoice with a calculating item, follow these steps:

Step 1.   From the *Customer Center* select the **Branch Opening** job for Cruz, Maria from the *Customers & Jobs* list.

Step 2.   Select **Invoices** from the *New Transactions* drop-down list; or, press Ctrl+ I.

Step 3.   The Branch Opening job for Cruz, Maria is already selected. Press **Tab**.

Step 4.   Enter *Walnut Creek* in the *Class* field and then press **Tab** twice.

Step 5.   The Academy Photo Service Invoice template in the *Template* drop-down list is already selected. Press **Tab**.

Step 6.   *1/26/2015* is already entered in the *Date* field. Press **Tab**.

Step 7.   Notice the *INVOICE #* is automatically entered for you with the next Invoice number (i.e. **2015-107**). Press **Tab** to skip to the next field.

Step 8.   Press **Tab** to skip the *Bill To* field.

Step 9.   Press **Tab twice** to skip the *P.O. No. and the Terms* fields.

Step 10.   Enter the two items shown in Table 2-3 in the body of the **Invoice**.

Item	Description	Qty	Rate	Amount
Camera SR32	Supra Digital Camera SR32	4	695.99	2,783.96
Lens	Supra Zoom Lens	1	324.99	324.99

Table 2-3 Data for use in the Invoice

Step 11.   On the third line of the body of the Invoice, in the **Item** column, enter *Subtotal* to sum the previous two item lines, and press **Tab** twice.

             Notice that QuickBooks automatically calculates the sum of the first two lines on the Invoice.

Step 12.   Enter *Disc 10%* in the **Item** column and press **Tab**.

             The *Disc 10%* Item is a special Calculating Item that calculates a percentage of the preceding line on sales forms. Since it is a **Discount Item**, QuickBooks performs the calculation and enters a negative amount for your discount. This subtracts the discount from the total of the Invoice and adjusts sales tax accordingly.

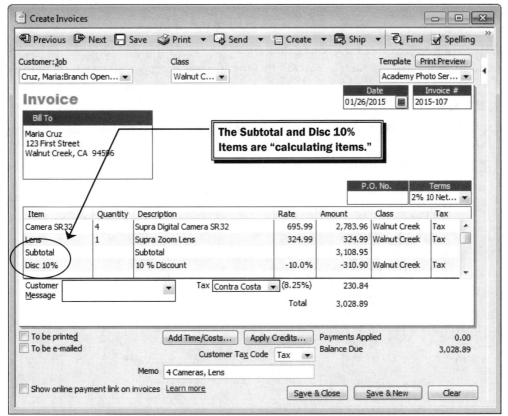

Figure 2-24 Completed Invoice with discount

> **Did You Know?**
> You can insert or delete lines on an Invoice (or any other form). To insert a line between two existing lines, click on the line that you want to move down and press Ctrl+INS (or select the **Edit** menu, and then select **Insert Line**). To delete a line, click on the line you want to delete and press Ctrl+Del (or select the **Edit** menu, and then select **Delete Line**).

Step 13.   Leave the *Customer Message* field blank.

Step 14.   Leave **Contra Costa** in the *Tax* field. Also leave **Tax** in the *Customer Tax Code* field.

Step 15.   Enter *4 Cameras, Lens* in the *Memo* field.

Step 16.   Verify that your screen matches Figure 2-24. To save the Invoice, click **Save & Close**.

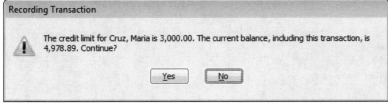

Figure 2-25 Recording Transaction window warns you about the customer's credit limit

Step 17.   If you see the *Recording Transaction* warning about Maria Cruz exceeding her credit limit (Figure 2-25), click **Yes**.

Open Invoices Report

Now that you've entered Invoices for your customers, QuickBooks' reports reflect the Invoices that are "open" and the "age" of each Invoice. The Open Invoices report is shown in Figure 2-26.

COMPUTER PRACTICE

Step 1.   Select the **Reports** menu, select **Customers & Receivables**, and then select **Open Invoices**.

Step 2.   Set the *Dates* field at the top of the report to *01/31/2015* and then press **Tab**.

Step 3.   Verify that your Open Invoices report matches Figure 2-26.

Step 4.   Close the report by clicking the (✕) in the upper right corner of the window.

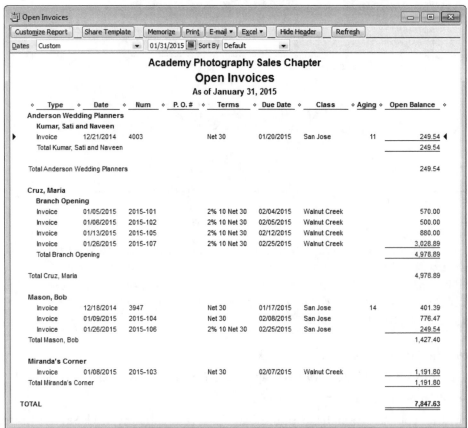

Figure 2-26 Open Invoices report

Step 5.   If you see a *Memorize Report* dialog box, click the **No** button.

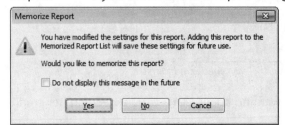

Figure 2-27 Memorized Reports window

> **Did You Know?**
> You can adjust the width of any column on the report by dragging the small
> diamond at the right of the column title to the left (narrowing the columns) or
> to the right (widening the columns).

Receiving Payments from Customers

Receiving Payments by Check

To record payments received from your customers and apply the payments to specific
Invoices, follow these steps:

COMPUTER PRACTICE

Step 1.   Click **Receive Payments** on the *Home* page.

Step 2.   Select **Mason, Bob** in the *Received From* field of the *Receive Payments* window (see
            Figure 2-28). Once a customer is selected, the *Customer Payment* window shows the
            open Invoices for that specific customer. This section shows the dates of the Invoices,
            along with the Invoice number, original amount, the last date for the prompt
            payment discount, and the amount due.

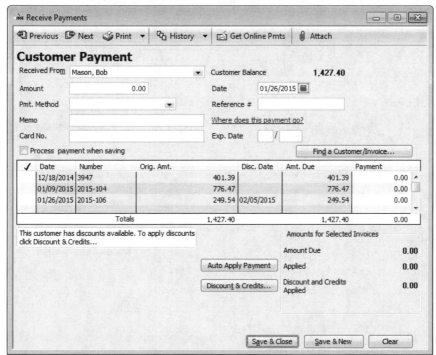

Figure 2-28 Receive Payments window

Step 3.   Enter 401.39 in the *Amount* field and then press **Tab**.

Step 4.   Enter *1/27/2015* in the *Date* field and then press **Tab** (see Figure 2-29).

Step 5.   Select **Check** from the *Pmt. Method* drop-down list and then press **Tab**.

Step 6.   Enter *5256* in the *Check No.* field and then press **Tab**.

Step 7.   Enter **Payment Received - Invoice #3947** in the *Memo* field and then press **Tab**.

            When entering a memo, type **Payment Received** followed by the Invoice number.
            Memos do not affect the application of payments to specific Invoices, but they are
            helpful in two very important ways. First, if you send your customers statements,

only the information in the *Check #, Date,* and *Memo* fields will show on statements, along with a three-letter code (PMT), representing the Payment transaction. Also, if you ever have to go back to the transaction and verify that you've applied the payment to the correct Invoice(s), you'll be able to look at the *Memo* field to see the Invoice(s) to which you *should* have applied the payments.

Step 8.   Confirm that **Invoice #3947** is already checked.

> **Note:**
> **When One Payment Applies to More than One Invoice**
> You can apply one check from a customer to multiple Invoices. When you receive payments, you can override the amounts in the **Payment** column to apply the payment to Invoices in whatever combination is necessary.
>
> **When You Don't Want to Apply the Entire Amount of the Payment**
> If you don't want to apply the entire amount of the customer's check to the Invoice, reduce the amount in the **Payment** column. You can apply the remaining balance of the customer's check to additional Invoices. If you do not, QuickBooks will give you a choice to either hold the remaining balance as a credit for the customer or refund the amount to the customer.

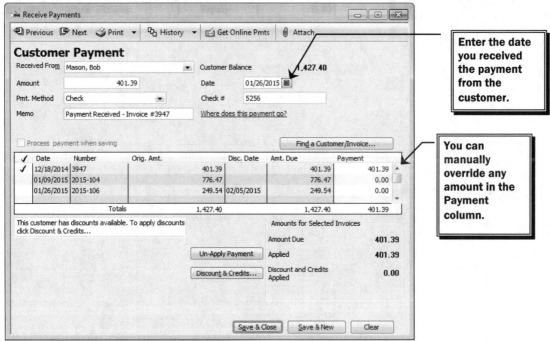

Figure 2-29 Completed Receive Payments window

Step 9.   Verify that the **Amount Due** and **Payment** columns for the selected invoice both show *$401.39*.

                The checkmark to the left of the **Date** column indicates the Invoice to which QuickBooks will apply the payment. QuickBooks automatically selected this Invoice because the amount of the customer's check is the same as the unpaid amount of the Invoice. See *Preferences for Applying Payments* on page 59. If applicable, you can deselect the Invoice by clicking on the checkmark. You can then select another Invoice from the list.

Step 10.   Verify that your screen matches Figure 2-29. If you see errors, correct them.

Step 11.   Click **Save & Close** to record the Payment transaction.

Handling Partial Payments

In the last example, Bob Mason paid Invoice #3947 in full.

However, if a customer pays only a portion of an Invoice, you should record the payment just as you did in the last example except that the amount would be less than the full amount due on any of the open Invoices. Apply the payment to the appropriate Invoice. QuickBooks will give the option to either leave the Invoice open or write off the unpaid amount. By clicking the *View Customer Contact Information* button, QuickBooks displays the *Edit Customer* window that allows you to see the customer's contact information. This is helpful if you need to contact the customer to ask a question about the partial payment (see Figure 2-30).

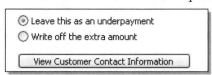

Figure 2-30 Partial Payment of Invoice

If you chose to leave the underpayment, the next time you use the **Receive Payments** function for that customer, the Invoice will show the remaining amount due. You can record additional payments to the Invoice in the same way as before.

Receiving Payments by Credit Card

The next example shows that Maria Cruz paid off the amount owing on the Branch Opening job. Maria Cruz used a credit card to pay her invoices, so this example shows how to receive credit card payments.

COMPUTER PRACTICE

Step 1.   From the *Customer Center* select the **Cruz, Maria:Branch Opening** job from the *Customers & Jobs* list. Select **Receive Payments** from the *New Transactions* drop-down list.

Step 2.   Enter data into the *Received From, Amount,* and *Date* fields as shown in Figure 2-31.

Step 3.   Enter **American Express** in the *Pmt. Method* field and then press **Tab**.

Step 4.   Leave the *Reference#* field blank. Press **Tab**.

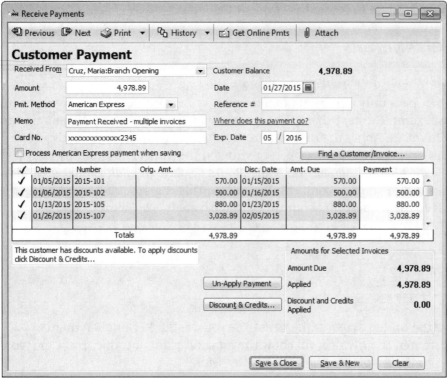

Figure 2-31 Customer Payment by Credit Card

Step 5.   Enter **Payment Received – multiple invoices** in the *Memo* field. Press **Tab**.

Step 6.   Enter **1234-123456-12345** in the *Card No.* field. Press **Tab**.

               QuickBooks shows the credit card number with some x's for security purposes.

Step 7.   Enter **05**, then press **Tab** and enter **2016** in the *Exp. Date* fields.

Step 8.   Verify that your screen matches Figure 2-31 and click **Save & Close**. If the Merchant Account Service Message appears, click the **Not Now** button.

> **Note:**
> If you want to keep a record of the customer's credit card information, including card number, expiration date, billing address and billing zip code, enter credit card information into the *Payment Info* tab of the Customer or Job record before you process the payment through the Receive Payments window. When you enter the customer or job name, QuickBooks will enter the credit card information automatically.

Where Do the Payments Go?

Recall the earlier discussion about **Undeposited Funds** beginning on page 46. Unless you turned off "Use **Undeposited Funds** as a default deposit to account" preference, QuickBooks does not increase your bank balance when you receive payments. Instead, when you record a payment transaction as shown above, QuickBooks reduces the balance in **Accounts Receivable** and increases the balance in **Undeposited Funds.** In order to have your payments show up in your bank account (and reduce **Undeposited Funds**), you must **Make Deposits.** See the section called *Making Bank Deposits* beginning on page 63.

> **The accounting behind the scenes:**
> Payments increase (debit) **Undeposited Funds** (or a bank/other current asset account) and decrease (credit) **Accounts Receivable**.

Preferences for Applying Payments

As soon as you enter the customer name at the top of the *Receive Payments* window and press **Tab**, QuickBooks displays all of the open Invoices for that customer in the lower section of the window. See Figure 2-32.

✓	Date	Number	Orig. Amt.	Disc. Date	Amt. Due	Payment
✓	01/05/2015	2015-101	570.00	01/15/2015	570.00	570.00
	01/06/2015	2015-102	500.00	01/16/2015	500.00	0.00
	01/13/2015	2015-105	880.00	01/23/2015	880.00	0.00
	01/26/2015	2015-107	3,028.89	02/05/2015	3,028.89	0.00
		Totals	4,978.89		4,978.89	570.00

Figure 2-32 Payment automatically applied to the oldest Invoice

Then, when you enter the payment amount, QuickBooks looks at all of the open Invoices for that customer. If it finds an amount due on an open Invoice that is the exact amount of the payment, it matches the payment with that Invoice. If there is no such match, it applies the payment to the *oldest* Invoice first and continues applying to the next oldest until the payment is completely applied. If this auto application of payments results in a partially paid Invoice, QuickBooks holds the balance on that Invoice open for the unpaid amount. This is a feature called *Automatically Apply Payments*.

If you select an Invoice in the Receive Payments form before entering an Amount Received, QuickBooks calculates the sum of the selected Invoice(s) and enters that sum into the Amount Received field. This feature is called *Automatically Calculate Payments*.

COMPUTER PRACTICE

To modify the **Automatically Apply Payments** and **Automatically Calculate Payments** setting, change the **Company Preferences** for **Payments**.

Follow these steps:

Step 1.　Select the *Edit* menu and then select **Preferences** (see Figure 2-33).

Step 2.　Select the **Payments** icon from the preference category in the list on the left. Then click the **Company Preferences** tab.

Step 3.　Check or uncheck the *Automatically apply payments* box to change it. For now, leave it checked.

With this feature disabled, in the Receive Payments window you will have to click Auto Apply Payment for each payment you process, or you will have to manually apply payments to Invoices by clicking in the column to the left of the Invoice and modifying the amount in the Payment column as necessary.

Step 4.　You can change the *Automatically calculate payments* box by checking or unchecking it. For now, leave it checked.

When this preference is on, QuickBooks will automatically calculate the payment received from the customer in the Amount field of the Receive Payments window as you select the Invoices. When this preference is off, QuickBooks does not automatically calculate payments.

Step 5.   Click OK.

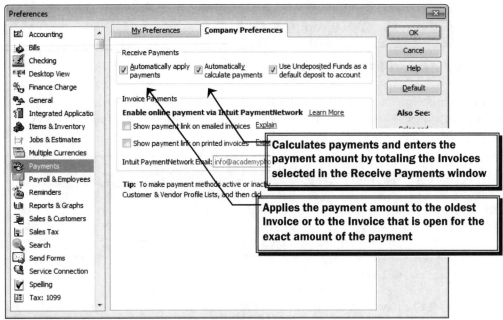

Figure 2-33 Preference for automatically applying payments

Recording Customer Discounts

What if your customer takes advantage of the discount you offer on your Invoice? In the next example, the payment you receive is less than the face amount of the Invoice because the customer took advantage of the 2% 10 Net 30 discount terms that Academy Photography offers.

COMPUTER PRACTICE

Follow these steps to record a payment on which the customer took a discount:

Step 1.   From the *Customer Center* select **Mason, Bob** from the *Customers & Jobs* list. Then select **Receive Payments** from the *New Transactions* drop-down list.

Step 2.   Enter all the customer payment information as shown in Figure 2-34. The customer is paying for Invoice #2015-106 after taking the discount allowed by the terms.

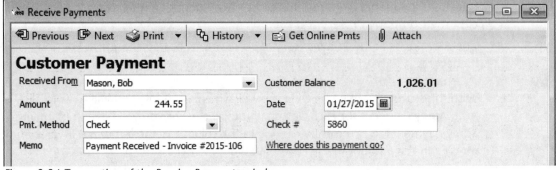

Figure 2-34 Top portion of the Receive Payments window

Step 3.   The bottom portion of the *Receive Payments* window (see Figure 2-35) displays the open Invoices for this customer. If the customer is eligible for discounts, a message will appear as shown just below the open Invoices. The **Disc. Date** column shows the date through which the customer is eligible to take a discount.

If the amount paid is not an exact match with any Invoice balance, QuickBooks will automatically apply the payment to the oldest Invoices. Here, Invoice #2015-104 is automatically selected since the amount $244.55 does not match any open invoices. The underpayment is also displayed. We'll fix this in the next step.

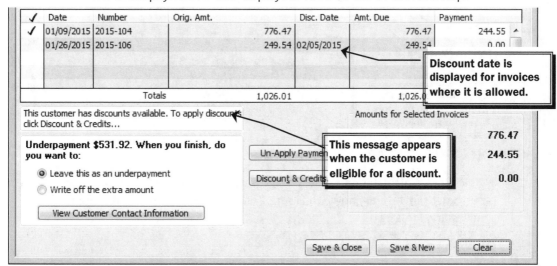

Figure 2-35 Bottom portion shows discount and credit information box, Invoice for payment and Underpayment

> **Note:**
> In the *Receive Payments* window the Underpayment amount is displayed with options to **Leave this as an underpayment** or **Write off the extra amount**. These options are displayed when the payment is less than the amount due on the selected Invoices. Similarly, Overpayment amounts are displayed with options to **Leave the credit to be used later** or **Refund the amount to the customer** when the payment is more than the amount due on the selected Invoices.
>
> **Tip:**
> If the payment amount doesn't add up exactly to the discounted amount, you'll need to make a choice. If the payment is too high, you could reduce the amount of the discount by lowering the amount in the *Discounts and Credits* window. If the payment is too low, you could raise the amount in the *Discounts and Credits* window. If the payment amount is significantly different, you can apply the amount of the payment and then send a Statement to the customer showing the balance due (if the payment is too low) or send a refund to the customer (if the payment is too high).

Step 4. Click in the column to the left of Invoice #**2015-104** to uncheck it and then click to check Invoice #**2015-106** (see Figure 2-36). This moves the payment so that it now applies to Invoice #2015-106. Make sure to uncheck #2015-104 before checking #2015-106, or you will see a Warning message.

✓	Date	Number	Orig. Amt.		Disc. Date	Amt. Due	Payment	
	01/09/2015	2015-104	776.47			776.47	0.00	▲
✓	01/26/2015	2015-106	249.54		02/05/2015	249.54	244.55	
								▼
	Totals		1,026.01			1,026.01	244.55	

Figure 2-36 Payment is now applied to the correct Invoice

Step 5.   Since the customer took advantage of the 2% 10 Net 30 terms that Academy Photography offered him, you'll need to reduce the amount due by 2%. To apply the discount to this Invoice, click **Discount and Credits** on the bottom of the *Receive Payments* window (see Figure 2-37).

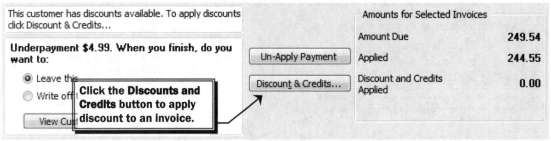

Figure 2-37 Discount and Credits Option

Step 6.   QuickBooks calculates and enters a suggested discount based on the terms on the customer's Invoice as shown in Figure 2-38. You can override this amount if necessary. Press **Tab**.

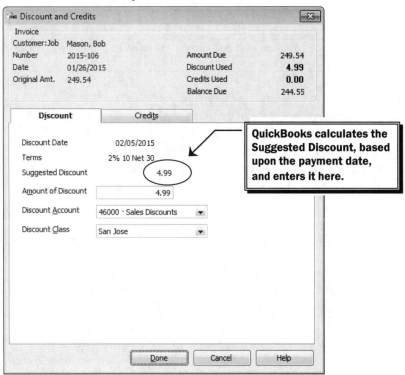

Figure 2-38 Discounts and Credits window

Step 7.   Select **46000 Sales Discounts** in *the Discount Account* field. Press **Tab**.

The *Discount Account* field is where you assign an account that tracks the discounts you give to your customers.

Step 8.   Enter *San Jose* in the *Class* field and then click **Done**.

Since Academy Photography uses class tracking, you will need to enter the appropriate class in this field. If you do not classify this transaction, QuickBooks will display the amount in an *Unclassified* column on the **Profit & Loss by Class** report. Refer to the Invoice you are discounting to determine the Class. Academy Photography uses the *San Jose* Class when recording Invoice 2015-106.

After recording the discount, the *Receive Payments* window reflects Total Discount and Credits Applied at the bottom of the Receive Payments window.

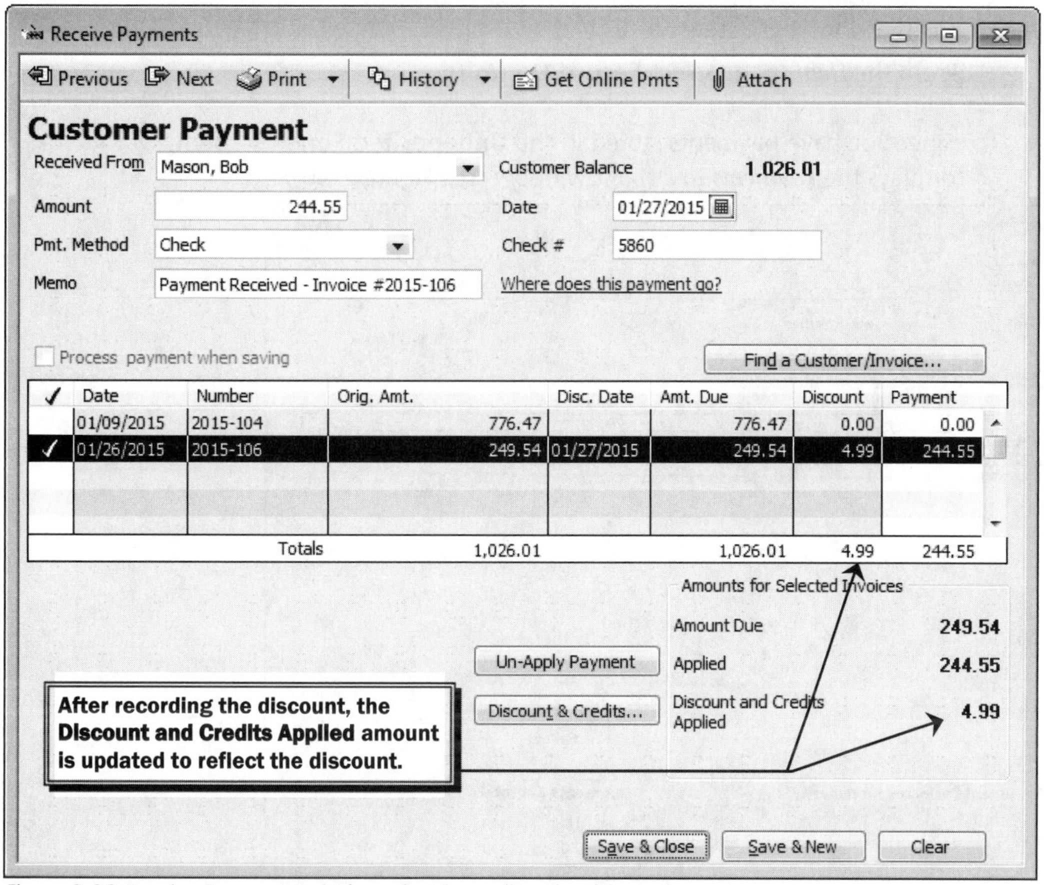

Figure 2-39 Receive Payments window after (recording the discount)

Step 9. Verify that your screen matches Figure 2-39.

Step 10. Click **Save & Close** to record the transaction.

Step 11. Close the Customer Center.

Making Bank Deposits

As you record payments from customers using the **Enter Sales Receipts** and **Receive Payments** windows, by default these payments are posted to a special QuickBooks account called **Undeposited Funds**. When you deposit these payments into your bank account, you will record a *Deposit* transaction. Deposit transactions move money from the **Undeposited Funds** account to the appropriate bank account. As you will see in this section, QuickBooks provides a special window (the *Payments to Deposit* window) to help you identify which payments are included on each deposit.

Since you will probably receive payments from your customers in several different ways (checks, cash, and credit cards), you'll want to record deposits of each payment type separately. This way, your deposits in QuickBooks will match what actually takes place at your bank, and your bank reconciliations will be much easier.

Therefore, when you make deposits, you'll deposit groups of each payment type together into deposits. Start with the checks and cash, followed by the MasterCard and VISA receipts, then the American Express receipts, and then the Discover receipts.

Depositing Checks and Cash

COMPUTER PRACTICE

To enter a deposit, follow these steps:

Step 1.   From the *Home* page select **Record Deposits**.

                      Since you have payments stored in the **Undeposited Funds** account, QuickBooks
                      displays the *Payments to Deposit* window (see Figure 2-40).

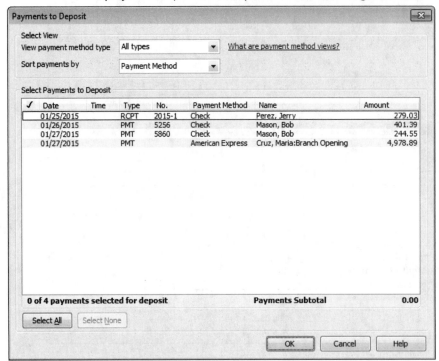

Figure 2-40 Select the payments to deposit

Step 2.   Select **Cash and Check** from the *View Payment Method Type* drop-down list (see
                      Figure 2-41).

                      Since the checks and cash you deposit in your bank account will post to your
                      account separately from credit card receipts, it is best to filter the report by payment
                      type and then create a separate deposit for each payment type. Depending on your
                      merchant service, you will probably need to create a single deposit for your
                      MasterCard and VISA receipts. Most merchant services combine MasterCard and
                      VISA receipts when they credit your bank account.

> **Tip:**
> Since you can filter the *Payments to Deposit* window by only one payment
> method at a time, using a single **Payment Method** for *Checks* and *Cash* will
> allow you to filter for both payment methods on this window. Depending on
> your merchant service, you may want to create a single **Payment Method** for
> *MasterCard* and *VISA* as well. To edit **Payment Methods** select the *Lists* menu,
> then select **Customer & Vendor Profile Lists**, and then select **Payment
> Methods List**. Once the *Payment Method List* window opens, select the Payment
> Method and select **Edit Payment Method** from the *Payment Method* menu.

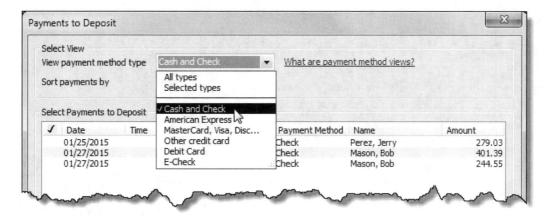

Figure 2-41 Cash and Check payments

Step 3.   Click **Select All** to select all of the cash and check deposits. See Figure 2-42. Click **OK**.

A checkmark in the column on the left indicates that QuickBooks will include the payment on the deposit.

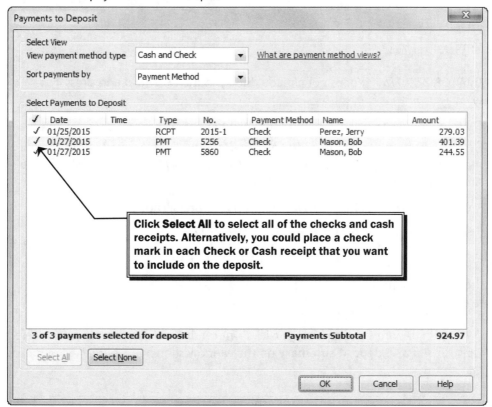

Figure 2-42 Select the payments to deposit

Step 4.   In the *Make Deposits* window, the **Checking** account is already selected in the *Deposit To* field (see Figure 2-43). The payments will be deposited to this bank account. Press **Tab**.

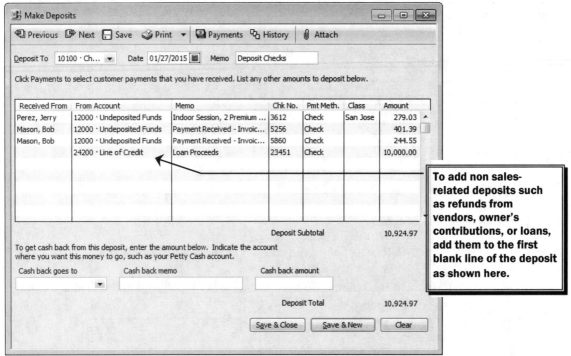

Figure 2-43 Make Deposits window

Step 5.   Enter *01/27/2015* if it does not already display in the *Date* field and press **Tab**.

Step 6.   Enter *Deposit Checks* in the *Memo* field and press **Tab**.

Step 7.   On this deposit, we will add a non-sales-related item, as follows:

    a)   On the first blank line, enter **Line of Credit** in the *From Account* column and press **Tab**. The *From Account* column on the *Make Deposits* window shows the account that the deposit is coming "from."

    b)   Enter **Loan Proceeds** in the *Memo* column and press **Tab**.

    c)   Enter *23451* in the *Chk No.* column and press **Tab**.

    d)   Enter **Check** in the *Pmt Meth.* column and press **Tab**.

    e)   Press **Tab** to skip the *Class* column.

    f)   Enter *10,000.00* in the *Amount* column.

Step 8.   If you wish to print the deposit slip, click **Print** on the *Make Deposits* window. Select **Deposit slip and deposit summary** on the window shown in Figure 2-44 and click **OK**.

> Note:
> QuickBooks can print deposit slips on preprinted deposit slips. To make this feature work for you, you'll need to order preprinted deposit slips that match the QuickBooks format.

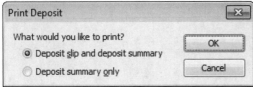

Figure 2-44 Print Deposit window for deposit slips

Step 9.   Click **Save & Close** to record the deposit.

> **The accounting behind the scenes:**
> In the deposit transaction (Figure 2-43) the checking account will increase (with a debit) by the total deposit ($10,924.97). All of the customer checks are coming from the **Undeposited Funds** account, and the loan proceeds are coming from the Line of Credit account. The customer checks will decrease (credit) the balance in **Undeposited Funds** and the loan from the owner will increase (credit) the balance in the Line of Credit account.

Holding Cash Back from Deposits

If you hold cash back when you make your deposits to the bank, fill in the bottom part of the deposit slip indicating the account to which you want to post the cash (see Figure 2-45).

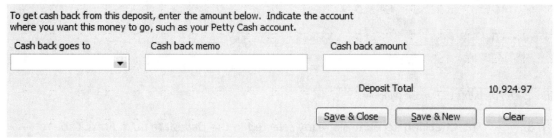

Figure 2-45 The bottom of the deposit slip deals with cash back

There are two ways you might use the cash back section of the deposit:

1.   If you're splitting the deposit between two different bank accounts, you could enter the other bank account and amount here. For example, if you send part of the funds from the deposit to the Money Market account, you could enter **Money Market** in the *Cash back goes to* field and the amount in the *Cash back amount* field.

2.   If you routinely hold back funds from your deposits and use them for several different purchases, you may want to set up a new QuickBooks bank account called **Petty Cash** and enter that account in the *Cash back goes to* field. The Petty Cash account is not really a bank account, but it's an account where you can track all your cash expenditures.

> **Tip:**
> It's not a good idea to hold cash back from deposits as "pocket money." If your business is a Sole Proprietorship, it's better to write a separate check (or ATM withdrawal) and then code it to **Owner's Draw**. This is a much cleaner way to track the money you take out for personal use. Discuss this with your QuickBooks ProAdvisor, or with your accountant.

Depositing Credit Card Payments

As mentioned previously, to ensure that your bank reconciliations go smoothly, you should always deposit your checks and cash separately from your credit card payments.

COMPUTER PRACTICE

Step 1.   Select the **Banking** menu, and then select **Make Deposits**. The *Payments to Deposit* window opens.

Step 2.   Click in the left column on the line to select the American Express receipt (see Figure 2-46). Then click **OK**. The *Make Deposits* window opens.

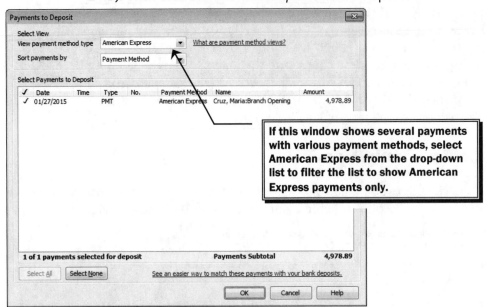

Figure 2-46 Payments to Deposit window

Step 3.   The **Checking** account is already selected in the *Deposit to* field. Press **Tab**.

Step 4.   Enter *01/27/2015* if it is not already entered in the *Date* field. Press **Tab**.

Step 5.   Enter *Deposit American Exp* in the *Memo* field.

As stated earlier, make sure you group together receipts in a way that agrees with the actual deposits made to your bank. This is a critical step in making your bank reconciliation process go smoothly.

Step 6.   On the first blank line of the deposit slip, enter *Bankcard Fees* in the **From Account** column and then press **Tab**.

You only need to create this line if your credit card processing company (or your bank) charges a discount fee on each credit card deposit rather than monthly.

Step 7.   Enter *Discount Fee* in the **Memo** column and then press **Tab**.

Step 8.   Press **Tab** to skip the **Chk No.** column.

Step 9.   Enter *American Express* in the **Pmt Method** column and then press **Tab**.

Step 10.   Enter *Walnut Creek* in the *Class* column and then press **Tab**.

Step 11.   You can use the QuickMath feature to enter the discount fee directly on the **Make Deposit** window. Enter *4978.89 * -.02* in the *Amount* column and press **Enter**.

QuickMath is a feature that helps you add, subtract, multiply, or divide in any QuickBooks Amount field. When you enter the first number (4978.89), it shows normally in the *Amount* column. Then when you enter the * (asterisk key or Shift+8), QuickMath shows a small adding machine tape on your screen (see Figure 2-47). Continue typing your formula for recording the discount fee. If the discount is 2%, enter *-.02* (minus point zero two) and press *Enter*. The result of the calculation shows in the *Amount* column (-99.58). **The minus sign makes the result a negative number and reduces the amount of your deposit.** This also increases (debits) your **Bankcard Fees** expense account.

Step 12.   Press **Tab** to have the total of the deposit updated automatically.

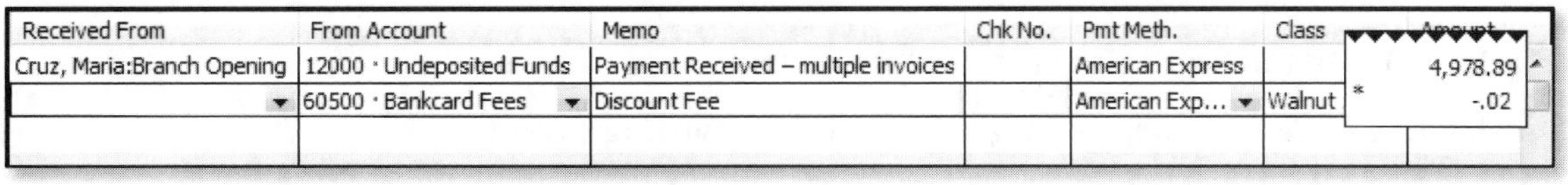

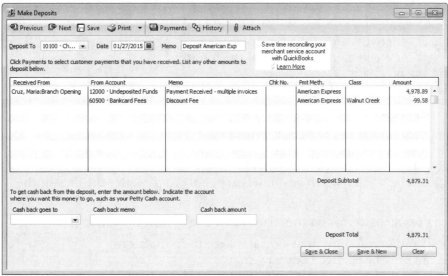

Received From	From Account	Memo	Chk No.	Pmt Meth.	Class	Amount
Cruz, Maria:Branch Opening	12000 · Undeposited Funds	Payment Received – multiple invoices		American Express		4,978.89
	60500 · Bankcard Fees	Discount Fee		American Exp...	Walnut	-.02

Figure 2-47 QuickMath makes an adding machine tape appear

Step 13.   Verify that your screen matches Figure 2-48. Click **Save & Close**.

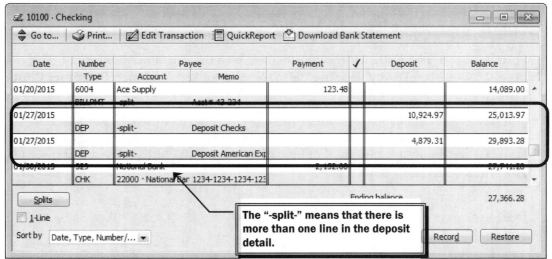

Figure 2-48 Make Deposits window after a credit card deposit

Now that you have entered your deposits, the checking account register shows each deposit and the updated balance in the account.

COMPUTER PRACTICE

To see the detail of a deposit, follow these steps:

Step 1.   Click the **Chart of Accounts** icon on the *Home* page.

Step 2.   Double-click on the **Checking** account in the *Chart of Accounts* window.

Step 3.   Scroll up until you see the two deposit transactions shown in Figure 2-49.

Step 4.   Close the *Checking* register and *Chart of Accounts*.

Figure 2-49 Checking register after entering deposits

Review Questions

Select the best answer(s) for each of the following:

1. In the *New Customer* window, you find everything except:

   a) Customer Name.
   b) Customer Bill To and Ship To address.
   c) Customer active/inactive status.
   d) Year-to-date sales information.

2. You should record a Sales Receipt when the customer pays:

   a) By cash, check, or credit card at the time of sale.
   b) By cash, check, or credit card at the end of the month.
   c) Sales tax on the purchase.
   d) For the order upon receipt of Invoice.

3. Which statement is false?

   a) Invoices are very similar to the Sales Receipt form.
   b) Invoices decrease Accounts Receivable.
   c) Sales Receipts have no effect on Accounts Receivables.
   d) Invoices should be created when customers are going to pay after the date of the initial sale.

4. You may specify payment Terms on the *New Customer* window; however:

   a) The payment Terms will only show on Sales Receipt transactions.
   b) The Terms can only be changed once a year.
   c) The sales representative must be informed.
   d) You are also permitted to override the Terms on each sale.

5. Your company has just accepted a payment for an Invoice. What should you do in QuickBooks to record this payment?

   a) Open the Invoice by clicking the **Invoices** icon on the *Home* page.
   b) Create a Sales Receipt by clicking the **Sales Receipt** icon on the *Home* page.
   c) Make a deposit by clicking the **Record Deposits** icon on the *Home* page.
   d) Receive the payment by clicking the **Receive Payments** icon on the *Home* page.

Sales-Problem 1

APPLYING YOUR KNOWLEDGE

> Restore the **Sales-12Problem1.QBM** file.

1. Enter your own name and address information into the Customer Center List. Then print the Customer List by selecting the *Reports* menu, **List**, and then **Customer Contact List**.

2. Enter a Sales Receipt using the data in Table 2-4. The payment will be automatically grouped with other payments in **Undeposited Funds** account. You'll need to create the customer record using Quick Add, or by setting it up in the list before adding the sale. Print the sale on blank paper.

Field	Data
Customer Name	Horwitz, Daniel
Class	Walnut Creek
Date	01/29/2015
Sale #	2015-1
Sold To	Daniel Horwitz 1695 Blue Sky Pkwy Walnut Creek, CA 94599
Check No	477
Payment Method	Check
Item	Camera SR32, Qty 2, $695.99
Item	Case, Qty 2, $79.99
Sales Tax	Contra Costa (8.25%) – Auto Calculates
Total Sale	$1,680.00
Customer Tax Code	Tax
Memo	2 Cameras, 2 Cases

Table 2-4 Use this data for a Sales Receipt in Step 2

3. Enter an Invoice using the data in the table below. Print the Invoice on blank paper.

Field	Data
Customer Name	Pelligrini, George: 1254 Wilkes Rd.
Class	San Jose
Custom Template	Academy Photo Service Invoice
Date	01/31/2015
Invoice #	2015-106
Sold To	Pelligrini Builders 222 Santana Ave. Los Gatos, CA 94482
PO Number	8324
Terms	Net 30
Item	Indoor Photo Session, Qty 6, $95/hour (Non-taxable)
Item	Retouching, Qty 1 (hrs), $95/hour (Non-taxable)
Sales Tax	Santa Clara (8.25%) – Auto Calculates
Total Sale	$665.00
Memo	6 Hour Session, 1 Hour Retouching

Table 2-5 Use this data for an Invoice in Step 3

4. Enter a second Invoice using the data in the table below. Print the Invoice on blank paper. You will need to add this customer either through *Quick Add* or entering the customer information in the *Customer Center*.

Field	Data
Customer Name	*Fuller, Nathan*
Class	*San Jose*
Custom Template	*Academy Photo Service Invoice*
Date	*01/31/2015*
Invoice #	*2015-107*
Sold To	*Nathan Fuller*
	99050 Market St.
	Santa Clara, CA 95111
PO Number	*736555*
Terms	*2% 10 Net 30*
Item	*Indoor Photo Session, Qty 3, $95/hour*
	(Non-taxable)
Sales Tax	*Santa Clara (8.25%) – Auto Calculates*
Total Sale	*$285.00*
Memo	*3 Hour Session*

Table 2-6 Use this data for an Invoice in Step 4.

5. Record a payment dated *2/15/2015* for *$285.00* from Nathan Fuller (check #5342) and apply it to Invoice **2015-107**.

6. On *2/15/2015,* you received a partial payment from George Pelligrini for the *1254 Wilkes Rd.* Job for $300. American Express payment, card #4321-654321-54321, expires in 5/2016.

7. On *2/15/2015*, deposit everything from the **Undeposited Funds** account using the following:

   a) Deposit Cash and Check payments together (Memo: Deposit Checks). Print **Deposit Slip and Deposit Summary** onto blank paper.

   b) Deposit American Express payments separately (Memo: Deposit American Express). Record a 2% bankcard discount fee (use QuickMath to calculate) on the credit card deposit number (Account - Bankcard Fee, Payment Method - American Express, Memo-2% Discount Fee). This amount should be a negative number. Print **Deposit Summary Only** onto blank paper.

Chapter 3
Tracking Revenue

Objectives

After completing this chapter, you should be able to:

- Process customer returns and credits (page 73)
- Write off customer *Invoices* (record bad debts) (page 77)
- Create customer *Statements* (page 80)
- Collect sales tax (page 81)
- Create sales reports (page 88)

Restore this File

This chapter uses Revenue-12.QBW. To open this file, restore the Revenue-12.QBM file to your hard disk. See page 8 for instructions on restoring files. If you are using QuickBooks Premier Accountant, we recommend that you toggle to QuickBooks Premier General Business as described on page x.

In the last chapter, you learned about sales forms and the accounts receivable process. In this chapter, you will learn how QuickBooks can help you record customer returns and refunds, create customer *Statements*, and process sales reports. The sales reports show details of each sale, or you can see summaries of sales by customer, job, sales rep, class, or item.

Recording Customer Returns and Credits

To record customer returns or credits, use QuickBooks *Credit Memos*. *Credit Memos* can be used in the following situations:

- To record the cancellation of an order that has already been invoiced.
- To record a return of merchandise from a customer.
- To record a credit-on-account for a customer.
- To record the first step of making a refund to a customer.

Key Term:
Credit Memos are sales forms that reduce the amount owed to your company by a customer.

The accounting behind the scenes:
Credit Memos reduce (credit) Accounts Receivable and reduce (debit) Income and, in some cases, Sales Tax Payable.

When you create a *Credit Memo* in QuickBooks, you must apply the credit to one or more *Invoices*, or use it to give a refund to the customer.

Refunding Customers

There are several situations when you may need to issue a refund to a customer:

1. When a customer pays for merchandise and then returns the merchandise.

2. When a customer requests a discount or refund on merchandise or services for which she has already paid.

3. When a customer overpays an *Invoice* and requests a refund.

If the customer paid with cash or check, you should issue a refund check. If the customer paid with a credit card, you should credit the customer's credit card.

COMPUTER PRACTICE

The first step in issuing a customer refund is to create a *Credit Memo* showing the detail of what is being refunded. Typically, the detail will include the products and/or services returned or discounted.

Bob Mason paid for but didn't use one hour of a photo session. In this exercise, you will create a *Credit Memo* directly from an *Invoice*. This has the advantage of including the details of the *Invoice* in the *Credit Memo*. Later, you will see other ways to create a *Credit Memo*, such as directly from the *Home* page.

Step 1.   Click **Customers** in the *Icon* bar to open the *Customer Center*.

Step 2.   Select **Mason, Bob** from the *Customer Center* list.

Step 3.   If necessary, choose **All** from the *Date* field in the list of transactions in the *Customer Center*. From the list of transactions displayed, double click on Invoice #2015-106. This will open the *Invoice*.

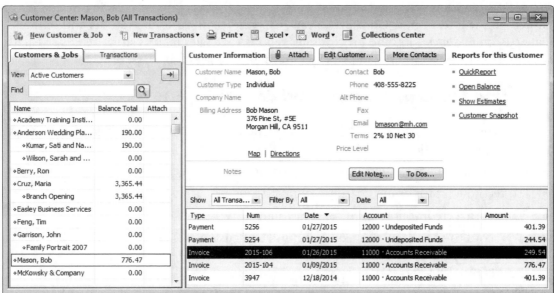

Figure 3-1 Opening Invoice from Customer Center

Step 4.   Click the **Create** button at the top of the *Create Invoices* window and choose **Create Credit Memo for this Invoice** from the drop down menu.

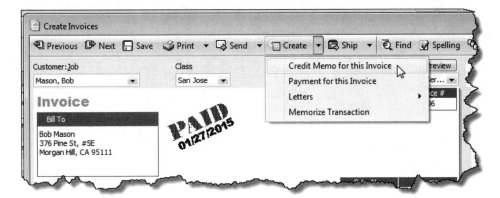

Figure 3-2 Create button in Create Invoices window

Step 5.   A *Credit Memo* opens with the information from the previous *Invoice* (see Figure 3-3).

           Credit Memos look similar to *Invoices,* but they perform the opposite function. That is, a *Credit Memo* reduces (debits) Sales, reduces (credits) Accounts Receivable, and in some cases reduces Sales Tax Payable. If Inventory is involved, a *Credit Memo* increases (debits) the Inventory asset and reduces (credits) the Cost of Goods Sold account.

Step 6.   Press **Tab** four times to move to the *Date* field and enter *2/15/2015*. Press **Tab**.

Step 7.   Enter *2015-106C* in the *Credit No.* field. Press **Tab** three times.

           This credit transaction is included on statements and customer reports, so using the *Invoice* number followed by a "C" in the *Credit No.* field helps identify which *Invoice* this *Credit Memo* should apply to.

Step 8.   Leave *Indoor Photo Session* in the *Item* field and tab to the *Qty* field. Change the *Qty* to *1*. Press **Tab** three times.

Step 9.   Press **Ctrl+Delete** to remove the *Standard Photo Package* from the *Credit Memo*.

Step 10.   Add *Refunded – 1 Hr Photo Session* to the *Memo* field.

Step 11.   Make sure your screen matches Figure 3-3. When done press **Save & New**.

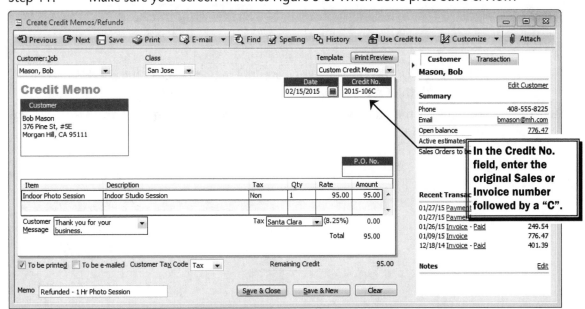

Figure 3-3 Use this data for the Credit Memo for Bob Mason

Step 12.   After you save the *Credit Memo,* QuickBooks displays the *Available Credits* window (see Figure 3-4). Select **Give a Refund** and click **OK**.

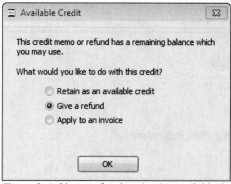

Figure 3-4 Give a refund option in Available Credit window

Step 13.   QuickBooks opens the *Issue a Refund* window (see Figure 3-5). Most of the information is already filled in. Enter **Refunded – 1 Hr Photo Session** in the *Memo* field. Click **OK** to record the refund check.

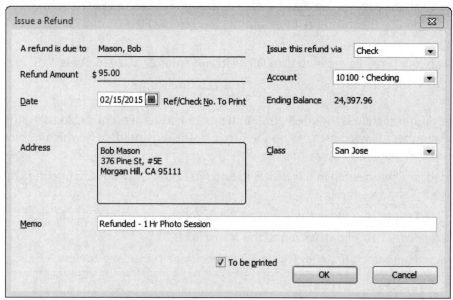

Figure 3-5 Issue a Refund for Photo Session

Step 14.   When you click **OK**, QuickBooks creates the refund check in the checking account and records the *Credit Memo.*

Step 15.   To redisplay the *Credit Memo,* click the **Previous** button in the *Credit Memo* window (see Figure 3-6).

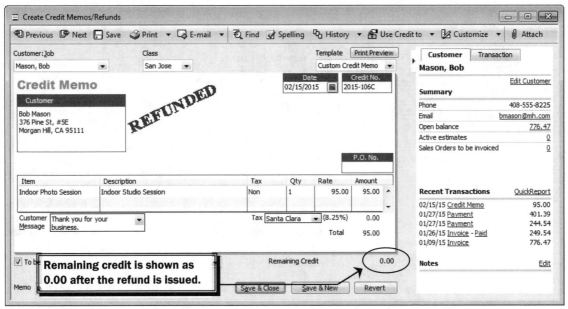

Figure 3-6 Credit Memo after the refund

Step 16.   Close the *Credit Memo* window. Close the *Invoice* window.

Step 17.   Although you will not do it now, this is when you would print the refund check.

Writing Off a Bad Debt

If an *Invoice* becomes uncollectible, you'll need to write off the debt. If you use the cash basis of accounting, the uncollectible *Invoice* has not yet been recognized as income on your *Profit & Loss* report, and therefore, you *could* simply delete the *Invoice* to remove it from your records. However, good accounting practice dictates that you enter a new entry to credit the customer balance and reverse the sale (and the sales tax if appropriate).

To properly write off the bad debt, use a *Credit Memo* and a *Bad Debt* Item as shown in the following practice. In the "Customizing QuickBooks" chapter, you'll learn more about Items, but for now, we'll set up a *Bad Debt* Item in the sample file.

COMPUTER PRACTICE

Step 1.   From the *List* menu select **Item List.**

Step 2.   Press **Ctrl+N** to display the *New Item* window.

Step 3.   If the *New Feature* window displays, click **OK** to bypass this window.

Step 4.   Create an *Other Charge* Item called **Bad Debt** as shown in Figure 3-7. Link the *Bad Debt* Item to the Bad Debts expense account. Click **OK.**

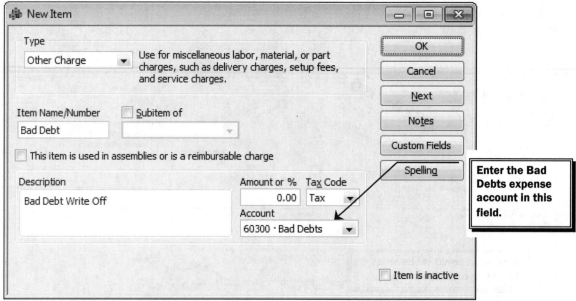

Figure 3-7 Bad Debt Other Charge Item

Step 5.   Select **OK** to close the *Item List*.

Step 6.   From the *Home* page select **Refunds & Credits**. This opens a *Credit Memo*.
              Alternatively, you could open the *Invoice* and create a *Credit Memo* from the *Create*
              button.

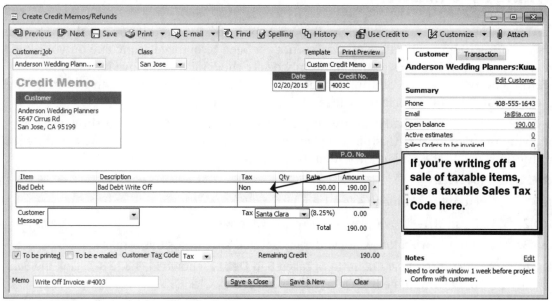

Figure 3-8 Write off a bad debt with a Credit Memo

Step 7.   Fill out the **Credit Memo** as shown in Figure 3-8. Choose ***Anderson Wedding
              Planners: Kumar, Sati and Naveen*** in the *Customer:Job* field.

Step 8.   QuickBooks displays a warning message because *Invoices* and *Credit Memos* normally
              increase or decrease Income accounts, rather than Expense accounts (see Figure
              3-9). Click **OK**.

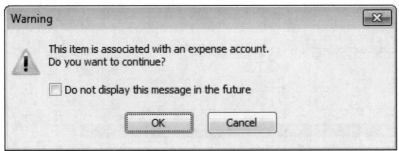

Figure 3-9 Warning about the Bad Debt Item pointing to an expense account

> **Note:**
> Under many circumstances, your Bad Debt write-off should not affect sales tax. However, if the sale you are writing off does need to affect your sales tax liability, you'll need to use two lines on the credit memo.
>
> On the first line of the *Credit Memo*, use the **Bad Debt** Item and enter the total of all taxable items in the sale (not including the sales tax) in the *Amount* column. Select **Tax** (or the appropriate Code) in the *Tax Code* column. QuickBooks will calculate the sales tax and reduce your liability by that amount.
>
> On the second line, use the same **Bad Debt** Item and enter the total of the non-taxable items from the original *Invoice*, including any shipping or miscellaneous charges (excluding sales tax). Select a non-taxable *Tax Code* for this line.

Step 9.   Click **Save & Close** to record the *Credit Memo*. The *Available Credit* window (see Figure 3-10) will be displayed. Select **Apply to an Invoice** option and click **OK**.

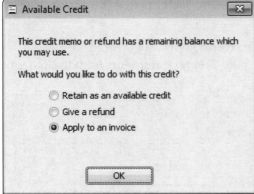

Figure 3-10 Apply to an Invoice option on Available Credit window

> **The accounting behind the scenes:**
> When you use the Bad Debt Item on a *Credit Memo*, the *Credit Memo* decreases (credit) Accounts Receivable and increases (debit) Bad Debts expense.

Applying the Bad Debt Credit Memo to an Open Invoice

COMPUTER PRACTICE

Step 1.   The *Apply Credit to Invoices* window is automatically displayed with Invoice #4003 **Check (✓)** column checked (see Figure 3-11).

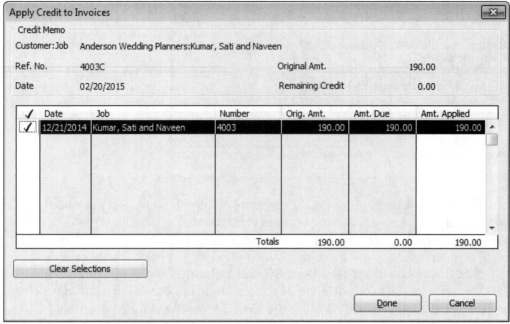

Figure 3-11 Apply Credit to Invoices window

Step 2.   Click **Done** to apply the bad debt to the selected *Invoice*.

Creating Customer Statements

QuickBooks Customer *Statements* provide a summary of the activity for an accounts receivable Customer during the period you specify. When you create *Statements*, you can show either all of the Customer's accounts receivable activity or just the transactions that are currently open.

COMPUTER PRACTICE

Step 1.   From the *Home* page click the **Statements** icon to open the *Create Statements* window (see Figure 3-12). Alternatively, click **Create Statements** from the *Customers* menu.

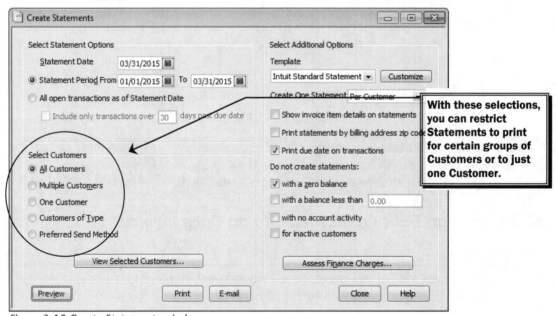

Figure 3-12 Create Statements window

Step 2.   Enter **03/31/2015** in the *Statement Date* field.

Step 3.   Set the *Statement Period From* and *To* fields to *1/1/2015* and *3/31/2015* respectively.

You need to include a *Statement Date* and a *Statement Period* because the *Statement Date* is the "current" date that will appear on the *Statement*, while *Statement Period* dates include the period for which accounts receivable transactions will show on the *Statement*.

Step 4.   Leave **All Customers** selected in the *Select Customers* section.

> **Note:**
> If you want to print only the open *Invoices* for each Customer, select **All open transactions as of Statement Date** at the top left of the *Create Statements* window. If you want to show the detail from the *Invoice*, make sure the *Show invoice item details on statements* option is selected.

Step 5.   Leave **Per Customer** selected in the *Create One Statement* drop-down list.

Step 6.   Check the **with a zero balance** box in the *Do not create statements* section.

Step 7.   Click **Preview**.

Step 8.   After previewing the three pages of statements in the *Print Preview* window (see Figure 3-13), click the **Close** button.

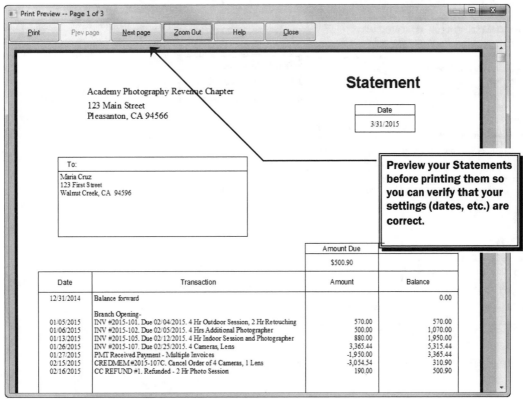

Figure 3-13 Preview your statements before printing

Collecting Sales Tax

If you sell products and certain types of services, chances are you will need to collect and remit sales tax. In many states, aside from the state tax, each county or city may impose an additional tax that businesses are required to track and report.

If you sell non-taxable goods and services, or if you sell to customers that are exempt from paying sales tax, your state will probably require a breakdown of non-taxable sales and the reason sales tax was not imposed.

These differing conditions may not apply in all jurisdictions, but QuickBooks allows you to track sales tax for all of these different situations. If you are not familiar with the sales tax rates or reporting requirements in your area, consult your state agency, your local QuickBooks ProAdvisor, or accountant for guidance.

Setting up Sales Tax

You must set up your **Sales Tax Preferences** before using the Sales Tax feature in QuickBooks.

COMPUTER PRACTICE

Step 1.   Click the **Manage Sales Tax** button on the *Home Page*. Or you can choose **Manage Sales Tax** from the *Sales Tax* option on the *Vendors* menu.

Step 2.   The *Manage Sales Tax* dialog box will appear (see Figure 3-14).

Step 3.   Click the **Sales Tax Preferences** button in the *Get Started* section. Alternatively, you could select **Preferences** from the *Edit* menu, then select the *Sales Tax Company* Preferences.

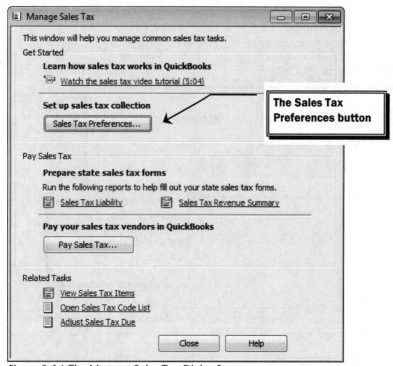

Figure 3-14 The Manage Sales Tax Dialog Box

Step 4.   The *Sales Tax Company Preferences* dialog box appears.

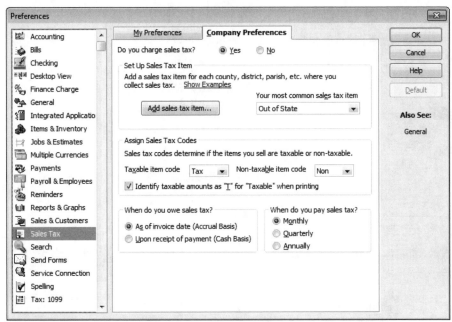

Figure 3-15 Sales Tax Company Preferences

Step 5.   Leave **Yes** selected in the *Do you charge sales tax?* section.

Step 6.   In the *Set Up Sales Tax Items* section, notice *Out of State* is selected in the *Your most common sales tax item* field. Change this field to **Contra Costa** (see Figure 3-16).

> **Note:**
> The sales tax item listed in the *Your most common sales tax item* field becomes the default sales tax item on new customer records, as well as on *Sales Receipts* and *Invoices*.

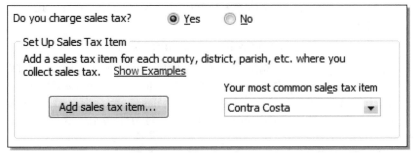

Figure 3-16 Select the Your most common sales tax item you use on sales forms

Step 7.   In the *Assign Sales Tax Codes* section, **Tax** is the default code in the *Taxable item code* field and **Non** is the default for the *Non-taxable item code* field. For more information about *Sales Tax Codes,* see page 85.

Step 8.   Review the remaining Preferences. When finished, click **OK** to save your changes and then **Close** to close the *Manage Sales Tax* window.

Sales Tax Items

Sales Tax Items are used on sales forms to calculate the amount of sales tax due on each sale. You can view the *Sales Tax Item* on the bottom of the form, separately from the rest of the *Items* (see Figure 3-17).

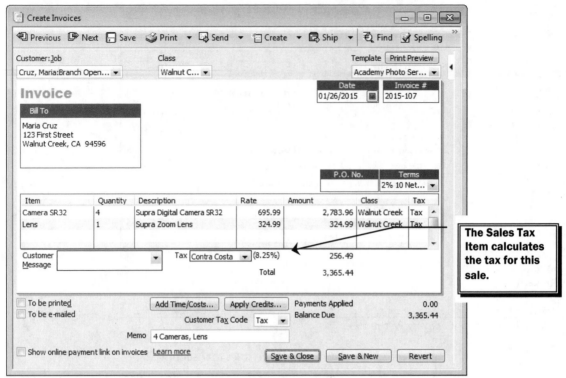

Figure 3-17 Invoice using the "Santa Clara" Sales Tax Item

To set up your Sales Tax Items, follow these steps:

COMPUTER PRACTICE

Step 1.   Select the *Lists* menu and then select **Item List**. Alternatively, click the **Items &
           Services** icon on the *Home* page.

Step 2.   To add a new Item, select the **Item** button at the bottom of the *Item List* and then
           select **New**. If you get a *New Feature* window, you may read it for information, but
           click **OK** to bypass it for now.

Step 3.   Select **Sales Tax Item** in the *Type* drop-down list and press **Tab**.

Step 4.   Enter the *Tax Name, Description, Tax Rate,* and *Tax Agency,* as shown in Figure 3-18.
           This item will track all sales activity (taxable and nontaxable) for Alameda County
           and will charge each customer 8.75% in sales tax. The sales taxes collected using the
           Alameda Sales Tax Item will increase the amount due to the *State Board of
           Equalization.*

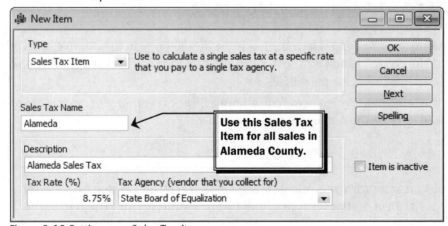

Figure 3-18 Setting up a Sales Tax item

Step 5. Click **OK** to save the Item.

> **The accounting behind the scenes:**
> **Sales Tax Items** automatically calculates the sales tax on each sales form by applying the sales tax rate to all taxable items on that sale. QuickBooks increases (credits) Sales Tax Payable for the amount of sales tax on the sale. Also, QuickBooks tracks the amount due (debits) by *Tax Agency* in the *Sales Tax Liability* report and in the *Pay Sales Tax* window.

Your sample file includes three additional *Sales Tax Items* for tracking sales in *Contra Costa* and *Santa Clara* counties, as well as *Out of State* sales. After you add the *Alameda Sales Tax Item*, your Item list will look like Figure 3-19.

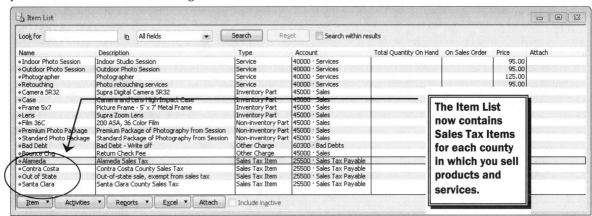

Figure 3-19 Item list

> **Note:**
> If you remit sales tax to **only one agency** (e.g., California's State Board of Equalization) but you collect sales tax in several different counties or cities, create a separate *Sales Tax Item* for each taxable location in which you sell products. This allows you to track different sales tax rates for each locale.
>
> **Note:**
> If you pay sales tax to **more than one agency**, you should use *Sales Tax Group*s to combine several different Sales Tax Items into a group tax rate.

Sales Tax Codes

Sales Tax Codes are an additional classification for calculating and reporting sales tax. A Sales Tax Code is assigned to each product or service Item, as well as to each Customer.

Sales Tax Codes serve two purposes. First, Sales Tax Codes indicate whether a specific product or service is taxable or non-taxable. Secondly, Sales Tax Codes categorize revenue based on the reason you charged or did not charge sales tax.

If your sales tax agency requires reporting for different types of tax-exempt sales, you may wish to create several non-taxable Sales Tax Codes for each type of non-taxable sale (e.g., **RSR** for non-taxable resellers).

Using Sales Tax Codes on Sales Forms

If you use a taxable *Sales Tax Code* in the *Customer Tax Code* field on sales forms, QuickBooks will apply sales tax (see Figure 3-20). If you use a non-taxable *Sales Tax Code*, QuickBooks will not apply sales tax unless you override the sales tax code (to a taxable code) on one of the lines in the body of the form.

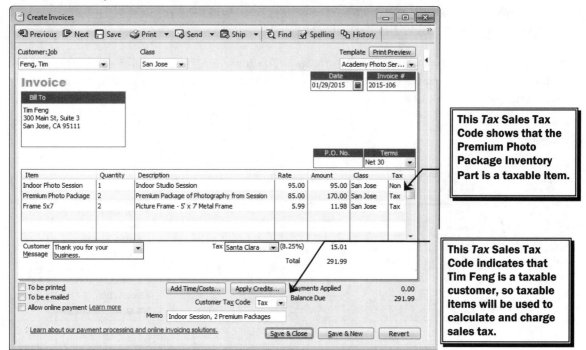

Figure 3-20 Invoice with taxable items

When you set up a Customer record, the *Sales Tax Code* you enter in the Customer record becomes the default in the *Customer Tax Code* field on sales forms.

Similarly, when you set up Items, the *Sales Tax Code* you enter in the *Item* record becomes the default Tax Code in the body of sales forms.

You can override the *Sales Tax Code* at the bottom of sales forms by using the *Customer Tax Code* drop-down list, or on each line in the body of the Invoice.

Setting up Sales Tax Codes

COMPUTER PRACTICE

One of your customers, Miranda's Corner, purchases various frames from Academy Photography to resell to her customers, and therefore does not pay sales tax.

Step 1.   From the *Lists* menu select **Sales Tax Code List**. QuickBooks displays the *Sales Tax Code List* window (see Figure 3-21).

Figure 3-21 Sales Tax Code List

Step 2.   This file already has two *Sales Tax Codes* (*Tax* and *Non*). To create a new *Sales Tax Code*, select **New** from the *Sales Tax Code* button at the bottom of the window.

Step 3.   Enter the information shown in Figure 3-22. This creates a Sales Tax Code for tracking customers who do not pay sales tax because they are resellers.

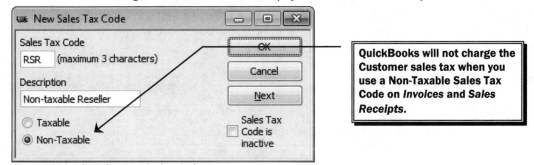

Figure 3-22 Edit Sales Tax Code window

Step 4.   Click OK to save this Sales Tax Code. .

Step 5.   Close the *Sales Tax Code List* window.

Step 6.   Open the *Customer Center*. Double click **Miranda's Corner** in the *Customer Center*. If you get a *New Feature* window, you may read it for information, but click **OK** to bypass it for now.

Step 7.   In the *Edit Customer* window, click on the **Additional Info** tab.

Step 8.   Select **RSR** from the *Tax Code* field in the *Sales Tax Information* section (see Figure 3-23).

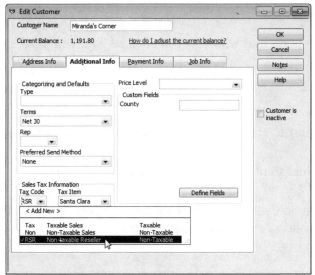

Figure 3-23 Changing the Customer Sales Tax Code

Step 9.   Click **OK** to close the *Edit Customer* window. Close the *Customer Center*.

Calculating Sales Tax on Sales Forms

When you properly set up your QuickBooks *Items*, *Customers*, *Sales Tax Codes*, and *Preferences*, QuickBooks automatically calculates and tracks sales tax on each sale.

As illustrated in Figure 3-24 and detailed in the steps above, each line on a sale shows a separate *Item* that is taxed according to the combination of how the *Item*, *Tax Code*, and Customer are set up. When you set up *Items*, you indicate which *Sales Tax Code* normally applies to that Item. In addition, when you set up a Customer record, you indicate the *Sales Tax Item* and *Sales Tax Code* to be used for that Customer.

Then, when you create a sale (*Invoice* or *Sales Receipt*), the *Customer Tax Code* and the *Sales Tax Item* are taken from the Customer's record and filled into the *Customer Tax Code* and *Tax* fields on the form. A non-taxable *Customer Tax Code* overrides the taxable *Tax Code* on each line item. If necessary, you can override the *Tax Code* on each line of the sales form or at the bottom of the form. The *Tax Item*, which can also be overridden, determines the rate to charge on the sum of all taxable line items on the sale.

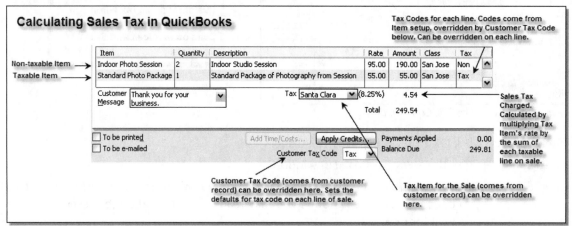

Figure 3-24 Calculating Sales Tax in QuickBooks

For more on paying the collected sales tax, see 131.

Creating Sales Reports

In this section, you'll learn how to create reports that will help you analyze your company's sales.

Customer Open Balance Report

You can create a *Customer Open Balance* report to view the open *Invoices* and the *Credit Memo* for this customer.

Step 1.   If necessary, display the **Customer Center** and then select **Cruz, Maria: Branch Opening** as shown in Figure 3-25.

Step 2.   Under the *Reports for this Job* section, select the **Open Balance** link (see Figure 3-25). You may need to expand the window to see the Reports section.

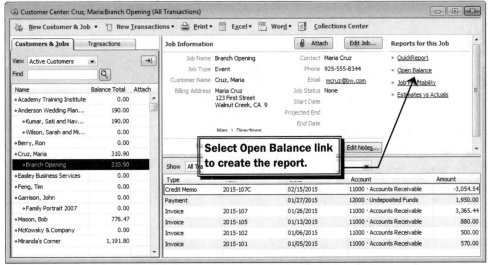

Figure 3-25 *Select the job and click the needed report in the Customer Center*

Step 3. The *Customer Open Balance* report opens (see Figure 3-26).

Step 4. Click the Close Window button ( ) at the top right of the window to close the report or press **Esc** to close the window.

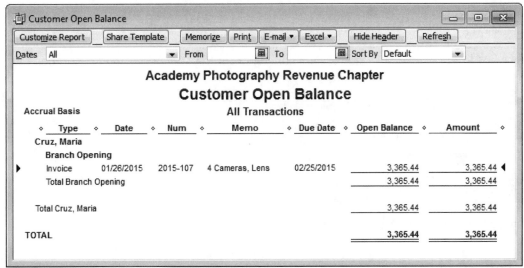

Figure 3-26 *Customer Open Balance report*

Sales by Customer Summary Report

The *Sales by Customer Summary* report shows how much you have sold to each of your customers over a given date range.

COMPUTER PRACTICE

To create this report, follow these steps:

Step 1. From the *Report Center* select **Sales** from the category list and then double click the *Sales by Customer Summary* report in the *Sales by Customer* section.

Step 2. Enter *01/1/2015* in the *From* date field and then press **Tab**.

Step 3. Enter *2/28/2015* in the *To* date field and then press **Tab**.

Figure 3-27 shows the *Sales by Customer Summary* report for the first two months of 2015.

Step 4.   To print the report, click **Print** at the top of the report.

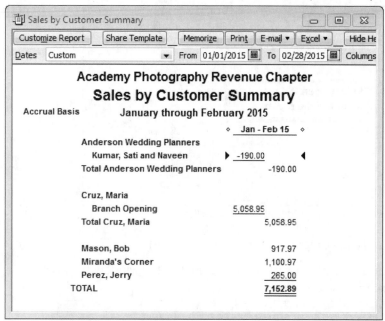

Figure 3-27 Sales by Customer Summary report

Step 5.   Close the *Sales by Customer Summary* report. If the *Memorize Report* dialog box opens, click **No** (see Figure 3-28).

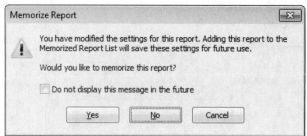

Figure 3-28 Memorize Report dialog box

Sales by Item Report

The *Sales by Item* report shows how much you have sold of each Item over a given date range. To create this report, follow these steps:

COMPUTER PRACTICE

Step 1.   From the *Report Center* select **Sales** from the category list and then double click the **Sales by Item Summary** sample in the *Sales by Item* section. You may need to scroll down.

Step 2.   Enter *1/1/2015* in the *From* date field and then press **Tab**.

Step 3.   Enter *2/28/2015* in the *To* date field and then press **Tab**.

Figure 3-29 shows the *Sales by Item Summary* report for the first two months of 2015.

Step 4.   To print the report, click **Print** at the top of the report.

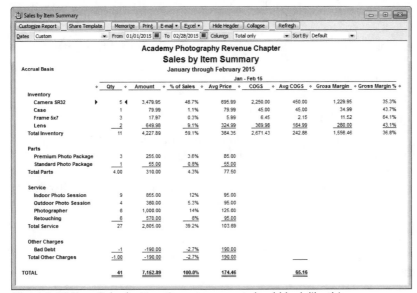

Figure 3-29 Your Sales by Item Summary report should look like this

Step 5. Close the *Sales by Item Summary* report. If the *Memorize Report* window opens, click **No**.

Review Questions

Select the best answer(s) for each of the following:

1. Customer *Statements*:
   a) Provide a summary of all accounts receivable activity for a Customer during the period you specify.
   b) Are not available in QuickBooks.
   c) Automatically assess and calculate finance charges for overdue accounts without any user action.
   d) Should only be created and mailed if the Customer's balance is over $500.

2. Which of the following options is not available on the *Available Credit* window?
   a) Give a refund.
   b) Retain as an available credit.
   c) Apply to an *Invoice*.
   d) Use with *Receive Payments*.

3. What is the best way to write off a bad debt?
   a) Delete the original *Invoice*.
   b) Create a *Credit Memo* using a *Bad Debt* Item and apply the credit to the past due *Invoice*.
   c) Create a *Credit Memo* for the amount of the past due *Invoice* and retain the available credit.
   d) Any of the above.

4. In which of the following situations would you create a *Credit Memo*?

a) You need to record a cancelled order that has already been invoiced but not paid.
b) A customer returns merchandise and wants the return credited to a future *Invoice*.
c) A customer requests a refund.
d) Any of the above.

5. The Credit Memo Number should be

a) The next number after the *Credit Memo Number* on the last *Credit Memo*.
b) The next number after the *Invoice Number* on the last *Invoice*, followed by a "C."
c) Any unique number.
d) The same number as the *Invoice* to which the *Credit Memo* is linked, followed by a "C."

Revenue-Problem 1

EXTENDING YOUR KNOWLEDGE

Restore the **Revenue-12Problem1.QBM** file.

1. On **Feb 7, 2015**, create **Invoice #2015-108** to Morris Consulting. Use the Walnut Creek class, terms 2% 10, Net 30. (Note: Special terms apply to this *Invoice* only.) The customer purchased a 2 hour Indoor Photo Session ($95 per hour) and 2 hours with a Photographer ($125 per hour). Use the Out of State Sales Tax Item. The *Invoice* total is $440.00. Print the *Invoice*.

2. On **Feb 9, 2015**, create **Invoice #2015-109** to Easley Business Services. Use the class San Jose. Terms are Net 30. The customer purchased 4 Camera ($695.99), 4 Lens ($324.99), and 4 Cases ($79.99). Use the Out of State Sales Tax Item. The *Invoice* total is $4,403.88. Print the *Invoice*.

3. On **Feb 10, 2015**, receive check **#58621** in the amount of $431.20 from Morris Consulting in full payment of Invoice #2015-108. He took a 2% discount of $8.80. Use the Sales Discount account and the Walnut Creek class.

4. On **Feb 15, 2015**, Donald Easley of Easley Business Services called and gave his VISA credit card number to pay off the balance on his open Invoices. The payment amount was $4,403.88; VISA #4444-3333-2222-1111; Exp. 05/2017.

5. On **Feb 23, 2015**, Morris Consulting requested a refund for two hours of Photographer services. Create **Credit Memo #2015-108C** and use the Walnut Creek class. Issue Morris Consulting a refund check.

6. On **Feb 26, 2015**, create a **Credit Memo** to write off Invoice 3696 to Ortega Services. You will need to create a Bad Debt item. Since Invoice 3696 included a taxable item, you will need to mark the Bad Debt item on the *Credit Memo* for the amount $695.99 and mark it as taxable. Use the Walnut Creek class. The entire amount of the write-off is $753.41.

7. On **Feb 27, 2015**, receive payment for **$1,191.80** from Miranda's Corner in payment of Invoice #2015-103. She uses her VISA card number 7777-8888-9999-0000 expiration date 12/2015, to pay this *Invoice*.

8. On **Feb 28, 2015**, issue **Credit Memo #2015-103C** to Miranda's Corner for Invoice #2015-103. The customer returned 1 Camera ($695.99). A 10% restocking fee applies. Use the San Jose class and the Santa Clara County sales tax. Issue a **refund** to Miranda's

Corner's VISA card on Credit Memo #2015-103C using the *Refunding Credit Cards* method discussed in the chapter. Total refund: **$683.81**. Print the *Credit Memo* after the refund.

9. Deposit the check in the **Undeposited Funds** account on **2/28/2015**. Total deposit amount is **$431.20**. Print the **Deposit Slip and Deposit Summary**.

10. Deposit all VISA receipts on **2/28/15**. Record a 2% **bankcard discount fee** (use QuickMath to calculate) on the credit card deposit. Total deposit amount is **$4,813.63**. Print the **Deposit Summary Only**.

11. Print **Sales by Customer Summary** for January through February 2015.

12. Print **Sales by Item Summary** for January through February 2015.

13. Create and print customer *Statements* for the period of **February 1, 2015** through **February 28, 2015**. Print *Statements* for all customers who have a balance due: one for Anderson Weddings and one for Bob Mason.

Chapter 4
Managing Expenses

Objectives

After completing this chapter, you should be able to:

- Set up vendors in the *Vendor List* (page 98)
- Understand how to use classes in QuickBooks (page 103)
- Use QuickBooks for job costing (page 105)
- Enter expense transactions in several different ways (page 105)
- Manage accounts payable transactions (page 110)
- Print checks (page 118)
- Void checks (page 122)
- Create and apply vendor credits (page 125)
- Track credit card charges and payments (page 128)
- Pay sales tax (page 131)
- Create reports about vendor transactions (page 133)

> **Restore this File**
>
> This chapter uses Expenses-12.QBW. To open this file, restore the Expenses-12.QBM file to your hard disk. See page 8 for instructions on restoring files. If you are using QuickBooks Premier Accountant, we recommend that you toggle to QuickBooks Premier General Business as described on page x.

In this chapter, we will discuss several ways to track your company's expenditures and vendors. We will start by adding vendors to your file, and then discuss several methods of paying them. In addition, this chapter shows you how to track expenses by job.

Entering Expenses in QuickBooks

QuickBooks provides several tools to help you track and manage the expenses in your business. These tools allow you to track your expenses in detail so that you can create extensive reports that help you manage your vendor relationships and control the costs in your business.

The Process of Entering Expenses in QuickBooks

The *Vendors* section of the *Home* page window provides you with a graphical flow of the steps involved in managing vendors, purchases, and payments (see Figure 4-1).

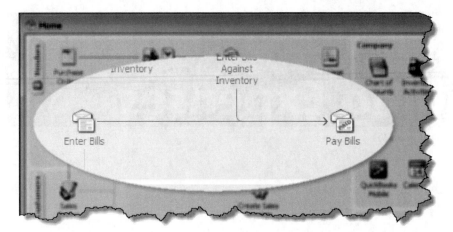

Figure 4-1 QuickBooks Home page

Clicking the *Vendors* icon on the *Home* page or the *Icon Bar* displays the *Vendor Center* (see Figure 4-2). The *Vendor Center* displays information about all of your vendors and their transactions in a single place. You can add a new vendor, add a transaction to an existing vendor, or print the *Vendor List* or *Transaction List*.

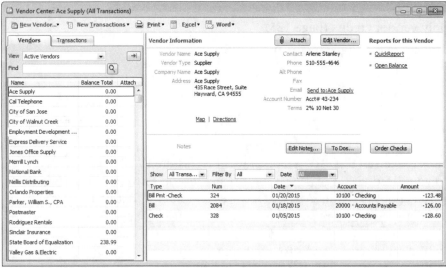

Figure 4-2 Vendor Center

In addition to the *Vendor Center*, the *Banking* section of the *Home* page contains options to help you navigate making deposits, writing checks, opening a check register, and reconciling with the bank statement. Figure 4-3 displays the *Banking* section of the *Home* page.

Figure 4-3 Banking section of the Home page

Table 4-1 shows many of the business transactions that might occur in dealing with vendors to process expenses in QuickBooks.

For illustrative purposes, we have defined two major groups of vendors – cash vendors and credit vendors. Table 4-1 shows how to enter transactions for each of these two groups of Vendors. The table also shows what QuickBooks does "behind the scenes" to record these transactions.

For some vendors, you will decide to track *Bills* and *Bill Payments*. This means the Accounts Payable account will be used to track how much you owe these vendors. We will refer to these as your credit vendors.

With other vendors, you will skip the Accounts Payable account and just write checks or otherwise pay them directly, coding the transactions to the appropriate expense accounts. We will refer to these as your cash vendors. Although you probably will not pay these vendors with actual cash, but with checks or credit cards, we will use the term cash vendor to distinguish them from credit vendors described previously.

Business Transaction	Cash Vendors		Credit Vendors	
	QuickBooks Transaction	Accounting Entry	QuickBooks Transaction	Accounting Entry
Recording a Purchase Order	Not usually used		[Purchase Orders]	Non-posting entry used to track *Purchase Orders*
Recording a Bill from a Vendor	Not usually used		[Enter Bills]	Increase (debit) **Expenses**, Increase (credit) **Accounts Payable**
Paying Bills	[Write Checks]	Increase (debit) **Expense**, Decrease (credit) **Checking**	[Pay Bills]	Decrease (debit) **Accounts Payable**, Decrease (credit) the **Checking Account**

Table 4-1 Steps for entering expenses

Recording Transactions

The first row in Table 4-1 references *Recording a Purchase Order*. Some vendors require *Purchase Orders* so they can properly process orders. When a *Purchase Order* is recorded, no accounting transaction is entered into QuickBooks; rather, a "memo" entry is made to track the *Purchase Order*. For details on using *Purchase Orders*, refer to the **Inventory** chapter beginning on page 233.

The second row references *Recording a Bill from a Vendor*. When you receive a bill from a vendor, you will record it using the *Enter Bills* window. Then, when it is time to pay your *Bills*, you will use the *Pay Bills* window in QuickBooks to select the *Bills* you want to pay. As shown below in Figure 4-4, both of these commands are available from the *New Transactions* drop-down menu in the Vendor Center.

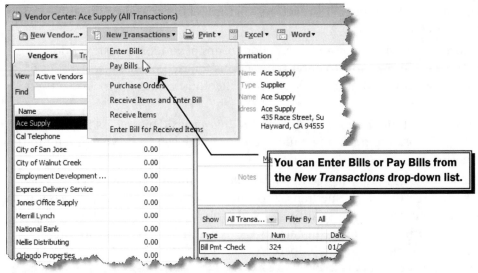

Figure 4-4 New Transactions Menu drop-down list in the Vendor Center

The third row references *Paying Bills*. Sometimes you will need to write a check that is not for the payment of a *Bill*. In that case, you will use the *Write Checks* window. *Write Checks* is accessible by clicking the **Check** icon in the icon bar, the **Write Checks** icon from the *Home* page, the **Write Checks** option from the *Banking* menu, or by pressing **Ctrl+W**.

Setting Up Vendors

Vendors include every person or company from whom you purchase products or services, including trade vendors, service vendors, and 1099 contract workers. Before you record any transactions to a Vendor in QuickBooks, you must set them up in the *Vendor Center*.

> **Tip:**
> When a vendor is also a customer, you will need to set up two separate records: a vendor record in the *Vendor Center* and a customer record in the *Customer Center*. The customer name must be slightly different from the vendor name. For example, you could enter Boswell Consulting as "Boswell Insulation-V" for the vendor name in the *New Vendor* window, and "Boswell Insulation-C" for the customer name in the *New Customer* window. The contact information for both customer and vendor record can be identical.

To set up a vendor, follow these steps:

COMPUTER PRACTICE

Step 1.   To display the *Vendor Center,* select the **Vendors** icon in the Vendors section of the *Home* page (see Figure 4-5). Alternately, click on the **Vendors** icon on the *Icon Bar.*

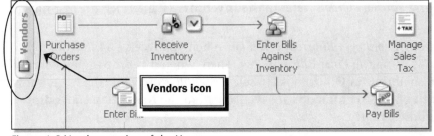

Figure 4-5 Vendors section of the Home page

Step 2.   Click the **New Vendor** button in the *Vendor Center* (see Figure 4-6) and choose **New Vendor** from the popup menu.

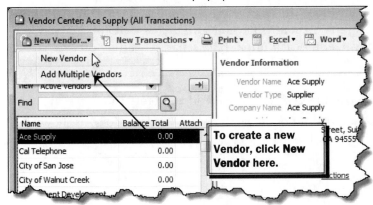

Figure 4-6 Add New Vendor to the Vendor list

Step 3.   The *New Vendor* window displays (see Figure 4-7). Notice there are three tabs labeled *Address Info, Additional Info* and *Account Prefill.*

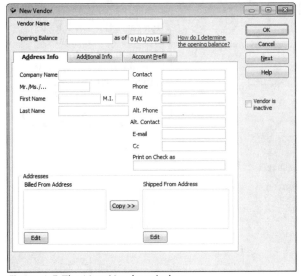

Figure 4-7 The New Vendor window

Step 4.   Enter *Boswell Consulting* in the *Vendor Name* field and press **Tab**.

> **Tip:**
> The *Vendor List* sorts alphabetically, just like the *Customer List*. Therefore, if your vendor is an individual person, enter the last name first, followed by the first name.

Step 5.   Press **Tab** twice to skip the *Opening Balance* and *as of* fields (see Figure 4-8).

The *Opening Balance* field shows only when you create a new *Vendor* record. You will not see this field on the *Edit Vendor* windows. The date in the *as of* field defaults to the current date. Since you will not enter an amount in the *Opening Balance* field, there is no need to change this date.

> **Important:**
> It is best *not* to use the *Opening Balance* field in the *New Vendor* window. If you *do* enter an opening balance for a vendor in the *Opening Balance* field, QuickBooks creates a *Bill* that increases (credits) Accounts Payable and increases (debits) Uncategorized Expense. Instead, enter each unpaid *Bill* separately after you create the vendor record.

Step 6.   Enter **Boswell Consulting** in the *Company Name* field and press **Tab**.

Step 7.   Continue entering data in the rest of the fields on the Vendor record, as shown in Figure 4-8. Press **Tab** after each entry.

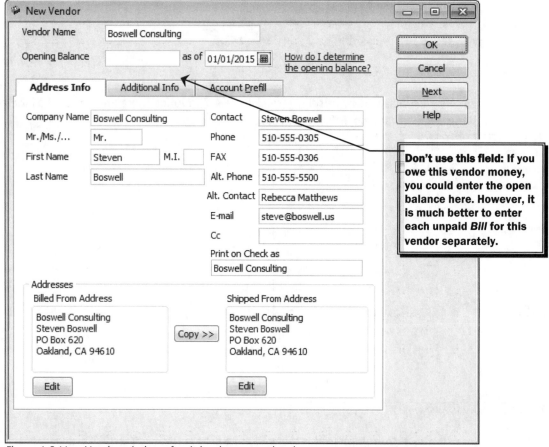

Figure 4-8 New Vendor window after it has been completed

Step 8.   Click the **Additional Info** tab to continue entering information about this vendor (see Figure 4-9).

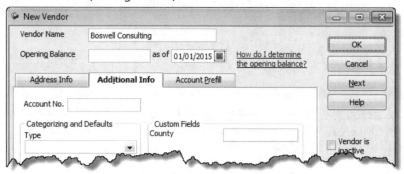

Figure 4-9 The Additional Info tab of the New Vendor window

Step 9.   Enter *66-112* in the *Account No.* field and press **Tab**.

In this field, you enter the number that your vendor uses to track you as a customer. If your vendor requires you to enter your account number on the checks you send, this is where you enter it. QuickBooks prints the contents of this field on the memo of the check when you pay this vendor's bill.

Select **Consultant** from the *Type* drop-down list and press **Tab**.

QuickBooks allows you to group your vendors into common types. For example, if you create a *Vendor Type* called Consultant and you tag each of your consultants' vendor records with this type, you could later create a report specific to this *Vendor Type*.

Step 10.   Select **2% 10 Net 30** from the *Terms* drop-down list and press **Tab**.

QuickBooks allows you to establish different types of default payment terms, including payment terms to accommodate discounts for early payment. In this example, the terms of 2% 10 Net 30 means that if you pay this vendor within 10 days of the invoice date, you are eligible for a 2% discount. In this field, you can set the payment terms default for this vendor. QuickBooks uses these default terms on all new *Bills* for this vendor. You can override the default terms on each *Bill* as necessary. When you create reports for accounts payable (A/P), QuickBooks takes into account the terms on each *Bill*. To learn more about the *Terms List*, and how to set up terms, see page 218.

Step 11.   Press **Tab** to leave the *Credit Limit* field blank.

Step 12.   Enter *123-12-1234* in the *TaxID* field.

The *Tax ID* field is where you enter the social security or taxpayer identification number of your Form 1099-MISC recipients. QuickBooks prints this number on the Form 1099-MISC at the end of the year.

Step 13.   Check the box next to *Vendor eligible for 1099*.

Select this box for all vendors for whom you expect to file a Form 1099-MISC.

Step 14.   Enter *Alameda* in the *County* field and press **Tab**.

The *County* field is a *Custom Field*. The *Define Fields* button on the *New Vendor* window, *Additional Information* tab allows you to define *Custom Fields* to track more information about your vendors. For this example, you will use the *County* field to tag each vendor with the county in which it is located. This allows you to create reports later that include geographic information about purchases from vendors. For more information on setting up and using *Custom Fields*, see page 223.

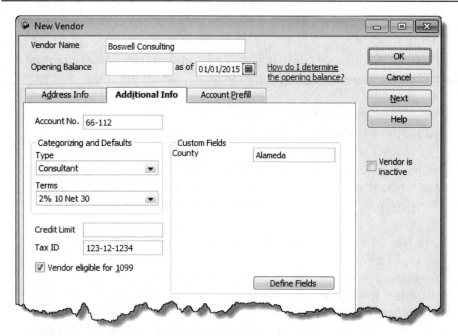

Figure 4-10 The Completed Boswell Consulting Additional Info tab

Step 15.   Verify that your screen matches Figure 4-10 (your *as of* date may differ), and then click the **Account Prefill** tab.

The *Account Prefill* tab allows you to set a default expense account for future transactions with this vendor.

Step 16.   Select **Professional Fees** from the first *Select accounts to pre-fill transactions* field (see Figure 4-11).

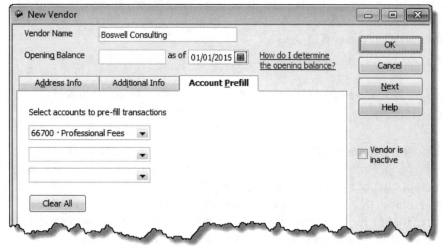

Figure 4-11 The completed Boswell Consulting Account Prefill tab

Step 17.   When finished, click **OK**.

If you were adding several vendors at this time, you would click **Next** instead, and begin adding another vendor, or you can begin by using the *Add Multiple Vendor* feature. Close the *New Vendor* window.

Activating Class Tracking

In QuickBooks, the *Class* field gives you a way to segregate your transactions other than by account name. You can use QuickBooks *Classes* to separate your income and expenses by line of business, department, location, profit center, or any other meaningful breakdown of your business. Alternatively, if your business is a not-for-profit organization, you could use *Classes* to separately track transactions for each program or activity within the organization.

For example, a dentist might classify all income and expenses as relating to either the dentistry or hygiene department. A law firm formed as a partnership might classify all income and expenses according to which partner generated the business. If you use *Classes*, you'll be able to create separate reports for each *Class* of the business. Therefore, the dentist could create separate Profit & Loss reports for the dentistry and hygiene departments, and the law firm could create separate reports for each partner.

In our sample company, Academy Photography uses *Classes* to track income and expenses for each of its stores - San Jose and Walnut Creek.

COMPUTER PRACTICE

Step 1.   Select the **Edit** menu, and then select **Preferences**.

Step 2.   Select the **Accounting** preference.

Step 3.   Select the **Company Preferences** tab, and make sure the box next to *Use class tracking* is checked (see Figure 4-12). When you use *Classes* on each transaction (*Checks, Bills, Invoices,* etc.), the *Profit & Loss by Class* report shows the income and expenses for each class.

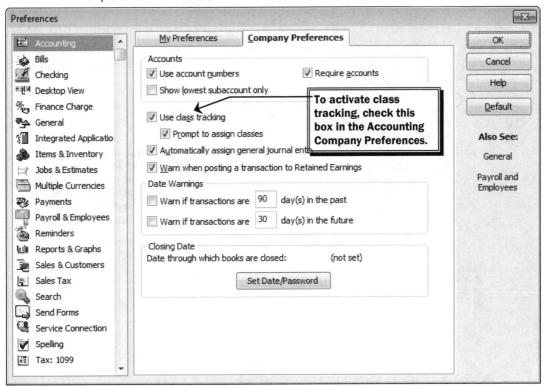

Figure 4-12 Activating class tracking in Accounting preferences

Step 4.   The *Prompt to assign classes* field is already checked. Leave the checkmark in this box.

With this setting, QuickBooks prompts you if you fail to assign a *Class* on any line of the transaction.

Step 5.   Click **OK**.

Figure 4-13 displays a *Bill* from Wong & Sons Video. The *San Jose* Class is selected in the *Class* column. This tracks the Subcontracted Services Expense to the *San Jose* Class (i.e., the San Jose store) so that the *Profit & Loss by Class* report shows the expense under the column for the *San Jose* Class.

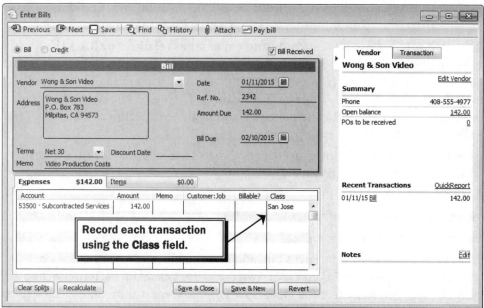

Figure 4-13 The Class field shows on many windows in QuickBooks, including Enter Bills

The *Profit & Loss by Class* report displays the income and expenses for each *Class*. Income and expenses for each Academy Photography store are displayed as separate columns. Note that the *San Jose* column includes the *Subcontracted Services*. For more information about the *Profit & Loss by Class* report, see page 170.

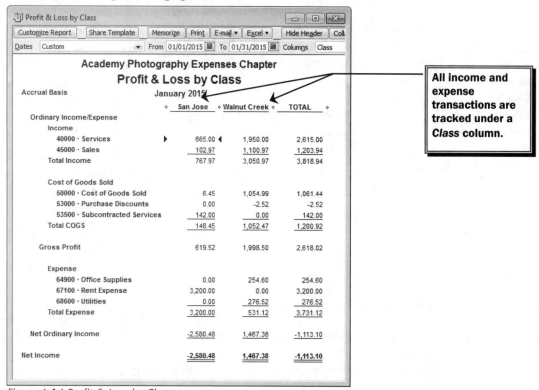

Figure 4-14 Profit & Loss by Class report

Tracking Job Costs

If you want to track the expenses for each *Customer* or *Job* (i.e., track job costs), link each expense with the *Customer* or *Job* to which it applies. In the following sections, you will learn about recording expense transactions in several different situations.

When you record an expense transaction, use the *Customer:Job* column to link each expense account or *Item* with a *Customer* or *Job* (see Figure 4-15).

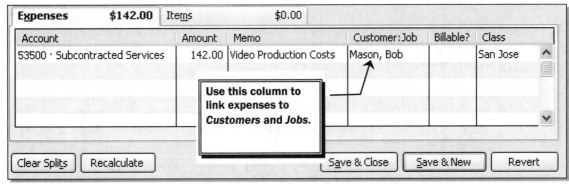

Figure 4-15 Linking expenses to Customers and Jobs (i.e., job costing)

When you track job costs, you can create reports such as the *Profit & Loss by Job* report that shows income and expenses separately for each *Job* (see Figure 4-16). For more information about the *Profit & Loss by Job* report, see page 173.

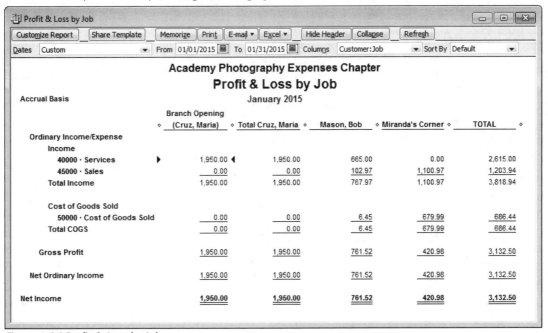

Figure 4-16 Profit & Loss by Job report

Paying Vendors

With QuickBooks, you can pay your vendors in several ways. You can pay by check, credit card, electronic funds transfer, or, though not recommended, cash.

Most of the time, you'll pay your vendors from a checking account, so this section covers three different situations for recording payments out of your checking account. The three situations are:

- Manually writing a check or initiating an electronic funds transfer and recording the transaction in a QuickBooks account register.

- Using the *Write Checks* function to record and print checks.

- Recording accounts payable bills through the *Enter Bills* window and using the *Pay Bills* function to pay these *Bills*.

Using Registers

In this example, you will manually write a check and then record the transaction in the QuickBooks checking account register.

COMPUTER PRACTICE

After you have written a manual check, or made a payment made by electronic funds transfer, you will record the transaction in QuickBooks.

Step 1.   Select the **Check Register** icon from the *Home* page. Alternatively, key **Ctrl+R** on your keyboard.

Step 2.   In the *Use Register* dialog box, make sure **Checking** displays in the *Select Account* field and click **OK** (see Figure 4-17).

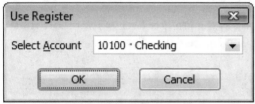

Figure 4-17 Use Register dialog box

Step 3.   Enter *02/08/2015* in the first empty line of *Date* column and press **Tab** (see Figure 4-18).

Date	Number	Payee		Payment	✓	Deposit	Balance
	Type	Account	Memo				
01/20/2015	324	Ace Supply		123.48			14,091.34
	BILLPMT	-split-	Acct# 43-234				
01/30/2015	329	National Bank		2,152.00			11,939.34
	CHK	22000 · National Bar 1234-1234-1234-123					
02/07/2015	330	Nellis Distributing		375.00			11,564.34
	BILLPMT	20000 · Accounts Pa					
02/08/2015		Payee		Payment		Deposit	
		Account	Memo				

Ending balance   11,564.34

Figure 4-18 Entering in manual check information

Step 4.   Enter *331* in the *Number* column and press **Tab**.

If you are entering a previously handwritten check, make sure this number matches the number on the physical check. If you are entering an electronic funds transfer or an ATM withdrawal, enter *EFT* in the check number field. Alternatively, if you are entering a Debit Card transaction, enter *Debit* in the *Number* column.

Step 5.   Enter **Bay Office Supply** in the *Payee* column and press **Tab**.

Since **Bay Office Supply** is not in the *Vendor List*, QuickBooks prompts you to *Quick Add* or *Set Up* the vendor (see Figure 4-19). Click **Quick Add** on the *Name Not Found* dialog box.

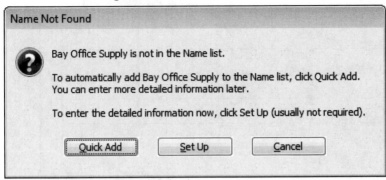

Figure 4-19 Name Not Found dialog box

Step 6.   Clicking **Quick Add** will add this vendor without entering the address and other information to completely set up the vendor. You can always go back later and add the other information by editing the vendor record. Click **OK** on the *Select Name Type* dialog box to add Bay Office Supply to the *Vendor Center* (see Figure 4-20).

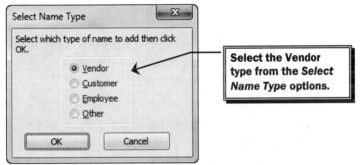

Figure 4-20 Select Name Type options - choose Vendor

Step 7.   Enter *128.60* in the *Payment* column and press **Tab**.

Step 8.   Enter **Office Supplies** in the *Account* column and press **Tab**.

After you enter the first few characters of the word "*Office*" in the *Account* field, notice that QuickBooks automatically fills in the rest of the field with "Office Supplies." This QuickFill feature helps you to enter data faster.

Step 9.   Enter **Printer Paper** in the *Memo* column.

Step 10.   Verify that you've entered all of the fields in the transaction correctly, and click **Record** to save the transaction (see Figure 4-21). If the *Set Check Reminder* dialog box opens, click **Cancel**.

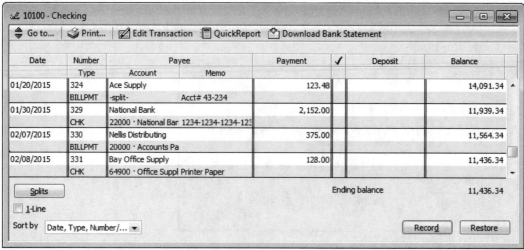

Figure 4-21 Bay Office Supply entry in the Checking register

Notice that QuickBooks automatically updates your account balance after you record the transaction.

Splitting Transactions

Sometimes you will need to split your purchase to more than one account. Let's say that the check you just wrote to Bay Office Supply was actually for the following expenses:

- $100.00 for printer paper, to be used in the San Jose store (*Class*).
- $28.60 for computer cables for the Walnut Creek store (*Class*).

In order to track your printing costs separately from your office supplies, you must *split* the expenses and assign each expense to a separate account.

COMPUTER PRACTICE

Step 1.   With the *Checking* register open, click on check **#331** to select it.

Step 2.   Click the **Splits** button as highlighted in Figure 4-22.

QuickBooks displays an area below the check where you can add several lines, memos, and amounts for *splitting* the expenses among multiple accounts.

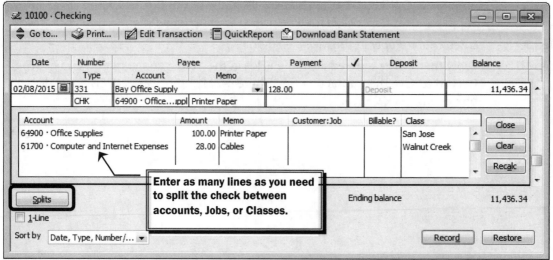

Figure 4-22 Split transaction window

Step 3. Change the amount on the first line from *128.60* to *100.00*. Then press **Tab**.

Step 4. Enter *Printer Paper* in the *Memo* column and press **Tab**.

Step 5. Skip the *Customer:Job* column by pressing **Tab**.

This is the column where you can optionally enter the Customer or Job name where this expense would apply.

Step 6. Enter *San Jose* in the *Class* column and press **Tab**.

Step 7. On the second line, enter *Computer and Internet Expenses* in the *Account* column and press **Tab**.

Step 8. QuickBooks calculates the amount **28.60** in the *Amount* column. This is correct so press **Tab** to leave it and move to the next field.

Step 9. Enter *Cables* in the *Memo* column and press **Tab**.

Step 10. Press **Tab** to skip to the **Class** column and enter *Walnut Creek*.

Step 11. Verify that your screen matches Figure 4-22, and then press **Record**.

Step 12. QuickBooks displays a dialog box asking if you want to record the changes to the previously recorded transaction. Click **Yes**.

Step 13. Close the *Checking* register.

Using Write Checks Without Using Accounts Payable

If you are tracking Job costs or *Classes* and are not using the accounts payable feature, it may be best to use the *Write Checks* window to record your expenses. If you use *Items* to track purchases and you are not using the accounts payable feature, you *must* use either *Write Checks* or the *Enter Credit Card Charges* window. See page 128 for more information about tracking credit cards.

COMPUTER PRACTICE

Step 1. To display the *Write Checks* window, click on the **Write Checks** icon on the *Home* page. Alternatively, press **Ctrl+W**.

Step 2. Make sure *Checking* is already selected in the *Bank Account* field. Press **Tab**.

Step 3. Enter *T* in the *No.* field and press **Tab**. QuickBooks will automatically fill in *To Print*. Alternately, click the **To be printed** box to the right of the *Items* tab.

This indicates that you want QuickBooks to print this check on your printer. When you print the check, QuickBooks will assign the next check number in the sequence of your checks.

Step 4. *02/08/2015* is already displayed in the *Date* field. Press **Tab**.

Step 5. Select **Orlando Properties** from the *Pay to the Order of* drop-down list and press **Tab**.

Notice that QuickBooks enters the name and address from the Vendor record as soon as you choose the Vendor name from the list.

Step 6. Enter *3200* in the *$* field and press **Tab**.

Step 7. Press **Tab** to skip the *Address*, *Memo*, *Online Payment*, and *To be printed* fields.

Step 8. Enter *Rent Expense* in the *Account* column of the *Expenses* tab if not already selected and press **Tab**.

> If necessary, when you enter your own expenses, use the bottom part of the check to split the payment between several different accounts, *Jobs,* and *Classes.*

Step 9.   Leave the *Amount* column set to *3,200.00* and press **Tab**.

Step 10.   Enter *San Jose Rent* in the *Memo* column, and press **Tab** twice.

Step 11.   Enter *San Jose* in the *Class* column and press **Tab**.

Step 12.   Verify that your screen matches Figure 4-23. Do not print the check now; we will print it later.

Step 13.   Click **Save & Close** to record the transaction.

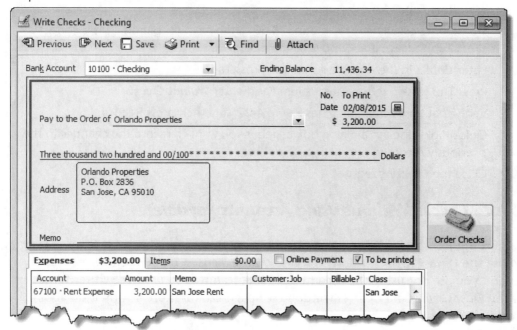

Figure 4-23 Write Checks window for Orlando Properties rent payment

> **Note:**
> In the example above, you recorded the check with a **To be printed** status, so that you can print it later, perhaps in a batch with other checks. If you wanted to print the check immediately after you entered it, you would have clicked **Print** at the top of the *Write Checks* window. QuickBooks would ask you to enter the check number.

Managing Accounts Payable

You can also use QuickBooks to track accounts payable.

When you receive a bill from a vendor, enter it into QuickBooks using the *Enter Bills* window. Recording a *Bill* allows QuickBooks to track the amount you owe to the vendor along with the detail of what you purchased. For a *Bill* to be considered paid by QuickBooks, you must pay it using the *Pay Bills* window, as discussed here.

Entering Bills

When a bill arrives from your vendor, enter it into QuickBooks using the *Enter Bills* window.

COMPUTER PRACTICE

Step 1.   Select the **Vendors** icon from the *Home* page to display the *Vendor Center*. Select the vendor **Ace Supply**, and then select **Enter Bills** from the *New Transactions* drop-down list (see Figure 4-24). Alternatively, you can click the **Enter Bills** icon on the *Home* page and select **Ace Supply** from the Vendor drop-down field.

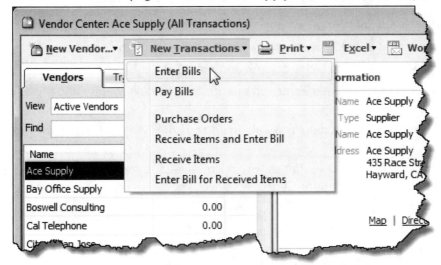

Figure 4-24 Selecting Enter Bills from the New Transaction drop-down list

Step 2.   In the *Enter Bills* window, verify that **Ace Supply** is displayed in the *Vendor* field and press **Tab**.

Notice that QuickBooks completes the *Bill Due, Terms,* and *Discount Date* fields automatically when you enter the *Vendor* name. QuickBooks uses information from the *Vendor* record to complete these fields. You can override this information if necessary. QuickBooks calculates the *Discount Date* and the *Bill Due* fields by adding the *Terms* information to the date entered in the *Date* field. If the terms do not include a discount, the *Discount Date* will not appear.

Step 3.   Enter *02/08/2015* in the *Date* field and press **Tab**.

Step 4.   Enter *2085* in the *Ref. No.* field and press **Tab**.

> **Tip:**
> When an A/P transaction increases what we owe, we call it a "bill." However, our vendors call them "invoices." Therefore, the *Ref. No.* field should match the number on the *Invoice* you received from the vendor. The *Ref. No.* field is important for two reasons. First, it is the number used to identify this *Bill* in the *Pay Bills* window, and second, it is the number that shows on the voucher of the *Bill Payment* check.

Step 5.   Enter *360.00* in the *Amount Due* field and press **Tab**.

Step 6.   Press **Tab** to skip the *Bill Due* field and to accept the due date that QuickBooks has calculated.

Step 7.   Press **Tab** to accept the **2% 10 Net 30** terms already selected.

Step 8.   Enter *Photo Materials for Jerry Perez Job* in the Memo field and press Tab.

> **Important:**
> If your vendor requires you to enter your account number on the checks you send, enter it in the *Account No.* field in the *Vendor* record. QuickBooks will print the contents of that field on *Bill Payments* to the vendor. If you enter a memo in this field on the *Bill*, it will override the *Account No.* field in the Vendor record.

Step 9.   Enter **Cost of Goods Sold** in the *Account* column of the *Expenses* tab and press **Tab**.

Step 10.   Press **Tab** to accept **360.00** already entered in the *Amount* column.

Step 11.   Enter **Photo Materials** in the *Memo* column and press **Tab**.

Step 12.   To job cost this purchase, enter **Perez, Jerry** in the *Customer:Job* column and press **Tab**.

Step 13.   Leave the *Billable?* field checked. Press **Tab** again and enter **Walnut Creek** in the *Class* column.

Step 14.   Verify that your screen matches that shown in Figure 4-25. Click **Save & Close** to record the **Bill**. Close the **Vendor Center** window.

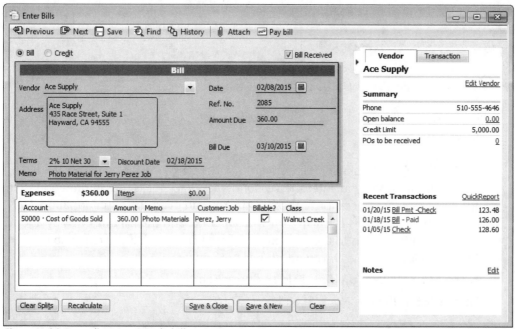

Figure 4-25 Recording Ace Supply bill

The Unpaid Bills Detail Report

To view a list of your unpaid *Bills*, use the *Unpaid Bills Detail* report.

COMPUTER PRACTICE

Step 1.   From the *Reports* menu, select **Vendors & Payables** and then select **Unpaid Bills Detail** (see Figure 4-26).

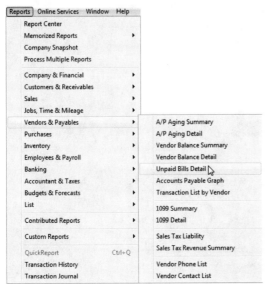

Figure 4-26 Selecting the Unpaid Bill Detail report

Step 2.   Enter *02/10/2015* in the *Date* field and press **Tab**.

Step 3.   Verify that your screen matches Figure 4-27. Close the report window. Click **No**, if the *Memorize Report* message appears.

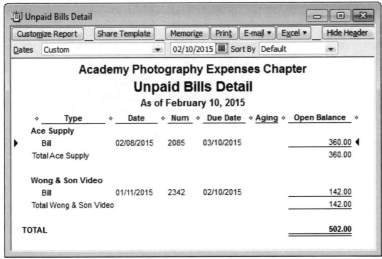

Figure 4-27 Unpaid Bills Detail report

Paying Bills

QuickBooks keeps track of all your bills in the Accounts Payable account. When you pay your bills, you will reduce the balance in Accounts Payable by creating *Bill Payment* checks.

COMPUTER PRACTICE

Step 1.   Select the **Vendors** icon from the *Icon Bar* to display the **Vendor Center**. Select **Pay Bills** from the *New Transactions* drop-down list (see Figure 4-28). You *do not* need to select a vendor first. Alternatively, you can click the **Pay Bills** icon on the *Home* page.

Figure 4-28 Selecting Pay Bills from the New Transaction drop-down list

Step 2.   QuickBooks displays the *Pay Bills* window.

Step 3.   Click on the radio button *Due on or before* and enter **03/10/2015** in the *Due on or before* date field (see Figure 4-29). QuickBooks allows you to filter the *Pay Bills* window so only the *Bills* due on or before a given date are shown.

> **Note:**
> The *Due on or before* field applies only to the *Bill* due date. There is no way to show only the *Bills* whose *discounts* expire on or before a certain date. However, you can sort the list of bills by the discount dates in the *Pay Bills* window by selecting **Discount Date** from the *Sort Bills by* drop-down list.

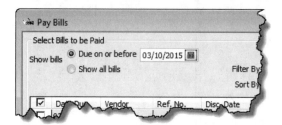

Figure 4-29 Entering the date in the Due on or before field

Step 4.   As shown in Figure 4-30, *Filter By* is set to *All vendors*. You can filter the *Pay Bills* window to only show specific vendors. Also, *Due Date* is already selected from the *Sort By* drop-down list. If you have several *Bills* from the same vendor, it is sometimes easier to see all of the *Bills* sorted by *Vendor*. You can also sort the bills by *Discount Date* or *Amount Due*.

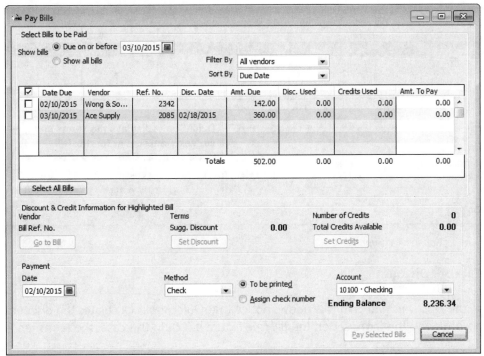

Figure 4-30 Pay Bills window

Step 5.   Leave **Check** in the *Payment Method* field selected. Ensure that the *To be printed* radio button is selected.

Step 6.   Leave **Checking** in the *Payment Account* field.

> **Note:**
> The *Payment Method* field allows you to choose to pay the bills by check or credit card. If you pay by check, QuickBooks automatically creates a check in your checking account for each bill selected for payment. To pay by credit card, select **Credit Card** and select the name of the credit card you want to use for the *Bill Payments*. QuickBooks will then create a separate credit card charge for each *Bill Payment*.

Step 7.   Enter **02/10/2015** in the Payment Date field.

Step 8.   Click the **Select All Bills** button in the middle to select both *Bills* that are displayed. Alternately, place a checkmark in front of the *Bills* you want to pay.

> **Tip:**
> If you want to display the original *Bill*, select the *Bill* on the *Pay Bills* window and click **Go to Bill**. This displays the original *Bill* so you can edit it if necessary.
>
> If you want to make a partial payment on a *Bill*, enter only the amount you want to pay in the *Amt. To Pay* column. If you pay less than the full amount due, QuickBooks will track the remaining amount due for that *Bill* in Accounts Payable. The next time you go to the *Pay Bills* window, the partially paid *Bills* will show with the remaining amount due.

Step 9.   To record a discount on the Ace Supply *Bill*, click on the *Bill* to select it. Notice the **Discount & Credit Information for Highlighted Bill** section (see Figure 4-31). Notice that QuickBooks displays the terms and a suggested discount for the *Bill*.

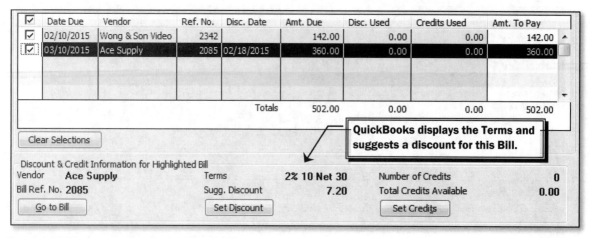

Figure 4-31 Discount section for Ace Supply bill

Step 10.   Click **Set Discount**.

In the *Discounts and Credits* window, notice that QuickBooks calculates the discount according to the terms set on the *Bill* (see Figure 4-32). In this case, the terms are *2% 10 Net 30*.

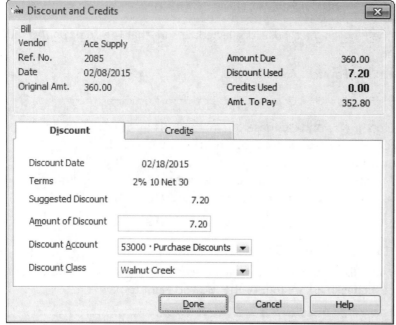

Figure 4-32 Discount and Credits window

Step 11.   Select **Purchase Discounts** in the *Discount Account* field to assign this discount to the proper account.

Step 12.   Enter *Walnut Creek* in the *Discount Class* field to assign this discount to the proper *Class*.

Refer to the *Bill* to determine the *Class*. The *Bill* being discounted was originally assigned to the *Walnut Creek Class* so the discount should use that class as well.

Step 13.   Click **Done**. This returns you to the *Pay Bills* window.

> **Note:**
> In some cases, it is better to use a *Bill Credit* instead of a discount. For example, when you want to associate the discount with a *Job*, or if you want to track discount items, use *Bill Credits* instead of using discounts in the *Pay Bills* process. You can record items, accounts, classes, and job information on the *Bill Credit*, just as you do on *Bills*. Then, in the *Pay Bills* window, click **Set Credits** to apply the *Bill Credit* to the *Bill*. To see how this would work, see the section on *Applying Vendor Credits* beginning on page 125.

Step 14.   Verify that your *Pay Bills* window matches that shown in Figure 4-33. Click **Pay Selected Bills** to record the *Bill Payments*.

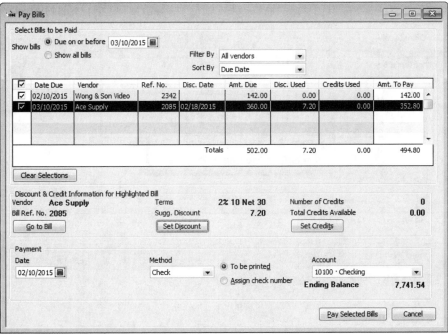

Figure 4-33 Pay Bills window after setting the discount

Step 15.   QuickBooks displays a *Payment* Summary dialog box as shown in Figure 4-34. Review the payments and click **Done**.

Step 16.   Close all windows except for the *Home* page.

Figure 4-34 Payment Summary dialog box

> **Note:**
> If you select more than one *Bill* for the same vendor, QuickBooks combines all of the amounts onto a single *Bill Payment*.

When you use a check to pay *Bills*, QuickBooks records each *Bill Payment* in the *Checking* account register and in the Accounts Payable account register (see Figure 4-35 and Figure 4-36). *Bill Payments* reduce the balance in both the Checking account (credit) and the Accounts Payable account (debit).

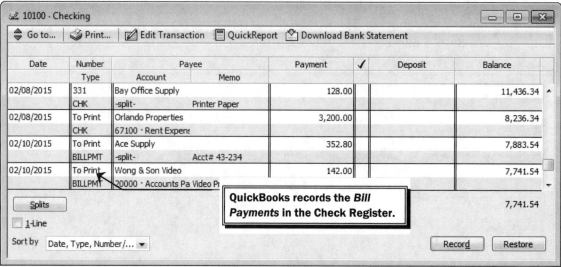

Figure 4-35 Checking account register after Bill Pay

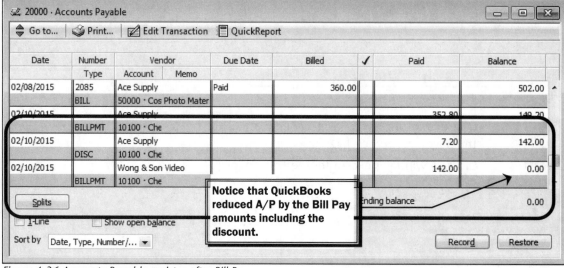

Figure 4-36 Accounts Payable register after Bill Pay

Printing Checks

COMPUTER PRACTICE

You do not need to print each check or *Bill Payment* separately. As you write checks and pay *Bills*, you have the option to record each check with a *To be printed* status. Follow these steps to print checks and *Bill Payments* that you have previously recorded with a *To be printed* status:

Step 1.   From the *File* menu, select **Print Forms** and then select **Checks**.

Step 2.   **Checking** in the *Bank Account* field is already selected (see Figure 4-37). This is the bank account on which the checks are written. Press **Tab**.

Step 3.   Enter *6001* in the *First Check Number* field, if necessary.

The *First Check Number* field is where you set the number of the first check you put in the printer.

> **Note:**
> QuickBooks assigns check numbers when it prints checks. You have the opportunity to set the check number just before you print the checks and after you assign a check number. QuickBooks keeps track of each check it prints and keeps the check number up to date.

Step 4.   QuickBooks automatically selects all of the checks for printing. Click **OK**.

To prevent one or more checks from printing, you can click in the left column to remove the checkmark for each check you don't want to print.

Since we did not print the rent check, it shows in Figure 4-37 along with the two *Bill Payments*. We will include it here so we can "batch print" all checks together.

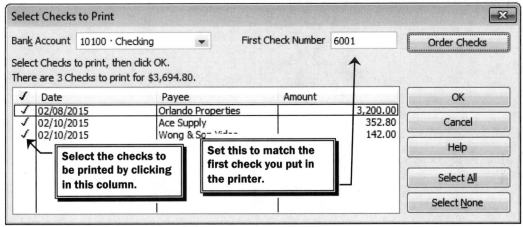

Figure 4-37 Select Checks to Print window

Step 5.   When the *Print Checks* window displays, click **Signature** on the right side of the window (see Figure 4-38).

You can automatically print singed checks by uploading a graphic file of a signature during the printing process.

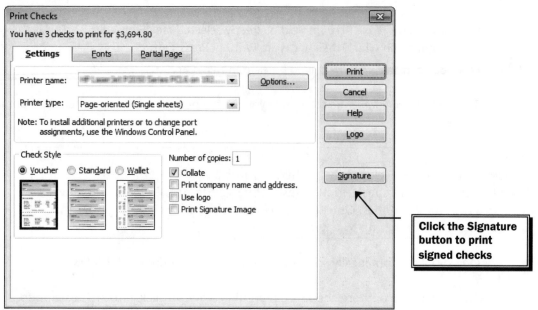

Figure 4-38 Signature Button in Print Checks window

Step 6.   In the *Signature* window, click the **File** button to upload the graphic file (see Figure 4-39).

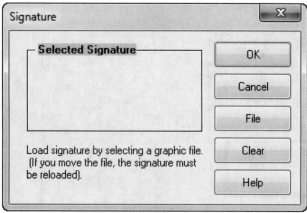

Figure 4-39 Signature window

Step 7.   In the *Open File* window, navigate to where you store your exercise files and open **Sign.png**. This file was included with the portable exercise files.

Step 8.   If QuickBooks displays a warning window, click **OK**. QuickBooks will copy the image file to a new folder called *Expenses-12 – Images*.

Step 9.   The *Signature* window now displays an image of the uploaded signature file (see Figure 4-40). Click **OK**.

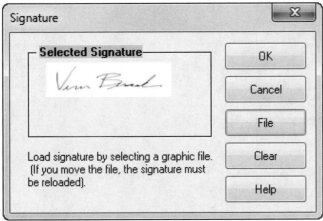

Figure 4-40 Signature window with file uploaded

> **Note:**
> Once you select the signature, QuickBooks will leave the box checked to always print the signature unless you uncheck the *Print Signature Image* shown in Figure 4-41.

Step 10.   Confirm your printer settings on the *Print Checks* window (see Figure 4-41), and click **Print** when you are ready to print. Your **Printer name** will most likely be different than what is displayed in Figure 4-41.

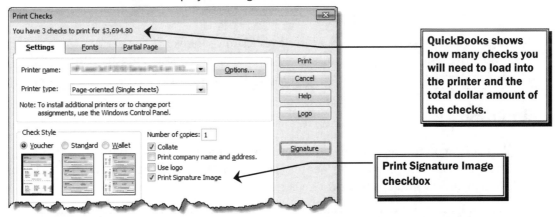

Figure 4-41 Print Checks window

> **Tip:**
> Make sure your checks are oriented correctly in the printer. With some printers, you feed the top of the page in first, and some you feed in bottom first. With some printers, you must insert the check face up, and with others, face down.

Step 11.   When QuickBooks has finished printing the checks, you will see the *Print Checks – Confirmation* dialog box in Figure 4-42.

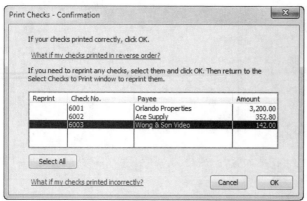

Figure 4-42 Print Checks - Confirmation dialog box

Step 12.   If the *Set Check Reminder* dialog box opens, click **Cancel**.

Step 13.   Click **OK**.

> **Note:**
> If your printer damages your checks and you select checks for reprinting, you will need to void each damaged check and re-enter a new check in the bank account register or on the *Write Checks* window.

> **Tip:**
> If you are paying multiple bills on a single check and you want the vendor to be able to identify these bills, you can print a *Bill Payment Stub* by choosing **Bill Payment Stub** from the *Print Forms* submenu on the *File* menu.

Voiding Checks

QuickBooks allows you to keep the information about voided checks so that you retain a record of these checks. It is important to enter each check into your register even if the check is voided. This will prevent gaps in your check number sequence.

> **Did You Know?**
> QuickBooks has a special report called *Missing Checks* that allows you to view all of your checks sorted by check number. The report highlights any gaps in the check number sequence. To view this report, select the **Reports** menu, then select **Banking**, and then select **Missing Checks**.

COMPUTER PRACTICE

Step 1.   Open the **Checking** account register and then select check 6003 by clicking anywhere on that record. You will be able to tell that the record has been selected as it will be outlined in the register.

Step 2.   From the *Edit* menu select **Void Bill Pmt-Check** (see Figure 4-43).

                When you void a check, QuickBooks changes the amount to zero, marks the check cleared, and adds **VOID** to the *Memo* field.

Step 3.   Click **Record** to save your changes.

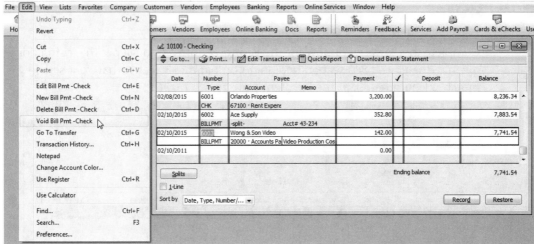

Figure 4-43 Voiding a check from the Edit menu

Since you are voiding a *Bill Payment*, QuickBooks warns you that this change will affect the application of this check to the *Bills* (see Figure 4-44). In other words, voiding a *Bill Payment* will make the *Bill* payable again.

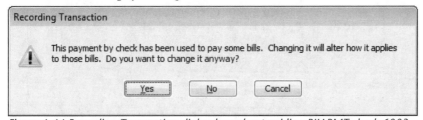

Figure 4-44 Recording Transaction dialog box about voiding BILLPMT check 6003

Step 4.   Click **Yes**.

               Notice that the transaction shows as cleared in the register, and that QuickBooks set the amount of the check to zero (see Figure 4-45).

Step 5.   Close all open windows except the *Home* page.

Date	Number	Payee		Payment	✓	Deposit	Balance	
	Type	Account	Memo					
02/08/2015	331	Bay Office Supply		128.00			11,436.34	▲
	CHK	-split-	Printer Paper					
02/08/2015	6001	Orlando Properties		3,200.00			8,236.34	
	CHK	67100 · Rent Expens						
02/10/2015	6002	Ace Supply		352.80			7,883.54	
	BILLPMT	-split-	Acct# 43-234					
02/10/2015	6003	Wong & Son Video		0.00	✓		7,883.54	
	BILLPMT	20000 · Accounts Pa	VOID: Video Producti					▼

Ending balance   7,883.54

Figure 4-45 Check register after voided transaction

To repay the *Bill*, repeat the bill paying, discount, and printing process by following the steps below.

COMPUTER PRACTICE

Step 1.   Select the **Pay Bills** icon on the *Home* page.

Step 2.   Complete the *Pay Bills* window for the **Wong & Son Video** *Bill* per the instructions given in the *Paying Bills* section beginning on page 113. Verify that your screen matches Figure 4-46. Set the Payment Date to *02/16/2015*.

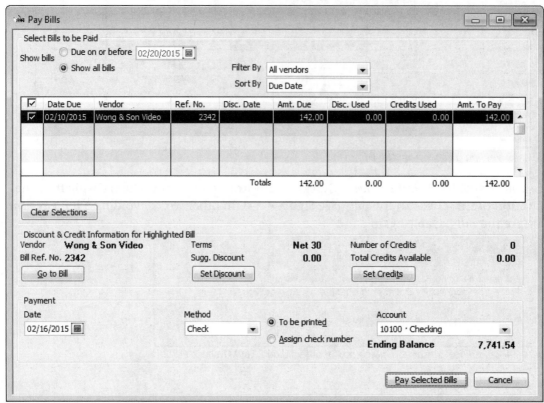

Figure 4-46 Completed Pay Bills window

Step 3.   Click **Pay Selected Bills** on the *Pay Bills* window to record the *Bill* payment.

Step 4.   Click **Done** on the *Payment Summary* dialog box.

Attaching Documents

There are many advantages to storing documents electronically. Going "paperless" increases efficiency and eliminates costly storage.

QuickBooks allows you to attach electronic documents to QuickBooks transactions, such as *Bills*, *Invoices*, and other QuickBooks forms. The attached documents can either be stored on your system for free, or on a secure server managed by Intuit using QuickBooks Document Management for a fee. To attach electronic documentation to a QuickBooks transaction, look for the *Attach* button in the upper section of the transaction window.

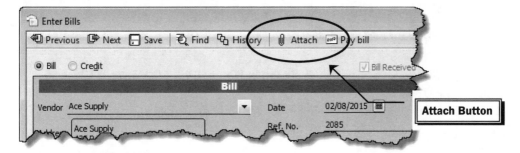

Figure 4-47 Attach button in Enter Bills window

Applying Vendor Credits

When a vendor credits your account, you should record the transaction in the *Enter Bills* window as a *Credit* and apply it to one of your unpaid *Bills*.

In some situations, it is best to use a *Bill Credit* instead of the *Discount* window to record certain vendor credits, because the *Discount* window does not allow you to record any of the following information:

- Reference numbers or memos – These may be important for reference later.
- Allocation of the credit to multiple accounts.
- Allocation to *Customers* or *Jobs* – This may be critical in many situations.
- Information using *Items*.

COMPUTER PRACTICE

First, create a *Bill* from Nellis Distributing for a Custom Window.

Step 1.   Click on the **Enter Bills** icon on the *Home* page.

Step 2.   Enter the Bill shown in Figure 4-48.

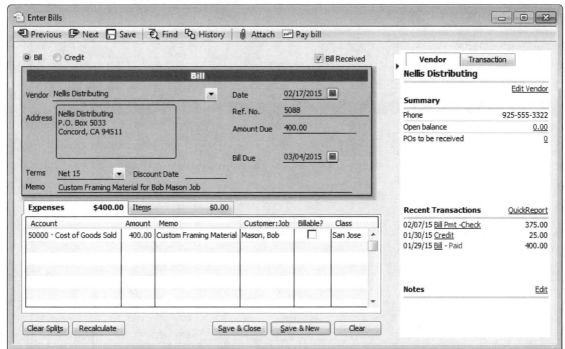

Figure 4-48 Bill from Nellis Distributing for Bob Mason job

Step 3.   When you're finished entering the data in Figure 4-48, click **Save & New**.

Now, enter a Bill Credit.

Step 1.   On the next (blank) *Bill* form, select the **Credit** radio button at the top right of the window.

Step 2.   Fill in the *Bill Credit* information as shown in Figure 4-49. Click **Save & Close** to record the credit.

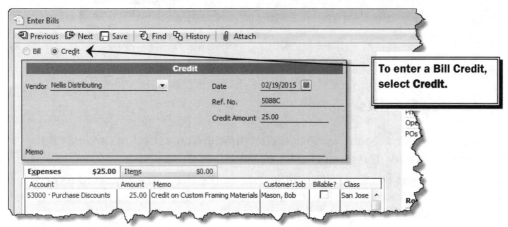

Figure 4-49 Creating a Bill Credit

> **The accounting behind the scenes:**
> When you record the **Bill Credit** shown in Figure 4-49, QuickBooks reduces (debits) Accounts Payable and reduces (credits) Purchase Discounts, a Cost of Goods Sold account.

Step 3.   To apply the *Bill Credit* to a *Bill* for that vendor, select **Pay Bills** from the *Home* page (See Figure 4-50).

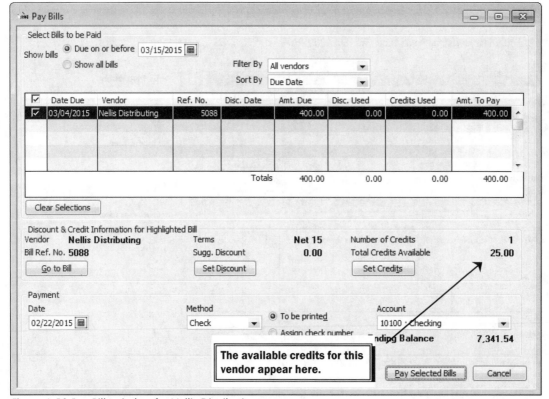

Figure 4-50 Pay Bills window for Nellis Distributing

Step 4. Enter *03/15/2015* in the *Due on or before* field and press **Tab**.

Step 5. Leave **Check** in the Payment Method field and **Checking** in the Payment Account field. Enter **02/22/2015** in the Payment Date field.

> **Important:**
> In order to apply a *Bill Credit*, the vendor name must be the same on both the *Bill* and the *Bill Credit*.

Step 6. Select the unpaid Bill for **Nellis Distributing** as shown in Figure 4-50.

When you select a *Bill* from a vendor for whom one or more unapplied credits exist, QuickBooks displays the total amount of all credits for the vendor in the *Total Credits Available* section. Notice the credit of $25.00 in Figure 4-50 for Nellis Distributing which we created above.

Step 7. Click **Set Credits**.

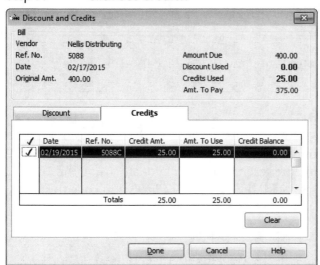

Figure 4-51 Discount and Credits window to set Bill Credit

On the *Discounts and Credits* window, QuickBooks automatically selected the credits to be applied to the *Bill*. You can override what is shown by deselecting the credit (removing the checkmark), or by entering a different amount in the *Amt. To Use* column.

Step 8. Leave the credit selected as shown in Figure 4-51 and click **Done**.

QuickBooks has applied the $25.00 credit to Bill #5088 and reduced the amount in the *Amt. To Pay* column to $375.00 (see Figure 4-52).

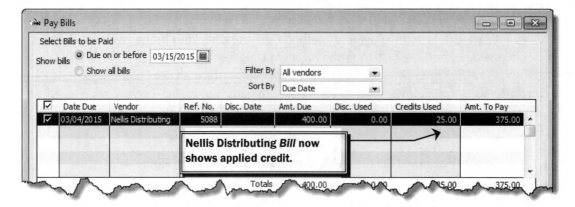

Figure 4-52 Pay Bills window after Bill Credit has been applied

Step 9.   Click **Pay Selected Bills** to pay the bill.

Step 10.   Click **Done** on the *Payment Summary* dialog box.

> **Note:**
> If you want to apply the credit without paying the *Bill*, reduce the *Amt. To Pay* column to zero.

Tracking Company Credit Cards

To track charges and payments on your company credit card, set up a separate credit card account in QuickBooks for each card. Then enter each charge individually using the *Enter Credit Card Charges* window. To pay the credit card bill, use *Write Checks* and code the check to the credit card account.

> **Another Way:**
> You can also pay your credit card bill by using *Pay Bills* after recording a *Bill* for the balance due, coded to the credit card liability account.
>
> **Did You Know?**
> Many credit cards allow you to download your credit card charges into QuickBooks through the Internet, eliminating the need to enter each charge manually. For more information about the QuickBooks Credit Card download, select the *Banking* menu, select *Online Banking*, and then select *Set Up Account for Online Services*.

Entering Credit Card Charges

Each time you use a company credit card, use the *Enter Credit Card Charges* window to record the transaction.

> **The accounting behind the scenes:**
> When you record credit card charges, QuickBooks increases (credits) your Credit Card Payable liability account and increases (debits) the expense account shown at the bottom of the window.

> **Note:**
> You will need to create an account on your *Chart of Accounts* for each company credit card. Use the *Credit Card* type when creating the account.

COMPUTER PRACTICE

Step 1. Click the **Enter Credit Card Charges** icon on the *Home Page*. Alternatively, from the *Banking* menu, select **Enter Credit Card Charges**.

Step 2. Press **Tab** to accept **National Bank VISA Gold** in the *Credit Card* field.

Step 3. **Purchase/Charge** is already selected. Press **Tab** twice.

If you used your card when receiving a refund or credit from a vendor, you would select **Credit** instead of **Charge** on this step. QuickBooks will then reduce the balance on your credit card when you record a Credit transaction.

Step 4. Enter *Bay Office Supply* in the *Purchased From* field and press **Tab**.

Step 5. Enter *02/24/2015* in the *Date* field. Press **Tab**.

Step 6. Enter *65432* in the *Ref No.* field and press **Tab**.

The *Ref No.* field is optional. Its purpose is to tag each charge with the number on the charge slip.

Step 7. Enter *86.48* in the *Amount* field and press **Tab**.

Step 8. Enter *Purchase Office Supplies* in *Memo* field and press **Tab**.

Step 9. Enter the *Account, Amount, Memo,* and *Class* fields as displayed in Figure 4-53.

Step 10. Verify that your screen matches Figure 4-53. Click **Save & New** to record the credit card charge.

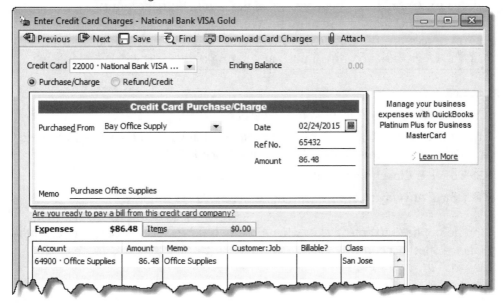

Figure 4-53 Enter Credit Card Charges window for Bay Office Supply purchase

Step 11. Enter another credit card charge that matches Figure 4-54. Click **Save & Close**.

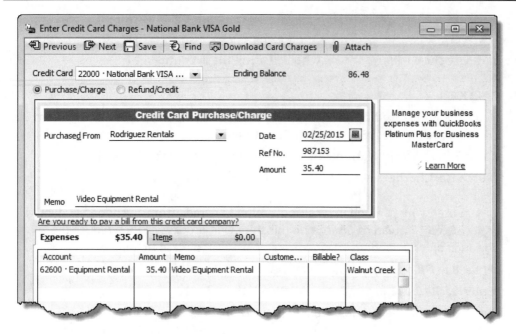

Figure 4-54 Enter Credit Card Charges window for equipment rental

Paying the Credit Card Bill

Follow the steps below to write a check to pay your credit card bill.

> **The accounting behind the scenes:**
> When you record a credit card payment, QuickBooks reduces (credits) the Checking account and reduces (debits) the Credit Card liability account.
> **Note:** There is another method of paying the credit card bill that is part of the reconciliation process. In the reconciliation chapter, you'll learn more about reconciling the credit card account, and then creating a *Bill* for the balance due.

COMPUTER PRACTICE

Step 1.   Click the **Write Checks** icon on the *Home* page.

Step 2.   Enter the check as shown in Figure 4-55. Notice that you will enter the credit card account name in the *Account* column of the *Expenses* Tab.

Step 3.   Click **Save & Close** to record the transaction.

Step 4.   Click **Save Anyway** to bypass *Items not assigned classes* window.

             You do not need to enter a class when posting to a credit card account or any other Balance Sheet account.

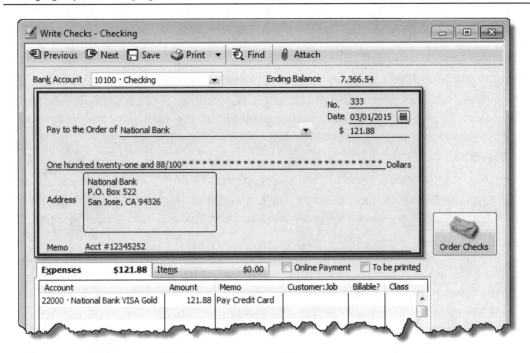

Figure 4-55 Write Checks window to pay credit card bill

To see the detail of your credit card charges and payments, look in the *National Bank VISA Gold* account register (see Figure 4-56). This register can be access by pressing **Ctrl+A** to open the Chart of Accounts, and then double-clicking on the *National Bank Visa Gold* credit card account. You can also pay credit cards as part of the reconciliation process. For more information, see 155.

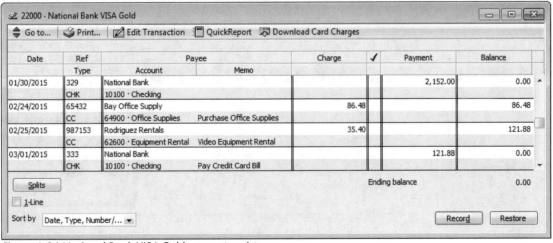

Figure 4-56 National Bank VISA Gold account register

Paying Sales Tax

Many QuickBooks users need to collect sales tax each time they sell products and certain types of services. This sales tax needs to be paid to the appropriate state or local agency. Academy Photography files its sales tax return to a single vendor called the State Board of Equalization. In this example, we will run reports for the first quarter of 2015. For more on collecting sales tax, see 81.

Paying Sales Tax

After you prepare your sales tax return and make necessary adjustments for discounts, interest, penalties or rounding, create a sales tax payment for the amount you owe.

When you pay your sales tax, do not use the *Write Checks* window because the payment will not affect the *Sales Tax Items*. It also will not show properly on the *Sales Tax Liability* reports. To correctly pay your sales tax liability, use the *Pay Sales Tax* window.

COMPUTER PRACTICE

Step 1.   From the *Home* page, select the **Manage Sales Tax** icon.

Step 2.   Click the **Pay Sales Tax...** button in the center of the *Manage Sales Tax* dialog box. Alternatively, from the *Vendors* menu, select **Sales Tax** and then select **Pay Sales Tax**.

Step 3.   The *Pay Sales Tax* window displays. In the *Pay From Account* field, **Checking** already displays so press **Tab**. This field allows you to select the account from which you wish to pay your sales tax.

Step 4.   Enter *04/15/2015* in the *Check Date* field and press **Tab**. This field is the date of *when* you are paying the sales tax.

Step 5.   Enter *03/31/2015* in the *Show sales tax due through* field and press **Tab**. In this field, enter the last day of the sales tax reporting period. For example, if you are filing your sales tax return for the first quarter, enter the last day of March in this field.

Step 6.   Leave **334** in the *Starting Check No.* field and press **Tab**. QuickBooks automatically enters the next check number sequentially.

Step 7.   Click in the **Pay** column (see Figure 4-57) on the line with a balance.

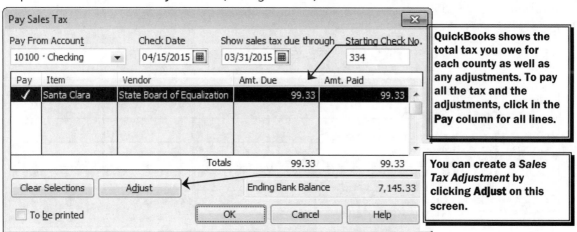

Figure 4-57 Pay Sales Tax window

Step 8.   Click **OK** to record the Sales Tax Payment.

Step 9.   Click **Close** on the *Manage Sales Tax* window.

After you record the sales tax payment, QuickBooks will create a special type of check called a *Sales Tax Payment* (TAXPMT) in your checking account for the total tax due to each sales tax agency (Vendor).

> **Important:**
> QuickBooks allows you to adjust the amounts in the *Amt. Paid* column.
> However, if you do you will retain an incorrect (overstated) balance *in Sales Tax Payable* for the period. If you need to change the amount of sales tax due, use a *Sales Tax Adjustment*. To quickly access *the Sales Tax Adjustment* window, click **Adjust** on the *Pay Sales Tax* window.

Accounts Payable Reports

QuickBooks has several reports that you can use to analyze and track your purchases and vendors. Following are two sample reports for you to create. See the Reports chapter for more information on creating reports.

Vendor Balance Detail

The **Vendor Balance Detail** report shows the detail of each *Bill* and *Bill Payment* to each vendor. However, this report only includes transactions that "go through" Accounts Payable. That is, it only shows transactions such as *Bills* and *Bill Payments*. If you write checks to your vendors directly, without first entering a *Bill*, those transactions will not show in this report.

COMPUTER PRACTICE

Step 1.   From the *Reports* menu, select **Vendors & Payables** and then select **Vendor Balance Detail** (see Figure 4-58).

Step 2.   To print the report, click **Print** at the top of the report. Close the report, and click **No** if the *Memorize Report* message appears.

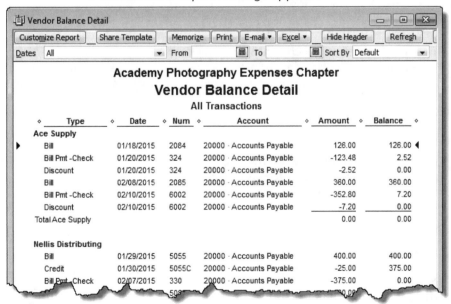

Figure 4-58 Vendor Balance Detail Report

Transaction List by Vendor

The *Transaction List by Vendor* report shows all transactions associated with your vendors, even if the transactions did not "go through" Accounts Payable (e.g., checks and credit card charges).

COMPUTER PRACTICE

Step 1.   From the *Reports* menu, select **Vendors & Payables** and then select **Transaction List by Vendor** (see Figure 4-59).

Step 2.   Set the date fields on the report to *01/01/2015* through *03/31/2015*.

Step 3.   Close all open windows and click **No** if the *Memorize Report* message appears.

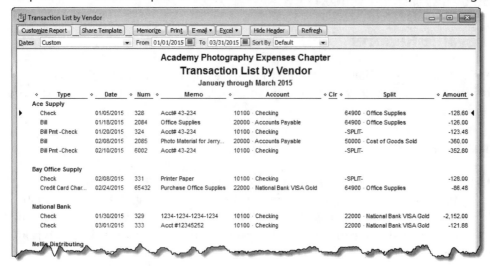

Figure 4-59 Transaction List by Vendor report

Review Questions

Select the best answer(s) for each of the following:

1. You may record payments to your vendors by:
    - a)   Recording a manual entry directly into the check register.
    - b)   Using *Write Checks* to write and print a check without using Accounts Payable.
    - c)   Using *Enter Bills* to record Accounts Payable and then using *Pay Bills* to pay open Bills.
    - d)   a, b, or c.

2. To display the *Vendor Center:*
    - a)   Click *Vendors* on the QuickBooks *Home* Page.
    - b)   Click the *Vendor Center* icon on the Navigation Bar.
    - c)   Select the *Vendor* menu and then select *Vendor Center*.
    - d)   a, b, or c.

3. You can add a vendor:
    - a)   Only at the beginning of the fiscal year.
    - b)   Only if you will purchase over $600 from that particular vendor and a Form 1099 will be issued.
    - c)   Only at the beginning of the month.
    - d)   At any time by selecting *New Vendor* in the *Vendor Center*.

4. Which statement is true?
    - a)   QuickBooks records each *Bill Payment* in a bank account register (or credit card account register) and the Accounts Payable register.
    - b)   *Bill Payments* increase the balance in both the Checking account and the Accounts Payable account.
    - c)   You should assign *Jobs* to all discounts taken.
    - d)   You cannot make partial payments on a *Bill*.

5. Which QuickBooks feature allows you to separate your income and expenses by line of business, department, location, profit center, or any other meaningful breakdown of your business?

   a)   Job costing.
   b)   Class tracking.
   c)   Customer types.
   d)   Vendor types.

Expenses-Problem 1

APPLYING YOUR KNOWLEDGE

> Restore the **Expenses-12Problem1.QBM** file.

1. Activate *Class* tracking in the data file.

2. Add a new vendor to the Vendor list using the data in the table below. Fields that are not provided below can be left blank.

Field Name	Data
Vendor Name	*Prado Photography Services*
Company Name	*Prado Photography Services*
Mr./Ms./...	*Ms.*
First Name	*Joy*
Last Name	*Prado*
Name and Address	*Prado Photography Services* *Joy Prado* *755 Market Ave.* *Castro Valley, CA 94500*
Contact	*Joy Prado*
Phone	*(510) 555-1414*
Email	*joy@pradophoto.biz*
Print on Check as	*Prado Photography Services*
Account #	*89766-46*
Vendor Type	*Consultant*
Terms	*Net 30*
Tax ID	*111-22-3333*
Check Box	*Vendor eligible for 1099*
County	*Alameda*
Account Prefill	*Professional Fees*

Table 4-2 Use this data to enter a new vendor

3. Print the **Vendor List**. (From the *Reports* menu, select **Vendors & Payables** and then select **Vendor Contact List**.)

4. Enter check #*331* directly in the **Checking** register on *01/12/2015* to *Carl's Hardware* for *$325.00*. Use **Quick Add** to add the Vendor. Split the expense to *$125.00* for **Office**

Supplies for the **San Jose** store and $*200.00* for **Repairs and Maintenance** for the **Walnut Creek** store.

5. Using **Write Checks**, enter a check (**to be printed**) to *Orlando Properties*, dated *01/12/2015* for *$1,500.00*, for **Rent** at the **San Jose** store. Make the check printable, but don't print the check.

6. Enter *Bill #1500* from *Nellis Distributing* on *01/18/2015* for *$922.00* with Terms of **Net 15**. The *Bill* is for the purchase of supplies for the Bob Mason job, so code the *Bill* to **Cost of Goods Sold**. Bob Mason is a customer in the San Jose store, so link the cost with the appropriate *Job* and *Class*.

7. Enter *Bill #3453* from *Sinclair Insurance* on *01/19/2015* for *$1,220.00* with Terms of **Net 30**. Code the *Bill* to **Insurance Expense**. Allocate 100% of the cost to the **San Jose** store.

8. Create and print an **Unpaid Bills Detail** report dated 1/20/2015.

9. Pay all of the **Bills** due on or before **02/28/2015**. Pay the **Bills** from the Checking account on 01/19/2015. Make the **Bill Payments** "printable" checks.

10. Print all of the checks that you recorded with a "to be printed" status. Print them on blank paper and start the check numbers at *6001*.

11. Enter a credit card charge on the **National Bank VISA** card from **Bay Office Supply** (Use *Quick Add* to add the vendor), reference *#1234*, dated *1/25/2015*. The purchase was for *$57.75* for office supplies for the Walnut Creek store.

12. Enter Bill *#4635* from *Ace Supply* on *01/25/2015* for *$1,440.62* with terms of **Net 30**. Code the *Bill* to **Cost of Goods Sold** since it was for supplies for the **Ron Berry** *Job*. Ron Berry is a *Customer* at the **San Jose** store. Keep the default terms for Ace Supply.

13. Enter a *Bill Credit* from *Ace Supply* on *01/30/2015* for *$450.00*. Use reference number *4635C* on the credit. Code the credit to **Cost of Goods Sold** and link the credit with the **Ron Berry** *Job* and the **San Jose** *Class*.

14. Apply the credit to Bill #4635 and pay the remainder of the Bill on 01/30/2015 using a printable check.

15. Print check #6005 on blank paper.

16. Print a **Vendor Balance Detail** report for **All** transactions.

Chapter 5
Bank Reconciliation

Objectives

After completing this chapter, you should be able to:

- Reconcile your checking account (page 138)
- Create bank reconciliation reports (page 144)
- Find errors during reconciliation (page 145)
- Correct errors found during reconciliation (page 148)
- Make corrections when QuickBooks automatically adjusts the balance in a bank account (page 149)
- Handle bounced checks (page 149)
- Reconcile credit card accounts and record a bill for later payment (page 155)
- Improve efficiency with Online Banking (page 158)

> **Restore this File**
>
> This chapter uses BankRec-12.QBW. To open this file, restore the BankRec-12.QBM file to your hard disk. See page 8 for instructions on restoring files. If you are using QuickBooks Premier Accountant, we recommend that you toggle to QuickBooks Premier General Business as described on page x.

As you write checks, withdraw money, make deposits, and incur bank charges, these transactions are recorded in QuickBooks. Then, at the end of each month, you must compare these transactions with your bank statement to ensure that each QuickBooks transaction matches the bank's records.

This process is called *reconciling*. It is a very important step in the overall accounting process and its primary goal is to ensure the accuracy of your accounting records.

In addition to reconciling bank accounts, you can also reconcile other accounts, such as credit card accounts, using the same process. For example, if you track each credit card transaction (charges, payments, interest charges, etc.) in a separate credit card liability account in QuickBooks, you should reconcile your QuickBooks credit card accounts with your monthly credit card statement.

In fact, you can reconcile almost any Other Current Asset, Fixed Asset, Credit Card, Other Current Liability, Long Term Liability, or Equity account using the same process presented in this chapter. However, even though QuickBooks *allows* you to reconcile many accounts, the primary accounts you'll reconcile are bank and credit card accounts since these types of accounts always have monthly statements.

In this chapter, you'll learn how to reconcile bank and credit card accounts, as well as how to find and correct errors in the reconciliation process.

Reconciling Bank Accounts

Figure 5-1 shows Academy Photography's bank statement for the checking account as of January 31, 2015. Before reconciling the account in QuickBooks, make sure you've entered all of the transactions for that account. For example, if you have automatic payments from your checking account (EFTs) or automatic charges on your credit card, it is best to enter those transactions before you start the reconciliation.

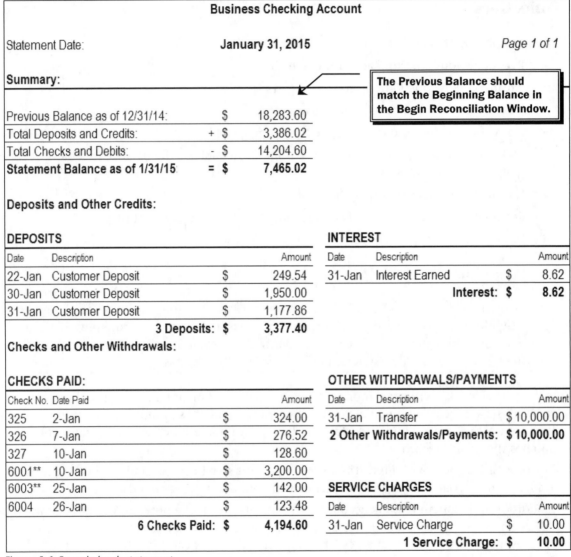

Figure 5-1 Sample bank statement

COMPUTER PRACTICE

Using the sample data file for this chapter, follow these steps to reconcile the QuickBooks Checking account with the bank statement shown in Figure 5-1.

Step 1.   Before you begin the reconciliation process, first review the account register to verify that all of the transactions for the statement period have been entered (e.g., deposits, checks, other withdrawals, and payments). You don't need to record the "bank-originated" transactions such as interest received and bank charges, because these transactions are recorded during the reconciliation process.

The Academy Photography sample data file for this section already has the deposits, checks, other withdrawals, and payments entered into the register.

Step 2. If the *Home* page is not already open, select the **Company** menu and then select **Home Page.**

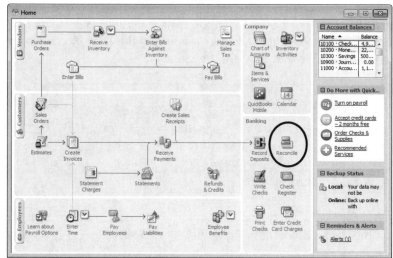

Figure 5-2 The Home Page

Step 3. Click the **Reconcile** Icon on the *Banking* section of the *Home* page (see Figure 5-2).

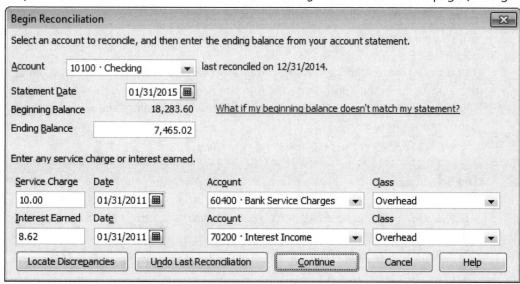

Figure 5-3 Begin Reconciliation window

Step 4. In the *Begin Reconciliation* window (see Figure 5-3), the *Account* field already shows *Checking*. The account drop-down list allows you to select other accounts to reconcile, however since *Checking* is the account you're reconciling, you don't need to change it now. Press **Tab**.

Step 5. Leave **01/31/2015** in the *Statement Date* field and press **Tab**.

The default statement date is one month after your last reconciliation date. Since this account was last reconciled on 12/31/2014, QuickBooks entered *01/31/2015*. Before proceeding to the next field, confirm that this date matches your bank statement date. Correct it if necessary.

> **Tip:**
> If your bank does not date statements at the end of the month, ask the bank to change your statement date to the end of the month. This makes it easier to match the bank statement with your month-end reports in QuickBooks.

Step 6.   Look for the *Previous Balance as of 12/31/14* on the bank statement (see Figure 5-1). Compare this amount with the *Beginning Balance* amount in the *Begin Reconciliation* window (see Figure 5-3). Notice that they are the same.

> **Note:**
> QuickBooks calculates the *Beginning Balance* field in the *Begin Reconciliation* window by adding and subtracting all previously reconciled transactions. If the beginning balance does not match the bank statement, you probably made changes to previously cleared transactions. See *Finding Errors During Bank Reconciliation* on page 145 for more information.

Step 7.   Enter *7,465.02* in the *Ending Balance* field. This amount is the *Statement Balance as of 1/31/15* shown on the bank statement in Figure 5-1. Press **Tab**.

> **Note:**
> If you already recorded bank charges in the check register, skip Step 8 through Step 11 to avoid duplicate entry of the charges.

Step 8.   Enter *10.00* in the *Service Charge* field and press **Tab**.

If you have any bank service charges or interest earned in the bank account, enter those amounts in the appropriate fields in the *Begin Reconciliation* window. When you enter these amounts, QuickBooks adds the corresponding transactions to your bank account register.

Step 9.   Leave **01/31/2015** in the *Date* field and press **Tab**.

The default date for the service charge is one month after your last reconciliation. Since this account was last reconciled on 12/31/2014, QuickBooks entered *01/31/2015*. Before proceeding to the next field, confirm this date matches your bank statement date. Correct it if necessary.

Step 10.   Select **Bank Service Charges** from the *Account* drop-down list and press **Tab**.

Each time you reconcile, this field will default to the account you used on the last bank reconciliation. Confirm that this is the correct expense account before proceeding to the next field.

Step 11.   Select **Overhead** from the *Class* drop-down list and press **Tab**.

> **Note:**
> If you already recorded interest income in the check register, skip Step 12 through Step 15 to avoid duplicate entry of the interest income.

Step 12.   Enter *8.62* in the *Interest Earned* field and press **Tab**.
Step 13.   Leave **01/31/2015** in the *Date* field and press **Tab**.
Step 14.   Select **Interest Income** from the *Account* drop-down list and press **Tab**.

Step 15.   Select *Overhead* from the *Class* drop-down list and click **Continue**.

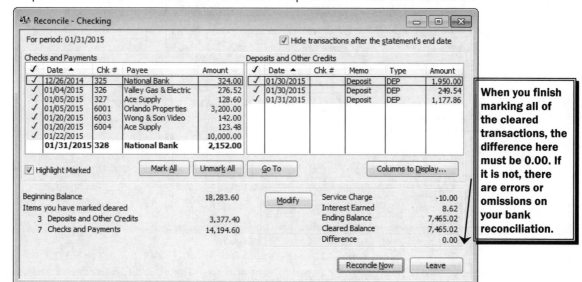

Figure 5-4 Reconcile – Checking window

Step 16.   At the top of the *Reconcile – Checking* window (see Figure 5-4), check the box labeled "Hide transactions after the statement ending date".

☑ Hide transactions after the statement's end date

This removes transactions dated after the statement date from being displayed on the screen. Since they could not possibly have cleared, this simplifies your life so you only have to look at transactions that *could* have cleared the bank as of the statement date.

Step 17.   In the *Deposits and Other Credits* section of the *Reconcile – Checking* window, match the deposits and other credits on the bank statement (see Figure 5-1 on page 138) with the associated QuickBooks transactions. Click anywhere on a line to mark it cleared. The checkmark (✓) indicates which transactions have cleared.

Step 18.   In the *Checks and Payments* section of the *Reconcile – Checking* window, match the checks and other withdrawals on the bank statement with the associated QuickBooks transactions.

Tip:
Notice that QuickBooks calculates the sum of your marked items at the bottom of the window in the *Items you have marked cleared* section. This section also shows the number of deposits and checks you have marked cleared. Compare the figures to your bank statement. If you find a discrepancy with these totals, you most likely have an error. Search for an item you forgot to mark or one that you marked in error.

Tip:
You can sort the columns in the *Reconcile - Checking* window by clicking the column heading. If you would like to change the columns displayed in the *Reconcile – Checking* window, click the *Columns to Display* button. This will allow you to select which columns you would like to see when you are reconciling (see Figure 5-5).

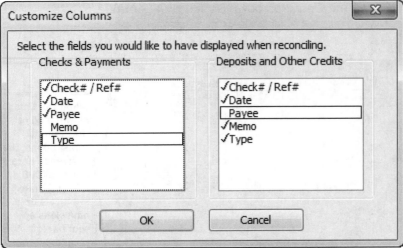

Figure 5-5 Customizing the Bank Reconciliation with Columns to Display

Step 19.   After you've marked all the cleared checks and deposits, look at the *Difference* field. It should be **0.00**, indicating that your bank account is reconciled.

If the *Difference* field is not zero, check for errors. For help in troubleshooting your bank reconciliation, see *Finding Errors During Bank Reconciliation* on page 145.

Tip:
If you need to wait until another time to complete the bank reconciliation, you can click **Leave**. When you click **Leave**, QuickBooks will save all of your changes so you can complete the reconciliation later.

Step 20.   If the *Difference* field is zero, you've successfully reconciled. Click **Reconcile Now**. If you see a window offering online banking, click **OK** to close.

Note:
It is very important that you do not click **Reconcile Now** unless the *Difference* field shows **0.00**. Doing so will cause discrepancies in your accounting records. See page 149 for more information.

Step 21.   The *Select Reconciliation Report* dialog box displays. The **Both** option is already selected, so click **Display** to view your reports on the screen (see Figure 5-6).

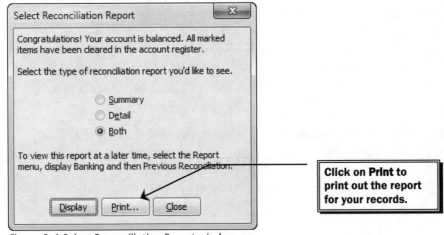

Figure 5-6 Select Reconciliation Report window

Step 22.   Click **OK** on the *Reconciliation Report* window (see Figure 5-7).

Figure 5-7 Reconciliation Report information window

Step 23.   QuickBooks creates both a *Reconciliation Summary* report (Figure 5-8) and a *Reconciliation Detail* report (Figure 5-9). The length of the detail report will depend upon how many transactions you cleared on this reconciliation and how many uncleared transactions remain in the account.

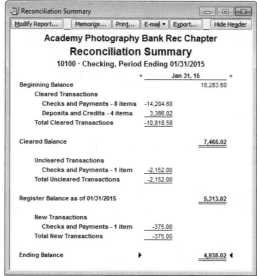

Figure 5-8 Reconciliation Summary report

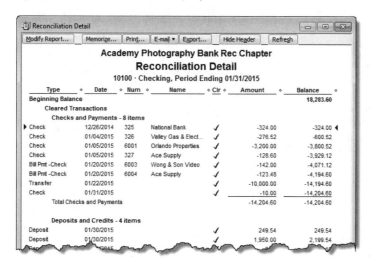

Figure 5-9 Reconciliation Detail report

Step 24.   Close all open report windows.

Bank Reconciliation Reports

Each time you complete a bank reconciliation, QuickBooks walks you through creating a bank reconciliation report for that reconciliation. You can recreate your bank reconciliation reports at any time by following the steps below.

> **Note:**
> If you are using QuickBooks Pro you can create Bank Reconciliation reports for the most recently reconciled month only. QuickBooks Premier allows you to view and print bank reconciliation reports for all bank reconciliations performed using QuickBooks versions 2002 or later. The examples and screenshots in this section apply to QuickBooks Premier.

COMPUTER PRACTICE

Step 1.   From the *Reports* menu select **Banking** and then select **Previous Reconciliation**. The *Select Previous Reconciliation Report* window displays (see Figure 5-10).

Step 2.   Confirm that **Checking** is selected in the *Account* field.

If you have more than one bank account, you can select another bank account using the *Account* drop-down list.

Step 3.   Confirm that **01/31/2015** is selected in the *Statement Ending Date* field.

QuickBooks automatically selects the report for your most recent bank reconciliation. You can select another report by highlighting the statement date in this section.

Step 4.   Confirm that **Detail** is selected in the *Type of Report* section.

Step 5.   Confirm that **Transactions cleared at the time of reconciliation** in the *In this report, include* section is selected. When you select this option, QuickBooks displays an Adobe Acrobat PDF file with the contents of the reconciliation report. The Acrobat (PDF) report does not include any changes you may have made to reconciled transactions. See Figure 5-10.

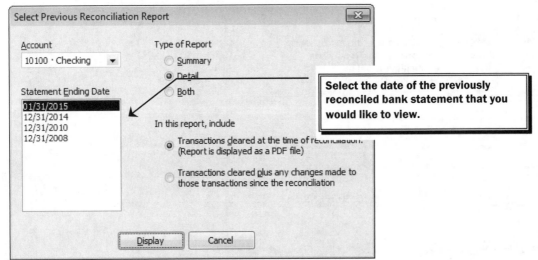

Figure 5-10 Printing a Previous Bank Reconciliation

Step 6.   Click **Display** to view your bank reconciliation reports on screen.

Note:

If your screen does not show the Balance column in the window shown in Figure 5-11, you need to set your Printer Setup settings to fit the report to 1 page wide before you perform the bank reconciliation. This is because Acrobat creates the report when you finish the reconciliation and uses the settings in your Printer Setup to determine how to lay out the page.

If you have already created the report, you can undo the reconciliation (see page 146) and then select *Printer Setup* from the *File* menu. When the *Printer setup* window displays, select *Report* from the *Form Name* drop down list. At the bottom of the window you can check the *Fit report to* option and enter *1* for the number of pages wide you want reports to display, as illustrated below.

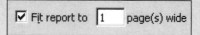

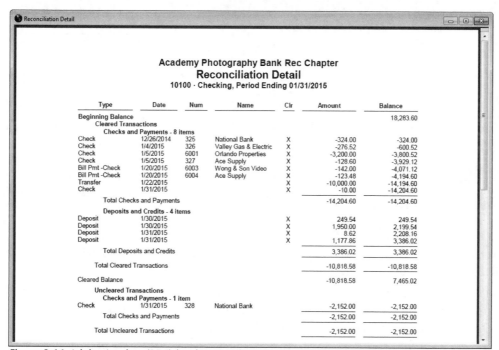

Figure 5-11 Adobe Acrobat (PDF) bank reconciliation report – your screen may vary

Step 7.   Close the *Reconciliation Detail* report.

Note:

If you prefer to create a normal QuickBooks reconciliation report (as opposed to an Acrobat PDF report), select the option, *Transactions cleared plus any changes made to those transactions since the reconciliation* in Step 5 above.

Finding Errors During Bank Reconciliation

If you have finished checking off all of the deposits and checks but the *Difference* field at the bottom of the window does not equal zero, there is an error (or discrepancy) that must be found and corrected. To find errors in your bank reconciliation, try the following steps:

Step 1: Review the Beginning Balance Field

Verify that the amount in the *Beginning Balance* field matches the beginning balance on your bank statement. If it does not, you are not ready to reconcile. There are two possibilities for why the beginning balance will no longer match to the bank statement:

1. One or more reconciled transactions were voided, deleted, or changed since the last reconciliation; and/or,
2. The checkmark on one or more reconciled transactions in the account register was removed since the last reconciliation.

To correct the problem you have two options:

Option 1: Use the Reconciliation Discrepancy Report to Troubleshoot

Review the report for any changes or deletions to cleared transactions. The *Type of Change* column shows the nature of the change to the transaction. Notice on the first line that a user deleted a cleared check. On the second line of the report a user changed the amount of a check.

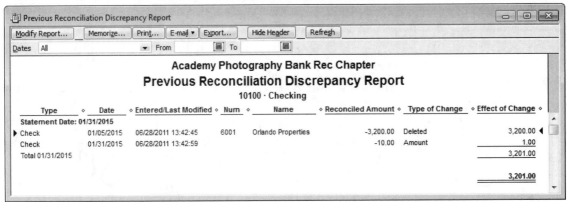

Figure 5-12 Reconciliation Discrepancy report

1. For each line of the report with "Deleted" in the *Type of Change* column, re-enter the deleted transaction. Then, use the *Bank Reconciliation* window to re-reconcile the transaction that had been deleted.

2. For each line of the report with "Amount" in the *Type of Change* column, double-click the transaction in the *Reconciliation Discrepancy* report to open it (i.e., QuickZoom). Then, change the amount back to the reconciled amount.

After returning all transactions to their original state (as they were at the time of the last reconciliation), you can then proceed to investigate whether the changes were necessary, and if so, enter adjustment transactions.

Option 2: Undo the Bank Reconciliation

The *Previous Reconciliation Discrepancy* report only shows changes to cleared transactions since your most recent bank reconciliation. If the beginning balance was incorrect when you performed previous bank reconciliations, the *Previous Reconciliation Discrepancy* report will not fully explain the problem.

If this is the case, the best way to find and correct the problem is to undo the previous reconciliation(s).

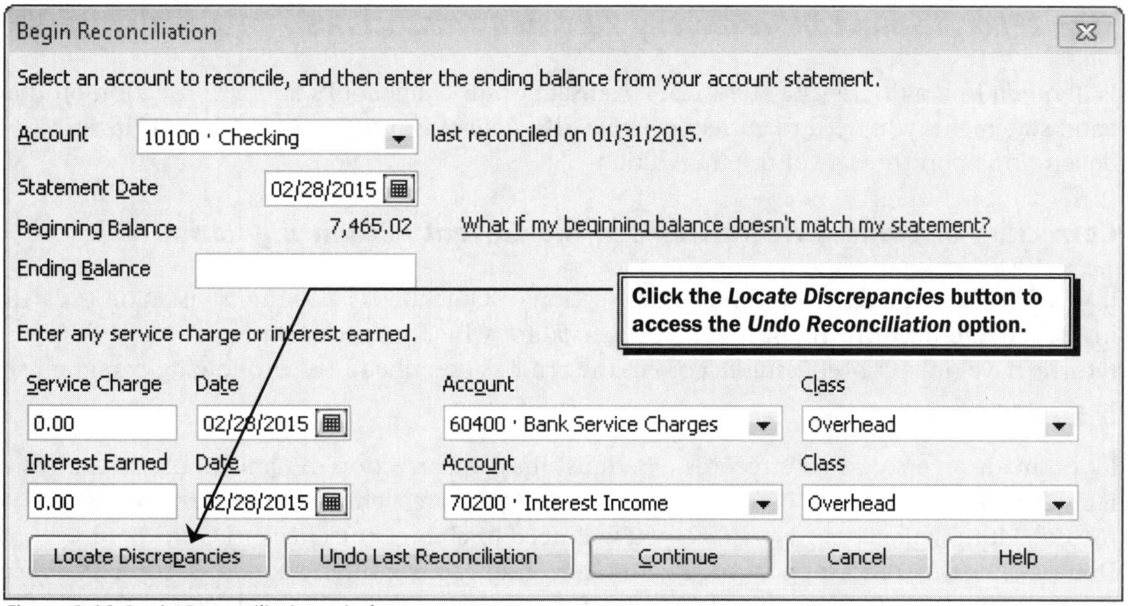

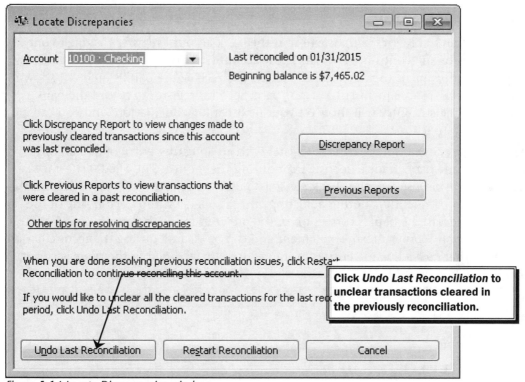

Figure 5-13 Begin Reconciliation window

Figure 5-14 Locate Discrepancies window

Note:
When you undo a reconciliation, QuickBooks resets your beginning balance to the previous period. However, the bank service charges and interest income that you entered in the prior reconciliation will remain in the check register and will not be deleted.

Therefore, do not enter bank services charges and interest income when repeating the bank reconciliation. Instead, clear those transactions along with the other checks and deposits when you re-reconcile the account.

Step 2: Locate and Edit Incorrectly Recorded Transactions

When you find a discrepancy between a transaction in QuickBooks and a transaction on the bank statement, you need to correct it. You will use different methods to correct the error, depending upon the date of the transaction.

Correcting or Voiding Transactions in the Current Accounting Period

If you find that you need to correct a transaction in QuickBooks and the transaction is dated in the **current accounting period** (i.e., a period for which financial statements and/or tax returns have not yet been issued), correct the error as described in the following paragraphs.

If You Made the Error

If you made an error in your records, you must make a correction in QuickBooks so that your records will agree with the bank. For example, if you wrote a check for $400.00, but you recorded it in QuickBooks as $40.00, you will need to change the check in QuickBooks. Double-click the transaction in the **Reconcile** window, or highlight the transaction and click **Go To.** Make the correction, and then click **Save & Close.** This will return you to the *Reconcile* window and you will see the updated amount.

If the Bank Made the Error

If the bank made an error, enter a transaction in the bank account register to adjust your balance for the error and continue reconciling the account. Then, contact the bank and ask them to post an adjustment to your account. When you receive the bank statement showing the correction, enter a subsequent entry in the bank account register to record the bank's adjustment. This register entry will show on your next bank reconciliation, and you can clear it like any other transaction.

For example, Figure 5-15 displays a check register with an adjusting entry of $90.00 on 1/31/2015 where the bank made a deposit error during the month. The $90.00 shortage is recorded on the *Payment* side of the check register so that the register will reconcile with the bank statement. Subsequently, another adjusting entry is made on the *Deposit* side of the check register to record the bank's correction of the previous month's deposit. The $90.00 deposit will show on February's bank statement and can be cleared during the reconciliation process. Notice that *both* adjusting entries in the register are recorded to the same account, *Reconciliation Discrepancies.*

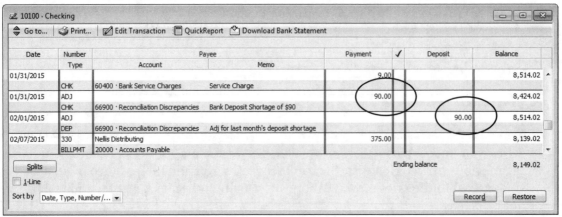

Figure 5-15 Adjusting entries for bank deposit error

Voiding Checks and Stop Payments

When you find a check dated in the **current accounting period** that you know will not clear the bank (e.g., if you stop payment on a check), you will need to void the check. Double-click the check from the **Reconcile** window. Select the **Edit** menu and then select **Void Check**. Click **Save & Close** to return to the *Reconcile* window.

When QuickBooks Automatically Adjusts your Balance

If the difference is not zero when you click **Reconcile Now** in the *Reconcile* window, QuickBooks creates a transaction in the bank account for the difference. The transaction is coded to the *Reconciliation Discrepancies* expense account. You should not leave this transaction in the register, but research why the discrepancy exists and properly account for it. A balance in this account usually indicates an over- or under-statement in net income.

Handling Bounced Checks

Banks and accountants often refer to bounced checks as NSF (non-sufficient funds) transactions. This means there are insufficient funds in the account to cover the check.

When Your Customer's Check Bounces

If your bank returns a check from one of your customers, enter an NSF transaction in the banking account register.

For example, Bob Mason bounced the check #2526 for $1,177.86 and the bank charged the Company $10.00. Complete the steps below to complete the NSF transaction.

COMPUTER PRACTICE

Step 1.   Open the **Checking** check register.

Step 2.   If necessary, choose **Date, Type, Number** from the *Sort by* drop down list at the bottom of the register.

Step 3.   Enter two transactions, both dated 2/8/2015, as shown in Figure 5-16 – one for the amount of the check that bounced and one for the fee charged by the bank.

Notice that the bounced check is coded to Accounts Receivable. This transaction creates a receivable from the customer that will show in your A/R reports and customer *Statements* until the customer repays you.

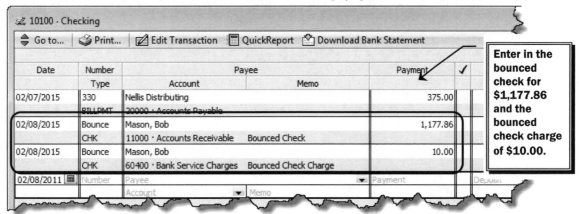

Figure 5-16 Add two transactions to your Checking register

> **Note:**
> If the bounced check was *not* a payment for one of your *Invoices* (i.e., not recorded to Accounts Receivable), skip Step 4 through Step 9.

Step 4.   After you enter the bounced check, select the **Reports** menu, select **Customers and Receivables,** and then select **Customer Balance Detail** (see Figure 5-17).

Step 5.   Double-click the payment transaction (#2526 on 01/30/2015) in the **Customer Balance Detail** report to view the *Receive Payments* window you used to record the check from your customer (see Figure 5-17). You may need to scroll to the bottom of the report.

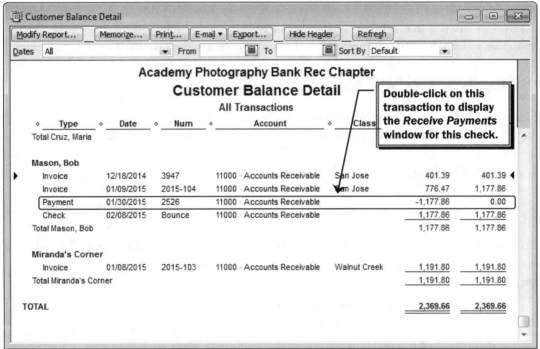

Figure 5-17 Customer Balance Detail report

Step 6.   In the *Receive Payments* window click in the check column (✓) next to the original *Invoices*, both 3947 on 12/18/2014 and 2015-104 on 1/9/2015 to un-apply the payments (see Figure 5-18).

Step 7.   Next, click in the checkmark column (✓) next to the bounced check transaction you recorded in Step 3 above. You'll see this transaction in the *Receive Payments* window.

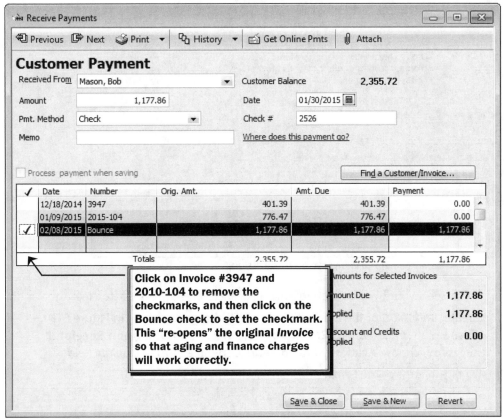

Figure 5-18 Select *the Bounced Check to apply to the original payment*

Step 8.   Click **Save & Close** and then click **Yes** in the *Recording Transaction* dialog box.

Step 9.   Close the **Customer Balance Detail** report.

> **Note:**
> The payment is reapplied to the bounced check so that the aging and finance charge calculations of the original *Invoice* are restored. If you did not edit the *Receive Payment* window in this way, the Accounts Receivable aging would be incorrect because QuickBooks would still think the original check (the one that bounced) had paid the *Invoice*. Since that check bounced, we want the original *Invoice* to show as unpaid until the customer actually makes a valid payment.

Next, if you charge your customers a service fee for processing their NSF check, create an *Invoice* for the customer as follows:

Step 10.   Create an **Other Charge** *Item* called **NSF Charge,** as shown in Figure 5-19.

   a)   Click the **Items & Services** icon on the *Home* Page.

   b)   Press **Ctrl+N** to display the *New Item* window.

   c)   Enter fields to make your screen match Figure 5-19. Click **OK** to create the new *Item*.

   d)   Close the *Item List.*

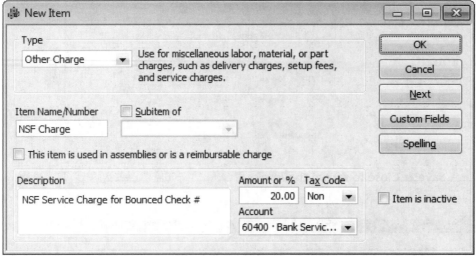

Figure 5-19 Use an Other Charge Item to charge your customers an NSF fee

Step 11.   If you see a window offering *Professional Service Forms,* press **OK** to clear the window.

Step 12.   Create an *Invoice* for the amount for the NSF charge as shown in Figure 5-20. Change the *Invoice #* to **2526Bounce** and the terms to **Due Upon Receipt**. If necessary, choose **Academy Photo Service Invoice** in the *Template* field.

Step 13.   Fill out the rest of the fields on the *Invoice* to match Figure 5-20.

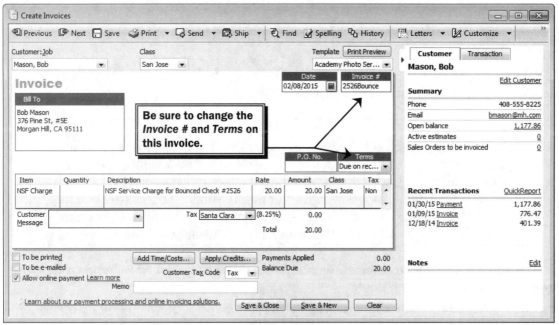

Figure 5-20 Invoice to charge the customer an NSF service charge

Step 14.   When you add the *NSF Charge Item* to the *Invoice,* QuickBooks displays a warning that says, "This item is associated with an expense account." Click **OK**.

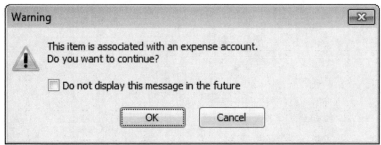

Figure 5-21 Warning dialog box

Step 15.   Click **Save & Close** to record the *Invoice*.

Step 16.   Since you changed the terms on this *Invoice* to *Due Upon Receipt*, QuickBooks asks if you want to make the *Due Upon Receipt* terms the default for Bob Mason. Click **No** on this window since you will use the *Net 30* terms on future *Invoices* for this customer.

> **Tip:**
> You will need to notify the customer of bounced check and the NSF fee. You can do this by sending the customer a *Statement*. For more information on printing *Statements*, see page 80
>
> **The accounting behind the scenes:**
> The bounced check you entered in the register increases (debits) Accounts Receivable and reduces (credits) the Checking account for the amount of the original check that bounced. The *Invoice* increases (debits) Accounts Receivable and decreases (credits) Bank Service Charges for the amount of NSF fees you are charging the customer.

Receiving and Depositing the Replacement Check

COMPUTER PRACTICE

To record the transactions for receiving and depositing a replacement check, follow these steps:

Step 1.   Select the **Customers** menu, and then select **Receive Payments**.

Step 2.   In this example, Bob Mason sent a replacement check #2538 on 2/10/15 for $1,197.86 that includes the amount of the check plus the NSF service charge of $20.00. Fill in the customer payment information as shown in Figure 5-22.

Make sure you apply the payment against the original *Invoices* and the service charge *Invoice* you just created in Figure 5-20.

Step 3.   Click **Save & Close**.

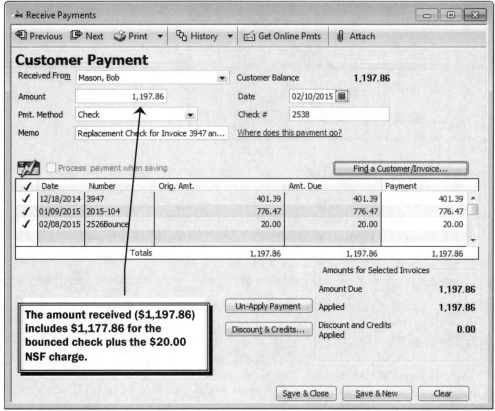

Figure 5-22 The Receive Payments window showing the replacement check

Next, add the replacement check to your next deposit just as you would any other check.

Step 4.   Select the **Banking** menu and then select **Make Deposits** (see Figure 5-23).

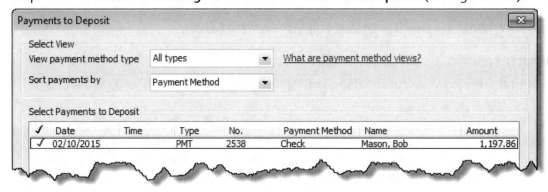

Figure 5-23 Add the replacement check to your deposit

Step 5.   In the *Payments to Deposit* window, select check #2538 as shown in Figure 5-23 and then click **OK** at the bottom of the window.

Step 6.   In the *Make Deposits* window, confirm that **Checking** in the *Deposit to* field is selected and that 02/10/2015 displays in the date field (see Figure 5-24). Then, click **Save & Close** at the bottom of the window.

Figure 5-24 Make Deposits window

Step 7.   Close the Checking register.

When Your Check Bounces

If you write a check that overdraws your account and your bank returns the check, follow these steps:

1.   Decide with your vendor how you will handle the NSF Check (e.g., send a new check, redeposit the same check, or pay by credit card).

2.   When the bank sends you the notice that your check was returned, there will be a charge from your bank. Enter a transaction in the bank account register. Code the transaction to Bank Service Charges and use the actual date that the bank charged your account.

3.   If your balance is sufficient for the check to clear, tell the vendor to redeposit the check.

4.   If your balance is not sufficient, consider other ways of paying the vendor, such as paying with a credit card. Alternatively, negotiate delayed payment terms with your vendor.

5.   If your vendor charges an extra fee for bouncing a check, enter a *Bill* (or use *Write Checks*) and code the charge to the Bank Service Charge account.

6.   If you bounce a payroll check, use the same process as described. It is good practice, and may be required by law, to reimburse your employee for any bank fees incurred as a result of your mistake.

Reconciling Credit Card Accounts and Paying the Bill

If you use a credit card liability account to track all of your credit card charges and payments, you should reconcile the account every month just as you do with your bank account. The credit card reconciliation process is very similar to the bank account reconciliation, except that when you finish the reconciliation, QuickBooks asks you if you want to pay the credit card immediately or if you want to enter a bill for the balance of the credit card.

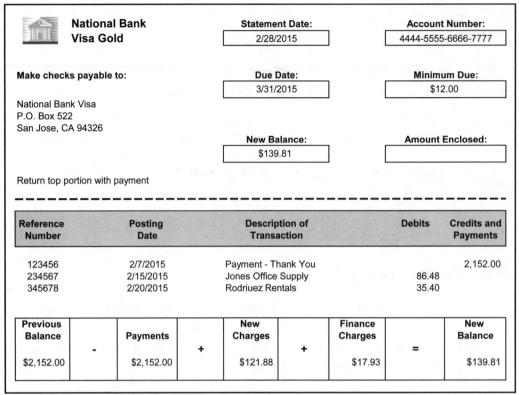

Reference Number	Posting Date	Description of Transaction	Debits	Credits and Payments
123456	2/7/2015	Payment - Thank You		2,152.00
234567	2/15/2015	Jones Office Supply	86.48	
345678	2/20/2015	Rodriuez Rentals	35.40	

Previous Balance		Payments		New Charges		Finance Charges		New Balance
$2,152.00	-	$2,152.00	+	$121.88	+	$17.93	=	$139.81

Figure 5-25 National Bank Visa credit card statement

Use the National Bank Visa Gold credit card statement shown in Figure 5-25 to reconcile your account.

COMPUTER PRACTICE

Step 1.   Select the **Banking** menu and then select **Reconcile**.

Step 2.   On the Begin Reconciliation window, enter the information from the Credit Card statement as shown in Figure 5-26. Click **Continue**.

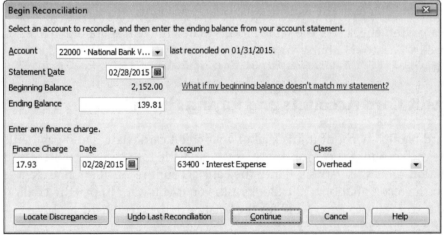

Figure 5-26 Enter your credit card statement information on the Begin Reconciliation window

Step 3.   Click each cleared transaction in the *Reconcile Credit Card* window as you match it with the credit card statement.

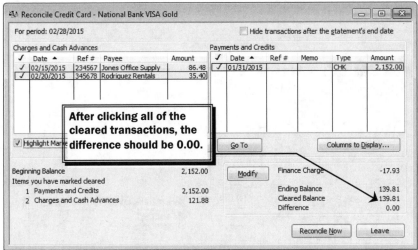

Figure 5-27 The Difference field should show a difference of 0.00 after reconciling

Step 4.   Verify that the *Difference* field shows **0.00** (see Figure 5-27). If it doesn't, look for discrepancies between your records and the credit card statement.

Step 5.   Verify that your screen looks like Figure 5-27 and click **Reconcile Now**.

Step 6.   On the *Make Payment* dialog box, click to select **Enter a bill for payment later** and click **OK** (see Figure 5-28).

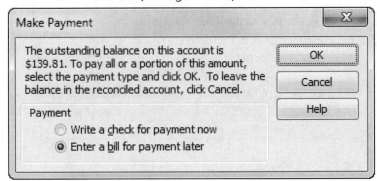

Figure 5-28 Make Payment window

Step 7.   On the *Select Reconciliation Report* window, click **Close.** Normally you would select **Both** and then click **Print**. However, for this exercise, skip this step. See page 144 for more information about Bank Reconciliation reports.

Step 8.   Enter the additional information to complete the **Bill** for the VISA payment as shown in Figure 5-29.

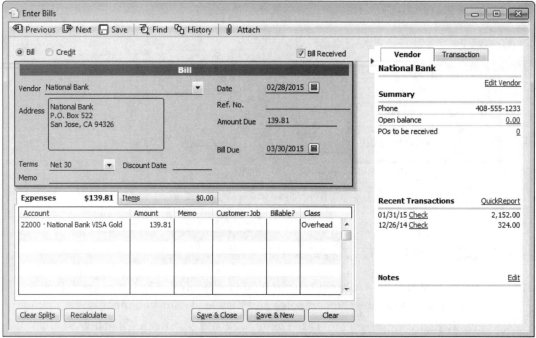

Figure 5-29 Use this data to pay the VISA Bill

> **The accounting behind the scenes:**
> QuickBooks selects the **National Bank VISA Gold** account on the Expenses tab.
> This reduces the Credit Card liability account (debit) and increases Accounts
> Payable (credit).
> **Note:**
> Although the bill in Figure 5-29 includes the Overhead class, the transaction will
> not affect the **Profit & Loss by Class** report because the bill does not post to any
> income or expense accounts.

Step 9.   Click **Save & Close** to record the Bill.

               This bill for $139.81 will display in the *Pay Bills* window the next time you select **Pay
               Bills** from the *Vendor* menu.

> **Important tip for partial payments of credit card bills:**
> If you don't want to pay the whole amount due on a credit card, don't just
> change the amount in the *Pay Bills* window. Instead, edit the original *Bill* to
> match the amount you actually intend to pay. By changing the *Bill*, you reduce
> the amount that is transferred out of the Credit Card account (and into A/P) to
> the exact amount that is paid. This way, the amount you don't pay remains in
> the balance of the Credit Card liability account and will match the account
> balance on your next credit card statement.

Online Banking

The QuickBooks Online Banking feature allows you to process online transactions, such as
payments and transfers, and download bank transactions into your QuickBooks file.
Downloaded transactions save you time by decreasing manual entry and increasing accuracy.
It is important to review each downloaded transaction to avoid bringing errors into your
company file.

Online Banking is secure. QuickBooks uses a secure Internet connection and a high level of encryption when transferring information from your financial institution.

Online Banking Setup

To begin to use Online Banking, you will need to set up the appropriate accounts to communicate with the bank. Steps vary by institution. To complete this process, refer to the QuickBooks help files or the video tutorial.

Processing Online Transactions

You may have the option to enter online transactions, such as online payments, bill payments, or transfers (depending on your financial institution). Figure 5-30 displays an example of an online payment. You can create an online payment by opening the **Write Checks** window and checking **Online Payment**. Notice that there are several differences between a standard check form and an online payment form. For example, the check number field displays the word *SEND*.

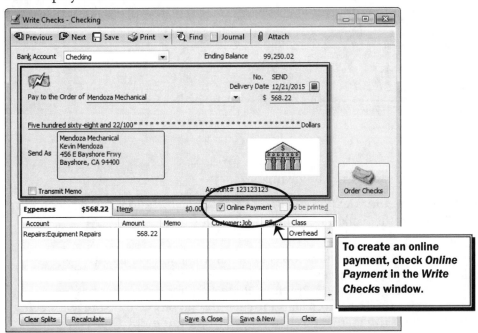

Figure 5-30 Check to be sent as an Online Payment

After saving an online payment, the transaction is queued up in the *Online Banking Center*. By clicking the *Send/Receive Transactions* button in the *Online Banking Center*, you can send the online payments and other online transactions to, as well as download transactions from, your financial institution.

Your financial institution may require additional steps. Follow any guidelines given after clicking the *Send/Receive Transactions* button. Do not click the *Send/Receive Transactions* button now.

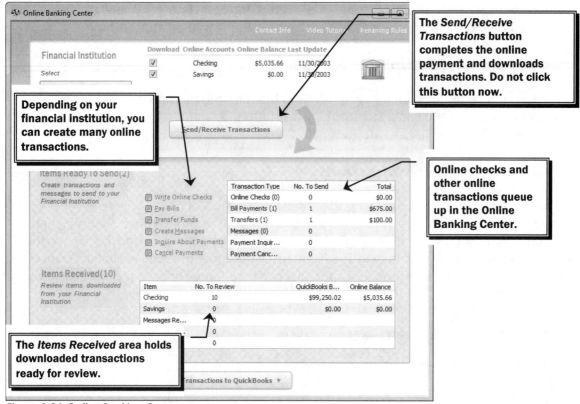

Figure 5-31 Online Banking Center – your screen may vary

Review Questions

Select the best answer(s) for each of the following:

1. When the *Beginning Balance* field on the *Begin Reconciliation* window doesn't match the beginning balance on the bank statement, you should:

    a)   Call the bank.

    b)   Change the amount in QuickBooks to match the bank's amount.

    c)   Click **Locate Discrepancies** in the *Begin Reconciliation* window. Click **Discrepancy Report** and/or **Previous Reports** to research what has been changed since the last reconciliation. Then fix the problem before reconciling.

    d)   Select the **Banking** menu and then select **Enter Statement Charges**.

2. Which statement is false?

    a)   You can enter bank service charges using *Enter Statement Charges*.

    b)   You can enter bank service charges on the *Begin Reconciliation* window.

    c)   You can enter bank service charges using the *Splits* button on a register transaction.

    d)   You can enter bank service charges using *Write Checks* before you start your reconciliation.

3. When you find an erroneous amount on a transaction while reconciling, correct the amount by:

    a)   Selecting the **Banking** menu and then selecting **Correct Error**.

    b)   Double-clicking on the entry and changing the amount on the transaction.

    c)   Selecting the entry in the **Reconcile** window, then clicking **Go To** and changing the amount on the transaction.

    d)   Performing either b or c.

4. To properly record a voided check from a closed accounting period:
   a) Delete the check in the register.
   b) Make a deposit in the current period and code it to the same account as the original check you want to void. Then delete both transactions in the **Reconciliation** window.
   c) Find the check in the register, select the **Edit** Menu, and then select **Void Check**.
   d) Change the amount of the check to zero.

5. Which of the following columns cannot be displayed in the *Checks and Payments* section of the *Reconcile* window?
   a) Check #.
   b) Class.
   c) Date.
   d) Payee.

Bank Rec-Problem 1

APPLYING YOUR KNOWLEDGE

Restore the **BankRec-12Problem1.QBM** file.

1. Using the sample bank statement shown below, reconcile the checking account for 01/31/2015.

Business Checking Account			
Statement Date:	**January 31, 2015**		Page 1 of 1

Summary:

Previous Balance as of 12/31/14:	$	18,283.60	
Total Deposits and Credits	+ $	4,561.08	
Total Checks and Debits	- $	8,076.12	
Statement Balance as of 1/31/15:	= $	**14,768.56**	

Deposits and Other Credits:

DEPOSITS

Date	Description		Amount
12-Jan	Customer Deposit	$	1,709.53
30-Jan	Customer Deposit	$	2,848.27
	2 Deposits: $		**4,557.80**

INTEREST

Date	Description		Amount
31-Jan	Interest Earned	$	3.28
	Interest: $		**3.28**

Checks and Other Withdrawals:

CHECKS PAID:

Check No.	Date Paid		Amount
325	2-Jan	$	324.00
326	7-Jan	$	276.52
327	17-Jan	$	128.60
6001**	25-Jan	$	3,200.00
6003**	25-Jan	$	142.00
	5 Checks Paid: $		**4,071.12**

OTHER WITHDRAWALS/PAYMENTS

Date	Description		Amount
31-Jan	Transfer	$	4,000.00
	1 Other Withdrawals/Payments: $		**4,000.00**

SERVICE CHARGES

Date	Description		Amount
31-Jan	Service Charge	$	5.00
	1 Service Charge: $		**5.00**

Figure 5-32 Bank statement for January 31, 2015

2. Print a **Reconciliation Detail** report dated 1/31/2015.

3. On **02/12/2015**, Maria Cruz's payment bounced (check #9563, received on 1/27/15 for Invoice #2015-105). The amount of the check was **$880.00**. The bank charged you an NSF Fee of **$10.00**. Using this information, record the following:

    a)   Enter the bounced check and NSF fee your bank charged you in your check register by using **Cruz, Maria:Branch Opening** as the *Payee*.

    b)   Unapply the original payment for *Invoice #2015-105* and then apply this same payment to the bounced check transaction you just created.

    c)   Create an *Other Charge* item called **NSF Charge** with an amount of $20.00. The description should read "***NSF Service Charge for Bounced Check #.***" Use the **Non** sales tax code, and associate the item with the **Bank Service Charge** expense account.

    d)   Create Invoice #*2015-105B* dated *2/12/2015* and code it to the **Walnut Creek** class for the **Cruz, Maria:Branch Opening**. Select the *NSF Charge Item* and charge Maria Cruz's job **$20.00** for the bounced check. Change the *Terms* to **Due Upon Receipt** for this *Invoice* only.

4. Enter the transactions necessary to record the receipt and redeposit of Maria Cruz's replacement check for $880.00 (Check #*9588*) that did not include the bounce charge. Date the payment *02/14/2015* and apply it to invoice #**2015-105**. Date the deposit on *02/14/2015*.

5. Using the sample bank statement shown below, reconcile the checking account for 02/28/2015.

	Business Checking Account				
Statement Date:	**February 28, 2015**			*Page 1 of 1*	
Summary:					
Previous Balance as of 1/31/15:	$	14,768.56			
Total Deposits and Credits: 6	+ $	5,720.20			
Total Checks and Debits: 7	- $	4,567.76			
Statement Balance as of 2/28/15:	= $	15,921.00			

Deposits and Other Credits:

DEPOSITS				INTEREST		
Date	Description		Amount	Date	Description	Amount
3-Feb	Customer Deposit	$	119.08	28-Feb	Interest Earned $	2.56
4-Feb	Customer Deposit	$	2,460.13		Interest: $	2.56
10-Feb	Customer Deposit	$	809.03			
11-Feb	Customer Deposit	$	753.41			
13-Feb	Customer Deposit	$	695.99			
14-Feb	Customer Deposit	$	880.00			
	6 Deposits: $		5,717.64			

Checks and Other Withdrawals:

CHECKS PAID:				OTHER WITHDRAWALS/PAYMENTS		
Check No.	Date Paid		Amount	Date	Description	Amount
329	14-Feb	$	2,152.00	12-Feb	Returned Item $	880.00
330	15-Feb	$	377.28	12-Feb	NSF Charge $	10.00
331	24-Feb	$	375.00		2 Other Withdrawals/Payments: $	890.00
332 **	28-Feb	$	645.00			
6004	2-Feb	$	123.48	**SERVICE CHARGES**		
	5 Checks Paid: $		3,672.76	Date	Description	Amount
				28-Feb	Service Charge $	5.00
					1 Service Charge: $	5.00

Figure 5-33 Bank statement for February 28, 2015

6. Print a *Reconciliation Detail* report dated 02/28/2015.

7. Print a customer *Statement* for Maria Cruz's Branch Opening job for the period 01/1/2015 through 02/28/2015.

Chapter 6
Reports and Graphs

Objectives

After completing this chapter, you should be able to:

- Describe several types of QuickBooks Reports (page 163)
- Set QuickBooks Preferences for cash or accrual basis reports (page 164)
- Create several different accounting reports (page 167)
- Create several different business management reports (page 177)
- Create graphs (page 182)
- Customize the look of reports and filter the data on reports (page 184)
- Memorize and group reports (page 190)
- Process and print multiple reports in batches (page 192)
- Use the *Search* command to find transactions (page 195)
- Use QuickZoom to see the "numbers behind the numbers" on reports (page 199)
- Export reports to spreadsheets for further analysis (page 201)

> **Restore this File**
>
> This chapter uses Reports-12.QBW. To open this file, restore the Reports-12.QBM file to your hard disk. See page 8 for instructions on restoring files. If you are using QuickBooks Premier Accountant, we recommend that you toggle to QuickBooks Premier General Business as described on page x.

QuickBooks reports allow you to get the information you need to make critical business decisions. In this chapter, you'll learn how to create a variety of reports to help you manage your business. Every report in QuickBooks gives you immediate, up-to-date information about your company's performance.

There are literally hundreds of reports available in QuickBooks. They allow you to work with the numbers so that you can look at your data in any way you wish. In addition to the built-in reports, you can *modify* reports to include or exclude whatever data you want. To control the look of your reports, you can customize the formatting of headers, footers, fonts, or columns.

When you get a report looking just the way you want, you can *memorize* it so that you can quickly create it again later.

Types of Reports

There are two major types of reports in QuickBooks – accounting reports and business management reports. In addition, most reports have both "detail" and "summary" styles. Detail reports show individual transactions and summary reports show totals for a group of transactions.

Accounting reports contain information about transactions and accounts. For example, the *Profit & Loss* report is a summary report of all transactions coded to income and expense accounts for a specified period of time. Your accountant or tax preparer will need several accounting reports from QuickBooks in order to provide accounting and tax services for your company.

Business management reports are used to monitor different activities of a business to help plan workflow and review transactions that have already occurred. These reports provide critical information that you need to operate your business. For example, the *Customer Contact List* report shows addresses, phone numbers, fax numbers, and other information about Customers. The *Collections* report provides information you need to follow up on *Invoices* that are past due. The *Sales by Item* report shows business managers how well each product and service is selling.

Report Type	Example Reports
Accounting	Profit & Loss, Balance Sheet, Trial Balance, Cash Flow Forecast, General Ledger, Trial Balance
Business Management	Open Invoices, Unpaid Bills Detail, Check Detail, Sales by Item Detail, Item Profitability, Customer Contact List, Item Price List, Time by Name, Stock Status by Item

Table 6-1 Types of QuickBooks reports

Cash Versus Accrual Reports

QuickBooks can automatically convert reports from the accrual basis to the cash basis, depending on how you set your Preferences or how you customize reports.

If you use cash basis accounting, you regard income or expenses as occurring at the time you actually receive a payment from a customer or pay a bill from a vendor. The cash basis records (or recognizes) income or expense only when cash is received or paid, no matter when the original transaction occurred. If you use accrual basis accounting, you regard income or expenses as occurring at the time you ship a product, render a service, or receive a bill from your vendors. Under this method, the date that you enter a transaction and the date that you actually pay or receive cash may be two separate dates, but income (or expense) is recognized on the day of the original transaction.

You can set the default for all QuickBooks summary reports to the cash or accrual basis by selecting *Cash* or *Accrual* in the *Summary Reports Basis* section of the *Reports & Graphs Preferences* window. Follow these steps:

COMPUTER PRACTICE

Step 1.   Select the **Edit** menu and then select **Preferences**.

Step 2.   Click on the **Reports and Graphs** preference.

Step 3.   Click the **Company Preferences** tab.

> **Note:**
> If you are in multi-user mode you will need to first switch to single-user mode to change company preferences.

Step 4.   To set the basis to match your company's finances, click **Cash** or **Accrual** in the *Summary Reports Basis* section (see Figure 6-1). For this chapter, leave the basis set to **Accrual**.

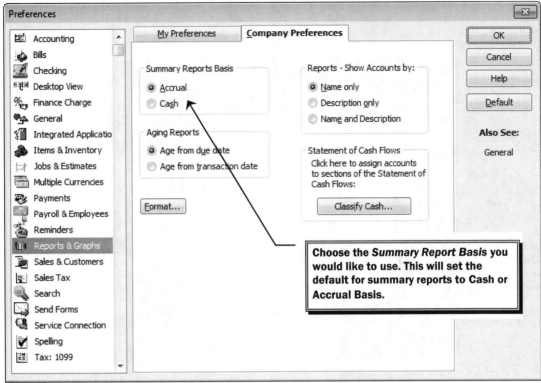

Figure 6-1 Preferences for Reports and Graphs

Step 5.   Click **OK** to save your changes (if any) and close the *Preferences* window.

> **Did You Know?**
> In QuickBooks, you can leave the *Reporting Preferences* set to the accrual basis for internal management reporting purposes and then create cash-basis reports for tax purposes.

Irrespective of the default setting in your *Preferences*, you can always switch between cash and accrual reports by modifying reports. To convert the report basis from accrual to cash on any report, follow these steps:

COMPUTER PRACTICE

Step 1.   Click the *Reports* icon on the *Icon Bar*. There are now three different views for previewing the reports, *Carousel, List,* and *Grid*.

Step 2.   Click on **Carousel View** in the upper right corner of the *Report Center*.

Step 3.   Select **Company & Financial** from the list on the left of the window, if it is not already selected. *Profit & Loss Standard* is the first report (see Figure 6-2).

You can choose other reports by moving the slider at the bottom the window. You can also choose a date range from the *Dates* fields at the bottom of the window.

Step 4.   Double click the **Profit & Loss Standard** report image in the *Report Center.*

Figure 6-2 Carousel View in the Report Center

Step 5. Click the **Customize Report** button at the top left of the *Profit & Loss* window.

Step 6. Set the *Dates* fields *From* **01/01/2015** and *To* **01/31/2015**. Press **Tab**.

Step 7. Click **Cash** in the *Report Basis* section (see Figure 6-3).

Step 8. Click **OK** to save your changes and display a Cash Basis *Profit & Loss* report for January 2015.

Step 9. Close the *Profit & Loss* report window.

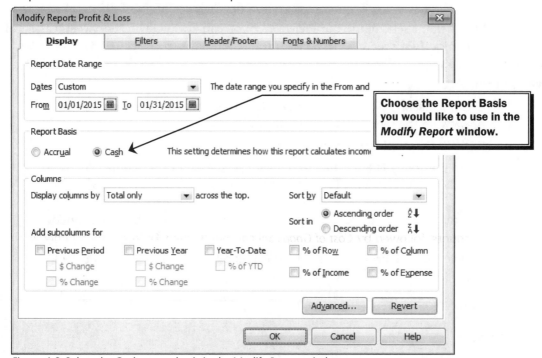

Figure 6-3 Select the Cash report basis in the Modify Report window

Accounting Reports

There are several built-in reports that summarize a group of transactions. These reports help you analyze the performance of your business.

Profit & Loss

The *Profit & Loss* report (also referred to as the *Income Statement*) shows all your income and expenses for a given period.

As discussed earlier, the goal of accounting is to provide the financial information you need to measure the success (or failure) of your organization, as well as to file proper tax returns. The *Profit & Loss* report is one of the most valuable sources of this financial information.

COMPUTER PRACTICE

Step 1.   From the *Report Center*, click **Grid View** to choose a report from a different view (see Figure 6-4).

Step 2.   Select **Company & Financial** from the list on the left of the window if it is not already selected, and then double click the **Profit & Loss Standard** report in the upper left of the Grid View.

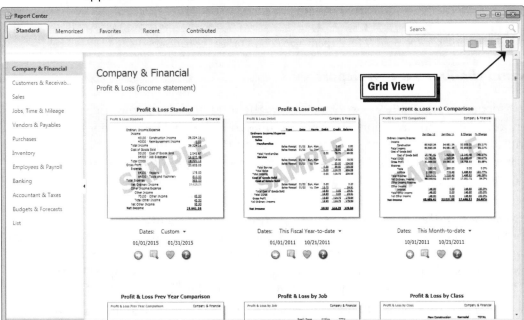

Figure 6-4 Grid View of the Report Center

Step 3.   Set the *Dates* fields *From **01/01/2015*** and *To **01/31/2015***. Press **Tab**.

Step 4.   The *Profit & Loss* report (see Figure 6-5) summarizes the totals of all your *Income* accounts, followed by *Cost of Goods Sold* accounts, then *Expenses*, then *Other Income*, and finally *Other Expenses*. The total at the bottom of the report is your *Net Income* (or loss) for the period you specified in the *Dates* fields. The *Profit & Loss* report is a company's operating results, normally for a period of 12 months or less.

Note that the window shown in Figure 6-5 is not the complete report. You will have to scroll down to see the remainder of the report. Do not close this report.

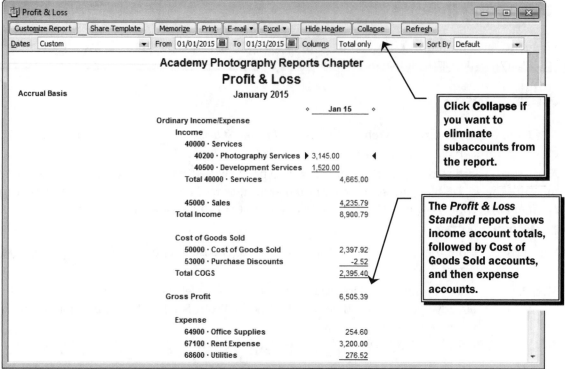

Figure 6-5 Upper portion of the Profit & Loss report (scroll down to see the remainder)

Analyzing the Profit & Loss Report

The first section of the *Profit & Loss* report shows the total of each of your income accounts for the period specified on the report. If you have subaccounts, QuickBooks indents those accounts on the report and subtotals them. Notice on Figure 6-5 that the *Services* income category has two subaccounts: *Photography Services* and *Development Services*. To hide subaccounts on this report (or any summary report), click the *Collapse* button at the top of the report.

The next section of the report shows your *Cost of Goods Sold* accounts. You use these accounts to record the costs of the products and services you sell in your business (e.g., inventory, cost of labor, etc.). If you use *Inventory Items*, QuickBooks calculates *Cost of Goods Sold* as each *Inventory Item* is sold, using the *average cost method*. (See the Inventory chapter beginning on page 233 for more information on how QuickBooks calculates average cost.)

The next section of the report shows your expenses of the business. Use these accounts to record costs associated with operating your business (e.g., rent, salaries, supplies, etc.). Expenses are generally recorded in QuickBooks as you write checks or enter bills, but can also be recorded directly into a register or as a journal entry.

The next section of the report shows your *Other Income/Expenses* accounts. Use these accounts to record income and expenses that are generated outside the normal operation of your business. For example, if you provide accounting services but sold an old business computer to a relative, the income generated from the sale would be classified as *Other Income* because it was generated outside the normal operation of your business.

At the bottom of the report, QuickBooks calculates your *Net Income* – the amount of your revenue less your Cost of Goods Sold and your operating expenses. You may want to view your expenses (such as rent, office supplies, employee salaries, etc.) as a percentage of total income to help you locate excessive expenses in your business.

COMPUTER PRACTICE

Step 1.   Click the **Customize Report** button at the top left of the *Profit & Loss* report.

Step 2.   Click the **% of Income** box (see Figure 6-6).

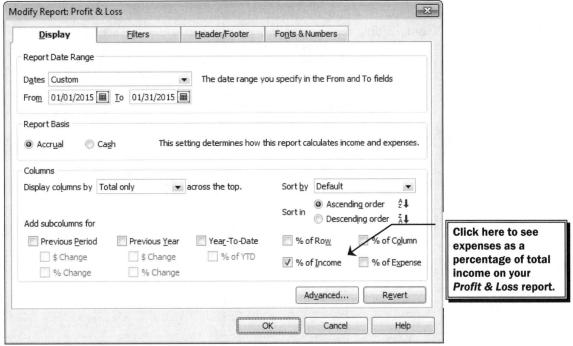

Figure 6-6 The Modify Report window

Step 3.   Click OK.

The *Profit & Loss* report now has a *% of Income* column (see Figure 6-7), allowing you to quickly identify numbers that deviate from the norm. Familiarize yourself with the percentages of expenses in your business and review this report periodically to make sure you stay in control of your expenses.

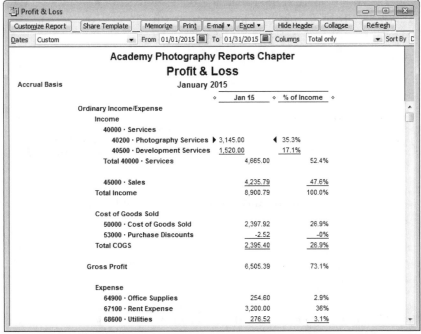

Figure 6-7 Modified Profit & Loss report

Step 4.   To find the details behind any of these numbers, you can use *QuickZoom* (explained on page 199). Double-click the *Cost of Goods Sold* line item amount of **2,397.92** in the report (see Figure 6-7).

The report shown in Figure 6-8 shows each transaction coded to the *Cost of Goods Sold* account. Double-click on any of these numbers to see the actual transaction.

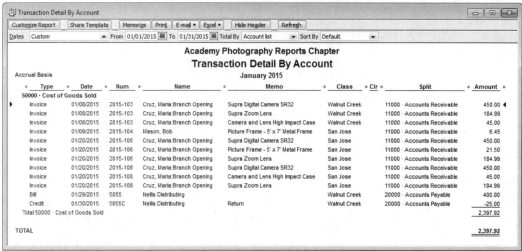

Figure 6-8 Transaction Detail by Account report for the Cost of Goods Sold account

Step 5.   Close both open reports.

Profit & Loss by Class Report

To divide your *Profit & Loss* report into departments (or Classes), use the *Profit & Loss by Class* report.

COMPUTER PRACTICE

Step 1.   From the *Report Center*, click the *List* view (see Figure 6-9)

Step 2.   Select **Company & Financial** from the menu on the left if it is not already selected, then double click the **Profit & Loss By Class** report in the *Profit & Loss (income statement)* section.

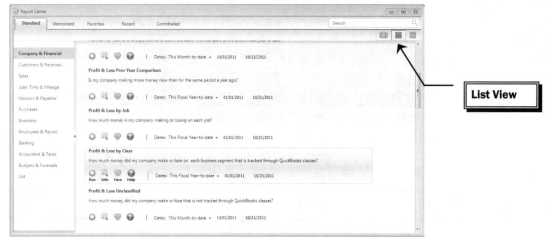

Figure 6-9 List View in the Report Center

Step 3.   Enter *01/01/2015* in the *From* field, enter *01/31/2015* in the *To* field at the top of the report, and press **Tab**.

Step 4.   Your report should look like the one shown in Figure 6-10. Notice that totals for each Class are displayed in a separate column.

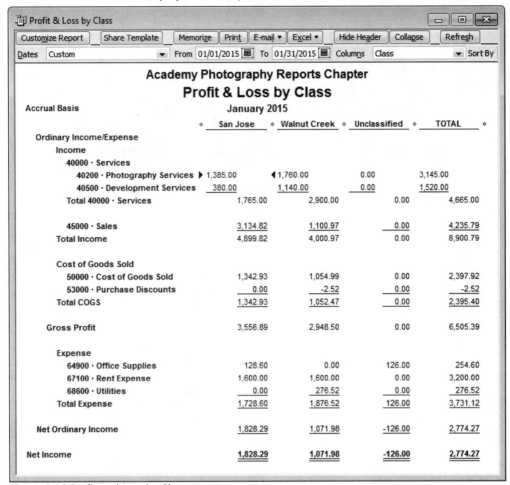

Figure 6-10 Profit and Loss by Class report

This report includes an *Unclassified* column, as shown in Figure 6-10, which means that some of the transactions were not assigned a Class. To classify the unclassified transactions, follow these steps:

Step 5.   Double-click to QuickZoom on the 126.00 amount in the *Unclassified* column under Office Supplies. This will bring up the *Transaction Detail by Account* report.

Step 6.   Double-click to QuickZoom on the 126.00 amount again. This opens the *Bill* from Ace Supply.

Step 7.   Assign the Class **Walnut Creek** to the *Bill* as shown in Figure 6-11.

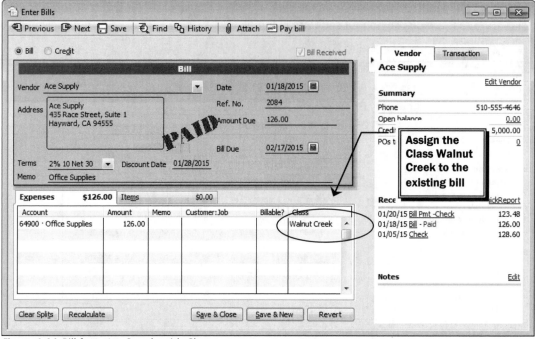

Figure 6-11 Bill from Ace Supply with Class

Step 8.   **Save and Close** the *Bill*.

Step 9.   The *Report needs to be refreshed* window appears. Click **Yes** to refresh the open reports.

Step 10.   Close the *Transaction Detail by Account* report. The *Profit & Loss by Class* report no longer has an *Unclassified* column (see Figure 6-12).

Step 11.   Close this report.

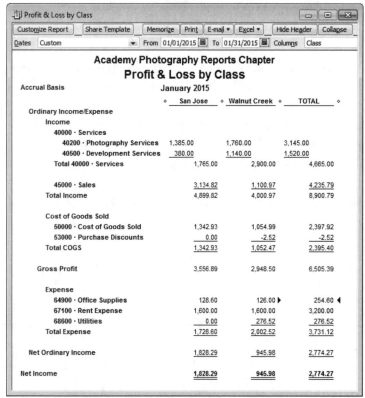

Figure 6-12 Profit & Loss by Class without Unclassified Column

> **Note:**
> When using Classes, be sure to always enter the Class as you are recording each transaction. This prevents any transaction from being recorded as "Unclassified." For transactions that do not fall within the normal operating activities of one of the classes in your company file, use a general Class such as *Overhead*.

To ensure that transactions are always assigned to Classes, set *Preferences* so that QuickBooks will prompt you to assign a Class before completing the transaction. To learn more about these *Preferences*, see page 205.

Profit & Loss by Job Report

To divide your *Profit & Loss* report into *Customers* or *Jobs*, use the *Profit & Loss by Job* report. This report, sometimes called the Job Cost report, allows you to see your profitability for each *Customer* or *Job*. This information helps you to spot pricing problems, as well as costs that are out of the ordinary. For example, if this report showed that you lost money on all the Jobs where you did an outdoor session, you would probably want to adjust your prices for outdoor photo shoots. Similarly, if the cost on one Job is significantly higher or lower than other Jobs of similar size, you might look closer at that Job to see if adjustments are needed to control costs.

COMPUTER PRACTICE

To create a *Profit & Loss by Job* report, follow these steps:

Step 1.   From the *Report Center*, select **Company & Financial** and then double click the **Profit & Loss By Job** link in the *Profit & Loss (income statement)* section.

Step 2.   Enter *01/01/2015* in the *From* field, enter *01/31/2015* in the *To* field, and press **Tab** (see Figure 6-13).

Step 3.   After you view the *Profit & Loss by Job* report, close all open report windows.

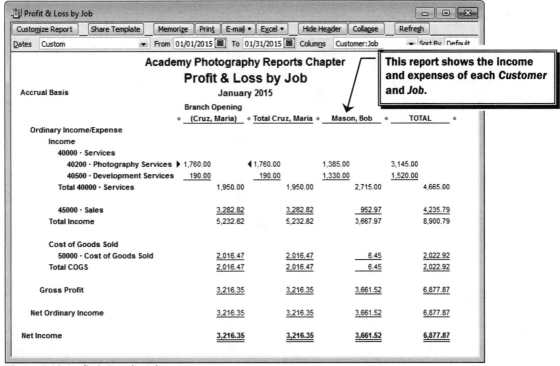

Figure 6-13 Profit & Loss by Job report

Balance Sheet

Another important report for analyzing your business is the *Balance Sheet*. The Balance Sheet shows your financial position, as defined by the balances in each of your assets, liabilities, and equity accounts on a given date.

COMPUTER PRACTICE

Step 1.   From the *Report Center*, select **Company & Financial** and then double click the **Balance Sheet Standard** report in the *Balance Sheet & Net Worth* section. You may need to scroll down.

Step 2.   Enter *01/31/2015* in the *As of* field and press **Tab**. In Figure 6-14, you can see a portion of the *Balance Sheet* for Academy Photography on 01/31/2015.

> **Tip:**
> Familiarize yourself with how your Balance Sheet changes throughout the year. Banks examine this report very closely before approving loans. Often, the bank will calculate the ratio of your current assets divided by your current liabilities. This ratio, known as the current ratio, measures your ability to satisfy your debts.

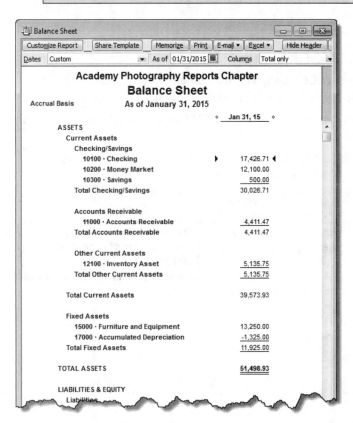

Figure 6-14 Balance Sheet for Academy Photography on 01/31/2015

Statement of Cash Flows

The *Statement of Cash Flows* provides information about the cash receipts and cash payments of your business during a given period. In addition, it provides information about investing and financing activities, such as purchasing equipment or borrowing. The *Statement of Cash Flows* shows the detail of how you spent the cash shown on the company's *Balance Sheet*.

COMPUTER PRACTICE

Step 1.   From the *Report Center*, select **Company & Financial** and then double click the **Statement of Cash Flows** report in the *Cash Flow* section.

Step 2.   Enter *01/01/2015* in the *From* field, enter *01/31/2015* in the *To* field, and press **Tab**.

On the report shown in Figure 6-15, you can see that although there was a net income of $2,774.27, there was a net decrease in cash of $532.89 during the first month of the year. Bankers look closely at this report to determine if your business is able to generate a positive cash flow, or if your business requires additional capital to satisfy its cash needs.

Step 3.   After you view the *Statement of Cash Flows* report, close all open report windows.

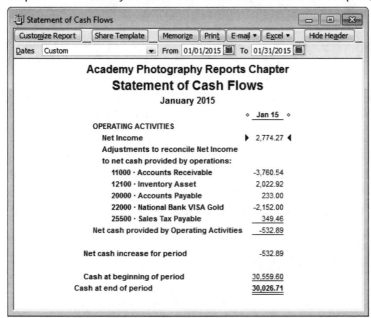

Figure 6-15 Statement of Cash Flows report

General Ledger

The *General Ledger* shows you all of the activity in all of your accounts for a specific period.

COMPUTER PRACTICE

Step 1.   From the *Report Center*, select **Accountant & Taxes** from the list of report categories on the left of the window and then double click the **General Ledger** report in the *Account Activity* section. If the *Collapsing and Expanding Transactions* window appears, read it and click **OK**.

Step 2.   Enter *01/01/2015* in the *From* field, enter *01/31/2015* in the *To* field, and press **Tab** (see Figure 6-16).

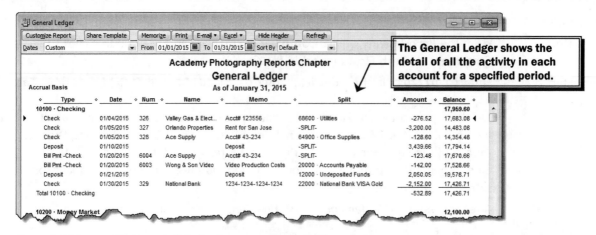

Figure 6-16 General Ledger - Activity in all accounts for a specific period

Trial Balance

The *Trial Balance* report shows the balance of each of the accounts as of a certain date. The report shows these balances in a Debit and Credit format. Your accountant will usually prepare this report at the end of each fiscal year.

COMPUTER PRACTICE

Step 1.　　From the *Report Center*, select **Accountant & Taxes** and then double click the **Trial Balance** report in the *Account Activity* section.

Step 2.　　Enter *01/01/2015* in the *From* field, enter *01/31/2015* in the *To,* field and press **Tab** (see Figure 6-17).

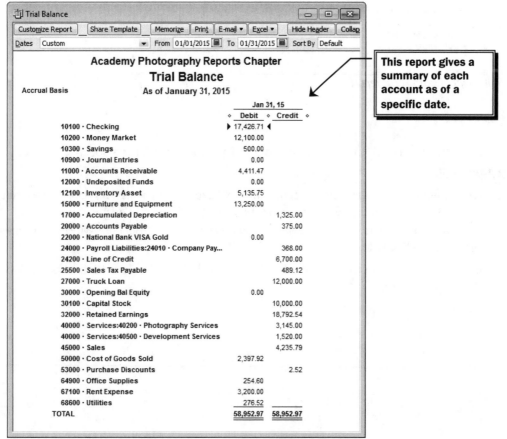

Figure 6-17 Trial Balance - Balance of each account as of a specific date

Step 3.   Close all open reports.

Voided/Deleted Transactions Summary Reports

The *Voided/Deleted Transactions Summary* report shows transactions that have been voided or deleted in the data file. This report assists accountants in detecting errors or fraud. This feature is very useful when you have a number of users in a file and transactions seem to "disappear" or change without explanation. The standard version of this report presents the transactions in a summary format (see Figure 6-18).

Figure 6-18 Voided/Deleted Transactions Report

The *Voided/Deleted Transactions Detail* report shows all of the line items associated with each affected transaction. This feature makes the original transaction information available so that it can be recreated if necessary (see Figure 6-19).

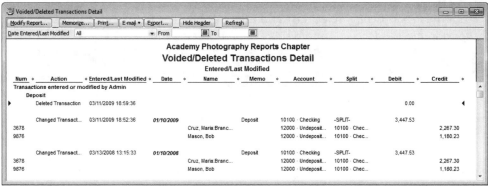

Figure 6-19 Voided/Deleted Transactions Detail Report

Business Management Reports

In the following Computer Practice exercises, you will use QuickBooks to create several different reports that help you manage your business.

Customer Phone List

The *Customer Phone List* shown in Figure 6-20 is a listing of each of your customers and their phone numbers. To create this report, follow these steps:

COMPUTER PRACTICE

Step 1.   From the *Report Center*, select **List** and then double click the **Customer Phone List** report in the *Customer* section to display the report (see Figure 6-20).

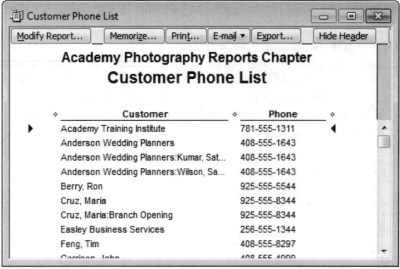

Figure 6-20 Customer Phone List report

Vendor Contact List

The *Vendor Contact List* shown in Figure 6-21 is a listing of your vendors along with each vendor's contact information. To create this report, follow these steps:

COMPUTER PRACTICE

Step 1.   From the *Report Center*, select **List** and then double click the **Vendor Contact List** report in the *Vendor* section to display the report (see Figure 6-21).

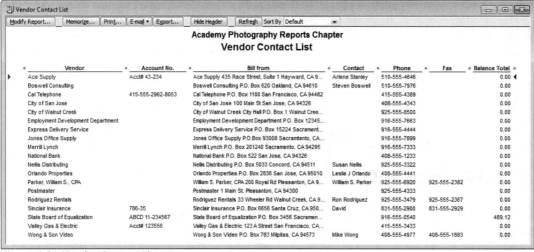

Figure 6-21 Vendor Contact List report

Item Price List

The *Item Price List* shown in Figure 6-22 is a listing of your *Items*. To create this report, follow these steps:

COMPUTER PRACTICE

Step 1.   From the *Report Center*, select **List** and then double click the **Item Price List** report in the *Listing* section to display the report (see Figure 6-22).

Step 2.   After viewing the **Item Price List** report, close all open report windows. Click **No** if QuickBooks prompts you to memorize the reports.

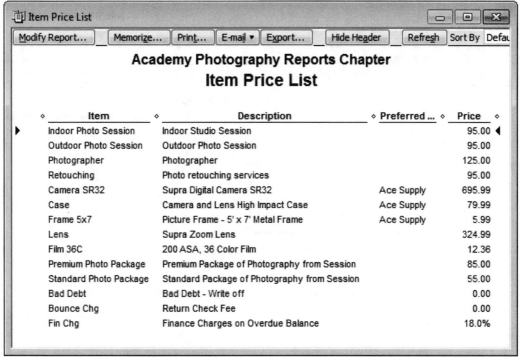

Figure 6-22 Item Price List report

Check Detail Report

The *Check Detail* report is quite valuable if you use accounts payable or payroll. It is frequently necessary to see what expense account(s) are associated with a bill payment. However, the *Register* report only shows that bill payments are associated with accounts payable. That's because a bill payment only involves the checking account and accounts payable. Similarly, paychecks only show in the register report as "Split" transactions because several accounts are associated with each paycheck. The *Check Detail* report shows the detailed expense account information about these types of transactions.

COMPUTER PRACTICE

Step 1.   From the *Report Center*, select **Banking** and then double click the **Check Detail** report in the *Banking* section.

Step 2.   Enter *01/01/2015* in the *From* field and enter *01/31/2015* in the *To* field. Then, press **Tab**.

Step 3.   Scroll down until you see Bill Pmt -Check 6004 (near the bottom of the report).

In Figure 6-23, notice bill payment number 6004. The report shows that QuickBooks split the total payment of $126.00 between the accounts payable account ($2.52) and the checking account ($123.48).

The amount for $-2.52 is the discount that you took when you paid the *Bill*. Although this report does not show it, you coded this amount to the Purchase Discounts account.

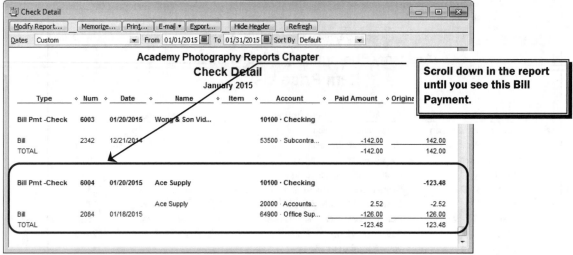

Figure 6-23 Check Detail report

Step 4.   Close all open report windows. Click **No** if QuickBooks prompts you to memorize the reports.

> **Tip:**
> In order to make your *Check Detail* reports easier to read and understand, consider recording your purchase discounts differently. Instead of taking the discount on the *Pay Bills* window (as you did in the example on page 115), consider recording your purchase discounts using *Bill Credits*.

Accounts Receivable and Accounts Payable Reports

There are several reports that you can use to keep track of the money that your Customers owe you (*accounts receivable*) and the money that you owe to your vendors (*accounts payable*).

Collections Report

The *Collections Report* is a report that shows each Customer's outstanding *Invoices* along with the Customer's telephone number.

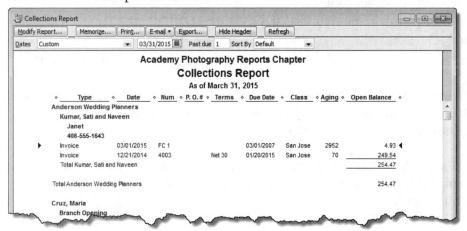

Figure 6-24 Accounts Receivable Collections Report

COMPUTER PRACTICE

Step 1.   From the *Report Center*, select **Customers & Receivables** and then double click the **Collections Report** in the *A/R Aging* section.

Step 2.   Enter *03/31/2015* in the *Dates* field and press **Tab** (see Figure 6-24).

Customer Balance Detail Report

Use the *Customer Balance Detail* report to see the details of each Customer's transactions and payments. This report shows all transactions that use the accounts receivable account, including *Invoices*, payments, discounts, and finance charges.

COMPUTER PRACTICE

Step 1.   From the *Report Center*, select **Customers & Receivables** and then double click the **Customer Balance Detail** report in the *Customer Balance* section (see Figure 6-25). The *Dates* field on this report defaults to *All*.

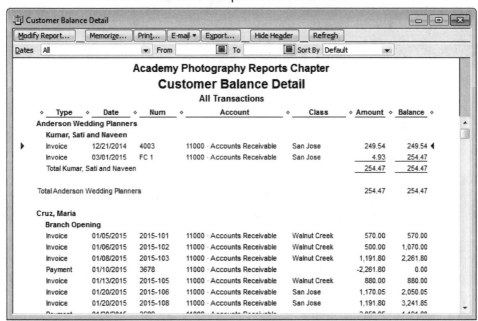

Figure 6-25 Customer Balance Detail report

Vendor Balance Detail Report

The *Vendor Balance Detail* report is similar to the *Customer Balance Detail* report, but it shows transactions that use *Accounts Payable*, including *Bills, Bill Credits, Bill Payments*, and discounts.

COMPUTER PRACTICE

Step 1.   From the *Report Center*, select **Vendors & Payables** and then double click the **Vendor Balance Detail** report in the *Vendor Balances* section (see Figure 6-26). The *Dates* field on this report defaults to *All*.

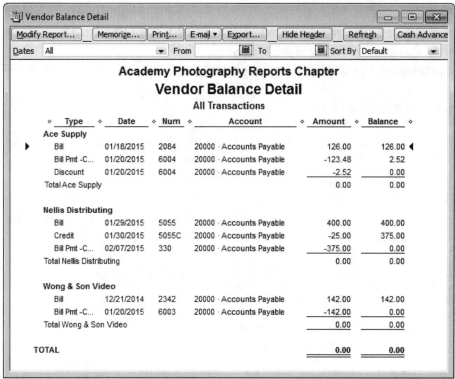

Figure 6-26 Vendor Balance Detail report

QuickBooks Graphs

One of the best ways to quickly get information from QuickBooks is to create a graph.

The *Income and Expense Graph* shows your income and expenses by month, and displays a pie chart showing a summary of your expenses.

COMPUTER PRACTICE

Step 1.   From the *Report Center*, select **Company & Financial** and then double click **Income and Expense Graph** in the *Income & Expenses* section.

Step 2.   Click **Dates** at the top left of the graph.

               QuickBooks will display the *Change Graph Dates* window (see Figure 6-27).

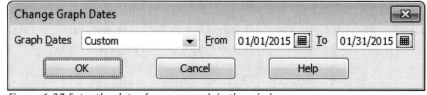

Figure 6-27 Enter the dates for your graph in the window.

Step 3.   Enter *01/01/2015* in the *From* field and enter *01/31/2015* in the *To* field. Then, click **OK**.

Step 4.   QuickBooks displays the graph shown in Figure 6-28.

Step 5.   After viewing the graph, close the graph window.

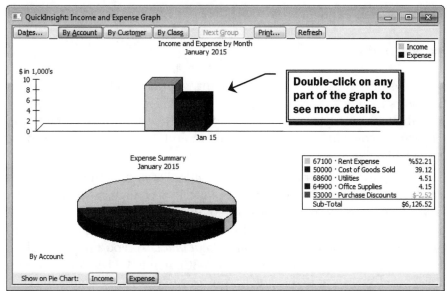

Figure 6-28 Income and Expense by Month graph

QuickBooks graphs highlight interesting facts about your company that are not easy to see from normal reports. For example, you can create a graph that shows your largest Customers or your biggest selling Items, and then you can visually inspect the relative sizes of each section of the graph.

COMPUTER PRACTICE

Step 1.   From the *Report Center*, select **Sales** and then double click **Sales Graph** in the *Sales by Customer* section (see Figure 6-29).

Step 2.   Click **Dates** at the top left of the graph. QuickBooks will display the *Change Graph Dates* window. Press **Tab**.

Step 3.   Enter *01/01/2015* in the *From* field, enter *02/28/2015* in the *To* field, and click **OK**.

Step 4.   Click the **By Customer** button on the top of the *QuickInsight: Sales Graph* window. This redraws the graph to show sales by Customer.

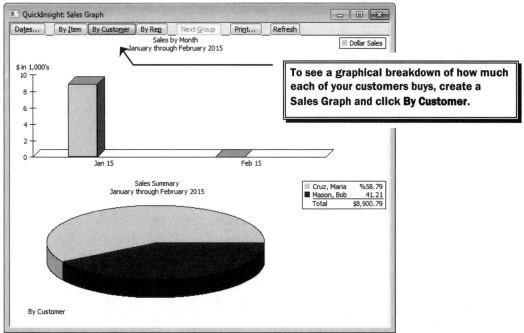

Figure 6-29 Create a Sales Graph by Customer

Step 5.   After viewing the graph, close the window.

Building Custom Reports

To make a reports that shows only the information you want, you can modify (i.e., customize) an existing report. All reports include at least some modification and filtering options, so familiarize yourself with the tabs in the *Modify Report* window as they are described below. In the Computer Practice section, you will create a sample report and then customize it using the *Modify Report* options available.

The *Modify Report* window displays when you click the *Customize Report* button on any report. Four tabs make up the *Modify Report* window. Use the *Display* tab to change the date range, select a report basis, add or delete columns, change how columns are displayed, or add subcolumns on a report. The *Display* tab will show different sections depending upon the report being modified. For example, the *Display* tab for a *Profit and Loss* report does not allow you to select or deselect columns for the report (see Figure 6-30), while the *Display* tab for an *Item Price List* only allows you to select or deselect columns for the report (see Figure 6-31). The *Display* tab shows those sections particular to the report being modified.

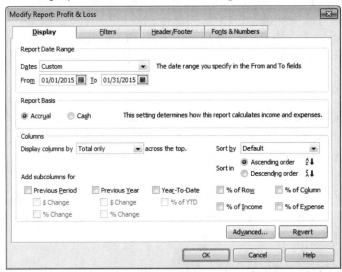

Figure 6-30 Display tab on the Modify Report: Profit & Loss window

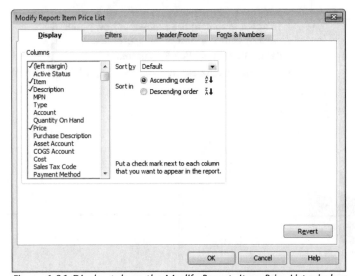

Figure 6-31 Display tab on the Modify Report: Item Price List window

Use the *Filters* tab to narrow the contents of the report so that you can analyze specific areas of your business. On the *Filters* tab, you can filter or choose specific accounts, dates, names, or Items to include in the report (see Figure 6-32).

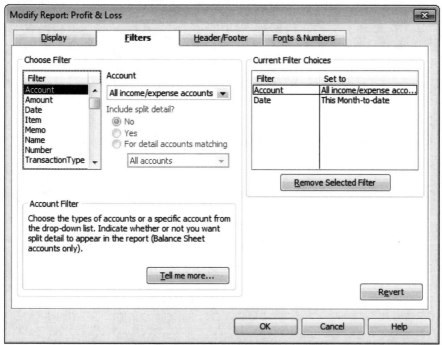

Figure 6-32 Filters tab on The Modify Report: Profit & Loss window

Use the *Header/Footer* tab to select which headers and footers will display on the report. In addition, the *Header/Footer* tab allows you to modify the *Company Name, Report Title, Subtitle, Date Prepared, Page Number,* and *Extra Footer Line* (see Figure 6-33).

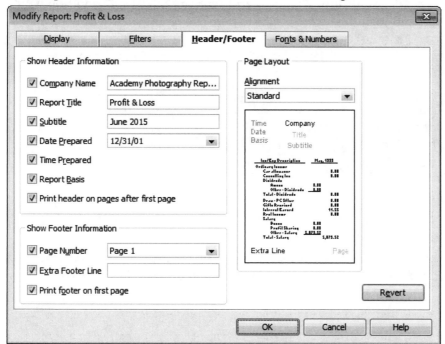

Figure 6-33 Header/Footer tab on The Modify Report: Profit & Loss window

Use the *Fonts & Numbers* tab to change the font and how numbers are displayed on the report. In addition, the *Fonts & Numbers* tab allows you to reduce numbers to multiples of 1000, hide amounts of 0.00, and show dollar amounts without cents (see Figure 6-34).

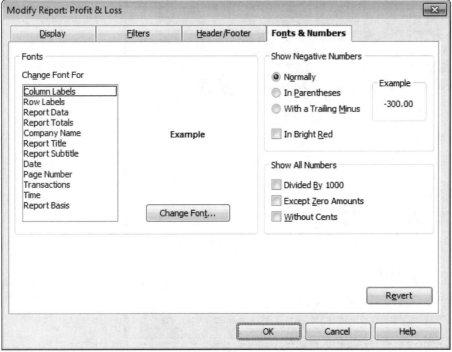

Figure 6-34 Fonts & Numbers tab on The Modify Report: Profit & Loss window

To practice modifying reports, suppose you want to get a report of all transactions that include all *Service Items* (*Photography Service* and *Development Services*) that you sold to Customers who live in *Walnut Creek* during January and February of 2015. In addition, you want QuickBooks to sort and total the report by Customer. The report should only display the type of transaction, the date, transaction number, customer name, city, Item, account, and amount. Finally, the report should be titled *Sales of Services to Walnut Creek Customers*.

> **Note:**
> Although Academy Photography uses Classes to track which store their Customers buy from, we want a report about where customers *live*. Specifically, we want the *City* from the Customer's address. This information comes from the field called "Name City" that is used as part of the Customer's billing address.

COMPUTER PRACTICE

Begin by creating a *Custom Transaction Detail* report and then modify the report so that it provides the information you need.

Step 1.   From the *Reports* menu, select **Transaction Detail** from the *Custom Report* submenu. The **Modify Report: Custom Transaction Detail Report** window displays.

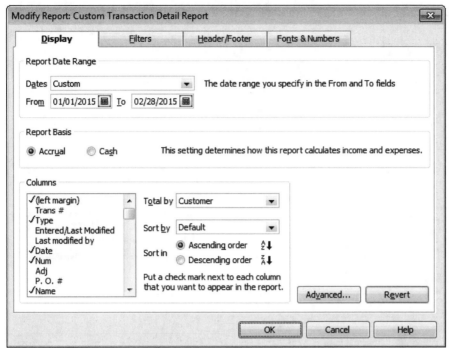

Figure 6-35 Modify Report: Custom Transaction Detail Report window

Step 2. Enter *01/01/2015* in the *From* field and enter *02/28/2015* in the *To* field.

Step 3. Select **Customer** from the *Total by* drop-down list and click **OK**.

This report will now show all transactions during January and February, totaled by Customer (see Figure 6-36).

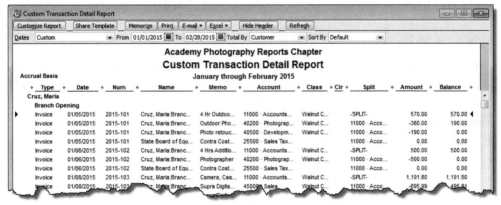

Figure 6-36 Transaction Detail by Account report totaled by Customer

For our purposes there are four problems with this report:

1. The report shows more columns than we want to display.
2. The report shows all transactions, not just the Service Items sold to Customers.
3. The report is not filtered to only show Customers who live in Walnut Creek.
4. The report has the wrong title.

We will modify the report to correct the four problems listed above.

Step 4. Click **Customize Report**.

Step 5. In the **Columns** section of the *Display* tab, notice that several fields have check marks (see Figure 6-37). The check marks indicate which columns show on the report.
Select **Name City** and **Item** to turn those columns on. Then deselect **Memo, Class,**

Clr, Split, and **Balance.** You will need to scroll up and down in the list to find each field.

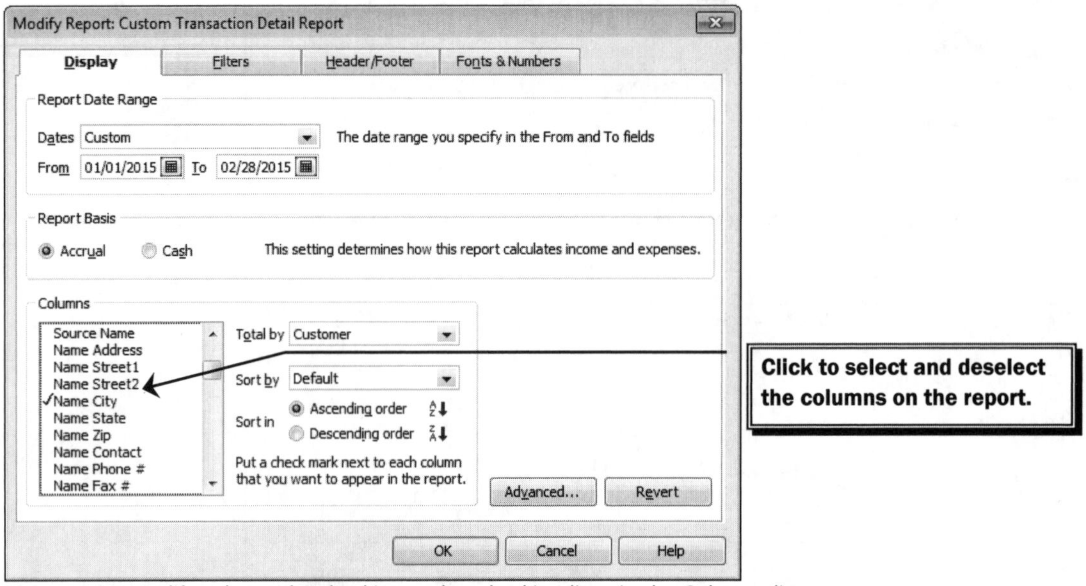

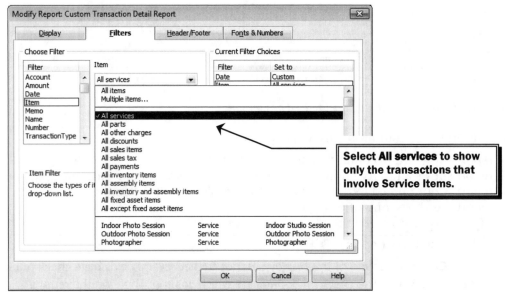

Figure 6-37 Modify columns by checking and unchecking lines in the Columns list

> **Note:**
> There are several other settings on the **Display** tab that you can choose if you want to modify the report further. For example, you could change the basis of the report from Accrual to Cash, or you could set the sorting preferences. Click the **Advanced** button for even more settings. Explore these settings to learn how they affect your reports. For descriptions of each selection, use the QuickBooks **Help** menu.

Step 6.   Click the **Filters** tab.

Step 7.   To filter the report so that it includes only Service Items, select the **Item** filter in the *Choose Filter* section and select **All services** from the *Item* drop-down list (see Figure 6-38).

Figure 6-38 Item drop-down list in the Filters window

Step 8.   To filter the report so that it includes only those Customers who live in Walnut Creek, scroll down the *Choose Filter* section and select the **Name City** filter. This displays a **Name City** field to the right of the *Choose Filter* section. Enter **Walnut Creek** in the **Name City** field (see Figure 6-39). Hit the **Tab** key.

> **Did You Know?**
> Many fields on the Filter tab act like wildcards. If you enter a portion of the text in a field for a particular filter, QuickBooks will display all records containing that text. For example, if you only type in *nut* or *eek* in the *City* field, all customer records in the city of Walnut Creek will still display, but other cities that contain *nut* or *eek* in their names will also appear. Therefore, be careful when using a wildcard in a field because it can produce an unintended result.

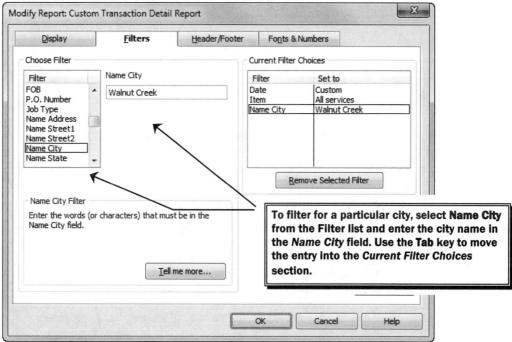

Figure 6-39 Entering a filter for a report

Step 9.   Click the **Header/Footer** tab on the *Modify Report* window.

Step 10.   To modify the title of the report so that it accurately describes the content of the report, enter *Sales of Services to Walnut Creek Customers* in the *Report Title* field as shown in Figure 6-40.

Step 11.   Click **OK** on the *Modify Report* window.

> **DO NOT CLOSE THE REPORT. YOU WILL USE IT IN THE NEXT PRACTICE.**

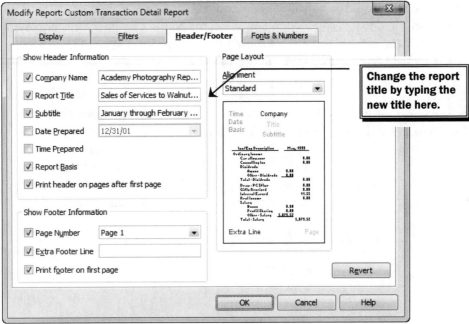

Figure 6-40 Change the report title on the Header/Footer tab

In Figure 6-41 you can see your modified report. Notice that its heading reflects its new content. You can modify the width of columns by dragging the diamond on the top right of the column to reduce or expand the width. Also, if you want to move a column left or right, move your curser over the column header until you see the hand icon. Then, hold your left mouse button down as you drag the column to the left or right.

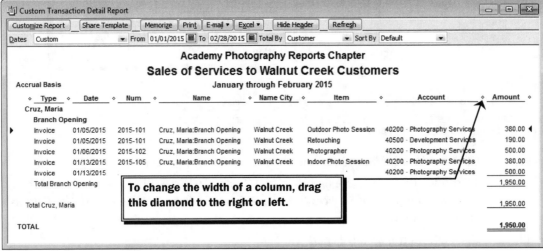

Figure 6-41 The customized report

Memorizing Reports

After you have modified a report, you can *memorize* the format and filtering so that you don't have to perform all of the modification steps the next time you want to view the report.

> **Note:**
> Memorizing a report does not memorize the data on the report, only the format, dates, and filtering.

If you enter specific dates, QuickBooks will use those dates the next time you bring up the report. However, if you select a *relative* date range in the *Dates* field (e.g., Last Fiscal Quarter, Last Year, or This Year to Date) before memorizing a report, QuickBooks will use the relative dates the next time you create the report.

For example, if you memorize a report with the *Dates* field set to *Last Fiscal Quarter*, that report will always use dates for the fiscal quarter prior to the date you run the memorized report (see Figure 6-42).

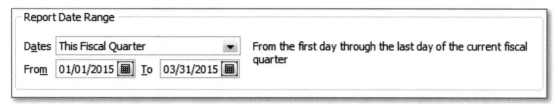

Figure 6-42 The Dates field showing a relative date range

COMPUTER PRACTICE

Step 1.   With the *Sales of Services to Walnut Creek Customers* report displayed, click **Memorize** at the top of the report.

Step 2.   In the *Memorize Report* window, the name for the report is automatically filled in. QuickBooks uses the report title as the default name for the memorized report (see Figure 6-43). The name can be modified if desired.

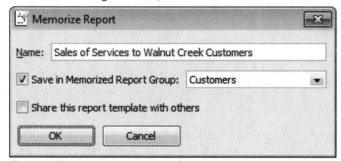

Figure 6-43 Memorize Report window

Step 3.   Click the Checkbox next to **Save in Memorized Report Group:** and select **Customers** from the drop-down list as shown in Figure 6-43.

You can group your reports into similar types when you memorize them. This allows you to run several reports in a group by selecting them in the *Process Multiple Reports* window.

Step 4.   Leave *Share this report template with others* unselected.

If checked, this feature would allow you to share your report template with the great QuickBooks user community. For more on *Contributed Reports*, see page 192.

Step 5.   Click **OK** and close the report.

Viewing Memorized Reports

The next time you want to see this report follow these steps:

Step 1.   From the *Report Center*, click on the **Memorized** tab at the top of the window.

Notice that QuickBooks displays the reports in groups according to how you memorized them.

Step 2.   Select the report you just memorized by selecting **Customers** on the menu on the left of the window and double click **Sales of Services to Walnut Creek Customers** (see Figure 6-44).

Figure 6-44 Memorized Report in the Report Center

Step 3.   Close all open report windows.

Contributed Reports

When you memorize a report, you are given the option of sharing the report template with others. You can access contributed reports from the Reports Center. Be aware that you may not be able to use certain reports if they utilize features that you do not use, such as multi-currency.

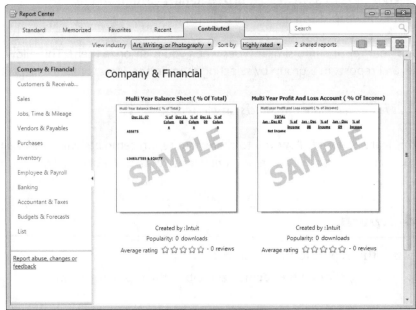

Figure 6-45 Contributed Reports in the Reports Center

Processing Multiple Reports

QuickBooks allows you to combine several reports into a group, so that you can later display and/or print the reports in the group as a batch.

You may want to use this feature to print a series of monthly reports for your files (e.g., monthly *Profit and Loss* and *Balance Sheet* reports).

COMPUTER PRACTICE

Step 1.　　From the *Reports* menu select **Process Multiple Reports** (see Figure 6-46).

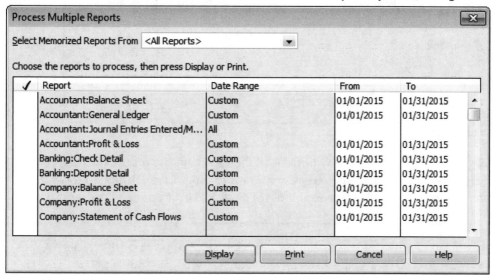

Figure 6-46 Process Multiple Reports window

> **Note:**
> Click in the column to the left of the report you want to include when you print or display your reports. Select the *From* and *To* date ranges of the report you wish to print in the columns on the right. Your date ranges will not match the ones displayed in Figure 6-46 and Figure 6-47. If you print the same group of reports on a regular basis, create a new Report Group in the *Memorize Reports List* window to combine the reports under a single group. Then you can select the group name in the *Select Memorized Reports From* field.

Step 2.　　Select **Customers** from the *Select Memorized Reports From* drop-down list (see Figure 6-47).

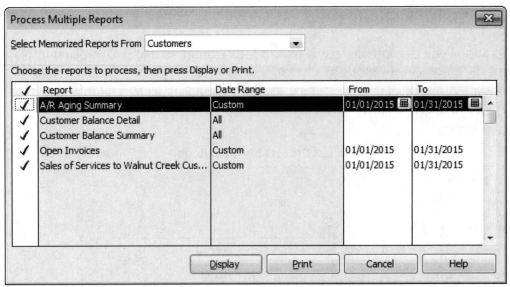

Figure 6-47 Customers Report Group

Step 3.   If you do not want to display or print all the reports in the group, uncheck (√) the left column to deselect the reports you want to omit. Click **Display** to show the reports on the window (see Figure 6-48) or click **Print** to print all the reports.

> If your *Home* page is maximized, make sure to **Restore Down** (⧉) the window so that your reports will display in the cascade style shown in Figure 6-48.

Step 4.   Close all open report windows. Click **No** if QuickBooks prompts you to memorize the reports.

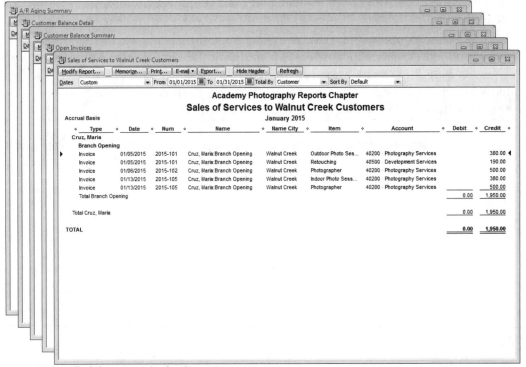

Figure 6-48 All of the reports in the Customer report group

Finding Transactions

There are several ways to find transactions in QuickBooks depending on what you are trying to find. Sometimes you only know the date of a transaction and other times you know only the Customer, Item, or amount. Some of the ways you can search for a transaction include finding it in the register, using the **Search** command, using **QuickReports**, or using **QuickZoom**.

Using the Search Command

If you are looking for a transaction and you do not know which register to look in, or if you want to find more than just a single transaction, you can use the **Search** command.

COMPUTER PRACTICE

You want to find a recent payment by Maria Cruz.

Step 1.   Enter **Cruz** in the *Search* field on the right side of the *Icon Bar* and select **Search company file** from the drop-down menu (see Figure 6-49). Click the **Search** icon.

Figure 6-49 The Search icon

Step 2.   The *Search* window opens. QuickBooks returns a keyword search including any transaction or *Name* record that contains the word, or string, "Cruz" (see Figure 6-50).

           You will notice that the search results include both the customer Maria Cruz, as well as Sinclair Insurance which is located in Santa Cruz, CA. Notice that different forms and name entries are included, such as Customers, Vendors, and *Invoices*.

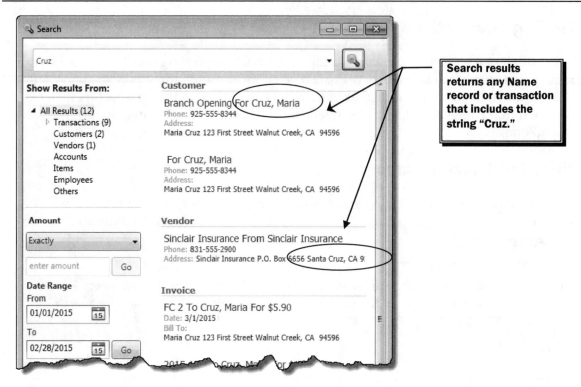

Figure 6-50 The Search Window

Step 3.   Close the *Search* window.

QuickReports

A *QuickReport* can quickly give you detailed transactions about an *Account, Item,* Customer, Vendor, or other payee. You can generate QuickReports from the *Chart of Accounts, Centers, Lists, Account Registers,* or forms. Table 6-2 shows different types of *QuickReports.*

When you are in...	The QuickReport shows you...
Chart of Accounts	All transactions involving that account
Centers and *Lists* (with an *Item* or *Name* selected)	All transactions for that *Item* or *Name*
Registers (with a transaction selected)	All transactions in that register for the same *Name*
Forms (*Invoice, Bill,* or *Check*)	All transactions for that particular customer, vendor, or payee within the same name as the current transaction

Table 6-2 Types of QuickReports

COMPUTER PRACTICE

Step 1.   Click the **Chart of Accounts** icon in the *Company* section of the **Home** page.

Step 2.   Select the **Inventory Asset** account.

Step 3.   Click the *Reports* button and select **Quick Report: Inventory Asset**. Alternatively, press **Ctrl+Q** (see Figure 6-51).

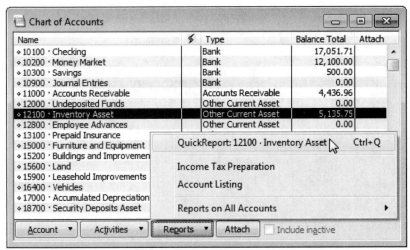

Figure 6-51 QuickReport of the Inventory Asset account

Step 4.   QuickBooks displays all transactions involving the **Inventory Asset** account (see Figure 6-52).

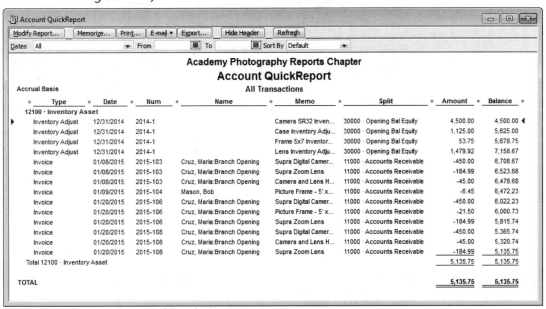

Figure 6-52 All transactions involving the Inventory Asset account

Step 5.   Close the *Account QuickReport* and *Chart of Accounts* window.

Step 6.   From the *Lists* menu select **Item List**.

Step 7.   Select **Camera SR32** from the *Item list*.

Step 8.   Click the *Reports* button and select **Quick Report: Camera SR32**. Alternatively, press **Ctrl+Q** (see Figure 6-53).

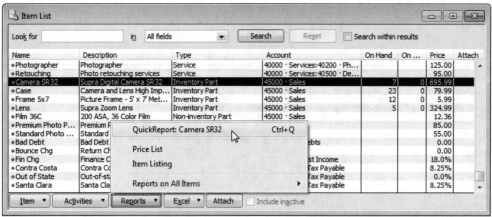

Figure 6-53 QuickReport for Camera SR32 Item

Step 9.   Change the *Dates* range to **All** by typing *A* in the Dates field. QuickBooks displays all
                transactions involving the **Camera SR32** Item (see Figure 6-54).

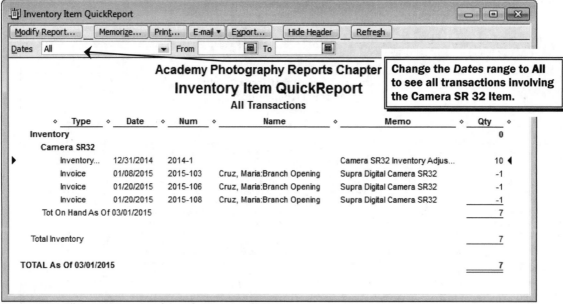

Figure 6-54 All transactions involving the Camera SR32 Item

Step 10.   Close the *Item QuickReport* and *Item List* window.

Step 11.   Click the **Check Register** icon in the *Banking* section of the *Home* page.

Step 12.   Confirm that *Checking* displays in the *Select Account* field of the *Use Register* dialog
                box. Click **OK**.

Step 13.   Scroll up and select **BILLPMT #6003**.

Step 14.   Click the **QuickReport** icon at the top of the register (see Figure 6-55) or press
                Ctrl+Q.

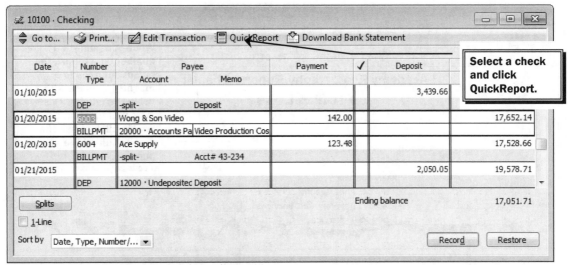

Figure 6-55 Select the Check and click QuickReport icon

Step 15.   QuickBooks displays a report of all transactions in the Checking register using the same name as the selected transaction (see Figure 6-56).

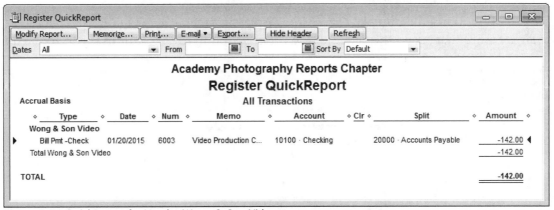

Figure 6-56 QuickReport for Vendor Wong & Son Video

Step 16.   Close the Register QuickReport and Checking register.

> **Did You Know?**
> You can also generate QuickReports from the Customer Center, Vendor Center, or Employee Center by selecting the Customer, Vendor, or Employee and clicking on the **QuickReport** link in the upper right-hand corner of the window.

Using QuickZoom

QuickBooks provides a convenient feature called *QuickZoom*, which allows you to see the details behind numbers on reports. For example, the Profit & Loss report in Figure 6-57 shows $3,145.00 of *Photography Services* income. Double-click on the amount to see the details behind the number.

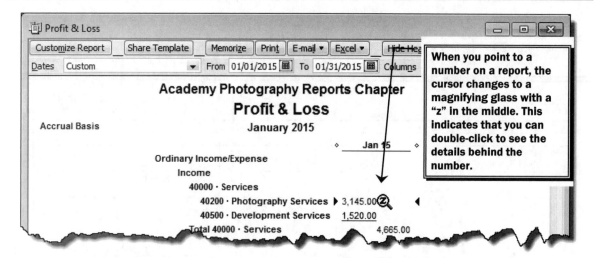

Figure 6-57 QuickZoom allows you to see the details behind a number

As your cursor moves over numbers on the report, it will turn into a magnifying glass with a "z" in the middle. The magnifying icon indicates that you can double-click to see the details behind the number on the report.

After you double-click the number, *QuickZoom* displays a *Transaction Detail By Account* report (see Figure 6-58) that shows the details of each transaction in the account that you zoomed in on.

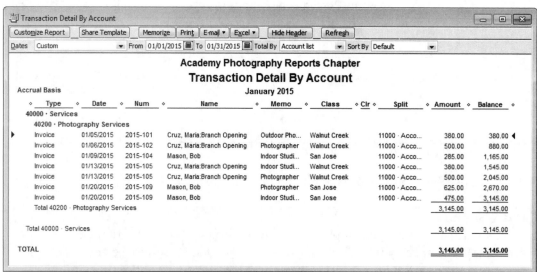

Figure 6-58 Transaction Detail by Account report

The columns in this report show the transaction *Type, Date, Num* (Number), *Name, Memo, Class, Clr* (Cleared), *Split, Amount,* and *Balance.* You can modify the report to add or delete columns as needed. See *Building Custom Reports* on page 184 for details on how to modify reports.

The *Clr* column on these reports shows a checkmark (√) when the transaction has a cleared status. If it is a transaction for a bank account, a checkmark means that the transaction has cleared the bank.

Exporting Reports to Spreadsheets

When you need to modify reports in ways that QuickBooks does not allow (e.g., changing the name of a column heading), you will need to export the report to a spreadsheet program.

> **Note:**
> *QuickBooks Statement Writer* is a utility for creating reports in Excel using live QuickBooks data. It is included in the Accountant editions of QuickBooks Premier and QuickBooks Enterprise Solutions.

Exporting a Report to Microsoft Excel

COMPUTER PRACTICE

Step 1.   From the *Report Center,* select **Sales** and then double click the **Sales by Customer Detail** report in the *Sales by Customer* section to display the report.

Step 2.   Enter *01/01/2015* in the *From* field and enter *01/31/2015* in the *To* field. Press **Tab** twice (see Figure 6-59).

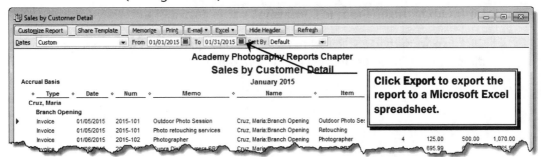

Figure 6-59 Click Export to export the report to a Microsoft Excel spreadsheet

Step 3.   Click **Excel** at the top of the report and choose **Create New Worksheet** from the dropdown menu.

Step 4.   In the *Send Report to Excel* window, make sure *Create new worksheet* and *in new workbook* are selected. This will export your report to a new Excel worksheet (see Figure 6-60).

> **Note:**
> The *Advanced* button of the *Send Report to Excel* window has many useful features for working with your QuickBooks data in Excel, including Auto Outline, which allows you to collapse and expand detail.

Figure 6-60 Send Report to Excel window

Step 5.   Click **Export** in the *Send Report to Excel* window. QuickBooks will export your report directly to an Excel spreadsheet (see Figure 6-61).

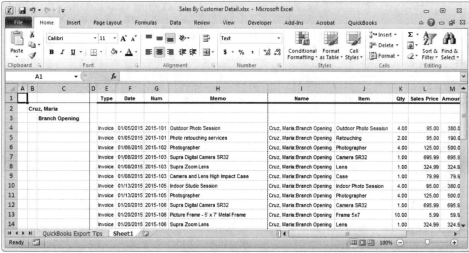

Figure 6-61 The report is now in an Excel spreadsheet.

> **Note:**
> After opening a QuickBooks exported report, Excel will display a QuickBooks Tips tab on the Excel ribbon. Once you save the file, you will able to use the *Update Report* feature to refresh the report with updated information from QuickBooks.

Review Questions

Choose the best answer(s) for each of the following:

1. What are the two major types of reports in QuickBooks?
   a) Register and List.
   b) Monthly and Annual.
   c) Accounting and Business Management.
   d) Balance Sheet and Profit & Loss.

2. Use the **Customize Report** button on any report to:
   a) Add or delete columns or change the accounting basis of the report.
   b) Change the width of columns on the report.
   c) Print the report on blank paper.
   d) Memorize the report for future use.

3. You cannot create a **QuickReport** for:
   a) Customers.
   b) Vendors.
   c) Items.
   d) Incorrectly posted entries.

4. To create a report that lists each of your vendors along with their address and telephone information:
   a) Display the *Vendor Contact List*.
   b) Open the *Search* window and do a search for Vendors and the corresponding Address and Phone Numbers.
   c) Customize the Vendor database.
   d) You must create a *Modified Report* to see this information.

5. In order to analyze the profitability of your company, you should:
   a) Only analyze if the company is profitable.
   b) Create a *Profit & Loss* report.
   c) Review all detailed transaction reports.
   d) Review the financial exceptions report.

Reports-Problem 1

APPLYING YOUR KNOWLEDGE

> Restore the **Reports-12Problem1.QBM** file.

1. Print the reports listed below for Academy Photography.
   a) Customer Phone List.
   b) Check Detail Report for January and February of 2015 with split detail, sorted by Num.
   c) Customer QuickReport for Bob Mason for January and February 2015.
   d) Profit & Loss Report (standard) for January through February 2015.
   e) Profit & Loss Report by Job for January through February 2015.
   f) Trial Balance Report for 01/31/2015.
   g) Balance Sheet Standard Report for January 31, 2015.

2. Create a custom report showing the customers who had paid an amount over $1,000 in January 2015. Modify the report so that it totals by Customer and includes the title and columns displayed in Figure 6-62.

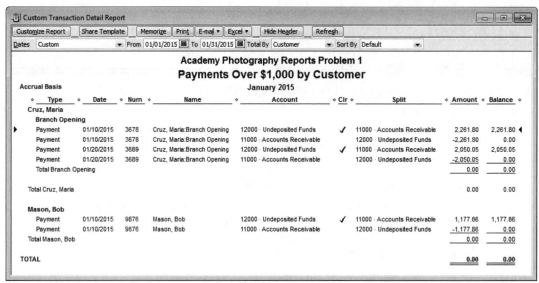

Figure 6-62   Customize your report to look like this.

> **Important:**
> When you complete #2, do not close the report. You will use the modified report in the next step.

3. Print the report you created in Step 2 and then memorize it in the Customers report group. Name the memorized report "Payments Over $1,000 by Customer."

4. Create and print a graph of your Income and Expenses (by Class) for January and February 2015.

Chapter 7 Customizing QuickBooks

Objectives

After completing this chapter, you should be able to:

- Modify QuickBooks *Preferences* (page 206)
- Customize QuickBooks menus and windows (page 208)
- Customize the *Icon Bar* and display settings (page 210)
- Use the *Item List* and other Lists (page 212)
- Use Custom Fields to track extra data on transactions (page 223)
- Create and customize sales forms (page 224)

> **Restore this File:**
> This chapter uses the Customizing-12.QBW. To open this file, restore the Customizing-12.QBM file to your hard disk. See page 8 for instructions on restoring files. If you are using QuickBooks Premier Accountant, we recommend that you toggle to QuickBooks Premier General Business as described on page x.

QuickBooks has many customizable options that allow you to configure the program to meet your own needs and preferences. This chapter introduces you to many of the ways you can make these configurations in QuickBooks using *Preferences*, customizing the *Home* page, menus, and toolbars, and creating templates for forms. This chapter also introduces some new lists, including the *Item List,* the *Terms List,* and the *Template List.*

QuickBooks Preferences

There are two types of *Preferences* in QuickBooks:

1. **User Preferences.** In QuickBooks, User Preferences are specific to the user who is currently logged on to the file. You can identify User Preferences on the *My Preferences* tab in the *Preferences* window. A user can make changes to his or her User Preferences as desired. The changes will not affect other users of the data file. Examples of User Preferences include changing displays setting (e.g., colors), report settings, and spell check settings.

2. **Company Preferences.** Use Company Preferences to make global changes to the features and functionality of an individual company's data file. For example, the *Preference* that turns Sales Tax Tracking on or off is a Company Preference. Only the *Administrator* of the data file can make changes to Company Preferences. Note that each company's *Preferences* are independent of the *Preferences* established for other QuickBooks companies on your computer.

In this section, you will learn about a few of these *Preferences* and how they affect QuickBooks. Clicking the *Help* button in the *Preferences* window will launch QuickBooks Help with specific topics relevant to the *Preference* in the open window.

> **Note:**
> Many of the *Preferences* are discussed in detail in other chapters. For example, the payroll preferences are discussed in the "Payroll Setup" chapter, beginning on page 299.

Setting User Preferences

COMPUTER PRACTICE

To access QuickBooks Preferences, follow these steps:

Step 1.　　　Select the **Edit** menu, and then select **Preferences**.

User Preferences – Desktop View

Use the *Desktop View* User Preferences ("*My Preferences*" tab)to customize the view of the current user.

Step 2.　　　Click the **Desktop View** icon. See Figure 7-1.

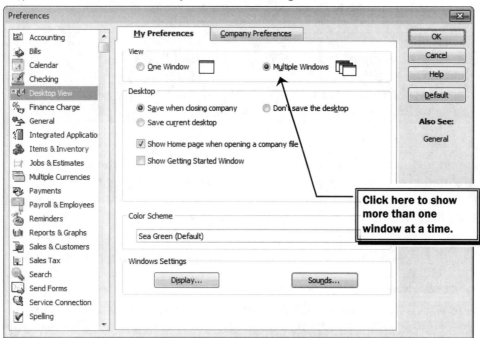

Figure 7-1 User Preferences - Desktop View

The user preferences for *Desktop View* allow you to customize the default windows that show when you open QuickBooks. We recommend selecting *Multiple Windows* as shown on Figure 7-1. When you first create a data file, QuickBooks selects *One Window* as the default Preference. Unless you change the Preference to *Multiple Windows*, you will not be able to display more than one QuickBooks window at a time, and you will not be able to change the size of QuickBooks windows. You will probably find the program much easier to navigate if you select *Multiple Windows*. You can also change the color and graphics of QuickBooks toolbars and windows by selecting a different default from the *Color Scheme* drop down menu.

There is also the *Show Home page when opening a company file* option. Activating this Preference causes the new *Home* page window to be displayed whenever the company file is opened.

> **Tip:**
> If you use QuickBooks in a multi-user environment, it may be best to select the *Don't save the desktop* radio button on the window shown in Figure 7-1. If you save the desktop, each time you open QuickBooks it will re-open all of the windows and reports you were viewing when you last used the program. If you save the desktop, this may negatively impact performance for other users when they open the data file.

Company Preferences – Desktop View

Administrators may use the *Company Preferences* tab in the *Desktop View* Preferences to control which icons display on the *Home* page. These settings will affect every user who uses this company file.

Step 3.   With the *Desktop View Preference* still selected, click the **Company Preferences** tab (see Figure 7-2).

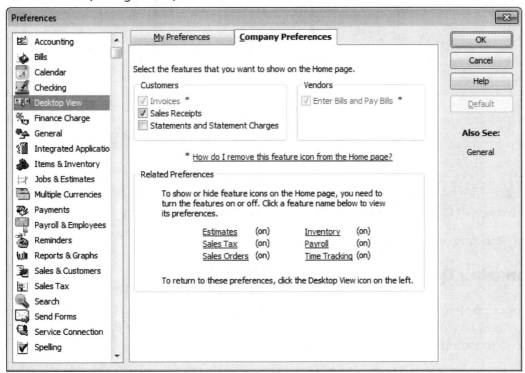

Figure 7-2 The Desktop View—Company Preferences window

Step 4.   Click the **Statements and Statement Charges** checkbox to deselect.

In this window, you can remove some icons from displaying on the *Home* page. Turning off the icon on the *Home* page does not disable the feature, since you can access the command using the appropriate menu. Some features, such as *Estimates, Sales Tax,* and *Sales Orders* listed in the lower portion of the *Desktop View Company Preference* window can only be removed from the *Home* page by disabling the feature using the appropriate *Preferences*. You can access the appropriate *Preference* through the links in the *Desktop View Company Preferences* window.

> **Note:**
> You cannot remove the icons for *Invoices, Enter Bills,* or *Pay Bills* from the *Home* page if certain other features are enabled. For example, the *Invoices* icon must be turned on if your company uses *Estimates* or *Sales Orders*. For a complete list of *Preferences*, see QuickBooks Help.

Step 5.　　Click **OK** to close the *Preferences* window. Click **OK** in the dialog box that appears about closing open windows.

Step 6.　　Click the **Home** button on the *Icon Bar*. Notice that the *Statements* branch of the *Customers* section of the *Home* page no longer displays (see Figure 7-3).

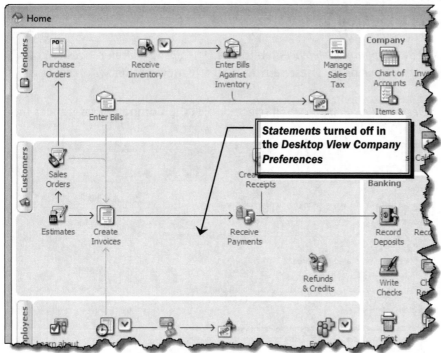

Figure 7-3 Home Page without Statements branch displaying

Customizing QuickBooks Menus and Windows

QuickBooks gives you the ability set up some special customized features. You can create a *Favorites Menu* for your regular activities. You can also customize the *Icon Bar*, which gives you easy access to various commands.

Favorites Menu

The *Favorites* menu is a customizable menu where you can place your common QuickBooks commands.

COMPUTER PRACTICE

Step 1.　　Locate the *Favorites* menu between the *Lists* and *Company* menus on the menu bar. (Those using QuickBooks Premier Accountant will see it between the *Lists* and *Accountant* menus).

　　　　　　If you do not see the *Favorites* menu, you can turn it on by selecting *Favorites Menu* from the *View* menu (see Figure 7-4).

Figure 7-4 Favorites Menu option in the View menu

Step 2. Select the **Customize Favorites** option from the *Favorites* menu (see Figure 7-5).

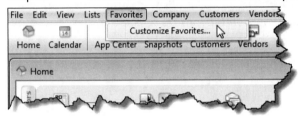

Figure 7-5 Customize Favorites option in the Favorites menu

Step 3. The *Customize Your Menus* window includes all available menu items. You can select a menu item to be easily accessed through the *Favorites* Menu. Click **Sales Rep List** and then click **Add** (see Figure 7-6).

You can use the *Sales Rep List* to identify employees who receive commission as a percentage of sales. This *List* is usually only available through the *Customer Vendor Profile Lists* submenu under the *Lists* menu. By adding it the *Favorites* menu, it can be accessed outside a submenu, more easily.

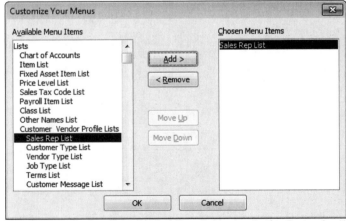

Figure 7-6 Sales Rep List added to Favorites menu in the Customize Your Menus window

Step 4. Click **OK** to close the *Customize Your Menus* window.

Step 5. Select the **Favorites** menu and chose **Sales Rep List** (see Figure 7-7).

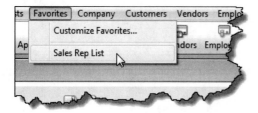

Figure 7-7 Sales Rep List in the Favorites menu

Step 6.   Close the **Sales Rep List**.

QuickBooks Icon Bar

The *Icon Bar* appears at the top of the screen below the menu (see Figure 7-8). The icons on the *Icon Bar* are shortcuts to QuickBooks windows. The *Icon Bar* allows you to create an icon shortcut to almost any window in QuickBooks. The *Icon Bar* can be selected or deselected from the *View* menu and can be customized.

Figure 7-8 Icon Bar

Customizing the Icon Bar

There are two ways to customize the *Icon Bar*: using the *Customize Icon Bar* window or using the *Add* "window-name" *to Icon Bar* option.

Using the Customize Icon Bar Window

Use the *Customize Icon Bar* window to add icons to the *Icon Bar* or to edit or delete existing icons. You can also use this window to add separators between icons and to reposition icons.

COMPUTER PRACTICE

Step 1.   Select **Customize Icon Bar** from the *View* menu. QuickBooks displays the *Customize Icon Bar* window shown in Figure 7-9.

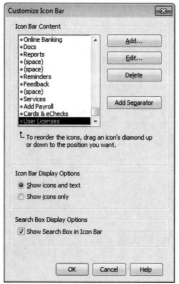

Figure 7-9 Customize Icon Bar window

Step 2.   To add an Icon to the *Icon Bar* click **Add**. QuickBooks opens the window shown in Figure 7-10.

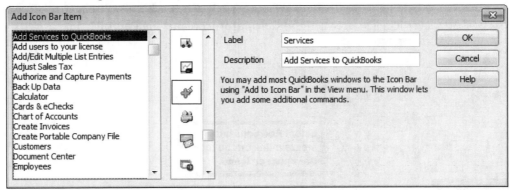

Figure 7-10 Add Icon Bar Item window

Step 3.   Select **Calculator** from the list of icons as shown in Figure 7-11. Notice that QuickBooks automatically selects the preferred icon for calculator and recommends the label name and description.

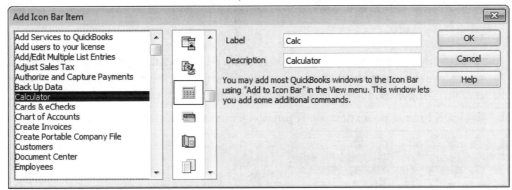

Figure 7-11 Add Icon Bar Item window with Calculator selected

Step 4.   Click **OK** to create the Calculator icon.

Step 5.   The order of the icons on this list dictates the order of the icons on the *Icon Bar*. To move the *Calc* icon, click the diamond next to **Calc** and then drag and drop *Calc* to move it above the **Add Payroll** icon as shown in Figure 7-12.

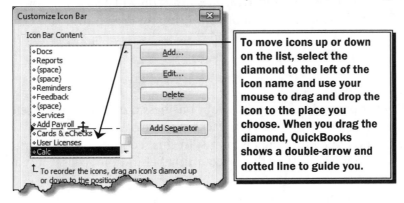

To move icons up or down on the list, select the diamond to the left of the icon name and use your mouse to drag and drop the icon to the place you choose. When you drag the diamond, QuickBooks shows a double-arrow and dotted line to guide you.

Figure 7-12 Use your mouse to move icons up or down in the list.

Step 6.   To remove an icon from the *Icon Bar*, select the icon in the list and click **Delete**. Highlight the **Feedback** item and then click **Delete**.

Step 7.   You may find it helpful to group the icons by type. To add a separator, select the **Calc** icon and then click **Add Separator**. QuickBooks will insert the word "(space)" below the **Calc** icon on the list (see Figure 7-13). On the *Icon Bar* itself, QuickBooks will add a vertical line between the **Calculator** icon and the **Payroll** icon.

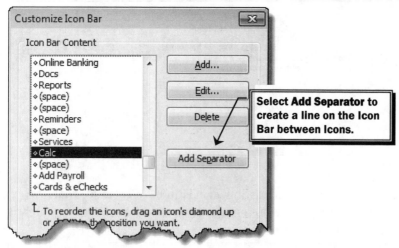

Figure 7-13 Icon List with Separator

Step 8.   To accommodate additional icons, or to reduce the height of your Icon Bar, you can select **Show icons only** in the *Display Options* section shown in Figure 7-13. For now, leave the **Show icons and text** option selected.

Step 9.   Click **OK** to save your changes. Figure 7-14 displays the customized *Icon Bar*.

Figure 7-14 Customized Icon Bar

QuickBooks Items and Other Lists

To help you track more details about your sales, QuickBooks provides several *Lists* that allow you to add more information to each transaction. In this section, you will learn how to create items in the *Item List*, *Terms List*, *Price Level List*, and *Templates List*. You will also learn how *Custom Fields* can be used to add more detail to several of your *Lists* and *Reports* in QuickBooks.

QuickBooks Items

The *Item List* is used to identify the products and services your business purchases and/or sells. *Items* in the *Item List* are also used as part of the sales tax tracking process as a means of generating subtotals and as a method of calculating discounts. In this section, you will learn more about QuickBooks *Items* and how they affect the "accounting behind the scenes" as you create transactions.

The *Item List* shows all *Items* you have already created (see Figure 7-15).

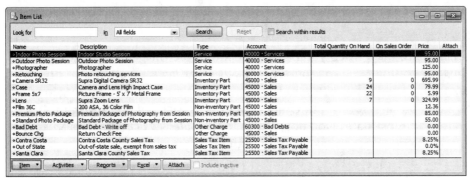

Figure 7-15 The Item list

Item Types

There are several different types of *Items* in QuickBooks (see Figure 7-16). When you create an *Item*, you indicate the *Item Type* along with the name of the *Item* and the *Account* with which the *Item* is associated.

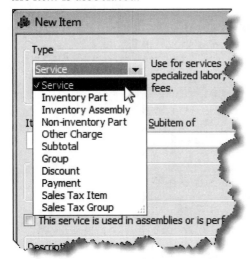

Figure 7-16 The Type menu in the New Item window

- *Service Items*: Used to track services you buy and/or sell.

- *Inventory Part Items*: Used to track your purchases and sales of inventory.

- *Inventory Assembly Items*: Used to track *Items* that contain assemblies of other *Items*. You must have QuickBooks Premier or QuickBooks Enterprise Solutions to use *Inventory Assembly Items*.

- *Non-inventory Part Items*: Used to track products you buy and/or sell but don't keep in inventory.

- *Other Charge Items*: Used to track miscellaneous charges such as shipping and finance charges.

- *Subtotal Items*: Used to calculate and display subtotals on sales forms.

- *Group Items*: Allows you to use one *Item* to "bundle" several *Items* together. *Group Items* are similar to *Inventory Assembly Items*, but Group items do not track quantity on hand (or sold) of the Group. Rather, each *Item* within the Group is tracked separately.

- *Discount Items*: Used to calculate and display discounts on sales forms.

- *Payment Items*: Used to show payments collected on the face of *Invoices* and refunds given on the face of *Credit Memos*.

- *Sales Tax Item*: Used to track sales taxes in each location where you sell taxable goods and services.

- *Sales Tax Group Items*: Used when you pay sales tax to more than one tax agency. The *Sales Tax Group Item* allows you to group several *Sales Tax Items* together into one total. The total tax from each *Sales Tax Item* in the group is the amount of tax charged when you use the group on sales forms, but QuickBooks tracks each *Sales Tax Item* in the group separately. In most states, you don't need to use *Sales Tax Groups*. Use *Sales Tax Group Items* only if you pay sales tax to more than one agency.

Service Items

Academy Photography sells photo sessions by the hour. To track the sales of a *Service Item*, create an *Item* called **Photo Session**, and associate the *Item* with the Services income account.

COMPUTER PRACTICE

Step 1.   Select the **Lists** menu and then select **Item List**.

Step 2.   Select the **Item** button and then select **New**.

Step 3.   Select **Service** from the *Type* drop-down list as shown in Figure 7-16 if it is not already selected, and fill in the detail of the *Item* as shown in Figure 7-17.

Step 4.   Click **OK** to save the Item.

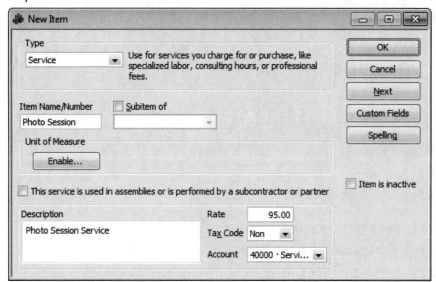

Figure 7-17 Selecting items

If the price for this service fluctuates, you can override this amount when you use it on a sales form. Therefore, when you set up the *Item*, enter the rate you normally charge.

Subcontracted Services

To track your subcontracted services, you can set up a special "two-sided" *Service Item* to track both the income and the expense of the subcontractor. By using a single *Item* to track both the income and expense for the subcontracted service, you can automatically track the profitability of your subcontractors. You might want to have a separate *Item* for each subcontractor.

COMPUTER PRACTICE

Step 1.   With the *Item List* displayed, press **Ctrl+N**. This is another way to set up a new *Item*.

Step 2. Select **Service** from the *Type* drop-down list if it is not already selected and press **Tab**.

Step 3. Enter **Video Photographer** in the *Item Name/Number* field and check the Subitem of box.

Step 4. Select **Photographer** from the *Subitem of* drop-down list.

Step 5. Check the box next to *This service is used in assemblies or is performed by a subcontractor or partner*.
Selecting this box allows you to use the same *Item* on purchase transactions and sales transactions, but have the *Item* affect different accounts depending on the transaction.

Step 6. Enter the *Description on Purchase Transactions, Cost* (purchase price), *Expense Account*, and *Preferred Vendor* for this *Item* as shown in Figure 7-18.

Step 7. Select **Non** in the *Tax Code* field.

Step 8. Enter the *Description on Sales Transactions, Sales Price*, and *Income Account* for this Item as shown in Figure 7-18.

Step 9. Click **Next** to save the *Item* and open another *New Item* window.

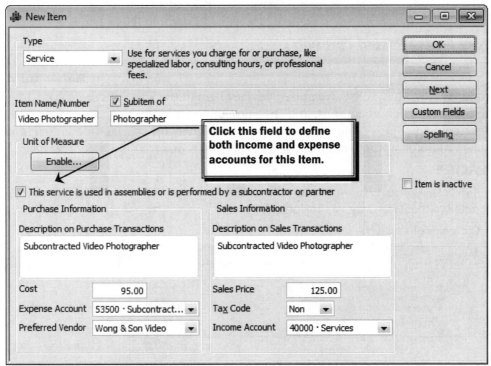

Figure 7-18 Subcontracted Service Item

Non-Inventory Parts

To track products that you buy and/or sell but don't monitor as inventory, set up *Non-Inventory Part Items*. Academy Photography doesn't track custom photo packages in inventory, so they use one generic *Item* called Custom Photo Package.

COMPUTER PRACTICE

Step 1. Select **Non-inventory Part** from the *Type* drop-down list.

Step 2. Enter **Custom Photo Package** in the *Item Name/Number* field.

Step 3. Fill in the detail of the *Item* as shown in Figure 7-19.

Step 4. Click **Next** to save the item.

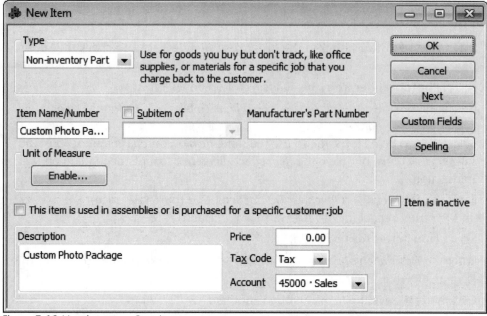

Figure 7-19 Non-inventory Part Item

Non-Inventory Parts - Passed Through

You can also specifically track the income and expenses for each *Non-Inventory Part*. In this case, you should create a "two-sided" *Non-inventory Part Item* to track the purchase costs in a Cost of Goods Sold (or Expense) account, and the sales amounts in an income account. This is particularly useful when you pass the costs on to your customers for special-ordered parts. For example, Academy Photography tracks camcorder orders with one *Non-Inventory Part Item*.

COMPUTER PRACTICE

Step 1.   If necessary, select **Non-inventory Part** from the *Type* drop-down list. Fill in the detail of the *Item* as shown in Figure 7-20.

Step 2.   Click **Next** to save the item.

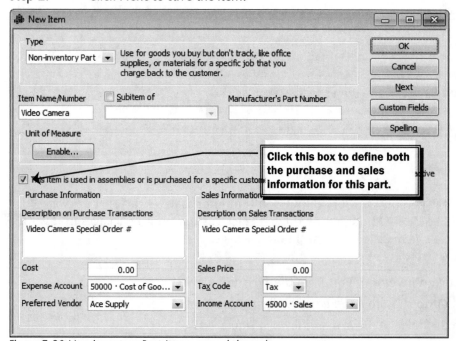

Figure 7-20 Non-inventory Part Item - passed through

Other Charge Items

To track charges like freight, finance charges, or expense reimbursements on your *Invoices*, use *Other Charge Items*.

COMPUTER PRACTICE

Step 1.   Select **Other Charge** from the *Type* drop-down list and fill in the detail of the *Item* as shown in Figure 7-21.

Step 2.   Click **Next** to save the Item.

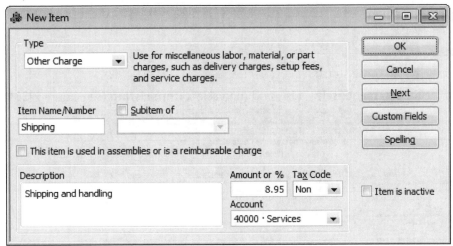

Figure 7-21 Track shipping charges with an Other Charge Item

Sales Tax Items

The *Sales Tax Items* are used to track sales tax.

COMPUTER PRACTICE

Step 1.   Select **Sales Tax Item** from the *Type* drop-down list and fill in the detail of the *Item* as shown in Figure 7-22.

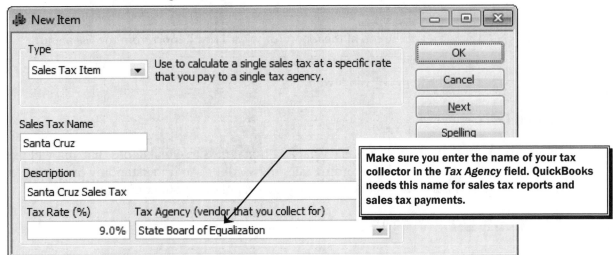

Figure 7-22 Track sales tax with the Sales Tax Item.

Step 2.   Click **OK** to save this *Item* and close the *New Items* window.

You should create a separate *Sales Tax* Item for each tax imposed by each taxing jurisdiction. For example, if you have both state and county sales taxes, then create *Sales Tax Items* for the state taxes and each of the county taxes. If multiple *Sales Tax Items* are to be billed on a particular sales transaction, then create a *Sales Tax Group Item* to join the individual *Sales Tax Items* together for billing purposes. This allows QuickBooks to correctly track sales taxes by taxing jurisdiction.

> Note:
> If you need to import a large number of *Items* (or other list entries) you can paste in a spreadsheet using the *Add/Edit Multiple List Entries* option, located in the *Lists* menu.

Printing the Item List

COMPUTER PRACTICE

To print the Item List, follow these steps:

Step 1.   Select the *Reports* menu, select **List**, and then select **Item Listing** (see Figure 7-23).

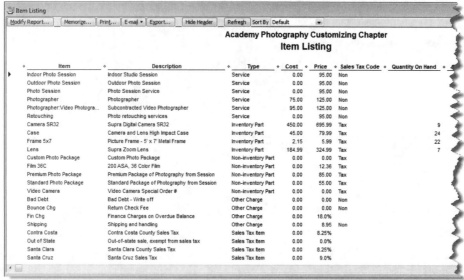

Figure 7-23 The Item Listing report

Step 2.   Click **Print** at the top of the report (or select **Print Report** from the *File* menu).

Step 3.   Close the **Item Listing Report**.

Step 4.   Close the **Item List** window.

Other Lists

In addition to the *Item List*, there are several additional *Lists* in QuickBooks that you will use when setting up customers and recording sales transactions. An understanding of how to set up and use these *Lists* is essential to operating QuickBooks for your company.

The Terms List

The *Terms List* is where you define the payment terms for *Invoices* and *Bills*. QuickBooks uses terms to calculate when an *Invoice* or *Bill* is due. If the terms specified on the transaction include a discount for early payment, QuickBooks also calculates the date on which the discount expires.

QuickBooks allows you to define two types of terms:

- *Standard Terms* calculate based on how many days from the *Invoice* or *Bill* date the payment is due or a discount is earned.
- *Date-Driven Terms* calculate based on the day of the month that an *Invoice* or *Bill* is due or a discount is earned.

You can override the default terms on each sale as necessary. When you create reports for *Accounts Receivable* or *Accounts Payable*, QuickBooks takes into account the terms on each *Invoice* or *Bill*.

COMPUTER PRACTICE

Step 1.   Select the *Lists* menu, select **Customers & Vendor Profile Lists**, and then select **Terms List** (see Figure 7-24).

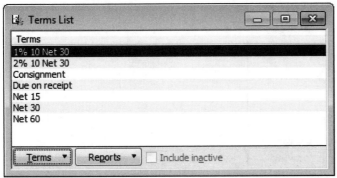

Figure 7-24 The Terms List window

Step 2.   The practice template file already includes several terms (see Figure 7-24). To set up additional terms, select the **Terms** menu from the *Terms List* window, and then select **New**, or press **Ctrl+N**.

Step 3.   To set up a standard term, complete the *New Terms* window as shown in Figure 7-25, and click **Next**.

The window in Figure 7-25 shows how the 2% 7 Net 30 terms is defined. It is a *Standard Terms Item* indicating that full payment is due in 30 days. If the customers pay within 7 days of the *Invoice* date, however, they are eligible for a 2% discount.

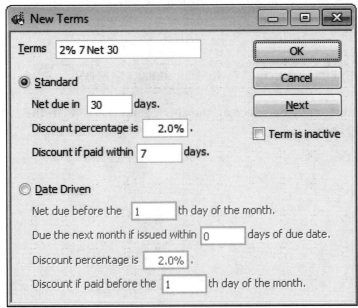

Figure 7-25 The New Terms window with standard terms

Step 4.   To set up a date-driven term, select the **Date Driven** radio button.

Step 5.   Fill in the fields as shown in Figure 7-26. Then click **OK**.

The terms in Figure 7-26 are an example of *Date Driven Terms,* where payment is due on the 10th of the month (e.g. February 10th). If the *Invoice* is dated less than 10 days before the due date, the *Invoice* (or *Bill*) is due on the 10th of the following month.

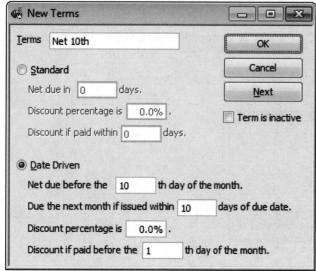

Figure 7-26 The New Terms window with date-driven terms

Step 6.   Close the **Term List** window.

Price Levels

> **Note:**
> *Per Item Price Levels* are only available in QuickBooks Premier and above.

Price Levels allow you to define custom pricing for different customers. Use *Price Levels* on *Invoices* or *Sales Receipts* to adjust the sales amount of particular items. There are several ways to use *Price Levels* on sales forms:

> **DO NOT PERFORM THESE STEPS NOW. THEY ARE FOR REFERENCE ONLY.**

1.   You can adjust each item individually by selecting the applicable *Price Level* in the *Rate* column drop-down list (see Figure 7-27).

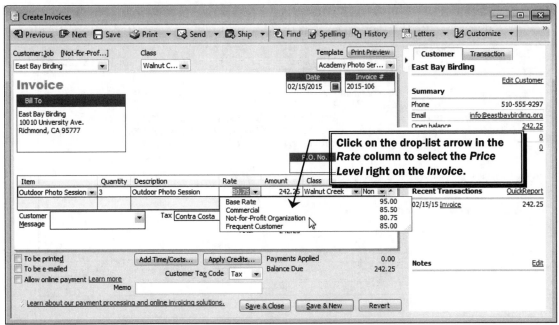

Figure 7-27 Selecting a Price Level on an Invoice

2. You can assign a *Price Level* to a Customer's record so that when you use the customer's name in a sales form, QuickBooks will change the default sales price for each *Sales Item* on the form (see Figure 7-28).

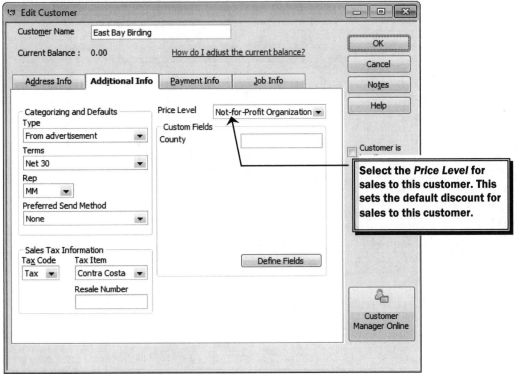

Figure 7-28 Setting a Price Level on a Customer's Record

You can create new *Price Levels* by opening the *Price Levels List* and selecting **New** from the *Price Levels Menu* or pressing **Ctrl+N** with the *Price Levels List* active. Depending on the type of *Price Level* you select, QuickBooks will:

- Increase or decrease the default sales price by a fixed percentage (see Figure 7-29). Fixed percentage *Price Levels* allow you to increase or decrease prices of *Items* for a

Customer or *Job* by a fixed percentage. For customers to whom you always give a discount, use this option so that the discount will be generated automatically.

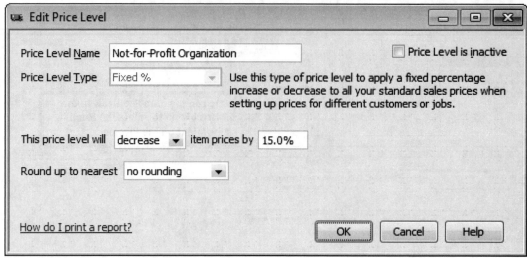

Figure 7-29 Defining a new price level

- Adjust the sales price to an amount you define when setting up the *Price Level*. *Per Item Price Levels* let you set different prices for *Items* that are associated with different *Customers* or *Jobs*.

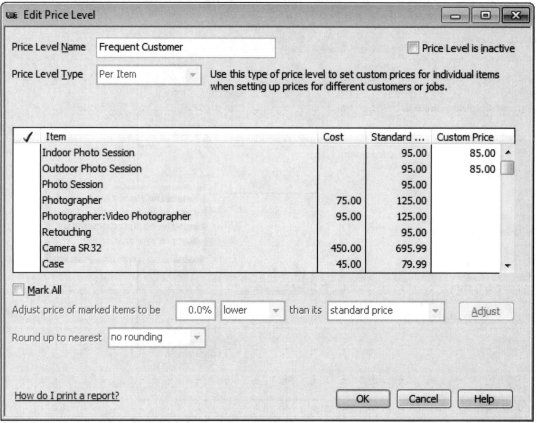

Figure 7-30 New Price Level window - Per Item Price Level Type

Custom Fields

When you set up a new *Customer* record, you can define *Custom Fields* for tracking additional information specific to your *Customers, Vendors,* and *Employees.*

Academy Photography tracks each *Customer* and *Vendor* by county in order to create reports of total purchases and sales in a city or county. This information allows them to determine the best area to expand business operations.

You can access the *Define Fields* button on the *Additional Info* tab of a *Customer* or *Vendor* record (see Figure 7-31).

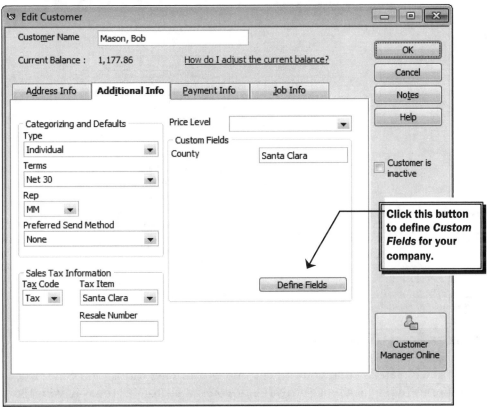

Figure 7-31 Click Define Fields in the Additional Info Tab.

In the window shown in Figure 7-32, you can define up to fifteen *Custom Fields* in the QuickBooks data file, and any one field, i.e., *Customer, Vendor,* or *Employee,* can have up to seven *Custom Fields.*

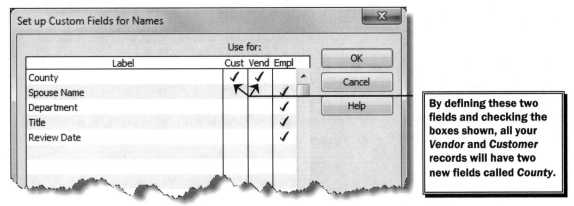

Figure 7-32 The Define Fields window

Adding Custom Field Data to Customer Records

After you have defined a *Custom Field* and checked the box in the *Customer:Job* column, the field appears on the *Customer* record (see Figure 7-33). Fill in the data just as you did for the other fields.

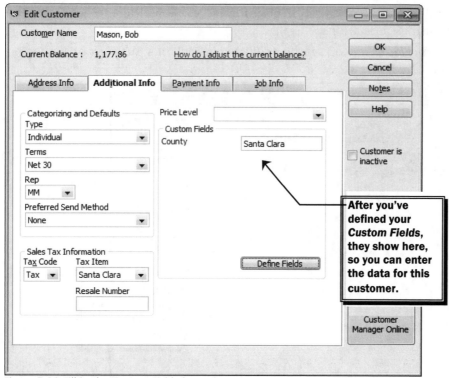

Figure 7-33 Fill in the Custom Fields for each customer.

Modifying Sales Form Templates

QuickBooks provides templates so that you can customize your sales forms. You can select from the standard forms that QuickBooks provides, or you can customize the way your forms appear on both the screen and the printed page. The first step in modifying your forms is to create a template for the form you want. The templates for all forms are in the *Templates List*.

> **Note:**
> In addition to modifying the templates described in this section, you can also download templates with particular designs for a fee from Intuit. To learn more about these downloadable templates, click the *Customize* button on a form.

COMPUTER PRACTICE

Step 1.   Select the *Lists* menu, and then select **Templates** (see Figure 7-34).

This list shows the standard templates that come with QuickBooks, as well as any form templates the user may have created.

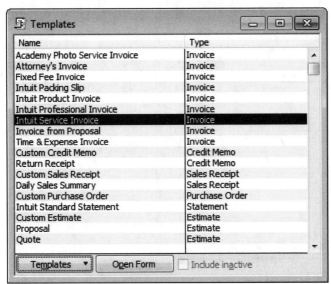

Figure 7-34 The Templates list

Step 2.   Select **Intuit Service Invoice**. Then select the **Templates** menu button and select **Duplicate**. The *Intuit Service Invoice* is the template you are using as the basis for your custom template.

Step 3.   Select **Invoice** on the *Select Template Type* window and click **OK** (see Figure 7-35).

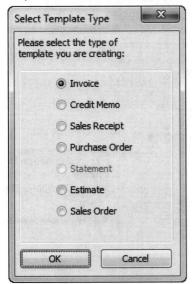

Figure 7-35 Select Template Type window

Step 4.   **Copy of: Intuit Service Invoice** should already be selected. Select the **Templates** menu and select **Edit Template**.

Step 5.   Click the **Manage Template** button in the *Basic Customization* window (see Figure 7-36).

Step 6.   In the **Manage Templates** window, enter *My Invoice Template* in the *Template Name* field (see Figure 7-37).

You must enter a unique template name. You must give your template a descriptive name so that you will easily recognize it when selecting it from a form list.

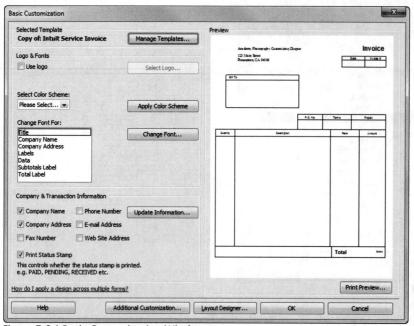

Figure 7-36 Basic Customization Window

> Note:
> You can download templates from the Intuit website – browse through the
> selection of pre-designed templates by clicking the *Download Templates* button
> on the *Manage Templates* window.

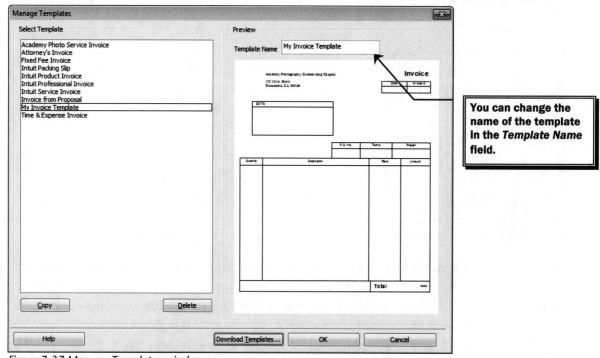

Figure 7-37 Manage Templates window

Step 7.   Click **OK** to accept the name change and close the *Manage Templates* window.

Step 8.   Click the **Additional Customization** button. The *Basic Customization* window
             changes to the *Additional Customization* window.

Step 9.   Review the fields in the *Header* tab. Do not edit any of the fields on this window.

You would click the boxes in the *Screen* and *Print* columns to indicate which fields will show on the screen and which fields will be printed. You could also modify the titles for each field by changing the text in the *Title* fields.

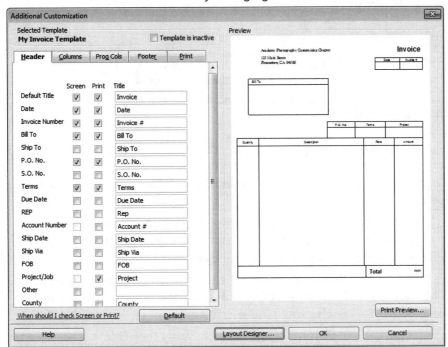

Figure 7-38 Additional Customization window showing the Header tab

Step 10.   Click the **Columns** tab to modify how the columns display on the *Invoice*. Change the order of the columns by entering the numbers in the *Order* column as shown in Figure 7-39. If you see the *Layout Designer* warning box, click **OK**.

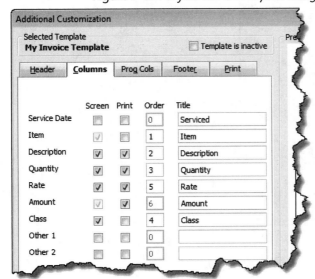

Figure 7-39 Additional Customization window showing the Columns tab

Step 11.   Click the **OK** button to return to the *Basic Customization* window.

Step 12.   Next, add a logo to the template by checking the **Use logo** checkbox (see Figure 7-40).

Adding a business logo to an *Invoice* helps customers familiarize themselves with your company. It can also help them identify your *Invoice*.

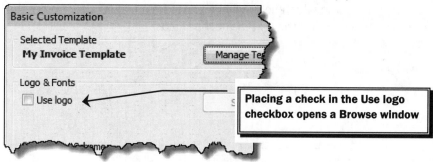

Figure 7-40 *The Use logo option in the Basic Customization window*

Step 13.   In the *Select Image* dialog box, navigate to your student files. Select **logo.gif** and click **Open**.

Step 14.   A dialog box warns that the logo graphic file will be copied to a subfolder of the location of your working file. Click **OK** to accept. You should see the logo in the upper left side of the preview pane of the *Managing Templates* window.

Step 15.   Click the **Select Color Scheme** drop down menu. You can choose six preset colors. Choose **Maroon** and then click the **Apply Color Scheme** button. The text and border lines on the *Invoice* change to the selected color.

Step 16.   Next, change the color of the *Invoice* title to black. Verify that **Title** is selected in the *Change Font For:* box and click the **Change Font** button.

Step 17.   The *Example* window opens (Figure 7-41). You can use this window to change font, size, style, and color of the title of the invoice. In the **Color** field, choose **Black**. When finished, click **OK**.

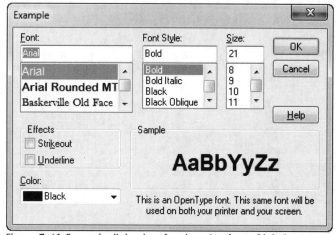

Figure 7-41 *Example dialog box for changing font of labels on a template*

Step 18.   Click **OK** to close the *Basic Customization* window.

Step 19.   Close the **Templates** window.

Step 20.   From the *Home Page*, click the **Create Invoices** icon.

Step 21.   To use the new template, choose **My Invoice Template** from the *Template* drop down list.

Step 22.   To view how the *Invoice* will print, click the down arrow next to **Print** button at the top of the *Create Invoices* window and select **Preview**.

Step 23.   Click **Close** to close the *Print Preview* window.

Step 24.   Close the **Create Invoices** window.

> **Note:**
> You can make further changes to the position of elements in the form by opening the *Layout Designer*. Click the **Layout Designer** button on the bottom of the *Basic Customization* window. From the *Layout Designer*, you can change the position of design elements, such as the textboxes and the logo.

Review Questions

Select the best answer(s) for each of the following:

1. You can create *Custom Fields* for:
    a)   *Customers.*
    b)   *Templates.*
    c)   *Vendors.*
    d)   Both a and c.

2. The two types of *Preferences* are:
    a)   *User* and *Company Preferences.*
    b)   *User* and *Accountant Preferences.*
    c)   *Favorite* and *General Preferences.*
    d)   Income *and Expense Preferences.*

3. If you don't see the *Favorites* menu in your menu bar, you can turn it on in the:
    a)   *Customize Templates* window.
    b)   *Customize Icon Bar* window.
    c)   *View* menu.
    d)   *Windows* menu.

4. Which of the following is not an available Template type in QuickBooks?
    a)   *Credit Memo.*
    b)   *Statement.*
    c)   *Check.*
    d)   *Sales Receipt.*

5. If you pay sales tax to more than one agency, you should use which of the following *Item* types?
    a)   *Sales Tax Group.*
    b)   *Group.*
    c)   *Inventory Assembly.*
    d)   *Subtotal.*

Customizing - Problem 1

APPLYING YOUR KNOWLEDGE

> Restore the **Customizing-12Problem1.QBM** file.

1. Set up the following *Terms*:

   a) 3% 7 Net 30
   b) 3% 10th Net 20th (Due next month if issued within 10 days of the due date)
   c) Net 45
   d) 3% 7th Net 30th (Due next month if issued within 10 days of the due date)

2. Create a **Terms Listing** report (Select the **Reports** menu, **Lists**, and then **Terms Listing**). Add the **Discount on Day of Month** and **Min Days to Pay** columns. Expand the columns so you can see the entire column headers. Print the report.

3. Add a *Custom Field* to your *Customers* called **Web Site**. Add the web sites to the following customer records:

Customer:Job Name	Web Site
Anderson Wedding Planners: Kumar, Sati and Naveen	*www.andweddingbliss.net*
Anderson Wedding Planners: Wilson, Sarah and Michael	*www.andweddingbliss.net*
Anderson Wedding Planners	*www.andweddingbliss.net*
Pelligrini, George	*www.pelligrinibuild.net*
Pelligrini, George:2354 Wilkes Rd	*www.pelligrinibuild.net*
Pelligrini, George: 4266 Lake Drive	*www.pelligrinibuild.net*

Table 7-1 Web site data for custom fields

4. Create a **Customer Contact List**, modified to display the *Customer Name* and *Web Site* only.

5. Create a **Sales Tax Item** for Santa Cruz, payable to the State Board of Equalization. The sales tax rate is 8.25%.

6. Create a duplicate **Invoice** of the *Intuit Service Invoice Template*. Then, make the following changes:

   a) Change the name of the template to *Academy Photo Invoice*.
   b) Add the **Web Site** custom field to the screen and printed *Invoice* using the *Additional Customization Header* tab.
   c) When prompted, click **Default Layout**.

7. Create a new *Non-inventory Part* called **Custom Package**. Set up the new *Item* using the following information:

Field Name	Data
Item Name/Number	*Custom Package*
Description	*Customized Photography Package from Session*
Price	*0 (leave 0 because it's a custom package)*
Tax Code	*Tax*
Account	*Sales*

Table 7-2 Item setup data

8. Create an **Invoice** for Pelligrini, George, for the 1254 Wilkes Rd job, using the *Academy Photo Invoice* template. Enter the following information on the header of the *Invoice*:

Field Name	Data
Class	*San Jose*
Date	*02/28/2015*
Invoice #	*2015-106*
Terms	*3% 7 Net 30*
Tax	*Santa Cruz*

Table 7-3 Use this data for the Invoice header.

9. Enter the following information into the body of the **Invoice**:

Item	Qty	Description	Rate	Amount	Tax
Outdoor Photo Session	*2*	*Outdoor Photo Session*	*95.00*	*190.00*	*Non*
Custom Package	*2*	*Customized Photography Package from Session*	*750.00*	*1500.00*	*Tax*

Table 7-4 Item descriptions

10. Accept the default for all other fields on the *Invoice*. Click **OK** if you get a pop-up window regarding custom price levels. Save and print the **Invoice**.

11. Save the new **Terms** and **Tax Items** when prompted.

Chapter 8
Inventory

Objectives

After completing this chapter, you should be able to:

- Activate the Inventory function (page 236)
- Set up Inventory Items in the Item List (page 237)
- Use QuickBooks to calculate the average cost of Inventory (page 242)
- Record sales of Inventory using sales forms (page 242)
- Use *Purchase Orders* to order Inventory (page 246)
- Receive Inventory against *Purchase Orders* (page 247)
- Enter *Bills* for received Inventory (page 253)
- Adjust your Inventory (page 257)
- Set up Group Items to bundle products and/or services (page 259)
- Create reports about Inventory (page 261)

> **Restore this File**
>
> This chapter uses Inventory-12.QBW. To open this file, restore the Inventory-12.QBM file to your hard disk. See page 8 for instructions on restoring files. If you are using QuickBooks Premier Accountant, we recommend that you toggle to QuickBooks Premier General Business as described on page x.

In this chapter, you will learn how to set up and manage your inventory in QuickBooks. QuickBooks has a number of tools for tracking goods and materials, including the *Inventory Center*.

QuickBooks Tools for Tracking Inventory

The *Vendors* section, located on the *Home* page, shows a graphical representation of the steps involved in purchasing and receiving Inventory. Figure 8-1 shows the purchasing process, beginning with creating a *Purchase Order* and ending with paying *Bills*.

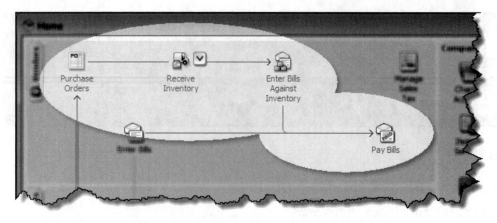

Figure 8-1 Vendors section of the Home page

Table 8-1 shows an overview of the **accounting behind the scenes** for different business transactions that involve Inventory. Familiarize yourself with this table, and refer to it when you encounter business transactions involving Inventory.

Business Transaction	QuickBooks Transaction	Accounting Entry	Comments
Purchasing Inventory with *Purchase Orders*	Purchase Orders	Non-posting entry used to record *Purchase Orders*.	You do not have to use *Purchase Orders*. If you do, QuickBooks tracks the status of your *Purchase Orders* and matches them with the *Bill* from your Vendor.
Receiving Inventory (Without Bill from Vendor)	Receive Inventory **Select Receive Inventory without Bill**	Increase (debit) **Inventory**, increase (credit) **Accounts Payable**. Increase Inventory quantities for each item received.	Use this transaction when you receive Inventory items that are not accompanied by a bill. This transaction enters an *Item Receipt* in the Accounts Payable account. Although it increases A/P, no bill shows in the *Pay Bills* window.
Receiving Inventory (With Bill from Vendor)	Receive Inventory **Select Receive Inventory with Bill**	Increase (debit) **Inventory**, increase (credit) **Accounts Payable**. Increase inventory quantities for each item received.	Use this transaction when you receive inventory accompanied by a bill from the Vendor.
Entering a Bill for Previously Received Inventory Items	Enter Bills Against Inventory	No change in debits and credits. This transaction only changes an *Item Receipt* transaction into a *Bill*.	When an *Item Receipt* is turned into a *Bill*, QuickBooks shows the *Bill* in the *Pay Bills* window.

Table 8-1 Summary of Inventory transactions

Tracking Inventory with QuickBooks

It is critical to think through your company's information needs before tackling Inventory. New users sometimes try to use Inventory parts to track products they don't really need to track in detail. You must separately enter every purchase and sale for each Inventory part. That might not seem like too much work at first, but if you have hundreds of small products with even a moderate turnover, you might overwhelm your bookkeeping system with detailed transactions.

When you use *Inventory Part Items* to track inventory, QuickBooks handles all the accounting for you automatically, depending upon how you set up *Inventory Part Items* in the *Item List*. Inventory is defined as goods that are purchased from a Vendor that will be sold at a future date. For example, a retailer has Inventory until they sell the merchandise to customers. When the Inventory is sold, it is removed from the *Inventory Asset* account and expensed through Cost of Goods Sold. This enables the sale to be properly matched to the expense in the right accounting period.

QuickBooks keeps a perpetual inventory, meaning that every purchase and every sale of Inventory immediately updates all your account balances and reports.

When QuickBooks Pro or Premier calculates the cost of Inventory, it uses the *average cost* method, explained on page 242. QuickBooks Pro and Premier do not support the first-in, first-out (FIFO) or last-in, first-out (LIFO) methods. New with the 2012 release, QuickBooks Enterprise Solutions does support FIFO as well as many other advanced Inventory features such as lot tracking and enhanced receiving. This chapter focuses on feature available with Pro and Premier.

> **Key Term:** *Perpetual inventory* in QuickBooks keeps a continuous record of increases, decreases, and balance on hand of Inventory items.
> **Key Term:** *Average Cost* method divides the cost of Inventory by the number of units in stock. It is most appropriate when prices paid for Inventory do not vary significantly over time, and when Inventory turnover is high (i.e., products sell through quickly). QuickBooks calculates the cost of Inventory using this method.

In order to keep your inventory system working smoothly, it is critical that you use *Inventory Parts* Items on all transactions involving Inventory. This means you must use the *Items* tab on every purchase transaction that involves *Inventory Part* type Items. Figure 8-2 illustrates entering a *Bill* using *Inventory Part* Items.

DO NOT ENTER THIS BILL NOW. IT IS FOR REFERENCE ONLY.

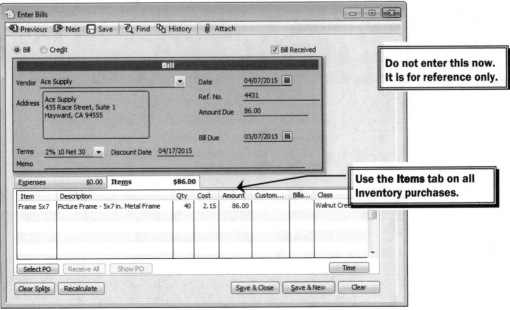

Figure 8-2 The Items tab is used for inventory transactions

Activating the Inventory Function

The first step in using QuickBooks for Inventory is to activate *Inventory* in your *Company Preferences*.

COMPUTER PRACTICE

Step 1.   Select **Preferences** from the *Edit* menu.

Step 2.   Select the **Items & Inventory** *Preference* and then select the **Company Preferences** tab.

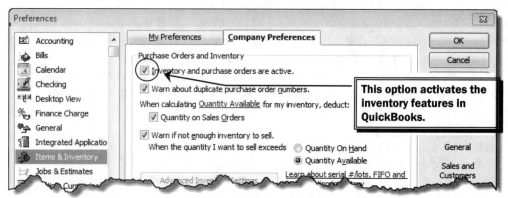

Figure 8-3 Company Preferences for Items & Inventory

Step 3.   Verify that **Inventory and purchase orders are active** is checked (see Figure 8-3).

> **Note:**
> When Inventory is activated, *Purchase Orders* are also activated. However, you are not required to use *Purchase Orders* when tracking Inventory.

Step 4.   Click the **OK** in the *Preferences* window.

After you activate the Inventory function, the Item List shows a new Item type called *Inventory Part* (see Figure 8-4). Only the *Inventory Part* Items are displayed in the *Inventory Center* (see Figure 8-5).

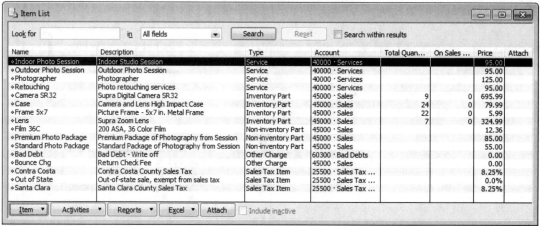

Figure 8-4 Item List window

The first time you create an *Inventory Part* Item in the Item List, QuickBooks automatically creates two accounts in your *Chart of Accounts*: An *Other Current Asset* account called Inventory Asset and a *Cost of Goods Sold* account called Cost of Goods Sold. QuickBooks uses these two important accounts to track Inventory (see Table 8-2). The *Inventory Asset* account holds the value of your Inventory until you sell it. The Cost of Goods Sold account records the cost of the Inventory *when* you sell it.

Accounts for Tracking Inventory	
Inventory Asset	A special *Other Current Asset* account that tracks the cost of each Inventory item purchased. This account increases (by the actual purchase cost) when Inventory is purchased, and decreases (by the weighted average cost) when Inventory items are sold.
Cost of Goods Sold	Cost of Goods Sold is subtracted from total Income on the *Profit & Loss Report* to show *Gross Profit*. QuickBooks automatically increases Cost of Goods Sold each time you sell an Inventory item.

Table 8-2 Two accounts that track inventory

Setting up Inventory Parts Items

To set up an inventory part in the *Item List*, follow these steps:

COMPUTER PRACTICE

Step 1.	In the *Company* section of the *Home* page, select **Inventory Activities** and choose **Inventory Center** from the menu (see Figure 8-5). Alternatively, select the **Vendors** menu and choose **Inventory Activities**, then select **Inventory Center**.

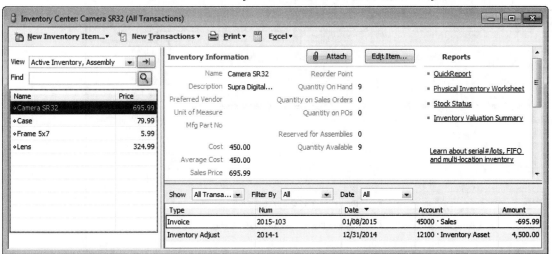

Figure 8-5 Inventory Center

Step 2.	Select the **New Inventory Item** button at the top of the *Inventory Center* and then select **New Inventory Item**. Alternatively, press **Ctrl+N**.

Step 3.	A *New Item* window opens with *Inventory Part* selected from the *Type* drop-down list. Press **Tab**.

Step 4.	Enter *Frame 8x10* in the *Item Name/Number* field and press **Tab**.

	You may optionally assign each item in your Inventory a part number, and then use the part numbers in the *Item Name/Number* field.

Step 5.	Skip the *Subitem of* field by pressing **Tab**.

	This field allows you to create subitems of items. If you use subitems, the *Sales by Item* reports and graphs will show totals for all sales and costs of the subitems.

> **Key Term:** *Subitems* help to organize the *Item List*. Use subitems to group and subtotal information about similar products or services in sales reports and graphs.

Step 6.   Skip the *Manufacturer's Part Number* field by pressing **Tab** again.

This field allows you to enter the part number that the Vendor uses or that is listed by the manufacturer. This enables you to reference the same number on *Purchase Orders* and *Bills* to eliminate confusion.

Step 7.   If necessary, press **Tab** to skip the *Enable* button under *Unit of Measure*.

Many businesses purchase items using one unit of measure and sell the same item using a different unit of measure. For example, a retail store may purchase items by the case, but sell the items individually (or by *each*). QuickBooks Premier and Enterprise includes the *Unit of Measure* feature to help in these situations.

Step 8.   Enter **Picture Frame - 8x10 in. Metal Frame** in the *Description on Purchase Transactions* field and press **Tab**.

The description you enter here appears as the default description when you use this item on *Purchase Orders* and *Bills*.

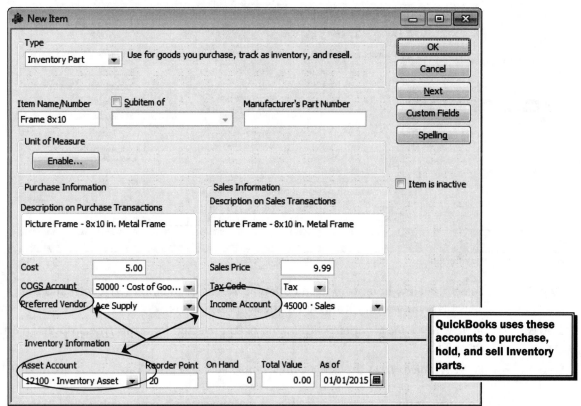

Figure 8-6 The completed New Item window

> **Note:**
> Notice that there are three account fields on the New Item window (*COGS*, *Asset*, and *Income*). In each of these fields, enter the accounts that QuickBooks should use when you purchase, hold, and sell this item. You are specifying how QuickBooks should account for the item when it is used in an Inventory transaction. Each field is covered separately in this chapter.

Step 9.   Enter *5.00* in the *Cost* field and press **Tab**.

Use this field to track the amount you pay to your Vendor (supplier) for the item. QuickBooks uses this amount as the default when you enter this item on *Purchase Orders* and *Bills*. If the cost changes, you can override the amount on the *Purchase Order* or *Bill*, or you can come back and edit the amount here.

Step 10.   In the *COGS Account* field, *Cost of Goods Sold* is already selected. Press **Tab**.

QuickBooks uses the *Cost of Goods Sold* account to record the average cost of this item when you sell it. For more information on average cost, see page 242.

Step 11.   Select **Ace Supply** from the *Preferred Vendor* drop-down list and press **Tab**.

The *Preferred Vendor* field is used to associate the item with the Vendor from whom you normally purchase this part. It is an optional field that you can leave blank without compromising the integrity of the system.

Step 12.   Press **Tab** to leave the *Description on Sales Transactions* field unchanged. The text in this field defaults to whatever you entered in the *Description on Purchase Transactions* field.

QuickBooks allows you to have two descriptions for this item: one for purchase forms and one for sales forms. If you'd like, you can use your Vendor's description when purchasing the item and a more customer-oriented description on your sales forms.

Step 13.   Enter *9.99* in the *Sales Price* field. Press **Tab**. The *Sales Price* is how much you normally charge your *Customers* for the item. You can enter a default here and later override it on sales forms if you need to.

In order for the *Sales Price* field to automatically calculate a price based on the cost of the item, you could modify the *Default Markup Percentage* field in the *Company Preferences* tab for the *Time & Expenses Preference* (See Figure 8-7).

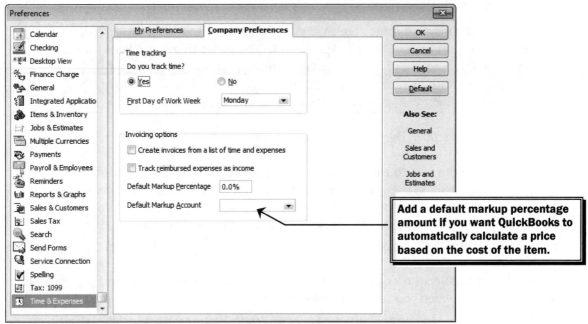

Figure 8-7 Modifying the default markup percentage in the Preferences window

Step 14.   The *Tax Code* is already selected. Press **Tab**.

Tax Codes determine the default taxable status of the item. Since the *Tax Code* called *Tax* is taxable, QuickBooks calculates sales tax on this item when it appears on sales forms. You can override the default *Tax Code* on each sales form. For more information on *Sales Tax Codes* see page 85.

Step 15.   Select **Sales** from the Income Account drop-down list. Press **Tab**.

This is the income account to which you want to post sales of this Item.

Step 16.   In the *Asset Account* field, **Inventory Asset** is already selected. Press **Tab**.

The *Inventory Asset* account is the account that tracks the cost of your inventoried products between the time you purchase them and the time you sell them.

> **The accounting behind the scenes:**
> When you purchase Inventory, QuickBooks increases (debits) the *Inventory Asset* account by the amount of the purchase price. When you sell Inventory, QuickBooks decreases (credits) the *Inventory Asset* account and increases (debits) the *Cost of Goods Sold* account for the average cost of that item at the time it is sold. For details on how QuickBooks calculates average cost, see page 242.

Step 17.   Enter *20* in the *Reorder Point* field and press **Tab** (see Figure 8-8).

The QuickBooks Reminders List will remind you when it's time to reorder Inventory items based on the *Reorder Point*.

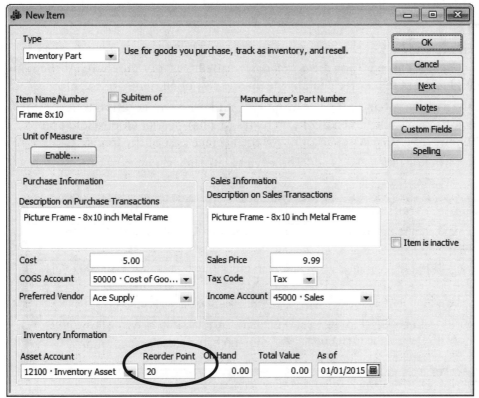

Figure 8-8 When Inventory drops below the reorder point, QuickBooks reminds you to reorder

Step 18.   Leave the *On Hand, Total Value,* and *As of* fields unchanged.

Note:
Do not enter the *On Hand, Total Value,* and *As of* fields. These fields are intended for use during the initial setup of the data file.

The accounting behind the scenes:
If you enter a quantity and value in this window, QuickBooks increases (debits) *Inventory* for the total value, and increases (credits) *Opening Bal Equity*.

However, even if you are setting up the data file it is better to leave the *On Hand* and *Total Value* fields set to zero when you set up the item. Then, as you will see later, use a single inventory adjustment transaction to set up the quantity and value on hand for *all* of the inventory items.

Step 19.   Click **OK** to save the new Item.

Tip:
Before setting up Inventory, think about what products you will track as *Inventory Parts*. It may not be necessary to separately track *every* product you sell as an *Inventory Part*. If you do not need detailed reports and Inventory status information about certain products you sell, consider using *Non-Inventory Part* Items to track those products. In general, use *Inventory Part* Items only when you really need to track the stock status of a product.

Calculating Average Cost of Inventory

When you use an Inventory item on a purchase form (e.g., a *Bill*), QuickBooks increases (debits) the *Inventory Asset* account for the *actual* cost of the Inventory purchase. At the same time, QuickBooks Pro and Premier recalculate the *average cost* of all items in Inventory.

When you use an Inventory item on a sales form (e.g., an *Invoice*), in addition to recording income and accounts receivable, QuickBooks increases (debits) Cost of Goods Sold and decreases (credits) the Inventory Asset account for the average cost of the items.

Table 8-3 shows how QuickBooks Pro and Premier calculate the average cost of Inventory items.

Situation/Transaction	Calculation
You have ten 8x10 picture frames in stock. Each originally costs $5.00.	10 units X $5.00 per unit = $50.00 total cost
You buy ten new 8x10 picture frames at $6.00 each.	10 units X $6.00 per unit = $60.00 total cost
The combined cost in inventory.	$50.00 + $60.00 = $110.00
The average cost per unit is equal to the total cost of Inventory divided by the total units in Inventory.	total cost/total units = average cost/unit $110.00 / 20 = $5.50 avg. cost/unit

Table 8-3 QuickBooks calculates the average cost of inventory items.

Each time you sell Inventory items, the average cost per unit is multiplied by the number of units sold. Then this amount is deducted from the Inventory Asset account and added to the *Cost of Goods Sold* account.

QuickBooks Pro and Premier only use the average cost method for calculating Inventory value. New with the 2012 release, QuickBooks Enterprise Solutions 12 can use the First In, First Out (FIFO) method for calculating Inventory value. If you need the FIFO method for calculating Inventory, consider upgrading to QuickBooks Enterprise Solutions.

Invoicing for Inventory Items

Selling Inventory Items Using an Invoice Form

When you sell Inventory, always use an *Invoice* or a *Sales Receipt* to record the sale. This ensures that QuickBooks updates your Inventory records and your financial reports at the same time.

COMPUTER PRACTICE

Step 1.   Enter the **Invoice** as shown in Figure 8-9, recording a sale of two 5x7 frames.

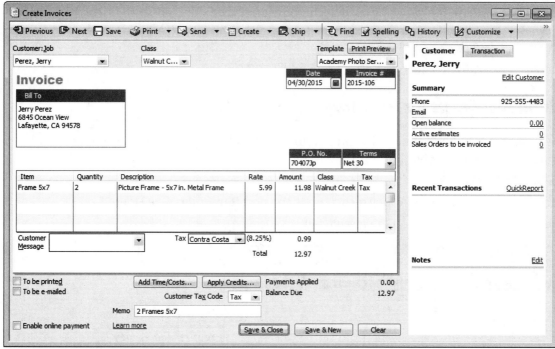

Figure 8-9 Enter this data in your Invoice.

Step 2. Click **Save & New** to save the *Invoice*.

Creating a Transaction Journal Report

To see how this Invoice affects the *General Ledger*, use a *Transaction Journal Report*.

COMPUTER PRACTICE

Step 1. Display the Invoice 2015-106 (shown previously in Figure 8-9).

Step 2. Select the *Reports* menu and then select **Transaction Journal** (or press Ctrl+Y).

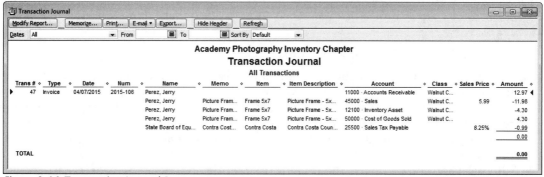

Figure 8-10 Transaction Journal Report

> **The accounting behind the scenes:**
> When you sell an *Inventory Part*, QuickBooks increases (credits) the income account defined for the item sold on the *Invoice* or *Sales Receipt* form. The *Transaction Journal Report* (Figure 8-10) shows the accounting behind the scenes of the *Invoice*. You can use the *Transaction Journal Report* to see the accounting behind *any* QuickBooks transaction.

Step 3.   Close the report by clicking the close box (☒) in the upper right corner. If the *Memorize Report* dialog box appears, check the *Do not display this message in the future* box and click **No**.

Step 4.   Close the **Invoice**.

Using Reminders for Inventory

Because you sold two Frame 5x7s and Inventory fell below 25 units (its reorder point), QuickBooks reminds you that it is time to reorder.

COMPUTER PRACTICE

Step 1.   Select the *Company* menu and then select **Reminders** (see Figure 8-11).

Step 2.   Double-click on the *Inventory to Reorder* line.

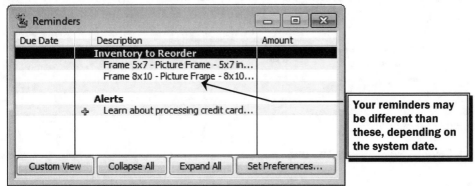

Figure 8-11 Reminders list

Step 3.   Close the window by clicking the close box (☒) in the upper right corner.

Purchasing Inventory

There are several ways to record the purchases of Inventory in QuickBooks. How you record receiving Inventory depends on *when* you receive the Inventory and *how* you intend to pay for it.

You have two options for purchasing Inventory:

1.   You could pay for items at the time you purchase and receive them. For example, you may be at your Vendor's store and write a check or charge your credit card for the items. In this case, you will use *Write Checks* or *Enter Credit Card Charges* to record your receipt of Inventory. This method is not generally advised for businesses that want a complete system for tracking purchases, receipts, and payments for Inventory purchases.

2.   Alternatively, you could use the Inventory ordering and receiving process displayed in the *Vendors* section of the *Home* page shown in Figure 8-12. If you choose this method for processing Inventory, you will issue a *Purchase Order* (PO) for each purchase and later receive part or all of the order by recording an *Item Receipt* or a *Bill*.

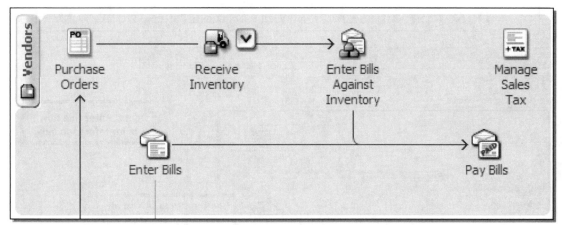

Figure 8-12 The Vendors section includes a flow chart for ordering and receiving Inventory

If the Vendor's bill does not accompany the shipment, use the *Receive Inventory without Bill* option from the *Receive Inventory* icon drop-down list (see Figure 8-13). This creates an *Item Receipt* in QuickBooks. When the bill comes, use the *Enter Bill for Received Items* option from the *Vendor* menu. This converts the *Item Receipt* into a *Bill*.

If you receive the bill when you receive the order, use the *Receive Inventory with Bill* option from the *Receive Inventory* drop-down list (see Figure 8-13). This creates a *Bill* in QuickBooks.

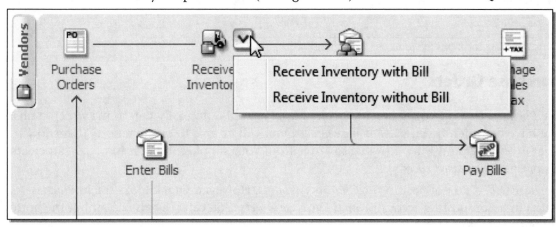

Figure 8-13 Receive Inventory drop-down list option

The *Receive Inventory* options from the *Receive Inventory* drop-down list and the *Receive Items* functions from the *Vendor* menu all record transactions that are *connected* to *Purchase Orders*. This connection is used by QuickBooks to track whether a purchase order is open or not.

Purchasing Inventory at a Retail Store with Check or Credit Card

If you buy Inventory at a retail store, use the *Write Checks* or *Enter Credit Card Charges* functions to record the purchase. Record the purchased items using the *Items* tab at the bottom of the check or credit card charge window (see Figure 8-14).

| DO NOT ENTER THIS CHECK NOW. IT IS FOR REFERENCE ONLY. |

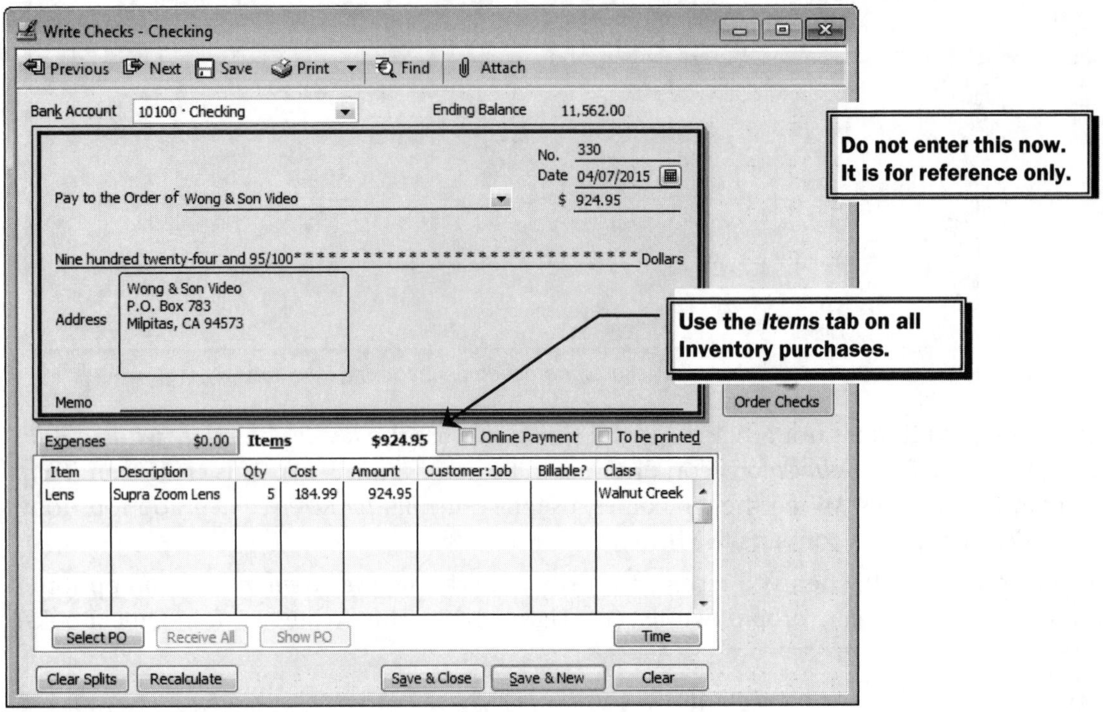

Figure 8-14 Use the Items tab to record a purchase.

Purchase Orders

Use *Purchase Orders* to track Inventory purchases, as well as to easily determine which items you have on order. If you use *Purchase Orders*, you will be able to create reports that show what is on order and when it is due to arrive from your supplier. In addition, you can create a list of open *Purchase Orders*.

Purchase Orders do not post to the *Chart of Accounts*. However, QuickBooks tracks *Purchase Orders* in a non-posting account called *Purchase Orders*. You can see this account at the bottom of your *Chart of Accounts*.

Creating a Purchase Order

Create a *Purchase Order* to reorder Inventory, filling out each item and quantity.

> **Note:**
> Since *Purchase Orders* are non-posting, QuickBooks does not include them on the *Pay Bills* windows.

COMPUTER PRACTICE

Step 1.   Select **Create Purchase Orders** from the *Vendors* menu. Alternately, click the **Purchase Orders** icon on the *Home* page. This displays the *Create Purchase Orders* window (see Figure 8-15).

Step 2.   Select *Ace Supply* from the *Vendor* drop-down list or type the name into the *Vendor* field. Press **Tab**.

Step 3.   Enter *Walnut Creek* in the *Class* field. Press **Tab**.

Step 4.   Press **Tab** three times to leave the *Ship To* field blank and to accept **Custom Purchase Order** as the default form template.

If you want the order shipped directly to one of your customers, select your customer from the drop-down list of the *Ship To* field next to the *Class* field. By default, QuickBooks enters your company's address from the *Company Information* window. To change your *Ship To* address, override it on this form here or select **Company Information** from the *Company* menu. Click the **Ship to Address** button to add your changes.

Step 5.   Enter *04/07/2015* in the *Date* field (if not displayed already) and press **Tab**.

Step 6.   Enter *2015-1* in the *P.O. No.* field and press **Tab**.
QuickBooks automatically numbers your *Purchase Orders* in the same way it numbers Invoices. It increases the number by one for each new *Purchase Order*. However, you can override this number if necessary.

Step 7.   Press **Tab** twice to accept the default *Vendor* and *Ship To* addresses. Enter the **Frame 5x7 (Qty 10)** and **Frame 8x10 (Qty 30)** items in the body of the **Purchase Order** as shown in Figure 8-15.

The Customer column allows you to associate your purchases with a particular *Customer* or *Job* to which you want to assign the expense for this purchase. Since you are purchasing Inventory, you do not know the customer information, so do not use this column.

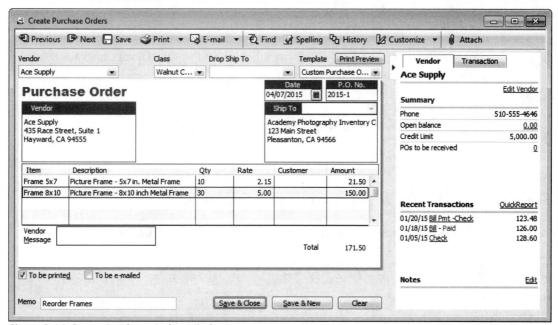

Figure 8-15 Create Purchase Orders window

Step 8.   Enter *Reorder Frames* in the *Memo* field.

Step 9.   Click **Save & Close**.

Receiving Shipments Against Purchase Orders

If you use *Purchase Orders* and you receive a shipment that is not accompanied by a bill, follow these steps:

COMPUTER PRACTICE

Step 1.   From the *Vendors* menu, select **Receive Items**. Alternatively, click **Receive Inventory** and then select **Receive Inventory without Bill** from the drop-down menu on the *Vendors* section of the *Home* page.

Step 2.   The *Create Item Receipts* window opens (see Figure 8-16). Enter *Ace Supply* in the *Vendor* field and press **Tab**.

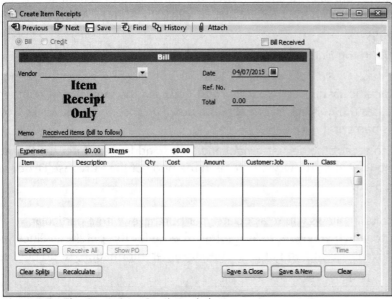

Figure 8-16 The Create Item Receipts window

Step 3.   Since there is an open *Purchase Order* for this Vendor, QuickBooks displays the message in Figure 8-17. Click **Yes**.

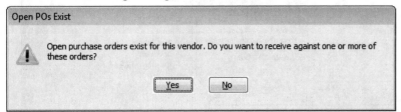

Figure 8-17 QuickBooks displays an Open POs Exist message, if applicable

Step 4.   Select the **Purchase Order** you are receiving against from the list in Figure 8-18 by clicking in the √ column. Then click **OK**.

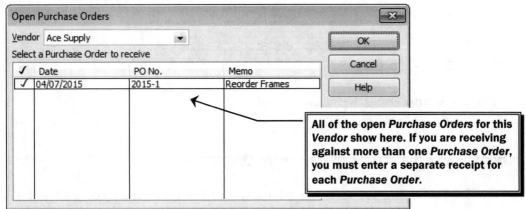

Figure 8-18 Open Purchase Orders window

Step 5.   QuickBooks fills in the *Item Receipt* with the information from the *Purchase Order* as shown in Figure 8-19.

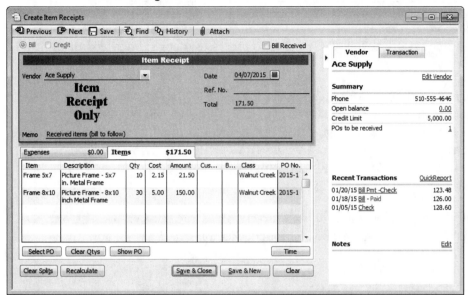

Figure 8-19 QuickBooks automatically completes the Item Receipt using the information from the Purchase Order

Step 6.   Leave *04/07/2015* in the *Date* field. Press **Tab**.

Step 7.   Enter *4431* in the *Ref. No.* field (see Figure 8-20).

         In the *Ref. No.* field you would enter the shipper number on the packing slip that accompanies the shipment. This helps you match the receipt with the *Vendor's* bill when you receive it.

Step 8.   **Tab** to the *Qty* column. Change the quantity to *5* for the Frame 5x7, and to *15* for the Frame 8x10 (see Figure 8-20).

         Do not worry about the Cost column. You have not received the bill yet, so QuickBooks uses the amounts you entered on the *Purchase Order*. When you get the actual bill for this shipment, you will correct or adjust the *Cost* column if necessary.

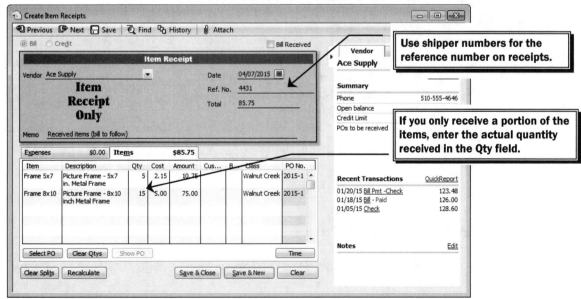

Figure 8-20 Use the shipper number in the Ref. No. field.

Step 9.   To save the Item Receipt, click **Save & Close**.

> **The accounting behind the scenes:**
> When you record an *Item Receipt*, QuickBooks increases (credits) *Accounts Payable* for the total amount of the *Item Receipt*. It also increases (debits) *Inventory* for the same amount.
>
> However, since you have not received the bill, your *Pay Bills* window will not yet show the bill, even though the balance in Accounts Payable was increased by the *Item Receipt*. This may seem strange at first because you normally expect the total in *Pay Bills* to match the balance in *Accounts Payable*. However, *Item Receipts* never show in the *Pay Bills* window. This properly accrues the liability in the right period.
>
> It turns out that *Item Receipts* and *Bills* are exactly the same transaction. The only difference is that the *Bill Received* box is not checked on *Item Receipts*, and it is checked on *Bills*.
>
> **Note:**
> You will see that *Item Receipt* does show up on the *Unpaid Bills Detail* and *A/P Aging* Reports. This lets you know that you have a payable to a Vendor for which you have not received a *Bill*. For cash forecasting purposes, it is important that these reports detail out everything you owe, even if a *Bill* has not yet been received.

Creating Open Purchase Orders Reports

COMPUTER PRACTICE

Step 1.   Select the *Reports* menu, select **Purchases**, and then select **Open Purchase Orders**.

This report (see Figure 8-21) shows the total dollar amount for *all* open *Purchase Orders*, not just the open balance of each *Purchase Order*. To see the open balance on a specific *Purchase Order*, double-click on it from this report.

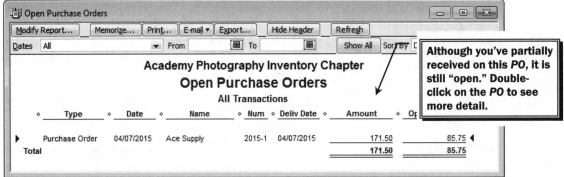

Figure 8-21 The Open Purchase Orders Report

Checking Purchase Order Status

To check the status of a *Purchase Order*, to change it, or to cancel it, edit the *Purchase Order* directly.

COMPUTER PRACTICE

Step 1.   Display the **Purchase Order** by double-clicking on it from the **Open Purchase Orders** report shown in Figure 8-21.

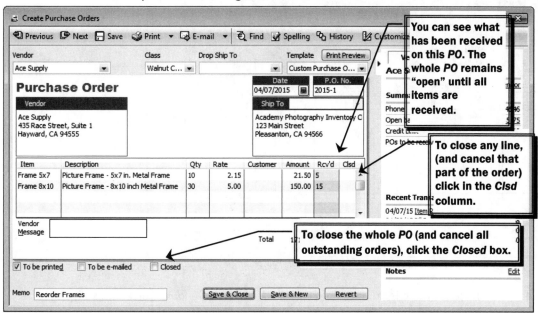

Figure 8-22 Edit the purchase order as necessary.

Step 2.   Review the quantity of each Item in the *Rcv'd* column.

On the *Purchase Order* in Figure 8-22, you can see that Academy Photography has received 5 Frame 5x7s and 15 Frame 8x10s.

If you know you will not receive the backorder items on a *Purchase Order*, you can close specific line items or close the whole order. To close any line of the order, click in the *Clsd* column. To close the whole order and cancel the rest of the order, click the *Closed* box at the bottom of the form. If you cancel an order, do not forget to notify the Vendor.

Step 3.   In this case, close the window without making any changes to the *Purchase Order*. Close the *Open Purchase Orders* report.

Entering the Final Shipment

When the final shipment arrives, enter another *Item Receipt*.

COMPUTER PRACTICE

Step 1.   Select the *Vendors* menu and then select **Receive Items**. Alternatively, click **Receive Inventory** and then **Receive Inventory without Bill** on the *Vendor* section of the *Home* page.

Step 2.   The *Create Item Receipts* window opens (see Figure 8-23).

Step 3.   Enter *Ace Supply* in the *Vendor* field and then press **Tab**.

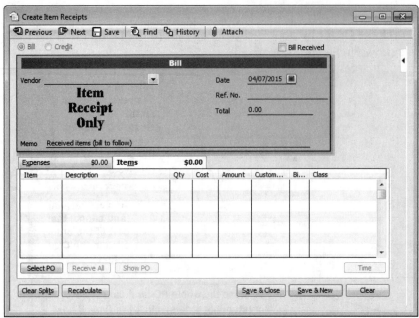

Figure 8-23 Enter the Vendor name in the Create Item Receipts window

Step 4.   Because there is an open *Purchase Order* for this *Vendor,* QuickBooks displays the
            dialog box shown in Figure 8-24. Click **Yes.**

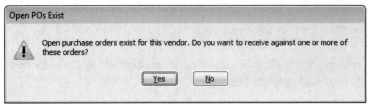

Figure 8-24 The Open PO's Exist window appears

Step 5.   Select the **Purchase Order** you are receiving against from the list (see Figure 8-25)
            and click **OK.**

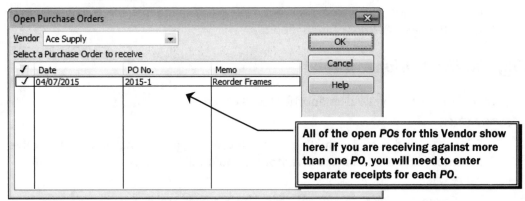

Figure 8-25 Open Purchase Orders window

Step 6.   QuickBooks automatically fills in the *Item Receipt* with the information from the
            Purchase Order.

Step 7.   Leave *04/07/2015* in the *Date* field.

Step 8.   Enter *4441* in the *Ref. No.* field (see Figure 8-26).

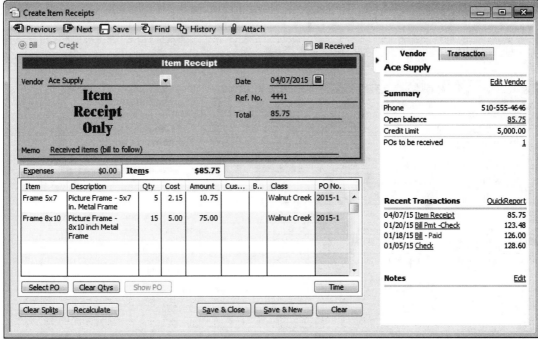

Figure 8-26 Item Receipt #4441

Step 9.   Click **Save & Close** to record the receipt.

Entering Bills for Received Inventory

Now that you have recorded *Item Receipts* for your Inventory shipments, the next step in the process is to record the bills when they arrive from the vendor.

Converting an Item Receipt into a Bill

COMPUTER PRACTICE

Step 1.   Select the *Vendors* menu and then select **Enter Bill for Received Items**. Alternatively, click **Enter Bills Against Inventory** icon in the *Vendor* section of the *Home* page.

Step 2.   Enter *Ace Supply* in the *Vendor* field and then press **Tab**.

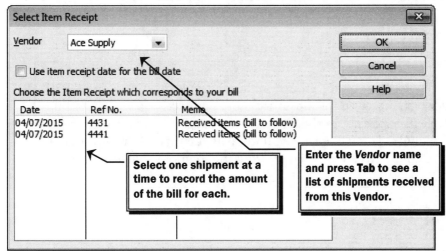

Figure 8-27 Select one shipment at a time

Step 3.   Select the first line on the window shown in Figure 8-27. Click **OK**.

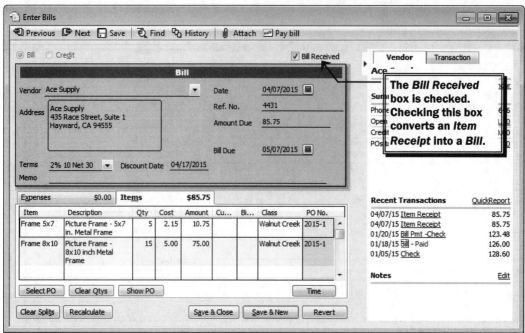

Figure 8-28 Enter Bills window

Step 4.   QuickBooks displays the *Item Receipt* and automatically checks the *Bill Received* box
                 (see Figure 8-28). Checking the *Bill Received* box converts the *Item Receipt* into a *Bill*.
                 Verify that the *Bill* matches your records and make changes to price, terms, due date,
                 or any other field that does not match the Vendor's bill.

> **Note:**
> QuickBooks does not add a new transaction when you use the *Enter Bill for
> Received Items* function. That is because you have already recorded an *Item
> Receipt*, which increases Inventory and Accounts Payable. This function simply
> converts your *Item Receipt* into a *Bill*.

Step 5.   Click **Save & Close** to record the **Bill**.

Step 6.   Click **Yes** if the *Recording Transaction* message displays.

Step 7.   Repeat Step 1 through Step 6 for Item Receipt #4441 and accept the defaults for all
                 quantities and amounts.

> **Note:**
> QuickBooks does not allow you to "group" multiple *Item Receipts* into one *Bill* if
> only one Vendor bill is received for the entire *PO*. If you receive one Vendor bill
> and have multiple *Item Receipts*, in the reference number of the *Bill* make sure to
> enter the same number. This will enable you to easily identify all the *Bills* that
> add up to the Vendor bill received when creating the Vendor's *Bill Payment*
> check.

Handling Overshipments

If your Vendor ships more than you ordered on a *Purchase Order*, you have three choices.

1.   You could refuse the extra shipment and send it back to the Vendor without recording anything in QuickBooks.
2.   You could receive the extra shipment into Inventory and keep it (and pay for it).
3.   You could receive the extra shipment into Inventory, and then send it back and record a *Bill Credit* in QuickBooks.

If you keep the overshipment (and pay for it):

DO NOT PERFORM THESE STEPS NOW. THEY ARE FOR REFERENCE ONLY.

1.   Override the number in the *Qty* column on the *Item Receipt* so that it exceeds the quantity on your *Purchase Order*. This increases the *Inventory Asset* and *Accounts Payable* accounts for the total amount of the shipment, including the overshipment.

2.   When the bill arrives from the Vendor, match it with the *Item Receipt* and pay the amount actually due. Unless you edit the *Purchase Order*, it will not match the *Item Receipt* or *Bill*. This may be important later when you look at *Purchase Orders* and actual purchase costs, so consider updating your *Purchase Order* to match the actual costs.

If you send the overshipment back after receiving it into Inventory:

DO NOT PERFORM THESE STEPS NOW. THEY ARE FOR REFERENCE ONLY.

1.   Override the number in the *Qty* column on the *Item Receipt* so that it exceeds the quantity on your *Purchase Order*. This increases the *Inventory Asset* and *Accounts Payable* accounts for the total amount of the shipment, including the overshipment. However, you do not plan to actually pay the Vendor for this "overshipment." Instead, you will return the extra items, and ask the Vendor to credit your account.

2.   When you return the excess items, create a *Bill Credit* for the Vendor. On the *Bill Credit*, enter the quantity returned and the cost for each item. We use a *Bill Credit* here because we want to reflect the proper financial transactions between us and our Vendor.

3.   At this point, the Vendor may apply your credit towards a future *Invoice* on items they send to you, or they may send you a refund if you have paid for the shipment.

4.   If you receive a refund from the Vendor, record the refund directly onto your next deposit transaction. You can manually add a line to the deposit using the Vendor's name in the *Received from* column, and Accounts Payable in the *From Account* column. Then, after recording the deposit, use the *Pay Bills* screen to apply the deposit line to the *Bill Credit*.

5.   To apply the *Bill Credit* to an unpaid bill for that Vendor, use the *Pay Bills* window.

Handling Vendor Overcharges

If you have a discrepancy between your *Purchase Order* and the Vendor's bill, there are several ways to handle it. If the Vendor overcharged you, the Vendor might agree to revise the bill and send you a new one. In this case, wait for the new bill before recording anything in QuickBooks. On the other hand, you might decide to pay the incorrect bill and have the Vendor adjust the next bill. In that case, use the *Expenses* tab on the *Bill* in QuickBooks to track the error. In this example, assume you were overcharged by $10.00.

COMPUTER PRACTICE

Step 1.   Select the *Vendors* menu and then select **Enter Bills**. Alternatively, click **Enter Bills** on the *Vendor* section of the *Home* page.

Step 2.   Click **Previous** on the *Enter Bills* window to display Bill #4441.

Step 3.   Select the **Expenses** tab to record a $10.00 overcharge from the Vendor. Use the **Cost of Goods Sold** account and the **Overhead** class to track the overcharge. Alternately, you could record the overcharge to a *Current Asset* account call **Due from Vendors** so that the error does not affect the Profit & Loss statement.

Step 4.   Click **Recalculate** to update the *Amount Due* field (see Figure 8-29). (Note that if you Tab into the next line, a negative $10 will appear. You will have to clear that amount in order to properly recalculate the Amount Due.)

Step 5.   Click **Save & Close**. Click **Yes** on the *Recording Transaction* message window.

Since the *Bill* in Figure 8-29 is $10.00 too much, contact the Vendor to discuss the overage on the *Bill*. The Vendor will either issue you a credit, or if you have already paid the *Bill*, send you a refund check. The Vendor may also apply the overpayment to your account to be applied to a future bill.

Depending upon the Vendor's action, do one of the following:

- If the Vendor refunds your money, add the refund directly onto your next deposit. Code the deposit to the *Cost of Goods Sold* account and the *Overhead* class (the account and class you used when you recorded the overage on the bill).

- If the Vendor sends you a credit memo, enter a **Bill Credit**. Code the *Bill Credit* to the *Cost of Goods Sold* account and *Overhead* class (the account and class you used when you recorded the overage on the *Bill*).

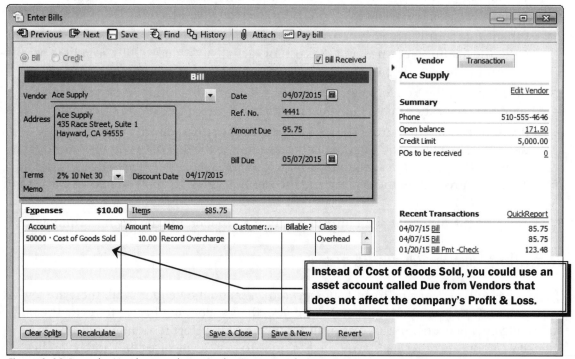

Figure 8-29 Record a Vendor overcharge in the Expenses tab

> **Note:**
> Always use the same account when you record the overcharge and the refund or credit. In the example above, the *Expenses* tab of the *Bill* for Ace Supply increases *Cost of Goods Sold* by $10.00 and the deposit or credit from the Vendor reduces *Cost of Goods Sold* by the same amount. Alternatively, you could use an *Other Current Asset* account called *Due from Vendors*, as discussed above.

Adjusting Inventory

QuickBooks automatically adjusts Inventory each time you purchase or sell *Inventory* items. However, it may be necessary to manually adjust Inventory after a physical count of your Inventory, or in case of an increase or decrease in the value of your Inventory on hand. For example, you might decrease the value of your Inventory if it has lost value due to new technology trends.

Adjusting the Quantity of Inventory on Hand

COMPUTER PRACTICE

Step 1.   Select the *Vendors* menu, select **Inventory Activities**, and then select **Adjust Quantity/Value on Hand**. Alternatively, click the **Inventory Activities** icon on the *Home* page and select **Adjust Quantity/Value on Hand** from the menu. QuickBooks displays the window shown in Figure 8-31.

Step 2.   If you need to, enter **Quantity** from the *Adjustment Type* field and press **Tab**.

Step 3.   Enter *04/30/2015* in the *Adjustment Date* field and press **Tab**.

Step 4.   Enter *Inventory Variance* in the *Adjustment Account* field and press **Tab**.

            QuickBooks adjusts the account you enter into the *Adjustment Account* field to offset the change in the *Inventory Asset* account balance. In this example, we are using *Inventory Variance*, a *Cost of Goods Sold* account, but you can use whichever account is best for your records.

Step 5.   The *Income or Expense expected* dialog box displays. Check the box next to *Do not display this message* in the future and click **OK** (see Figure 8-30).

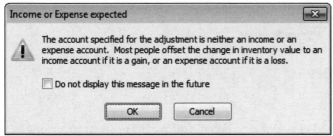

Figure 8-30 Income of Expense expected dialog box

> **Note:**
> The dialog box displays because QuickBooks is looking for an expense account to record the offsetting decrease in the Inventory asset. Although the entry can be made to an expense account (decrease in Inventory) or an income account (increase in Inventory), many people find that offsetting Inventory variances to the Cost of Goods Sold account (for either Inventory increases or decreases) more accurately reflects the recording of variances.

Step 6.   Enter *2015–1* in the *Ref. No.* field and press **Tab** twice to skip the *Customer: Job* field.

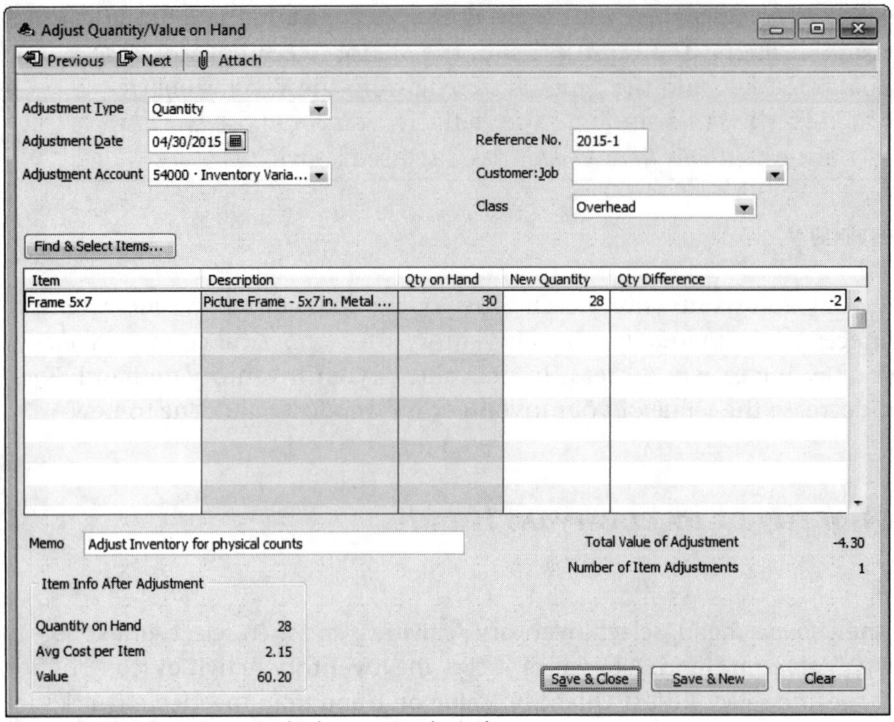

Figure 8-31 Adjust Quantity/Value on Hand window

Step 7.   Enter **Overhead** in the *Class* field and press **Tab**.

Step 8.   Enter **Frame 5x7** in the *Item* column and press **Tab**.

Step 9.   Enter **28** in the *New Quantity* column and press **Tab**.

                 Notice that QuickBooks calculates the quantity difference (-2) in the *Qty Difference*
                 column. Also, notice that QuickBooks automatically calculates the *Total Value of
                 Adjustment* in the bottom right corner. QuickBooks Pro and Premier use the *average
                 cost method* to calculate this value. Look at the *Inventory Valuation Detail Report* later
                 in this chapter to see how the average cost changes each time you adjust Inventory
                 in this way.

Step 10.   Enter **Adjust Inventory for physical counts** in the *Memo* field.

Step 11.   To save the adjustment, click **Save & New**.

Adjusting the Value of Inventory

COMPUTER PRACTICE

With the Adjust Quantity/Value on Hand window displayed, follow these steps to record a
value adjustment to your inventory.

Step 1.   Enter **Quantity and Total Value** from the *Adjustment Type* field and press **Tab**.

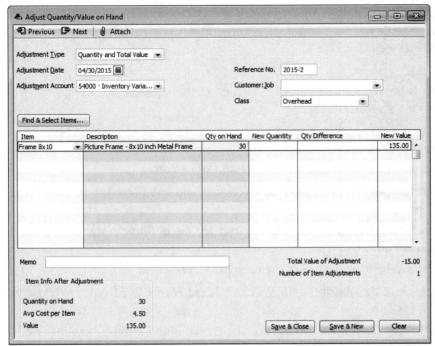

Figure 8-32 Click on the Value Adjustment box to change inventory value

Step 2.   Confirm that **04/30/2015** is already selected in the *Adjustment Date* field. Press **Tab**.

Step 3.   Confirm that **Inventory Variance** is already selected in the *Adjustment Account* field.

Step 4.   Leave *2015-2* in the *Ref. No.* field.

Step 5.   Leave the *Customer:Job* field blank.

Step 6.   Enter *Overhead* in the *Class* field.

Step 7.   Enter *Frame 8x10* in the *Item* column. Press **Tab** three times.

Step 8.   Enter *135.00* in the *New Value* column on the Frame 8x10 line and press **Tab**. Notice that QuickBooks calculates the Total Value of Adjustment.

Step 9.   Enter *Adjust Inventory Value of Frame 8x10* in the *Memo* field.

Step 10.   Click **Save & Close** to save the adjustment.

QuickBooks will post the amount of this adjustment ($15.00) to the *General Ledger*. Since this adjustment lowers the value of the Frame 8x10 item, it reduces the average cost of each unit on hand. Therefore, the next time you sell a Frame 8x10, QuickBooks will transfer the new (lower) average cost out of *Inventory* and into *Cost of Goods Sold*.

The accounting behind the scenes:
Inventory value adjustments always affect your *Inventory Asset* account. If the *Total Value of Adjustment* is a positive number, the *Inventory* account increases (debits) by that amount and the *Adjustment* account decreases (credits). If the *Total Value of Adjustment* is a negative number, the debits and the credits are reversed.

Setting up Group Items

Sometimes, you sell items in bundles. For example, every time Academy Photography sells three hours of services for retouching, it also includes a 5x7 metal frame. Academy

Photography uses *Group* Items to bundle products and/or services on sales forms. You may also purchase items in a bundle from a Vendor, so setting up a *Group* Item may make the purchasing process easier as well.

COMPUTER PRACTICE

Step 1.   Click **Items & Services** on the *Company* section of the *Home* page, or select the *Lists* menu and then select **Item List**.

Step 2.   Select the **Item** button at the bottom of the *Item List* window and select **New**. Alternatively, press **Ctrl+N**.

Step 3.   Select **Group** from the *Type* drop-down list and press **Tab**.

Step 4.   Enter **5x7 Retouching** in the *Group Name/Number* field and press **Tab** to advance to the *Description* field.

Step 5.   Enter **Retouching photograph and placing in a 5x7 metal frame** in the *Description* field and press **Tab**.

Step 6.   Click the *Print items in group* box (see Figure 8-33). Press **Tab**.

Step 7.   On the first line at the bottom of the window, select **Frame 5x7** from the *Item* drop-down list. Press **Tab**.

Step 8.   Enter **1** in the *Qty* column and press **Tab**. The *Qty* column indicates how many of each item is included in the *Group*.

Step 9.   On the second line at the bottom of the window, select **Retouching** from the *Item* drop-down list. Press **Tab**.

Step 10.   Enter **3** in the *Qty* column. Press **Tab**.

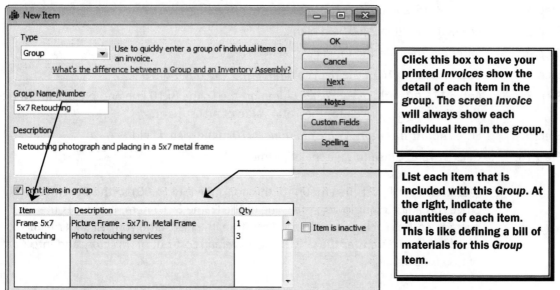

Figure 8-33 Specify Items in the group and whether to print Items on the sales form

> **Note:**
> The *New Item* window in Figure 8-33 does not include a *Sales Price* field. When you enter a *Group* Item on sales forms, QuickBooks uses the sales prices of the items within the *Group* to calculate a total price for the *Group*. You can override the price of each item within the *Group* directly on the sales form.
>
> In addition, the printed sales form will show the *Group* Item detail only if the *Print items in group* box is checked. However, you will always see the items in this *Group* on the screen version of the sales form.

Step 11.   Click **OK** to save the *Group* Item and then close the *Item List* window.

Inventory Assemblies

QuickBooks Premier includes an *Item Type* called *Inventory Assemblies* which is quite useful if you want to track individual *Items* and then group them into an assembly. *Inventory Assembly Items* help to track Inventory that is created from raw materials that are themselves tracked as *Items*.

The feature is similar to *Groups*, but it allows you to combine several *Inventory Items* into a single *Item*. They are different from *Group Items* because the parts are removed from *Inventory* as soon as an *Inventory Assembly Item* is assembled.

An *Inventory Assembly* is defined by specifying which components (must be *Inventory Part, Inventory Assembly, Non-inventory Part, Service,* or *Other Charge* type items) are needed to produce it. Essentially, you define the *Bill of Materials* for each *Inventory Assembly Item* when you set up the item.

Inventory Reports

QuickBooks provides several reports for Inventory analysis, all of which are customizable in ways similar to other reports.

For daily management of Inventory, use the *Stock Status by Item Report*, the *Stock Status by Vendor Report*, or the *Inventory Valuation Summary Report*. These reports give a quick overview of Inventory counts, Inventory values, and pending orders.

For detailed research about transactions involving Inventory, use the *Inventory Item QuickReport* or the *Inventory Valuation Detail Report*.

Inventory Item QuickReport

The *Inventory Item QuickReport* is useful for seeing all transactions involving an *Inventory Item*.

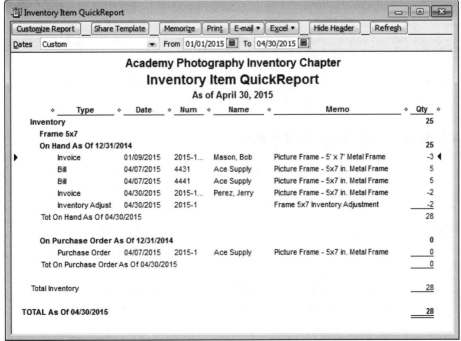

Figure 8-34 Inventory Item QuickReport

COMPUTER PRACTICE

Step 1.   From the *Home* page, click the **Inventory Activities** icon and choose **Inventory Center.**

Step 2.   Click on the **Frame 5x7** Item to select it in the left side of the *Inventory Center.*

Step 3.   Click the **QuickReport** link from the right side of the *Inventory Center.*

Step 4.   Set the *From* date to *01/01/2015* and the *To* date to *04/30/2015* and press **Tab**. The *QuickReport* for the Frame 5x7 displays (see Figure 8-34).

Step 5.   Close the report by clicking the close box (☒) in the upper right corner of the window. Leave the *Inventory Center* open.

Inventory Stock Status by Item Report

The *Stock Status by Item Report* is useful for getting a quick snapshot of each Inventory part, as well as the number of units on hand and on order. In addition, this report gives you information about your Inventory turnover, showing a column for sales per week.

COMPUTER PRACTICE

Step 1.   Click the **Stock Status** link on the right side of the *Inventory Center.* Alternatively, select the *Reports* menu, select **Inventory**, and then select **Inventory Stock Status by Item**.

Step 2.   Set the *From* date to *01/01/2015* and the *To* date to *04/30/2015* and press **Tab**. The Inventory Stock Status by Item report displays (see Figure 8-35).

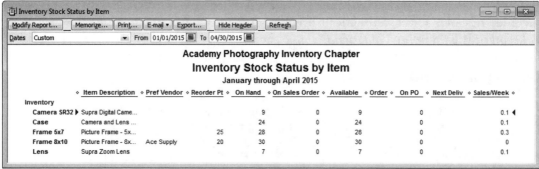

Figure 8-35 Inventory Stock Status by Item report

Step 3.   To close the report, click the close box (☒) at the top right corner of the window. Click **No** if you are prompted to memorize the report.

Inventory Stock Status by Vendor Report

The *Stock Status by Vendor Report* gives you information about your Inventory parts, including how many are on hand, and how many are on order. This *Report* is sorted by the *Preferred Vendor* field in the item.

COMPUTER PRACTICE

Step 1.   Select the **Reports** menu, select **Inventory**, and then select **Inventory Stock Status by Vendor.**

Step 2.   Set the *From* date to *01/01/2015* and the *To* date to *04/30/2015* and press **Tab**. The *Inventory Stock Status by Vendor Report* displays (see Figure 8-36).

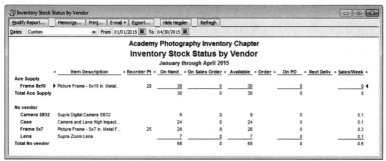

Figure 8-36 Inventory Stock Status by Vendor Report

Step 3.   To close the report, click the close box (![X]) at the top right corner of the window. Click **No** if you are prompted to memorize the report.

Inventory Valuation Reports

The *Inventory Valuation Summary Report* gives you information about the value of your Inventory items on a certain date. This report shows each item in Inventory, the quantity on hand, the average cost, and the retail value of each item.

COMPUTER PRACTICE

Step 1.   Click the **Inventory Valuation Summary** link on the right side of the *Inventory Center*. Alternatively, select the **Reports** menu, select **Inventory**, and then select **Inventory Valuation Summary**.

Step 2.   Set the *Date* field to *04/30/2015* and press **Tab** (see Figure 8-37).

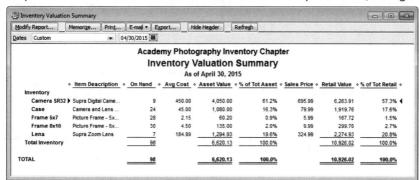

Figure 8-37 Inventory Valuation Summary report

Step 3.   To close the report, click the close box (![X]) at the top right corner of the window. Click **No** if you are prompted to memorize the report.

Review Questions

Select the best answer(s) for each of the following:

1. If your Vendor ships more than you ordered on a *Purchase Order* (an overshipment), which of the following actions would not be appropriate?

    a)   You could refuse the extra shipment and send it back to the Vendor without recording anything in QuickBooks.

    b)   You could receive the extra shipment using an *Inventory Adjustment* transaction.

    c)   You could receive the extra shipment into Inventory and keep it (and pay for it).

    d)   You could receive the extra shipment into Inventory, and then send it back and record a *Bill Credit* in QuickBooks.

2. When setting up a *Group* Item, where do you enter the sales price?

   a) Enter the price in the *Sales Price* field.
   b) Enter the price in the *Item Pricing* list.
   c) The *Group* Item does not include a *Sales Price* field.
   d) Enter the price in the *Set Price* window.

3. To activate QuickBooks Inventory:

   a) Select the **File** menu and then select **Preferences**.
   b) Select **Purchases - Vendors**.
   c) Consult your accountant to determine the proper Inventory valuation method.
   d) Select the **Edit** menu, then select **Preferences**, then click on the **Items & Inventory** *Preference* and then click the **Company Preferences** tab. Finally, click on the option that activates Inventory.

4. The Inventory asset account:

   a) Tracks open *Purchase Orders* of Inventory items.
   b) Decreases when Inventory is purchased.
   c) Increases when Inventory is sold.
   d) Increases when Inventory is purchased.

5. In QuickBooks Pro and Premier, Inventory can do all of the following except:

   a) Provide reports on the status of each item in Inventory including how many are on hand and how many are on order.
   b) Use the LIFO or FIFO method of determining Inventory cost.
   c) Calculate gross profit on Inventory sold.
   d) Track the open *Purchase Orders* for every Inventory item.

Inventory Problem 1

APPLYING YOUR KNOWLEDGE

Restore the **Inventory-12Problem1.QBM** file.

1. Create new **Inventory Items** in the Item List with the following data.

Item Type	Inventory Part
Item Name	Frame 4x6 Black
Purchase Description	Picture Frame - 4x6 Black
Cost	$4.95
COGS Account	Cost of Goods Sold
Preferred Vendor	Leave blank
Sales Description	Picture Frame - 4x6 Black
Price	$9.99
Tax Code	Tax
Income Account	Sales
Asset Account	Inventory Asset
Reorder Point	25
Qty on Hand	Leave zero
Total Value	Leave zero
As of	Leave current date

Item Type	Inventory Part
Item Name	Frame 4x6 White
Purchase Description	Picture Frame - 4x6 White
Cost	$4.49
COGS Account	Cost of Goods Sold
Preferred Vendor	Leave blank
Sales Description	Picture Frame - 4x6 White
Price	$8.99
Tax Code	Tax
Income Account	Sales
Asset Account	Inventory Asset
Reorder Point	25
Qty on Hand	Leave zero
Total Value	Leave zero
As of	Leave current date

2. Create **Purchase Order** #2015-1 dated 04/06/2015 to Ace Supply using the *Walnut Creek Class* for 10-Frame 5x7, 40-Frame 4x6 Black, and 40-Frame 4x6 White. Leave the *Ship To* drop-down field at the top blank. The total *PO* amount is $399.10. Print the *Purchase Order* on blank paper.

3. Record the transactions below. On these transactions, unless you're told differently, keep all defaults on transactions for *Date*, prices, and *Sales Tax*.

April 10, 2015	Create an **Item Receipt** for 10-Frame 5x7, 15-Frame 4x6 Black, and 20-Frame 4x6 White from Ace Supply against PO #2015-1. The product came without a bill, but the packing slip number was #3883. The total *Item Receipt* amount is $185.55.
April 13, 2015	Create an **Item Receipt** for the remaining items from Ace Supply against PO #2015-1. The product came without a bill, but the packing slip number was #7622. The total *Item Receipt* amount is $213.55.
April 17, 2015	Create **Invoice** #2015-106 to Jerry Perez for 5-Frame 5x7 (use list price). Use the *Walnut Creek* Class. The total *Invoice* amount is $32.42.
April 20, 2015	Received bill for *Item Receipt* #3883 from Ace Supply. Additional $8.50 delivery charges were added to the bill. Use the *Expenses* tab on the bill to record delivery charges (coded to *Postage and Delivery* expense) and allocate the cost to the *Walnut Creek Class*. The total *Bill* amount is $194.05. (*Hint:* Use the **Recalculate** button if necessary to adjust the *Amount Due*.)
April 20, 2015	Received bill for *Item Receipt* #7622 from Ace Supply. The total **Bill** amount is $213.55.
April 30, 2015	Enter an **Inventory Adjustment** for a Frame 5x7 item. Use the *Inventory Variance* account and the *Walnut Creek* class to record the adjustment. *Inventory Adjustment Reference* # 2015-101. *Quantity on hand* is 26. The total *Value of Adjustment* is -$2.15.

4. Create and print the following reports:

    a)   **Frame 5x7 Item QuickReport** with the *Dates* field set to **All**

    b)   **Inventory Stock Status by Item** for 01/01/2015 through 04/30/2015

    c)   **Inventory Valuation Summary** as of 04/30/2015

Chapter 9
Time and Billing

Objectives

After completing this chapter, you should know:

- What makes an expense Billable, not Billable, or Billed (page 267)
- How to add reimbursable Expenses, Items, and Time to *Invoices* (page 269)
- How to use two-sided Items to track reimbursable expenses (page 275)
- How to use two-sided Items to track subcontracted services (page 281)
- Activate Time Tracking (page 284)
- Pass Billable time onto an *Invoice* (page 287)
- Create reports to analyze timesheet data (page 291)

> **Restore this File**
>
> This chapter uses TimeBilling-12.QBW. To open this file, restore the TimeBilling-12.QBM file to your hard disk. See page 8 for instructions on restoring files. If you are using QuickBooks Premier Accountant, we recommend that you toggle to QuickBooks Premier General Business as described on page x.

This chapter covers billable expenses, including time tracking and <u>*Two-Sided Items*</u>. QuickBooks helps you track these expenses from when they occur through to billing the client.

Reimbursable (Billable) Expenses

QuickBooks allows you to pass expenses through to customers for reimbursement.

To track a reimbursable cost, you'll first need to record the expense. Enter a transaction such as a *Bill*, *Check* or *Credit Card Charge* to record the original expense, and then assign the Customer or Job to which the expense applies.

On expense transactions, the *Billable?* option indicates that the expense will be passed through to the *Customer* or *Job* (see Figure 9-1). In other words, this option indicates that the expense can be billed to the Customer when a sales form is created. This option only appears after you enter a name into the *Customer:Job* field in the *Expenses* (or *Items*) tab area of the expense transaction. Also, the *Billable?* option only appears if you code the transaction to one of the following account types:

- *Other Current Asset*
- *Expense*
- *Other Expense*

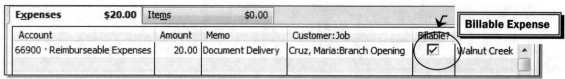

Figure 9-1 Billable Expense item

> **Note:**
> The *Billable?* option will NOT appear if you code the expense transaction to an *Income* or *Cost of Goods Sold* type account.
> **Tip:**
> If you need to use the pass-through process for *Cost of Goods Sold* transactions, you can create an *Item* that points to a *Cost of Goods Sold* account and then use that *Item* on the original transaction by clicking on the *Items* tab. This will allow you to pass the expense through to *Invoices*. See *Using Two-Sided Items* on page 275 for an example of using *Items* to track pass-throughs.

Sometimes you want to assign expenses to *Jobs* so you can track all of the related costs to the *Job*, but you do not intend to pass them through for reimbursement. In this case, you can uncheck the *Billable?* option so that the line item is "non-billable."

COMPUTER PRACTICE

For simplicity, in this example, we'll use an expense account called *Reimbursable Expenses* to hold the expenses until they are reimbursed. However, you may want to use an *Other Current Asset* type account to hold all of your reimbursable expenses. If you're unsure about which account type to use for your reimbursable expenses, consult with your accountant.

Step 1.   Select the **Write Checks** icon on the *Banking* section of the *Home* page.

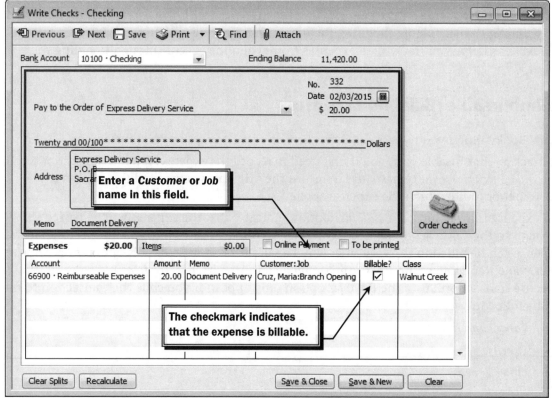

Figure 9-2 Record a reimbursable expense

Step 2.   From the *Write Checks* window, enter the *Check* shown in Figure 9-2.

When you select the Branch Opening *Job* for Maria Cruz in the *Customer:Job* column of the *Expenses* tab, the *Billable?* option appears with the checkmark already selected.

Step 3.   Click **Save & Close** to record.

The next time you create an *Invoice* for the customer, you can pass the cost through to the *Invoice* by following the next steps.

Step 4.   Select the **Invoices** icon on the *Customer* section of the **Home** page.

Step 5.   Enter **Cruz, Maria: Branch Opening** for the *Customer:Job* field.

Once the name is entered, the message in Figure 9-3 appears to prompt you to select the expenses that you designated as billable.

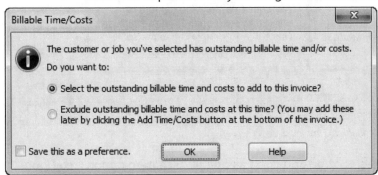

Figure 9-3 Billable Time/Costs option window

Step 6.   Click **OK**.

Step 7.   The *Choose Billable Time and Costs* window opens for Maria Cruz's Branch Opening *Job* (see Figure 9-4).

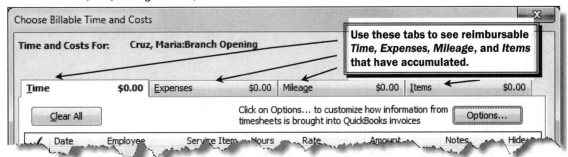

Figure 9-4 Top section of the Choose Billable Time and Costs screen

Step 8.   The top section of the *Choose Billable Time and Costs* screen shows four tabs where you can view pass-through expenses. The *Expenses* tab will show the billable expenses (such as the check you just wrote) that were recorded using the *Expenses* tab on checks, bills, and credit card charges.

Step 9.   Click the **Expenses** tab (see Figure 9-5).

Step 10. Verify that *20%* is entered in the *Markup Amount or %* field.

The *Markup* will increase the amount due by the *Customer* to cover the costs of processing this expense. You can either enter a static dollar amount or a percentage that will change depending on the amount. *Default Markup* can be set in the *Time & Expense Company Preference*.

Step 11. Enter **Expense Markup** in the *Markup Account* field.

Step 12.   In the middle section of the *Expenses* tab (see Figure 9-5), click a checkmark in the far left column on the line for **Express Delivery Service** to pass the expense, with the 20% markup, to Maria Cruz's *Invoice*.

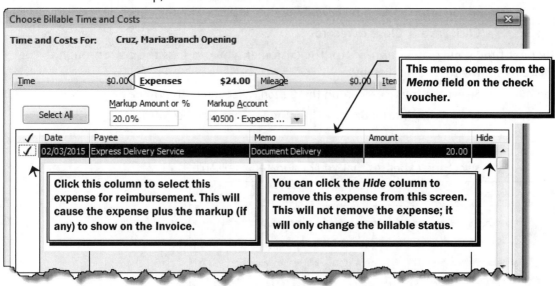

Figure 9-5 Middle section of the Choose Billable Time and Costs screen

Step 13.   Select the **Print selected time and costs as one invoice item** option (see Figure 9-6). Then click **OK**.

When you select this option, QuickBooks prints all reimbursable expenses on a single line in the body of the *Invoice* rather than listing each expense separately. You'll always see the *details* of the reimbursable expenses, including the markup, on the screen even if you chose *Print selected costs as one invoice Item*.

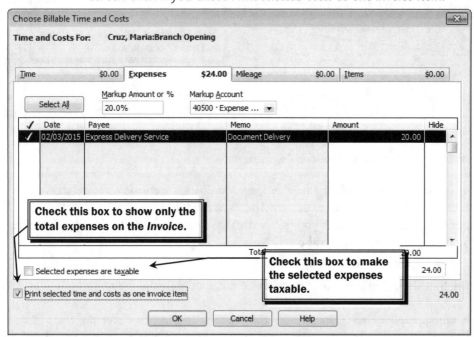

Figure 9-6 The Expenses tab of the Choose Billable Time and Costs screen

Step 14.   Once you are returned to the *Invoice*, enter the **Template**, **Class**, **Date**, and **Invoice** # as shown in Figure 9-7. The *Invoice* now includes the reimbursable expense.

Step 15. To see what the *Invoice* will look like when you print it, click **Print**, and then click **Preview** (see Figure 9-8).

Step 16. When you are finished reviewing, click **Close** in the *Print Preview* window, and click **Save & Close** to record the *Invoice*.

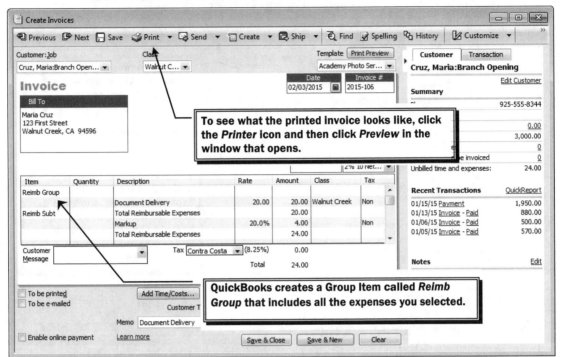

Figure 9-7 Reimbursable expenses shown on an Invoice

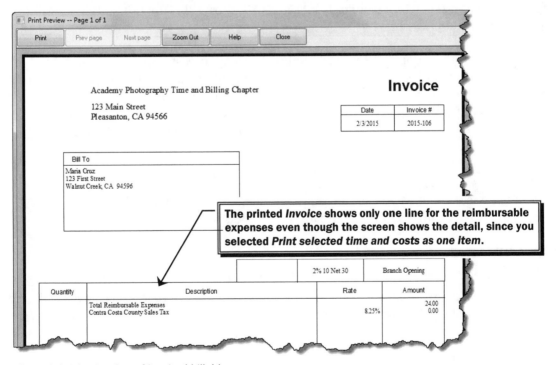

Figure 9-8 Print Preview of invoiced billable expenses

The completed example of pass-through expenses shows on your Profit & Loss statement with the date range set for February 3rd, 2015 to February 3rd, 2015 so as to only include the transaction entered earlier in this chapter and as shown in Figure 9-9.

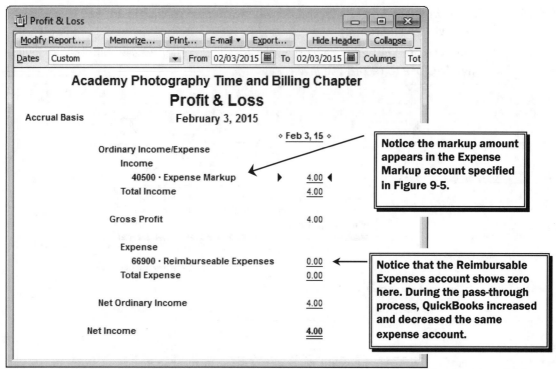

Figure 9-9 Reimbursable Expenses on the Profit & Loss report

> **The Accounting Behind the Scenes:**
> The *Reimbursable Expenses* account has a zero balance because QuickBooks increased (debited) the balance when you recorded the *Check* shown in Figure 9-2 and then decreased (credited) the account when you recorded the *Invoice* shown in Figure 9-7.

Sometimes it is more appropriate to track reimbursable expenses in one account and the reimbursements in another account. For example, you could record all reimbursable expenses in the expense account called "Reimbursable Expenses," and you could track the reimbursements in an income account called "Expenses Reimbursed." For QuickBooks to handle reimbursements in this way, you will need to make changes to your *Time & Expense Company Preferences*.

> **Note:**
> Ask your accountant if you should treat reimbursements as income before making these changes to your company's QuickBooks file.

COMPUTER PRACTICE

Step 1.   Select the **Edit** menu and choose **Preferences**.

Step 2.   Select **Time & Expense** on the left icon bar (you may have to scroll down on the left side of the *Preferences* window to access that selection).

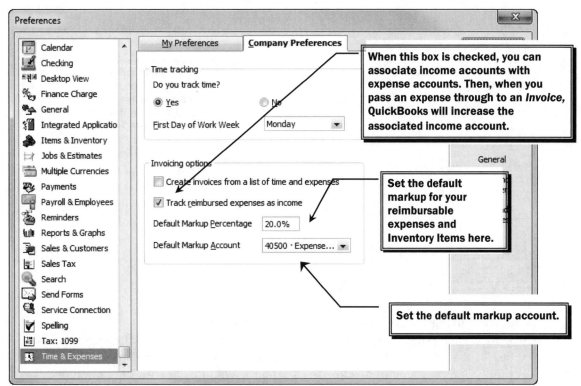

Figure 9-10 Time & Expense Company Preferences

Step 3. Select the **Company Preferences** tab.

Step 4. Notice that the box next to **Track reimbursed expenses as income** is checked.

Step 5. Notice the **20%** in the *Default Markup Percentage* field is preselected.

This field sets the default markup percentage for pass-through expenses.

Step 6. Notice that Expense Markup is selected as the *Default Markup Account*

Step 7. Click **OK** to close the window.

Now you need to associate each reimbursable expense account with an appropriate income account. You should note that for each reimbursable expense account you create, you will need to create a separate income account. You cannot have multiple reimbursable expense accounts that tie to only one income account.

Step 1. Display the *Chart of Accounts* list and select the **Reimbursable Expenses** account (See Figure 9-11).

Step 2. Select the *Edit* menu and then select **Edit Account**, select the **Account** button at the bottom of the *Chart of Accounts* window and choose **Edit Account**, or press **Ctrl+E**.

Step 3. Click **Track reimbursed expenses in Income Acct.** and then select the **Expenses Reimbursed** income account from the *Income Account* field drop-down menu.

Step 4. Click **Save & Close** to save your changes.Close the Chart of Accounts.

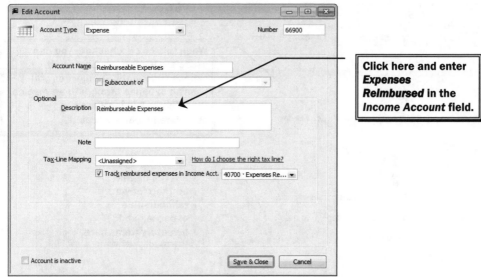

Figure 9-11 Edit the Reimbursable Expense account.

The Accounting Behind the Scenes:
Now when you post an expense to *Reimbursable Expenses* and pass the expense through on an *Invoice*, QuickBooks will increase the *Expenses Reimbursed* income account. From our previous example, the results would be as seen in Figure 9-12.

Important accounting consideration:
If you used an existing expense account in a closed accounting period (a period for which you have filed tax returns or prepared financial statements), do not select the **Track Reimbursed Expenses in Income Acct.** option on that account. Doing so will cause discrepancies between your QuickBooks reports and the company's tax returns and/or financial statements. Instead, create a new account for tracking reimbursable expenses and make the change to that account.

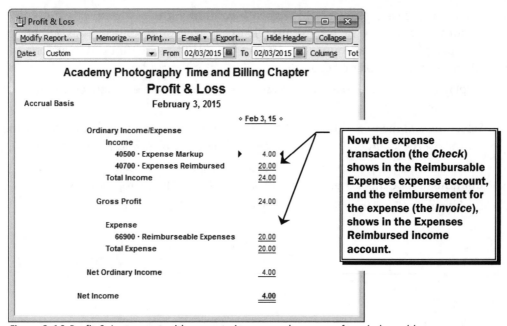

Figure 9-12 Profit & Loss report with separate income and expenses for reimbursable expenses

Using Two-Sided Items

QuickBooks allows you to use the same Item on expense forms (e.g., *Checks* and *Bills*) and sales forms (e.g., *Invoices* and *Sales Receipts*). When you use Items to track both expenses and revenue, you can generate reports showing the profitability of each Item.

> **Key Term: Two Sided Item** – An *Item* used on both types of forms (expenses and sales) is commonly called a "Two-Sided Item" because the *Item setup* screen includes purchase information on the left side (expense account field) and sales information on the right (income account field).

Possible uses of two-sided Items include:

- **Reimbursable Expenses:** If you have numerous reimbursable expenses and you need detailed reports about those expenses (such as a report showing which expenses have or have not been reimbursed), or if you want the ability to summarize Billable costs on *Invoices* by category. To summarize by category, you can create two-sided *Other Charge Items* to designate categories of expenses (e.g., transportation, clerical, or material expenses). Use these Items on both expense transactions and sales forms as on described in the *Reimbursable (Billable) Expenses* section beginning on page 267.

- **Custom Ordered Parts:** If you sell custom-ordered parts, you might want to create two-sided *Non-Inventory Part Items* to track both the purchase and the sale of each part. Doing so will show you which of the sales were profitable, and by how much.

- **Subcontracted Labor:** If you hire subcontractors, you probably want to use two-sided *Service* Items to track both the expense and the revenue for the work they perform. Then, you can find out which subcontracted services are profitable, and by how much.

- **Cost of Goods Sold Postings:** As discussed earlier, if you use the *Expenses* tab on expense transactions (*Bills*, *Checks*, *Credit Card Charges*), you can only record a pass-through expense when you code the transaction to an *Other Current Asset, Expense,* or *Other Expense* account type. If *Cost of Goods Sold* (or another account type) is the appropriate choice for your reimbursements, create a two-sided item with Cost of Goods Sold in the *Expense Account* field.

Our first example of the use of two-sided Items is for tracking custom orders. This example also shows how Cost of Goods Sold postings can be passed-through.

Tracking Custom Orders

If you sell products that you don't hold in inventory, you can use QuickBooks "two-sided Items" function to automatically track the revenue and costs for each Item.

COMPUTER PRACTICE

Step 1.   Open the *Item List* and select **New Item** from the *Item* menu (or use **Ctrl+N** to access the *New Item* window).

Step 2.   Choose **Non-inventory Part** and enter the *Custom Camera* Item as displayed in Figure 9-13. Make sure you select the checkbox next to *This item is used in assemblies or is purchased for a specific Customer:Job.*

When you select this option, QuickBooks provides the following additional fields: *Description on Purchase Transactions, Cost, Expense Account* and *Preferred Vendor.*

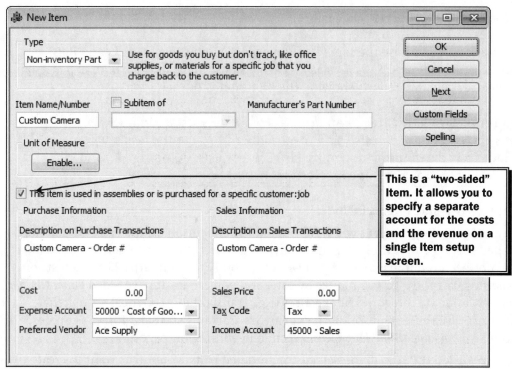

Figure 9-13 A "two-sided" Non-inventory Part Item

The Accounting Behind the Scenes:
When you use a two-sided item on expense forms, QuickBooks increases (debits) the Expense account you enter in the *Expense Account* field. When you use a two-sided item on sales forms, QuickBooks increases (credits) the Income account you enter in the *Income Account* field.

Step 3.   Notice that the *Cost* and *Sales Price* for this item are both **0.00**.

Custom-ordered parts will have a different cost and sales price every time you sell them. If you enter cost and sales price amounts in the original item, you'll need to override the numbers for each individual purchase or sale. For this reason, it's best to just leave them zero.

Step 4.   Complete the fields as shown above, and click **OK** to close this window.

Tip:
Once you set up the *Custom Camera* Item, you can use the Item for all special orders of cameras, regardless of the make or model. You can override the description of the item each time you use it on a transaction.

After creating the two-sided *Non-Inventory Part*, you are now ready to use the Item on expense forms.

Step 1.   Select the **Purchase Orders** icon on the *Vendors* section of the *Home* page, or choose **Create Purchase Orders** from the *Vendors* drop-down menu.

Step 2.   Prepare a **Purchase Order** as shown in Figure 9-14.

Notice that QuickBooks uses the default description you entered when setting up the item. Add the number in the *P.O. No.* field to the end of this description. Choose **No** when asked whether you want to update the *Custom Camera* item with a new cost.

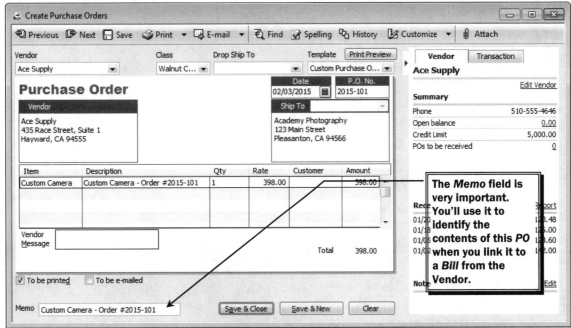

Figure 9-14 A Purchase Order for a two-sided Non-inventory Part

> **Tip:**
> Make sure you enter the description in the *Memo* field so that you'll be able to identify the *Purchase Order* in the list of *Open Purchase Orders* when you receive the *Bill*.
>
> **Tip:**
> Use the Windows copy and paste commands to duplicate the description to the Memo field at the bottom of the *Purchase Order* and other forms. To do so, highlight the completed description on the *PO* form and press **Ctrl+C**. Then click in the *Memo* field and press **Ctrl+V**.

Step 3.   Click **Save & Close** to record the *Purchase Order*.

When you receive a bill from the Vendor, record it as follows:

Step 1.   Chose the **Enter Bills** icon on the **Vendor** section of the *Home* page, or choose **Enter Bills** from the *Vendor* drop-down menu.

Step 2.   On the Bill, enter **Ace Supply** in the *Vendor* field. Then press **Tab**.

Step 3.   Because there are open *Purchase Orders* for Ace Supply, QuickBooks displays the message shown in Figure 9-15. Click **Yes**.

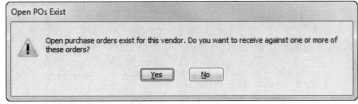

Figure 9-15 Open POs exist message

Step 4.   Select PO #2015-101 by placing a checkmark in the column to the left of the date and click **OK**.

If you had several open *Purchase Orders* for this Vendor, each would appear in the list shown in Figure 9-16.

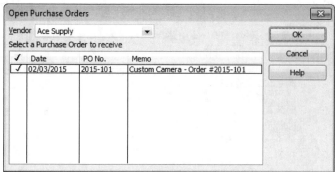

Figure 9-16 Select on open Purchase Order from the list

Step 5.   QuickBooks automatically fills out the bill with the data from your *PO* as shown in
                 Figure 9-17.

                 Continue filling out the rest of the fields on the Bill.

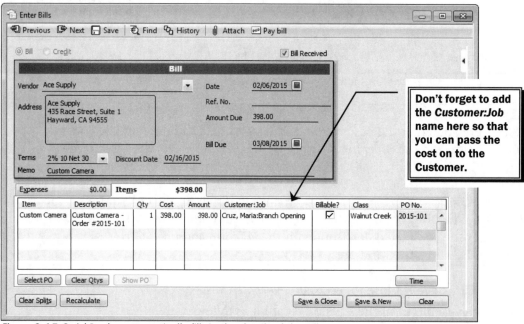

Figure 9-17 QuickBooks automatically fills in the details of the Bill.

Step 6.   Verify that **Cruz, Maria:Branch Opening Job** is in the *Customer:Job* column of the
                 Items tab.

Step 7.   Click **Save & Close** to record the *Bill*.

> **The Accounting Behind the Scenes**
> This *Bill* increases (credits) Accounts Payable and increases (debits) Cost of
> Goods Sold. Cost of Goods Sold is the account in the *Expense Account* field of the
> *Custom Camera* Item.

When you create an *Invoice* for this job, you can pass the cost of the *Custom Camera* Item
through to the customer's *Invoice* and mark it up.

Step 1.   Select the **Create Invoices** icon on the *Customer* section of the *Home* page. Use the
                 Academy Photo Service Invoice.

Step 2.   Enter **Cruz, Maria:Branch Opening** for the *Customer:Job* field.

Step 3.   Click **OK** on the *Billable Time/Costs* reminder message.

Step 4. The *Choose Billable Time and Costs* screen opens for Maria Cruz's Branch Opening Job. Choose the **Item** tab (see Figure 9-18).

Step 5. Click the far left column on the first line to select the **Custom Camera** Item (see Figure 9-18). Then click **OK**.

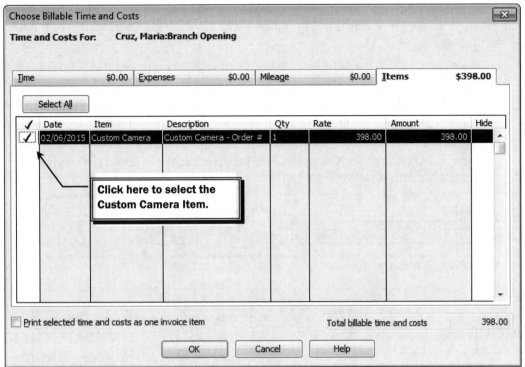

Figure 9-18 Select the Custom Camera Item.

Step 6. When you click **OK**, QuickBooks adds the Custom Camera Item to the customer's *Invoice*. Enter the *Invoice* information as seen in Figure 9-19.

Step 7. Complete the description so it reads **Custom Camera Order #2015-101** and copy this information to the *Memo* field.

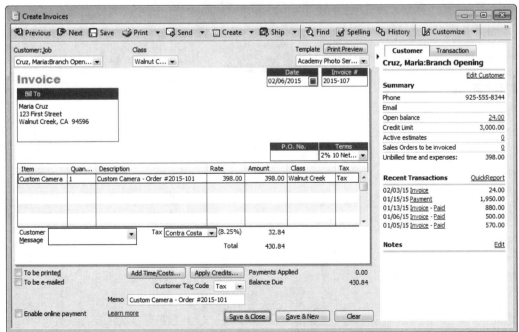

Figure 9-19 The Custom Camera Item now shows in the Customer's Invoice.

Since the Custom Camera Item shown in Figure 9-13 doesn't include an amount in the *Sales Price* field, the item passes through at the cost amount recorded on the *Bill* shown in Figure 9-17, in this case $398.00.

To record the markup you'll need to manually adjust the price that shows on the *invoice*. You can use the *QuickMath* function that allows you to do calculations without using your calculator. In this example, the Custom Camera cost was $398. Using *QuickMath*, we'll mark this item up by 20%.

Step 8.   Place the cursor in the **Rate** column on the *Invoice* (anywhere in this field).

Step 9.   Press the ***** (asterisk) key on the keyboard to access the *QuickMath* multiplication function. Since your cursor was in the rate field when you pressed the asterisk, QuickBooks copies the first number ($398) onto the adding machine tape (see Figure 9-20).

Step 10.   Enter **1.2** (multiply by 120%) and press **Tab** to insert the adjusted (calculated) amount into the *Rate* column.

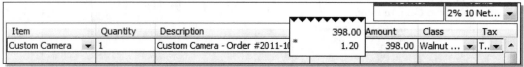

Figure 9-20 The QuickMath adding machine tape

> **Note:**
> The asterisk (*) opens the QuickMath feature because QuickBooks recognizes the asterisk as a multiplication key. You can also access QuickMath by typing a plus (+), minus (-), or back slash (/) to add, subtract or divide by any number, respectively.

Step 11.   The *Invoice* now includes the adjusted amount of **$477.60** (see Figure 9-21). Press **Tab** again to have the *Amount* and *Balance Due* fields. You may receive a *Did you know…* window, which you can read and then click **OK**.

Step 12.   Click **Save & Close** to save the *Invoice*.

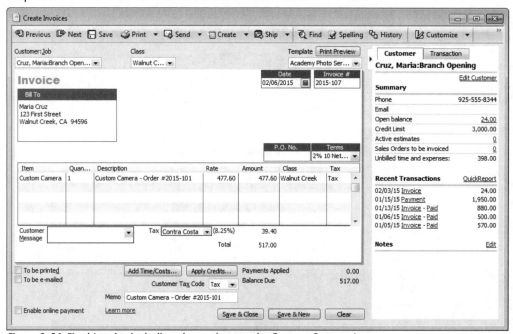

Figure 9-21 Final Invoice including the markup on the Custom Camera Item

Using Service Items to Track Subcontracted Labor

If you hire subcontractors, you may want to create a two-sided *Service Item* for each subcontracted service. This will allow you to pass subcontractor costs through to *Invoices* and it will allow you to create reports showing the profitability of your subcontracted services.

COMPUTER PRACTICE

In this example, we'll use a two-sided Service Item for photographer services that are subcontracted to East Bay Photographers. The item is already set up.

Step 1.　　　Open the *Item List* and double-click the **Photographer** Item. This will open the *Edit Item* screen for this item (see Figure 9-22).

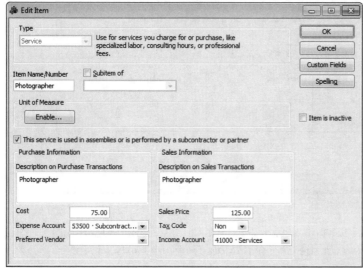

Figure 9-22 A "two-sided" Service Item for tracking subcontracted labor

Step 2.　　　Notice that the box entitled *This service is used in assemblies or is performed by a subcontractor or partner* is selected.

　　　　　　　Just as in the last example, when this box is clicked, QuickBooks opens the other side of the item revealing fields for entering the *Description on Purchase (and Sales) Transactions, Cost, Expense Account, Preferred Vendor, Sales Price, Tax Code, and Income Account.*

Step 3.　　　Click **OK** to close the *Photographer* item.

When you receive a bill from, write a *Check* to, or enter credit charges for a subcontractor, use the *Photographer* Item to record the expense.

Step 4.　　　Select the **Enter Bills** icon on the *Vendors* section of the *Home* page.

Step 5.　　　Enter a Bill for **East Bay Photographers** as shown in Figure 9-23.

　　　　　　　Select the Items tab to complete the form. The checkmark in the *Billable?* column to the right of the *Customer:Job* column indicates that each line of the *Bill* is billable (i.e., available for pass-through).

Step 6.　　　Click **Save & Close** to record the Bill.

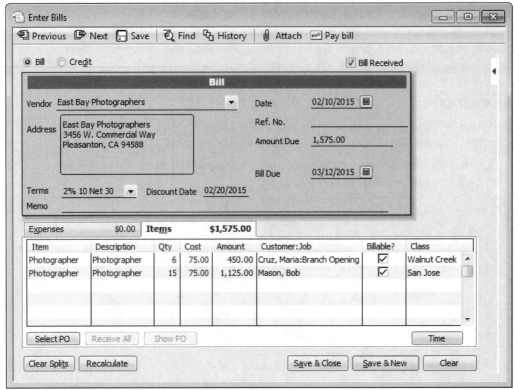

Figure 9-23 Enter a Bill for subcontracted services.

The next time you create an *Invoice* for Bob Mason or Maria Cruz's Branch Opening Job, the *Photographer Service* Item will show on the *Choose Billable Time and Costs* screen.

Step 1.   Select the **Create Invoices** icon on the *Customer* section of the *Home* page.

Step 2.   Enter **Cruz, Maria:Branch Opening** for the *Customer:Job* field.

Step 3.   Click **OK** on the *Billable Time/Costs* reminder message. The *Choose Billable Time and Costs* screen opens.

Step 4.   Click the *Items* tab. Figure 9-24 shows the *Photographer Service* Item you recorded on the bill shown in Figure 9-23. Notice that the *Rate* column shows $125.00/hour, not the purchase price of $75.00/hour. The $125.00 amount comes from the *Sales Price* field on the Item setup screen (see Figure 9-22).

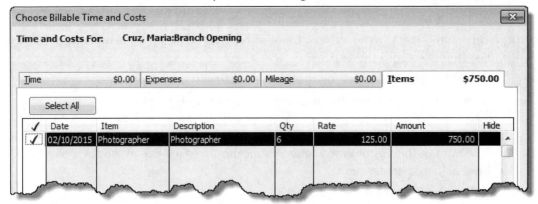

Figure 9-24 The Billable Time and Costs screen shows the two-sided Service Item.

Step 5.   Click the far left column on the first line to select the *Photographer* Item (see Figure 9-24). Then click **OK**.

QuickBooks adds the Photographer Item in the body of the *Invoice* as shown in Figure 9-25.

Step 6.   Once you are returned to the *Invoice*, verify that the **Template**, **Class**, **Date**, and **Invoice #** are the same as shown in Figure 9-25.

Step 7.   Click **Save & Close** to record the *Invoice*.

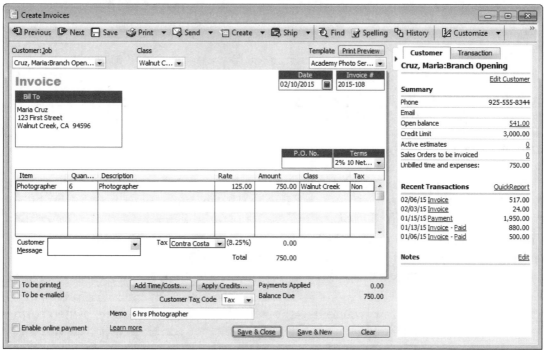

Figure 9-25 The Invoice with the subcontracted service passed-through.

> **Another Way:**
> If you want to track subcontractors' time, you can record timesheets for each subcontractor (being sure to mark the transactions as *Billable*) just as you do with your employees. You can then pass the time information through to the *Invoice* instead of passing the expense from the *Bill*. In this case, when you later enter the Vendor name in the *Bill* or *Check* window, QuickBooks will prompt you to use the time you entered in the timesheet. If you choose to do so, the payment Item will populate with the Item you entered from the timesheets. This time will come through with a non-billable status which is correct. If you choose not to pass the time through to the payment, you should still enter the *Job* name on the *Bill*, but you should mark the expense not billable by unchecking the *Billable?* option.

Unbilled Costs by Job Report

Create an *Unbilled Cost by Job* report to view all of the billable expenses and *Items* that you haven't passed through to invoices.

COMPUTER PRACTICE

Step 1.   Select the **Reports** menu, choose **Jobs, Time & Mileage,** and then choose **Unbilled Costs by Job**. Review this report.

Step 2.   Close the report.

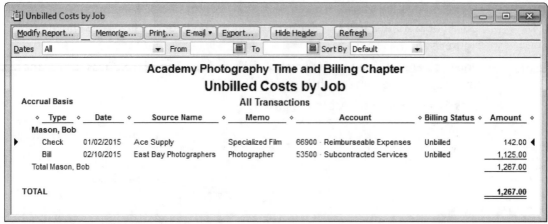

Figure 9-26 The Unbilled Costs by Job report

Billable Time

If you enter timesheet information into QuickBooks that includes a *Customer* or *Job* name, you can pass the time through to the Customer's *Invoice*. This example shows how to pass billable hours on timesheets through to *Invoices*.

The time tracking feature in QuickBooks is quite simple on the surface, but very powerful for streamlining businesses that pay hourly employees through QuickBooks Payroll, or for businesses that provide time-based services to customers. The time tracking feature requires QuickBooks Pro or above.

The time tracking feature allows you to track how much time each employee, owner, partner, or subcontractor spends working on each *Job*. In addition, you can track which service the person performs and to which *Job* and/or *Class* the time should apply. Then, once you record timesheet information, you can use it to calculate paychecks and create *Invoices* for the billable time.

When you use timesheets as the basis for paychecks and/or for invoicing, QuickBooks tracks everything required to create detailed job cost reports based on the timesheets.

Although the time tracking features in QuickBooks are quite powerful, there are also several "add-ons" (extra costs apply) to QuickBooks that provide even more features for time tracking, and their data can be synchronized with QuickBooks. For example, there are additional products that provide time clock integration, web-based time data entry, and even more flexible tracking features than you can find in QuickBooks. For a complete list of add-ons, go to http://marketplace.intuit.com, and search for time tracking.

Activating Time Tracking in QuickBooks

Before you can use the Time Tracking feature, you must activate Time Tracking in the *Company* tab of the *Time & Expense Preferences* window.

COMPUTER PRACTICE

To activate the Time Tracking feature, follow these steps:

Step 1.   Select the **Edit** menu and then select **Preferences**. Select the **Time & Expense** item on the left and click the *Company Preferences* tab (see Figure 9-27).

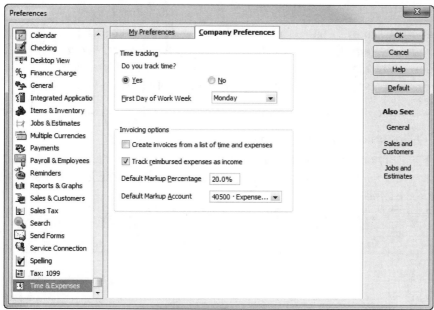

Figure 9-27 Time & Expense preferences

Step 2.   Confirm that **Yes** in the *Do you Track Time?* section is already selected.

When working with your company's data file you will need to turn on Time Tracking by clicking **Yes** either on the window shown in Figure 9-27 or in the EasyStep Interview.

Step 3.   Confirm that **Monday** is selected in the *First Day of Work Week* field. Monday is the first day that QuickBooks will display on the *Weekly Timesheet*

Step 4.   Click **OK** to close Preferences.

Entering Time on Timesheets

To track your employees' time, you'll enter *activities* on timesheets.

An *activity* is the time spent by a single person performing a single service on a single date. For example, an attorney might enter an activity on the timesheet to record a phone conversation that she will bill to one of her clients. When an hourly employee performs a service for a customer you should include the *Customer* or *Job* name in the time activity. Each activity is recorded on a separate line of the timesheet, and you can mark each time activity as Billable if you wish to pass that activity through to a customer's *Invoice*.

A *Weekly Timesheet* is a record of several activities performed during a one-week period by a single employee, owner, or subcontractor. Enter *Weekly Timesheet* information using the *Weekly Timesheet* window.

COMPUTER PRACTICE

To enter time *activities*, follow these steps:

Step 1.   Select the **Employees** menu, select **Enter Time**, and then select **Use Weekly Timesheet**.

Alternatively, you can click the **Enter Time** button in the *Employee Center*.

Step 2.   Enter *Mike Mazuki* in the *Name* field.

> **Note:**
> If you need to enter the same activities for multiple employees, you can select *Multiple Names* from the *Name* field. This will open the *Select Employee, Vendor or Other Name* window, where you can check multiple names. Any activities listed in the *Weekly Timesheet*, including billable activities, will apply to each *Employee* or other you selected.

Step 3.   Click the **Calendar icon** and choose *January 12, 2015*.

Step 4.   Enter each activity on a separate line in the timesheet as shown in Figure 9-28. Be sure to select the *Kumar* job for *Anderson Wedding Planners* and the job for Maria Cruz in the *Customer:Job* column.

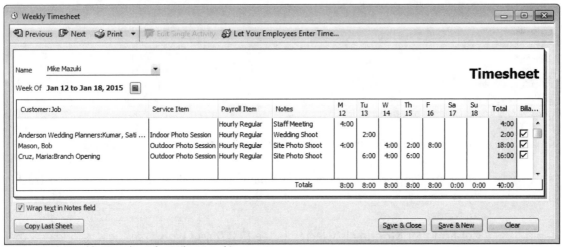

Figure 9-28 Weekly timesheet for Mike Mazuki

Step 5.   Click **Save & Close** to record the timesheet activity.

> **Note:**
> If you plan to use timesheets to create Paychecks, you should record all of the time for each employee, including non-billable time (e.g., sick, vacation, and administrative time).

Printing Timesheets

In some companies, you may need to print several copies of your employees' timesheets for review by owners or managers.

COMPUTER PRACTICE

To print timesheets, follow these steps:

Step 1.   From the *File* menu, select **Print Forms** and then select **Timesheets**.

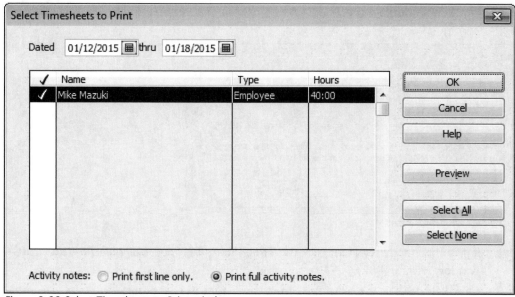

Figure 9-29 Select Timesheets to Print window

Step 2.   Set the dates to *01/12/2015* through *01/18/2015* (see Figure 9-29).

Step 3.   Select **Print full activity notes** at the bottom of the window and then click **OK** (see Figure 9-29).

Step 4.   Click **Print** on the *Print Timesheets* window (see Figure 9-30).

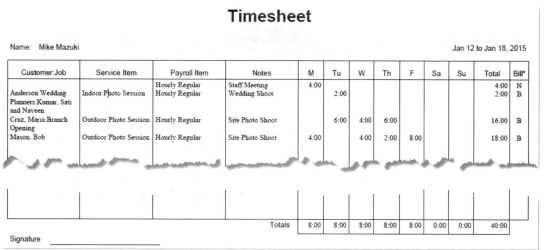

Figure 9-30 Printed timesheet for Mike Mazuki

Invoicing Customers for Time

You can also pass timesheet information through to *Invoices*. When you mark time activities as "Billable," QuickBooks allows you to transfer the time information onto the next *Invoice* for that Customer.

COMPUTER PRACTICE

To create an *Invoice* to a Customer, and pass the timesheet data onto the *Invoice*, follow these steps:

Step 1.   From the *Customer* menu, select **Create Invoices** or click **Create Invoices** on the *Home* page.

Step 2.   In the *Customer:Job* section select **Cruz, Maria:Branch Opening**.

Step 3.   QuickBooks displays the *Billable Time/Costs* window (see Figure 9-31). Click **OK** to continue.

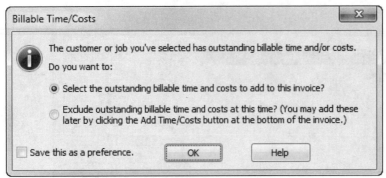

Figure 9-31 Billable Time/Cost window

Step 4.   If it is not already selected, click the **Time** tab in the *Choose Billable Time and Costs* window (Figure 9-32).

Step 5.   Click **Select All** to use all of the time activity for this Customer.

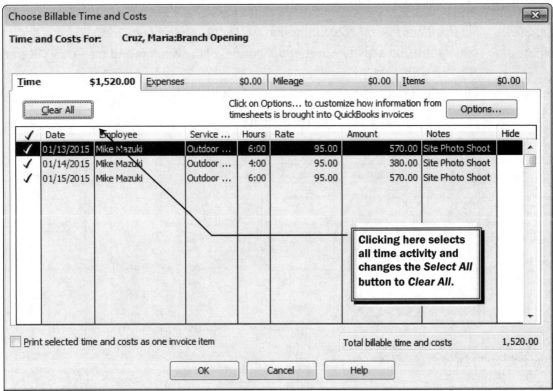

Figure 9-32 Billable time for Maria Cruz's Branch Opening job

Step 6.   Click **Options** to modify the way time activities are passed through to *Invoices*.

This window allows you to change the way time is transferred onto *Invoices*. The default setting is shown below, and you'll probably want to leave the setting alone. However, you can modify it to use either the information from the *Notes* field on the employee's timesheet or the information from the *Description* field of the Service Items. This information will show in the *Description* column of the completed *Invoice*. If you check **Combine activities with the same service item and rate,**, your *Invoices* will not show any notes from individual time records.

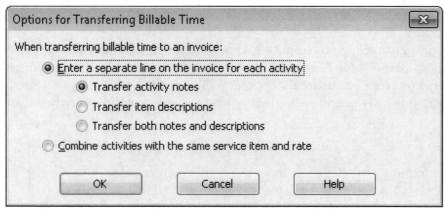

Figure 9-33 Options for Transferring Billable Time window

Step 7.   Leave *Enter a separate line on the invoice for each activity* and *Transfer activity notes* selected. Click **OK** to close the *Options for Transferring Billable Time* window. Click **OK** to close the *Choose Billable Time and Costs* window to transfer the time to the *Invoice*.

Step 8.   The *Invoice* now shows the time activity from Mike Mazuki's timesheets. Enter **Walnut Creek** in the *Class* field and 2/10/15 for the date so your *Invoice* matches Figure 9-34.

Figure 9-34 Invoice with billable time passed through

> **Note:**
> After you post timesheet information to paychecks and *Invoices*, the timesheet will affect income (because of the *Invoice*), expenses (because of the paycheck), and job cost reports (because of the job information on both the paycheck and the *Invoice*).

Step 9.   Click **Save & Close** to record the *Invoice*.

Making Activities Billable Again

After you pass time (or *Items*) through to an *Invoice*, QuickBooks removes the check in the *Billable* column in the *Choose Billable Time and Costs* window and replaces it with a small gray *Invoice* icon. If you void or delete an *Invoice* that contains billable time or items, you'll need to go back to the original time activity and click the gray icon to make the time activity billable again.

> **Note:**
> When you transfer time activities onto an *Invoice*, QuickBooks changes the billable status of the time activities to "billed." However, if you void or delete the *Invoice*, QuickBooks **does not automatically** change the status backed to "unbilled."
>
> **Tip:**
> If you have billable time, cost, or *Item* activity that you wish to clear from your unbilled reports (e.g., Unbilled Costs by Job), you can pass the time through to an *Invoice*, save the *Invoice*, and then delete the *Invoice*. This method is much faster than editing each billable item, cost, or time activity individually.

COMPUTER PRACTICE

To make time activities billable again, edit each time activity as described in the following steps. Note that usually the *Invoice* would first be cancelled, but we will not do that for this example.

Step 1.   Select the *Employees* menu, select **Enter Time**, and then select **Use Weekly Timesheet**.

Step 2.   Enter **Mike Mazuki** in the *Name* field.

Step 3.   Click the **calendar icon** and choose *01/12/2015*

Because you already passed this time through to an *Invoice*, QuickBooks replaced the *Billable?* checkmark with an *Invoice* icon on the timesheet activity for Maria Cruz's Branch Opening job (see Figure 9-35).

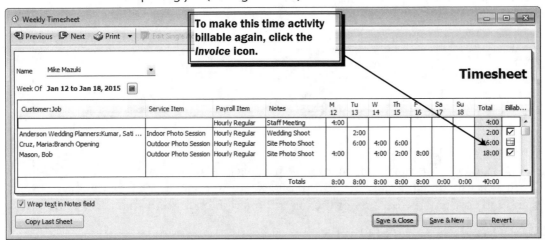

Figure 9-35 Timesheet for Mike Mazuki showing that the time for Maria Cruz's Job has been billed

Step 4.   Click the *Invoice* icon in the *Billable* column to make the time activity for the Branch Opening job billable again.

Step 5.   Click **Yes** on *Billing Status* window shown in Figure 9-36.

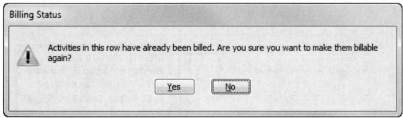

Figure 9-36 Billing Status window

Step 6. Click **Save & Close** on the *Weekly Timesheet* window to save your changes.

Time Reports

There are several reports that help you summarize and track time activities.

Time by Name Report

The *Time by Name Report* shows how many hours each employee, owner, or partner worked for each *Customer* or *Job*.

COMPUTER PRACTICE

To create the *Time by Name* report, follow these steps:

Step 1. From the *Reports* menu, select **Jobs, Time & Mileage**, and then select **Time by Name**.

Step 2. Set the date range for the report to *01/01/2015* through *01/31/2015*.

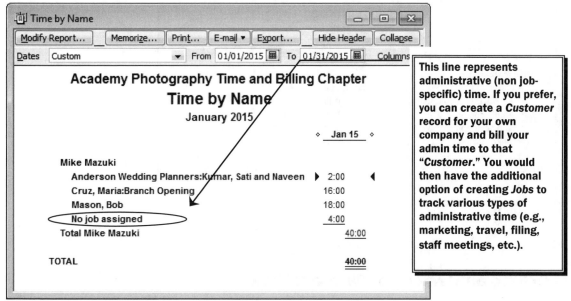

Figure 9-37 Time by Name report

Step 3. Click the **Customize Report** button in the upper left corner of the *Time by Name* report window.

Step 4. Click the checkbox next to the **Billed** and **Unbilled** options in the *Modify Report* window (see Figure 9-38). Click **OK**.

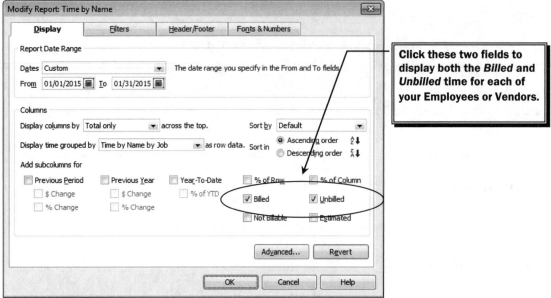

Figure 9-38 Modify the Time by Name report to include Billed and Unbilled columns.

Step 5.   The *Time by Name* report now differentiates between the **Billed** and **Unbilled** time.

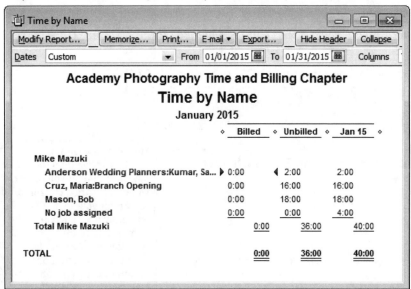

Figure 9-39 The customized Time by Name report

Step 6.   Close the report. Do not memorize it.

Tracking an Owner's or Partner's Time

In some businesses, owners and partners do not receive paychecks, but they still need to track their time activity, record the labor costs to specific Jobs, and then pass the time through to their Customers' *Invoices*.

COMPUTER PRACTICE

To track an owner or partner's time for billing purposes, follow these steps:

Step 1.   Display the *Other Names* list by selecting the **Lists** menu and then selecting **Other Names List**.

Step 2. Select **New** from the **Other Names** menu at the bottom of the *Other Names List* window.

Step 3. Create an *Other Name* record for Vern Black, the owner of Academy Photography as shown in Figure 9-40.

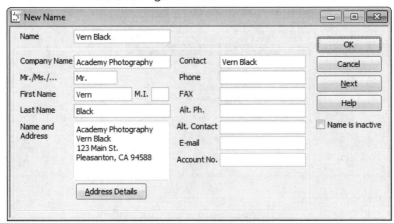

Figure 9-40 Other Name record for owner Vern Black

Step 4. Click **OK** to save Vern Black's record, and then close the *Other Names* list.

Step 5. Open the **Weekly Timesheet** window and enter the timesheet activity for Vern Black as shown in Figure 9-41.

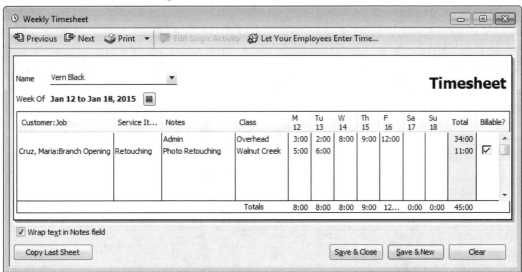

Figure 9-41 Time activity for Vern Black

Step 6. Click **Save & Close** to record the timesheet activity.

Step 7. To pass this time through to an *Invoice* for the Customer, open the *Create Invoices* window and enter the **Maria Cruz's Branch Opening Job** in the *Customer:Job* field. Click **OK** in the *Billable Time/Costs* window.

Step 8. If you need to, click the **Time** tab in the *Choose Billable Time and Costs* window (see Figure 9-42). Notice that QuickBooks shows the time for Vern Black as well as the timesheet activity for Mike Mazuki that you made billable again on the *Weekly Timesheet* window shown in Figure 9-35.

Step 9. Click **Select All** and then click **OK** to transfer the timesheet information through to the Customer's *Invoice* (see Figure 9-42).

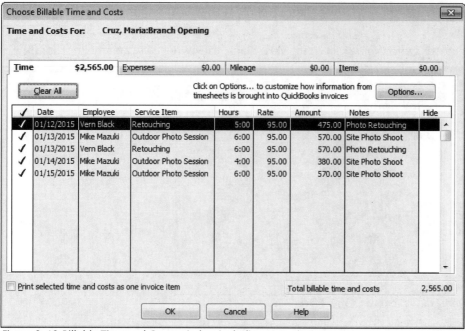

Figure 9-42 Billable Time and Costs window including owner's time

Step 10.   Enter the *Class* and *Date* information so that your *Invoice* matches Figure 9-43.

Step 11.   Click **Save & Close** to record the *Invoice*.

Step 12.   The *Recording Transaction* window displays that Maria Cruz is over her credit limit. Click **Yes**.

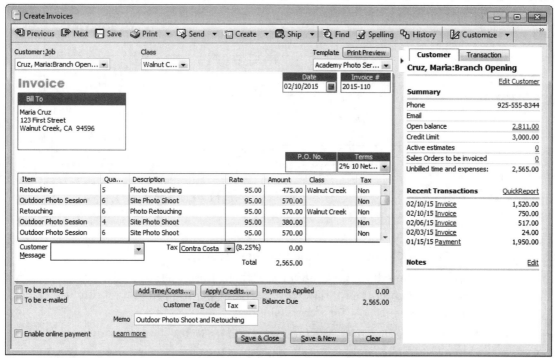

Figure 9-43 The Invoice now shows the time activity for Mike Mazuki and Vern Black.

> **Note:**
> You will not usually "pay" the owner for their time because owners generally take a "draw" (a check coded to Owner's Drawing) instead of getting paid through Payroll. Therefore, the timesheet information for Vern Black will not get recorded as labor costs on Maria Cruz's Branch Opening *Job*.

Review Questions

Select the best answer(s) for each of the following:

1. In QuickBooks you are allowed to pass through billable expenses to Customers:
    a) Only if you paid by credit card.
    b) If you paid by check or credit card, but you don't assign the Customer or Job to the expense.
    c) If you used a *Bill, Check,* or *Credit Card Charge* and assign the *Customer* or *Job* to which the expense applies.
    d) None of the above.

2. Which account types CANNOT be used in the expense tab of a purchase transaction to make the expense *Billable?*
    a) Cost of Goods Sold.
    b) Expense.
    c) Other Expense.
    d) All the above.

3. If you want to assign expenses to a *Customer:Job*, but do not want to pass them through for reimbursement, do the following in a purchase transaction:
    a) Do not assign the *Customer:Job*; just enter the information in the *Memo* field.
    b) Assign the *Customer:Job*, and then click the checkbox in the *Billable* column to remove the checkmark.
    c) Delete the *Invoice* icon.
    d) a or b.

4. Which of the following tabs appear in the *Choose Billable Time and Costs* window:
    a) Items.
    b) Expenses.
    c) Time.
    d) All of the above.

5. In an *Invoice*, you can automatically markup the pass-through expenses using the *Markup Account* option. It is available in the *Choose Billable Time and Costs* window on:
    a) Items tab.
    b) Expenses tab.
    c) Time tab.
    d) All of the above.

Time and Billing Problem 1

APPLYING YOUR KNOWLEDGE

Restore the **TimeBilling-12Problem1.QBM** file.

1. Create the following two-sided *Other Charge* Item:

Field	Data
Item Type	Other Charge
Item Name	Freight & Delivery
Option Selected	This is used in assemblies or is a reimbursable charge
Description on Purchase	Freight and Delivery Charges
Description on Sales	Freight and Delivery Charges
Cost	$20
Sale Price	$45
Expense Account	Reimbursable Expenses
Tax Code	Non
Income Account	Services

Table 9-1 Details of the Other Charge Item

2. Create the following two-sided *Non-inventory Part* Item:

Field	Data
Item Type	Non-inventory Part
Item Name	Custom Lens
Option Selected	This item is used in assemblies or is purchased for a specific Customer:Job
Description on Purchase	Custom Lens Order #
Description on Sales	Custom Lens Order #
Cost	$0
Sale Price	$0
Expense Account	Cost of Goods Sold
Tax Code	Tax
Income Account	Sales

Table 9-2 Details of the Non-inventory Part Item

3. Create a *Purchase Order* by entering the following, Total: **$2,080.00**:

Field	Data
Vendor	Ace Supply
Class	Walnut Creek

Date	4/1/15
P.O. No.	2015-101
Item	Custom Lens
Description	Custom Lens Order #2015-101
Qty	4
Rate	$520
Customer	Cruz, Maria: Branch Opening
Memo	Custom Lens Order #2015-101

Table 9-3 Details of the Purchase Order

4. A new partner, Clara Mercado, has joined Academy Photography. Open the **Other Names List** and add Clara Mercado to the list.

5. Enter a *Bill* (**Ref # A1234**) on **4/5/2015** from **Ace Supply** after receiving the custom lens order. Use the *P.O. No.* **2015-101**, *Customer:Job:* **Maria Cruz's Branch Opening**, *Class:* **Walnut Creek**, *Memo:* **Custom Lens Order #2015-101**. This Item expense is billable. Add freight charge of **$20.00** using the **Freight & Delivery** Item, *Customer:Job:* **Maria Cruz's Branch Opening** and *Class:* **Walnut Creek**. This Item expense is also *Billable*. Total: **$2,100.00**.

6. Print **Unbilled Costs by Job Report** for all transactions.

7. Using the *Academy Photo Service Invoice*, create an *Invoice* on **4/5/2015** for **Maria Cruz's Branch Opening** *Job*, *Class:* **Walnut Creek**, *Invoice #:* **2015-106**, *Description* and *Memo:* **Custom Lens order #2015-101**. Select all the open *Billable* Items for this *Job*. Use **QuickMath** to markup the Custom Lens Item by **20%**. Total **$2,746.92**. Print the **Invoice**.

8. Use the *Weekly Timesheet* to record hours from the table below for Clara Mercado from 04/20/15 through 04/26/15.

Date	Day	Hrs	Customer:Job	Service	Notes	Class	Billable
4/20/15	Mon	8.0	Anderson Wedding Planners: Wilson, Sarah and Michael	Indoor Photo Session	Photo Shoot	Walnut Creek	Yes
4/21/15	Tues	8.0	Anderson Wedding Planners: Wilson, Sarah and Michael	Indoor Photo Session	Photo Shoot	Walnut Creek	Yes
4/22/15	Wed	8.0	Perez, Jerry	Outdoor Photo Session	Photo Shoot	Walnut Creek	Yes
4/23/15	Thurs	8.0			Admin	San Jose	No
4/24/15	Fri	8.0	Miranda's Corner	Indoor Photo Session	Product Photos	San Jose	Yes

Figure 9-44 Clara Mercado's time log

9. Create a *Sales Receipt* for Anderson Wedding Planners' Wilson *Job*.

    a)   Include all of Clara Mercado's time, and post it to the *Sales Receipt*.

    b)   *Class* is **Walnut Creek**.

    c)   *Date* is **04/27/2015**.

    d)   *Sale No.* is **2015-101**.

    e)   *Check No.* is **10987**.

    f)   *Payment Method* is **Check**.

    g)   Add one (1) **Photographer** Item for **$125.00** to the *Sales Receipt*.

    h)   *Sales Receipt* total is **$1,645.00**.

10. Print the Profit and Loss by Job for April, 2015.

Chapter 10
Payroll Setup

Objectives

After completing this chapter, you should be able to:

- Set up Payroll accounts in the *Chart of Accounts* (page 300)
- Understand Payroll Items (page 301)
- Use the *Payroll Setup Interview* to add Payroll Items (page 302)
- Use the *Payroll Setup Interview* to add Employee records (page 313)
- Set up Employee Defaults (page 322)
- Run Employee Reports (page 327)

> **Restore this File**
> This chapter uses PRSetup-12.QBW. To open this file, restore the PRSetup-12.QBM file to your hard disk. See page 8 for instructions on restoring files. If you are using QuickBooks Premier Accountant, we recommend that you toggle to QuickBooks Premier General Business as described on page x.

In this chapter, you will learn how to set up QuickBooks to track your Payroll. In order to use QuickBooks to track your Payroll, you must properly set up your *Payroll Accounts*, *Payroll Items*, *Employees*, and *Opening Balances*. If you plan to process payroll manually or use an outside payroll service, you will still need to set up QuickBooks to correctly record your Payroll transactions.

You have five choices for using QuickBooks to track your Payroll:

1. **Manual Payroll.** You can prepare your own Payroll manually in QuickBooks without the use of any tax tables. This option is not recommended for most users, but it is provided if you want to manually calculate your Payroll. You may also want to prepare Payroll manually if you use an outside Payroll service other than Intuit (e.g., ADP or Paychex). With an outside Payroll service you would be required to re-enter Payroll details into QuickBooks. *This chapter uses Manual Payroll.*
2. **Basic Payroll.** You can prepare your own Payroll in-house using QuickBooks Standard Payroll. This option is recommended for users who want a cost-effective way to maintain control and flexibility of their Payroll process. Basic Payroll utilizes up-to-date tax tables that automatically calculate Employee deductions, and fills out the company's federal tax forms.
3. **Enhanced Payroll.** This option is recommended for users who need a comprehensive in-house Payroll solution that offers all the features of Standard Payroll plus additional features like state Payroll forms, workers' compensation tracking, and one-step net-to-gross calculations. Like the Basic Payroll option, Enhanced Payroll utilizes up-to-date tax tables that automatically calculate Employee deductions, and fills out the company's federal tax forms.
4. **Online Payroll.** Intuit Online Payroll offers many of the same features as Enhanced Payroll, including state Payroll forms, workers' compensation tracking, and tax tables. Because it is available online, this Payroll option doesn't require QuickBooks and can be accessed when you are away from your QuickBooks data.

5.   **Assisted Payroll.** This option is recommended for users who want all the flexibility of processing their own Payroll found in Enhanced Payroll, but would like Intuit to complete all of their tax filings, deposits, and W-2s.

For detailed information on the differences between these options, select the *Employees* menu, select **Payroll**, and then select **Learn About Payroll Options**. Intuit occasionally makes changes to their Payroll options between version releases, and there may be changes since the publication of this book.

Checklist for Setting up Payroll

Like the setup of your company file, the proper setup of your Payroll is the most important factor in getting it to work well for you. Table 10-1 provides you with a checklist for your Payroll setup. Make sure that you complete each step in the order given unless it really does not apply.

Payroll Setup Checklist

1.   Gather information about each of your employees, including the name, address, social security number, and W-4 information.

2.   Activate the Payroll function in *Preferences*.

3.   Set up Payroll Accounts in the *Chart of Accounts*. Example accounts: Gross Wages, Payroll Tax Expense, Federal PR Tax Liabilities, and State PR Tax Liabilities.

4.   Enable your QuickBooks file for Payroll processing, either manually or by signing up for one of QuickBooks Payroll services.

5.   Using the *Payroll Setup Interview*, set up Payroll Items, Payroll Vendors, Employee defaults, Employee records, and year-to-date Payroll figures.

6.   Add additional Payroll Items directly from the Payroll Item list.

7.   Edit Payroll Items to modify the Vendor information and the way the Items affect the *Chart of Accounts*.

8.   If setting up mid-year, enter year-to-date information for additional Payroll Items on the Payroll list for each Employee, and enter year-to-date liability payments.

9.   Verify Payroll Item setup, Employee setup, and the Vendor list.

10.   Proof your setup. Use the *Payroll Checkup* wizard and compare reports with your accountant's or Payroll service's reports. The *Payroll Checkup* wizard is not covered in this chapter.

Table 10-1 Payroll Setup Checklist

> **Key Term - W-4:** Form W-4 is the IRS form that each of your employees must complete when you hire them. The IRS requires employees to provide you with their name, address, social security number, and withholding information on this form. The Internal Revenue service has many payroll forms available online at **www.irs.gov**. For form W-4, enter **W4** in *Search* field.

Payroll Accounts

In your *Chart of Accounts*, confirm that you have all of the accounts you want to see on your *Balance Sheet* and *Profit and Loss Reports*. Academy Photography uses the following accounts for Payroll. These accounts are already set up in the practice file.

Example Liability Accounts for Payroll

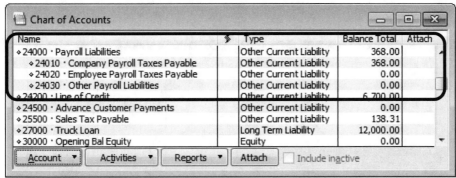

Figure 10-1 Payroll Liability Accounts

Example Expense Accounts for Payroll

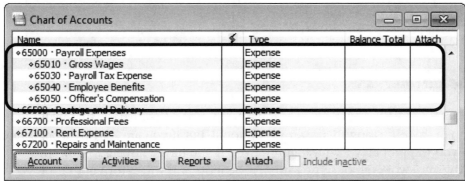

Figure 10-2 Payroll Expense Accounts

If you are not sure which accounts you should include in your *Chart of Accounts*, ask your accountant. However, you should normally have only a few subaccounts associated with the *Payroll Liabilities* account, and a few subaccounts associated with the Payroll Expenses account. Do not add unnecessary accounts and subaccounts to the *Chart of Accounts*, since the detailed tracking of Payroll comes from *Payroll Items* and not accounts.

If your *Chart of Accounts* already has too many accounts or subaccounts, you can merge some accounts until you have a manageable number of accounts.

Payroll Items

Payroll Items are used to track the compensation, additions, deductions, and other employer-paid expenses listed on the employee's paycheck. These Items include wages, commissions, tips, benefits, taxes, dues, retirement plans, and any other additions and deductions to an employee's paycheck. Like other QuickBooks Items, Payroll Items are connected to the *Chart of Accounts* so that as paychecks are created, the accounting behind the scenes is handled automatically. In addition, Payroll Items are used to accumulate Payroll Liabilities. Figure 10-3 shows the Payroll Item List after the *Payroll Setup Interview*, which is discussed beginning on page 302, has been completed.

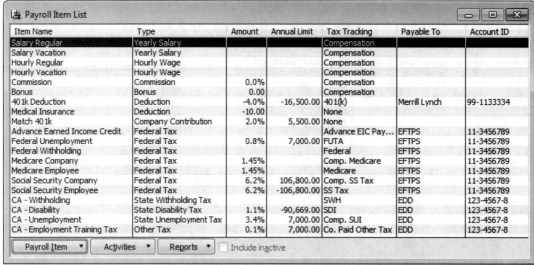

Figure 10-3 Payroll Item List

The *Payroll Setup Interview*

The *Payroll Setup Interview* is a set of windows similar to the *EasyStep Interview* that walks you through the setup of Payroll. Using this wizard is optional, but if you are starting from scratch (as shown here), you will probably find it helpful. Even if you have existing Payroll, the wizard can take the guesswork out of setting up new benefits and wages for your Employees.

COMPUTER PRACTICE

Step 1.   From the *Employees* menu, select **Payroll Setup**.

Step 2.   QuickBooks displays the *QuickBooks Payroll Setup* window shown in Figure 10-4. Click **Continue**.

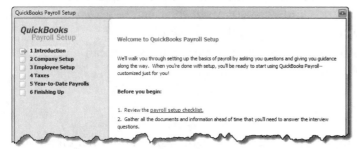

Figure 10-4 Payroll Setup Interview window

Setting up Compensation and Benefits Payroll Items

In this section of the setup wizard, you will set up compensation Items (i.e., hourly wages, salary wages, bonuses, commissions, etc.).

COMPUTER PRACTICE

Step 1.   QuickBooks displays the Compensation and Benefits section in shown in Figure 10-5. Click **Continue**.

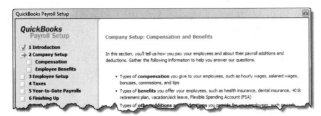

Figure 10-5 Payroll Setup Interview – Step 2 - Compensation and Benefits

Step 2.   QuickBooks displays the *Add New* window and pre-selects *Salary, Hourly wage and overtime,* and *Bonus, award, or one-time compensation* (see Figure 10-6). Select the **Commission** *Other compensation* Item and click **Next**.

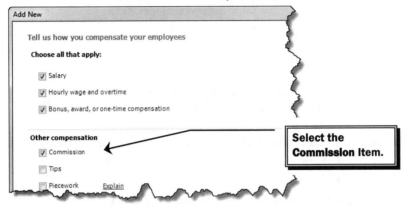

Figure 10-6 Payroll Setup Interview - Add New compensation options

Step 3.   In the next screen, QuickBooks wants to know how commissions should be calculated. Select **Percentage of sales (or other amount)** and click **Finish** (see Figure 10-7).

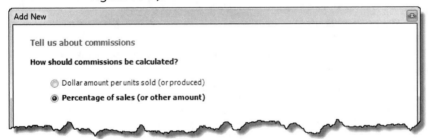

Figure 10-7 Payroll Setup Interview – commissions calculations

Step 4.   QuickBooks displays the *Compensation list* shown in Figure 10-8. At this point, we need to modify this list by editing some of the names and adding new ones.

Figure 10-8 Payroll Setup Interview – Review the Compensation list

Step 5.   To change the name of the Hourly Payroll Item to *Hourly Regular*, select **Hourly** from the *Compensation list* and click **Edit**.

Step 6.   Type ***Hourly Regular*** in the *Show on paychecks as* field (see Figure 10-9) and select **Payroll Expenses:Gross Wages** from the *Account name* drop-down list. Then click **Finish**.

Figure 10-9 Edit Hourly Pay window

Step 7.   Edit or delete the rest of the default compensation Items, renaming and editing the accounts to match the table shown in Table 10-2. Leave all other fields set to their defaults as you edit the Items.

Default Item Name	Change to this Name	Change to this Account
Double-time hourly	**Delete this Item**	**Delete this Item**
Hourly	Hourly Regular	Payroll Expenses:Gross Wages
Overtime (x1.5) hourly	**Delete this Item**	**Delete this Item**
Salary	Salary Regular	Payroll Expenses:Gross Wages
Bonus	Bonus	Payroll Expenses:Gross Wages

Table 10-2 Compensation Item Names and Accounts

Step 8.   When you're finished editing the default Payroll Items, your list will look like the one in Figure 10-10.

Compensation	Description
Hourly Regular	Hourly
Salary Regular	Salary
Bonus	Bonus
Commission	Commission

Figure 10-10 Compensation Items after renaming

Step 9.   Click **Continue** to set up Employee benefits.

Medical Insurance Deduction

Step 1.   QuickBooks displays the *Set up employee benefits* window. Click **Continue**.

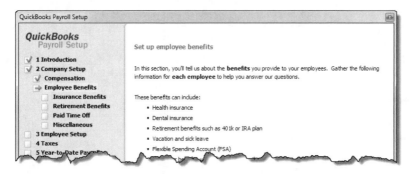

Figure 10-11 Payroll Setup Interview – Set up Employee benefits

In this section of the setup wizard, you will set up the benefits you offer (health insurance, dental insurance, retirements plans, etc.), and any other additions or deductions that affect the Employees' gross income (e.g., expense reimbursements, dues, garnishments, etc.). If your company provides benefits, there are three options for allocating the costs between the company and the Employee. First, the company could pay the entire expense; second, the company and Employee could share the expense; and third, the Employee could pay the entire expense.

If your company pays the entire expense, Payroll is usually not involved. However, there are certain circumstances when you would need to adjust the W-2s to include the benefits. Check with your tax professional.

If the costs are shared between the company and the Employees, or if the Employees pay for the entire cost via Payroll deductions, use a *Deduction Item* to track the deductions. The following method is the simplest way to handle this type of deduction in Payroll:

Now, we will resume the exercise.

COMPUTER PRACTICE

Step 1.   In the *Set up insurance benefits* page (Figure 10-12), click **Health insurance** and then click **Next.**

Figure 10-12 Set up insurance benefits page

Step 2.   Select the option for **Both the employee and company pay portions,** as shown in Figure 10-13, and then click **Next.**

Even though Academy Photography pays most of the health insurance costs, this Item will be set up to deduct a portion of the expense after taxes from paychecks. We'll have to modify it later to connect the Payroll Item to the health insurance expense account. Make sure to leave the **Payment is deducted after taxes** option selected.

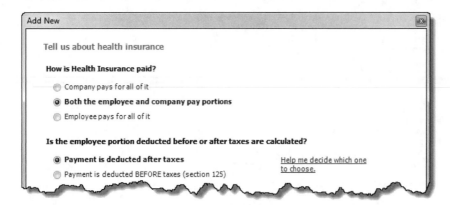

Figure 10-13 The health insurance Payroll Item setup screen

Step 3.   In Figure 10-14 the *Payroll Setup Interview* asks if you want to setup the Payee, Account #, and Payment frequency. Leave **I don't need a regular payment schedule for this item** selected and click **Finish**.

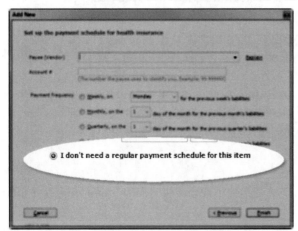

Figure 10-14 Setting up the payment schedule window

Step 4.   The *Insurance Benefits* list window displays.

Figure 10-15 Insurance Items list

Notice in Figure 10-15 that QuickBooks has added two Payroll Items. One Item, *Health Insurance (company paid),* was added to track the accruals for the employer portion of the health insurance costs, and the other Item, *Health Insurance (taxable),* to track the Employee deductions. However, for our example, the employer pays the health insurance bill by directly coding the bill to Health Insurance expense. Then, the employer deducts the Employees' portion of the health insurance costs from their paychecks. So we'll delete the *Health Insurance (company paid)* Item because we won't accrue the employer's portion of the health insurance costs through Payroll.

Step 5.   Select the *Health Insurance (company paid)* Item (see Figure 10-15), and then click **Delete**.

Step 6.   Click **Yes** on the *Delete Payroll Item* window.

Step 7.   Next, select the *Health Insurance (taxable)* Item and click **Edit** (see Figure 10-16). Change the name to **Medical Insurance** in the *Show on paychecks as* field and click **Next**.

Figure 10-16 Edit: After-Tax Employee-Paid Health window

Step 8.   Click **Next** to skip the option to edit the payment schedule and move to the next window.

Step 9.   In the *Edit After-Tax Employee-Paid Health* section, change the *Account type* to **Expense**. Ignore the warning displayed next to the *Account name* that the Account type must be a liability account, and select **Insurance Expense:Health Insurance Expense** from the *Account name* drop-down list (see Figure 10-17). Then click **Next**.

Figure 10-17 Account type and Account name window

Step 10.   Leave the defaults in the tax tracking type window and click **Next** (see Figure 10-18).

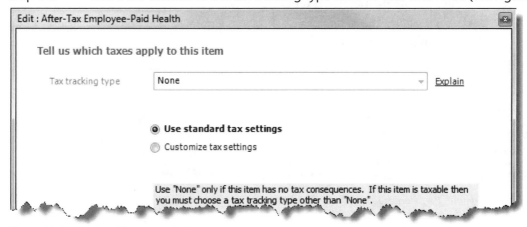

Figure 10-18 Tax tracking type window

Step 11.   Change the default rate to 100.00 and click **Finish** (see Figure 10-19).

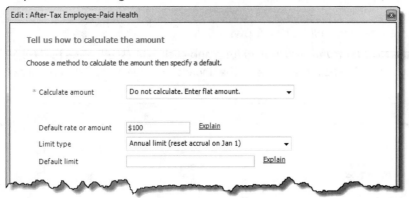

Figure 10-19 Setting the default rate

Step 12.   You will return to the *Insurance Benefits list*. Click **Continue**.

401(k) Employee Deduction and Company Match Items

If you have a 401(k) plan, you can set up Payroll Items to track the employer contributions and the Employee contributions (salary deferral) to the plan.

COMPUTER PRACTICE

Step 1.   On the *Tell us about your company retirement benefits* screen (Figure 10-20), click on the **401(k)** Item and click **Next**.

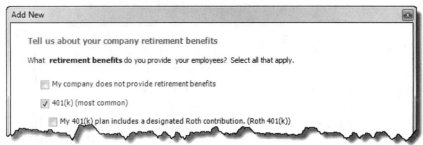

Figure 10-20 Adding the 401(k) Payroll Items

Step 2.   Click **Finish** to accept the default selection and not set up a regular payment schedule for the 401(k) at this time.

Step 3.   Next, edit each of the default Items shown in Figure 10-21. First, select the *401k Co. Match* Item and click **Edit**.

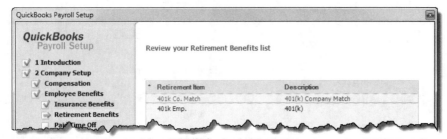

Figure 10-21 The default Item names for 401k

Step 4.   Type **Match 401k** in the *Show on paychecks as* field (see Figure 10-22). Click **Next**.

Figure 10-22 Modifying the Company Match Item name for 401k

Step 5.   Type **Merrill Lynch** in the *Payee (Vendor)* field and **99-1133334** in the *Account #* field and click **Next** (see Figure 10-23).

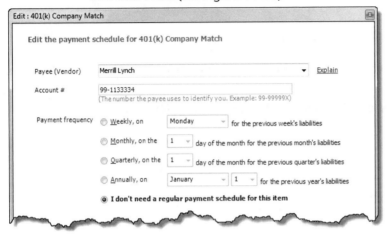

Figure 10-23 Modifying the Company Match Item Payee and Account # for 401k

Step 6.   In the *Expense account* section, select **Payroll Expenses: Employee Benefits** from the drop-down list in the *Account name* field. You may need to scroll up to find this selection. In the *Liability account* section, select **Payroll Liabilities: Other Payroll Liabilities** from the drop-down list in the *Account name* field. (See Figure 10-24.) Click **Next**.

Figure 10-24 Modifying the Expense account and Liability account information

Step 7.   On the next window, leave the **Use standard tax settings** checked and click **Next**.

Step 8.   On the *Tell us how to calculate the amount* screen, enter the information shown in Figure 10-25 and then click **Finish**.

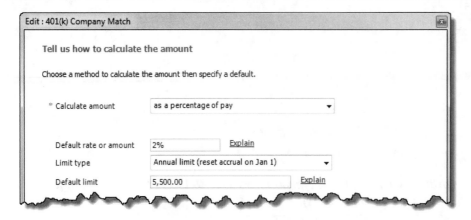

Figure 10-25 Setting the calculation method, amounts, and limit for 401(k) contribution Item

Step 9.   You will return to the <u>Retirement Benefit list</u> window. Select the **401k Emp. Item** and click **Edit**.

Step 10.   Enter the data as shown in Figure 10-26 and then click **Next**.

Figure 10-26 401(k) Deduction Item

Step 11.   Enter the data as shown in Figure 10-27 and then click **Next**.

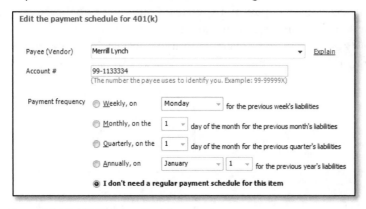

Figure 10-27 401(k) Payee and Account #

Step 12.   Enter the data as shown in Figure 10-28 and then click **Next**.

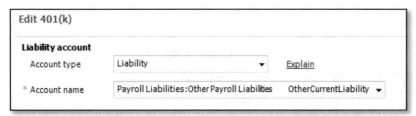

Figure 10-28 Setting the payee and account for the 401(k) Deduction Item.

Step 13.   Leave the *Use standard tax settings* checked and click **Next**.

Step 14.   Enter the data as shown in Figure 10-29 and then click **Finish**.

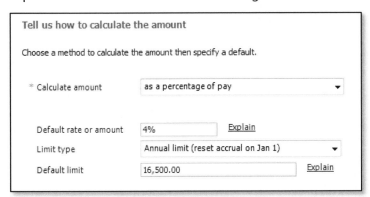

Figure 10-29 Setting the calculation method, amounts, and limit for 401(k) deduction Item

You're now finished with setting up the retirement benefits portion of your Payroll Item list. Your *Payroll Setup Interview* should now look like Figure 10-30.

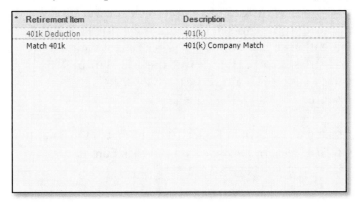

Figure 10-30 Progress in the Payroll Setup Interview.

Step 15.   Click **Continue** to proceed to the next section of the setup.

> **Note:**
> If you have 401(k) deductions for several Employees, you'll probably want to set up separate Deduction Items for each Employee. Enter the Employee's account number in the **Enter the number that identifies you to agency** field. That way, when you pay your liabilities, the voucher of the liability check lists deductions separately for each Employee. Alternatively, you could use just one Deduction Item and send a printout of your *Payroll Summary Report* with your payment to the 401(k) administrator. Filter that report to show only the *401(k) Deduction* and the *Match 401(k)* Items. You'll have to handwrite the account numbers for each Employee on the report.

Paid Time Off Payroll Items

If you pay Employees for time off, the *Payroll Setup Interview* will walk you through creating Items to track and pay vacation or sick pay.

COMPUTER PRACTICE

Step 1.   On the *Set up paid time off* screen (Figure 10-31), click on the **Paid vacation time off** Item and click **Finish**.

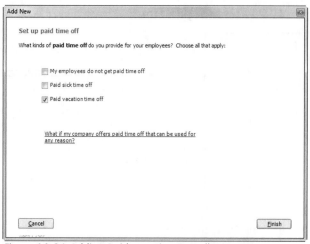

Figure 10-31 Adding Paid vacation Payroll Items

> **Note:**
> If you have a "Paid Time Off (PTO)" policy instead of separate sick and vacation
> time, you can use either Sick or Vacation time to keep track of how much PTO
> you offer your Employees. Rename it on the Payroll *Preferences* so that when it
> prints on your paychecks and pay stubs, it appears as Paid Time Off. Within
> QuickBooks, however, it continues to appear as either Sick or Vacation,
> depending on which one you choose.

Step 2.   Next, edit each of the default Items shown in Figure 10-32 to match the data shown
            in the subsequent screens. First, select *Hourly Vacation* and click **Edit**.

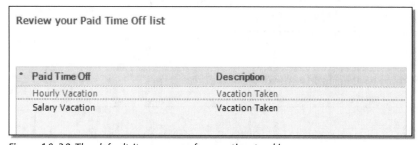

Figure 10-32 The default Item names for vacation tracking

Step 3.   Set the expense account to **Payroll Expenses:Gross Wages** as shown in Figure
            10-33. Then click **Finish**.

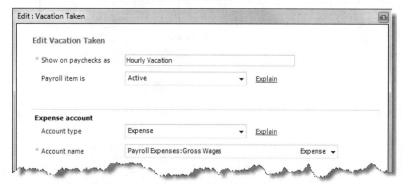

Figure 10-33 Modifying the Hourly Vacation Item

Step 4.   Next, edit the Salary Vacation Item to match the *Account* shown in Figure 10-34.
            Then click **Finish**.

Figure 10-34 Modifying the Salary Vacation Item

You're now finished with setting up the Paid Time Off portion of your Payroll Item list. Your *Payroll Setup Interview* should now look like Figure 10-35.

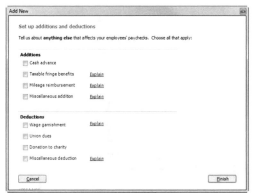

Figure 10-35 Progress in the Payroll Setup Interview.

Step 5.   Click **Continue** to proceed to the next section of the setup.

In the next section, you can set up other types of additions and deductions that are relevant to your company. The process is similar to the earlier steps and you can follow the onscreen instructions.

Figure 10-36 Other additions and deductions screen

Step 6.   Click **Finish** to skip the screen shown in Figure 10-36.

Step 7.   Click **Continue** to advance to setting up Employees.

Setting up Employees

COMPUTER PRACTICE

After you have set up your Payroll Items, the setup wizard takes you through setting up Employees.

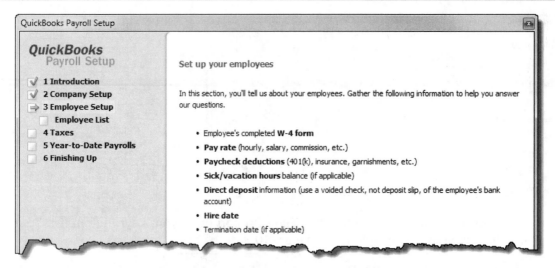

Figure 10-37 Set up Employees starting point in the Payroll Setup Interview.

Step 1.   On the *Set up Employees* window (Figure 10-37), click **Continue**.

Step 2.   Enter the information shown in Figure 10-38 and then click **Next**.

Figure 10-38 Entering Kati Reynolds' address information

> **Note:**
> QuickBooks uses the Employee name fields (first name, middle initial, then last name) to distinguish between Employees. Therefore, if two Employees have the same name, you must not use their exact names in the Employee list. If necessary, add or omit a middle initial to distinguish between different Employees with the same name.

Step 3.   In the *hiring information* window, enter the data as shown in Figure 10-39 and then click **Next**.

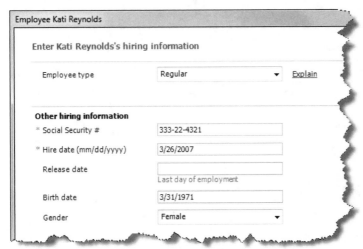

Figure 10-39 Hiring information window for Kati Reynolds

Step 4. In the *wages and compensation for Kati Reynolds* window, enter the information as shown in Figure 10-40. Then click **Next**.

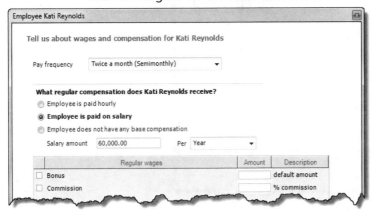

Figure 10-40 Pay frequency and compensation window for Kati Reynolds

Step 5. Select the benefit Items as shown in Figure 10-41. Then click **Next**.

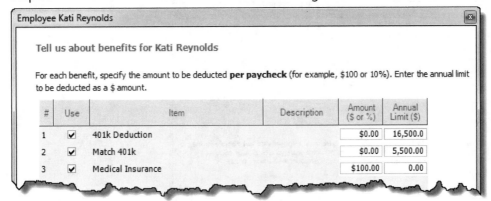

Figure 10-41 Selecting the benefits Items to add to Kati Reynolds' paychecks

Step 6. Enter the vacation time calculation method for Kati Reynolds as shown in Figure 10-42. Leave the Current balances blank. Then click **Next**.

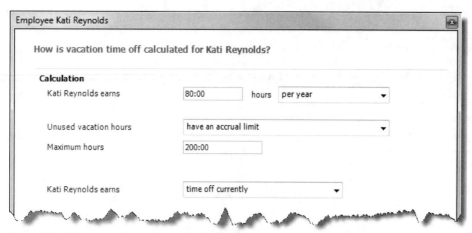

Figure 10-42 Vacation time calculation for Kati Reynolds

Step 7.   Click **Next** to skip the *direct deposit information* screen.

Step 8.   Enter the information shown in Figure 10-43 and then click **Next**.

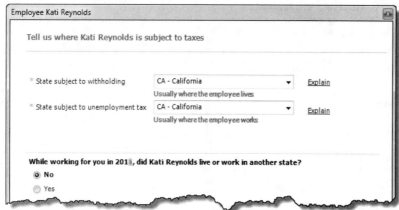

Figure 10-43 State information for Kati Reynolds

Step 9.   Enter the federal tax information as shown in Figure 10-44 and then click **Next**.

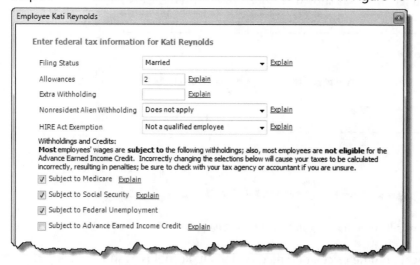

Figure 10-44 Kati Reynolds' federal tax information

Step 10.   Enter the state tax information as shown in Figure 10-45 and then click **Next**.

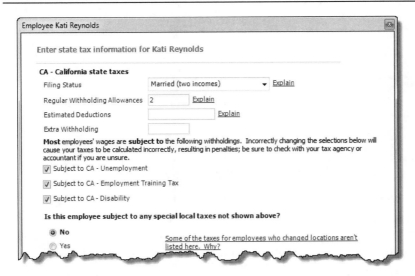

Figure 10-45 Kati Reynolds' state tax information

Step 11.   Choose S (State Plan for Both UI and DI) from the *Setup wage plan information for Kati Reynolds* as shown in Figure 10-46.

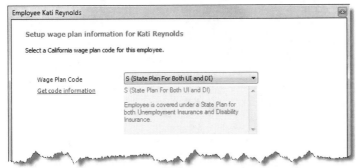

Figure 10-46 Setup wage plan information for Kati Reynolds

Step 12.   Click **Finish**.

Step 13.   You've finished setting up Kati Reynolds, your screen should look like Figure 10-47.

Figure 10-47 Progress in the Payroll Setup Interview.

Payroll Tax Item Setup

COMPUTER PRACTICE

The next section of the *Payroll Setup Interview* helps you set up the Payroll tax Items. Continue on with the *Payroll Setup Interview*, following these steps:

Step 1.   The first screen of the Payroll taxes setup is shown in Figure 10-48. Click **Continue**.

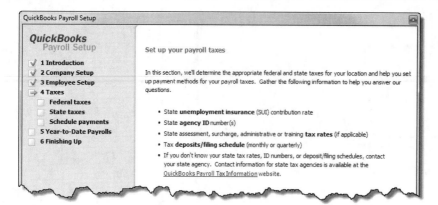

Figure 10-48 Setting up Employees completed

Step 2.   QuickBooks displays the federal Payroll tax Items that have been set up for you (see Figure 10-49). Click **Continue**.

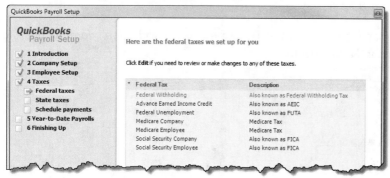

Figure 10-49 Federal Payroll tax Items

Step 3.   In the company file you are using, QuickBooks displays the *Set up state payroll taxes* window because the *Unemployment Company Rate* must be entered in manually (since we are processing Payroll manually). Enter **3.4%** in the *CA – Unemployment Company Rate* field (see Figure 10-50). Press **Tab** to accept the entry and **Finish** to move to review your state taxes.

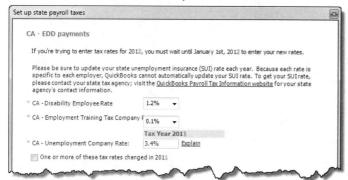

Figure 10-50 Entering in 3.4% in the California Unemployment Company Rate field – your screen may vary

Step 4.   Review the state Payroll tax Items shown in Figure 10-51. Then click **Continue**.

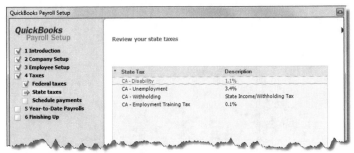

Figure 10-51 State Payroll tax Items

Scheduling Your Tax Payments

COMPUTER PRACTICE

The next section of the *Payroll Setup Interview* helps you to schedule your tax payments. Continue on with the *Payroll Setup Interview* following these steps:

Step 1.   The first screen in the Payroll taxes section is shown in Figure 10-52. This is where you set up the Vendor name for the payee on federal tax payments for Federal 940. The default Vendor name is United States Treasury. However, since you'll most likely make payments using the Electronic Federal Tax Payment System (EFTPS), the sample data file has already been set up with a vendor called EFTPS. Select **EFTPS** as the *Payee* (Vendor) you use to pay your liabilities for Federal taxes. In addition, select **Quarterly** from the drop down list in the *Deposit Frequency* field. Click **Next**.

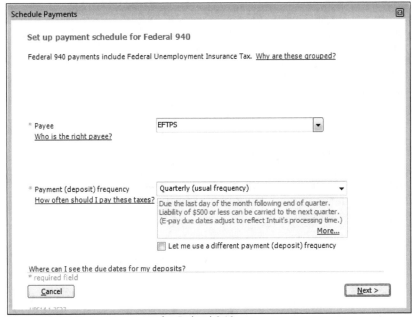

Figure 10-52 Set up payments for Federal 940

Step 2.   To set up payments for Federal 941/944, enter in the data shown in Figure 10-53 and click **Next**.

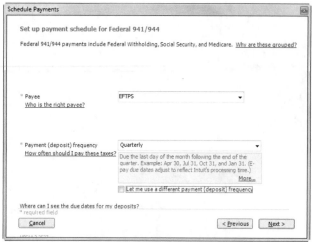

Figure 10-53 Set up payments for Federal 941/944

Step 3.   To set up payments for California Withholding and Disability Insurance, enter in the data shown in Figure 10-54 and click **Next**.

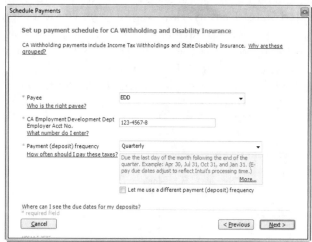

Figure 10-54 Set up payments for CA UI and Employment Training Tax

Step 4.   To set up payments for California Unemployment Insurance (UI) and Employment Training Tax, enter the data shown in Figure 10-55 and click **Finish**.

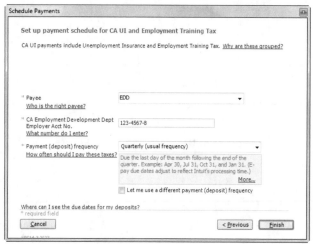

Figure 10-55 Set up payments for CA Withholding and Disability Insurance

Step 5.   QuickBooks returns you to window where you can review the list of your scheduled tax payments (see Figure 10-56). Click **Continue** to set up your year-to-date amounts.

Figure 10-56 Review your Scheduled Tax Payments list

Setting up Year-to-Date Payroll Amounts

COMPUTER PRACTICE

Step 1.   Click **Continue** on the *Enter Payroll history for the current* year window (Figure 10-57).

Figure 10-57 Entering YTD Payroll Amounts

Step 2.   On the window shown in Figure 10-58, click **No** and then click **Continue**.

If you were setting up your own Payroll in the middle of the year, you would click **Yes** on this page and then QuickBooks would lead you down a set of screens where you would set up each Employee's Payroll history for the current year. However, this example assumes that you're setting up Payroll at the beginning of the year, so click **Continue**.

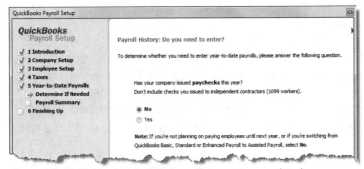

Figure 10-58 Finished with YTD Payroll Amounts completed

Finishing Up the *Payroll Setup Interview*

COMPUTER PRACTICE

Step 1.   Click **Go to Payroll Center** on the Setup is complete window (see Figure 10-59).

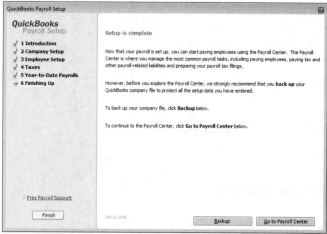

Figure 10-59 The Congratulations window

Step 2.   The *Employee Center* is shown in Figure 10-60.

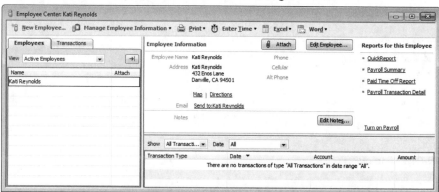

Figure 10-60 Employee Center

> **Note:**
> Because we are processing Payroll manually, the Employee Center does not display the Payroll tab. This tab displays only when Payroll is activated using a Payroll activation key.

Setting Up Employee Defaults

The *Employee Defaults* feature allows you to define defaults for your Employee records so that each time you add a new Employee, you don't have to enter the same information over and over. For example, if you pay all your Employees weekly, you can set up the defaults for weekly Payroll and that way you won't have to enter the pay period on each new Employee record. You don't have to use the *Employee Defaults*, but if you do, it will save you time and reduce the likelihood of errors.

COMPUTER PRACTICE

To set up the *Employee Defaults*, follow these steps:

Step 1.   From the *Employee Center*, select the *Manage Employee Information* drop-down and select **Change New Employee Default Settings** as shown in Figure 10-61.

> **Note:**
> Setting up *Employee Defaults* only applies to new Employees you will set up after default settings are in place.

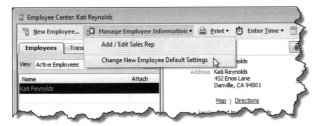

Figure 10-61 Selecting Employee Defaults from the Employee Center

Step 2.   In the *Employee Defaults* window, Select **<Add New>** from the *Payroll Schedule* drop-down list as shown in Figure 10-62.

The *Payroll Schedule* function allows you to group together Employees with the same pay frequency (i.e., weekly, bi-weekly, monthly, etc.) in order to make processing Employees with various Payroll schedules convenient and easy.

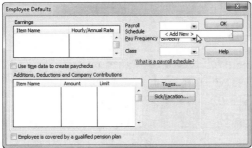

Figure 10-62 Adding a new Payroll Schedule

Step 3.   QuickBooks displays the *New Payroll Schedule* window. Complete the schedule based upon entries in Figure 10-63. Click **OK** to continue.

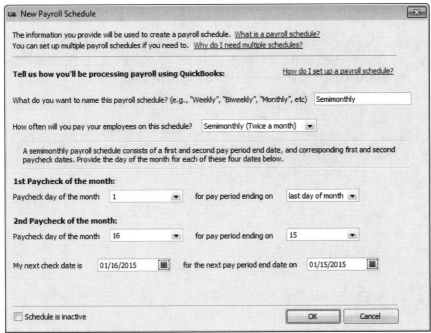

Figure 10-63 New Payroll Schedule

Step 4.   If QuickBooks displays the dialog box asking if the date is correct, click **Yes**.

Step 5.   In Figure 10-64 QuickBooks asks if you would like to assign the new schedule to all Employees with the Semimonthly pay frequency. Click **Yes**.

Figure 10-64 Assign Payroll Schedule dialog box

Step 6.   Figure 10-65 displays the number of Employees assigned to the new schedule. This information is helpful because it can alert you to assignment errors. Unfortunately, there is no way to undo global assignments. Click **OK**.

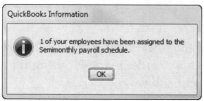

Figure 10-65 Number of Employees assigned a schedule dialog box

> **Note:**
> The Payroll Schedules list can be viewed in the *Payroll* tab of the Employee Center, which requires a Payroll subscription service from QuickBooks. In addition, Payroll Schedules cannot be deleted or modified without a Payroll subscription from QuickBooks.

Step 7.   Complete the remaining information as shown in Figure 10-66, by clicking the fields directly in the *Additions, Deletions and Company Contributions* section of the *Employee Defaults* window. Also make sure to check the box, **Use time data to create paychecks**, so that timesheet data can automatically transfer to the Employee's *Preview Paycheck* window.

Use the *Employee Defaults* window to set up the Payroll information that most of your Employees have in common. In the pay period, enter how often most Employees are paid. These are only defaults, so entering something here does not preclude you from overriding your choices for an individual Employee.

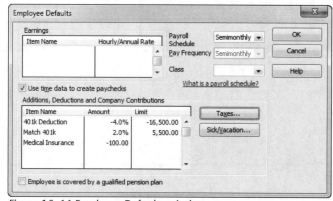

Figure 10-66 Employee Defaults window

Step 8.   Verify that your screen matches Figure 10-66, and then click **Taxes**.

Default settings for taxes

COMPUTER PRACTICE

Step 1.   In the *Taxes Defaults* window, leave the default *Federal* tax settings as shown in Figure 10-67 and click the **State** tab.

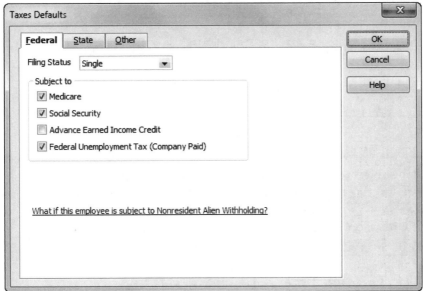

Figure 10-67 Taxes Defaults - Federal

Step 2.   On the *State* taxes default window, select **CA** from the *State* drop-down list in both the **State Worked** and **State Subject to Withholding** sections (see Figure 10-68). This window will vary depending on the states you choose. Then click the **Other** tab.

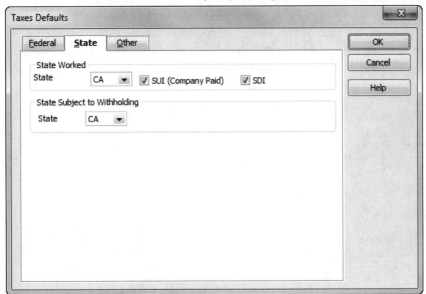

Figure 10-68 Taxes Defaults - State

Step 3.   Select **CA – Employment Training Tax** in the *Item Name* section as shown in Figure 10-69. Then click **OK**.

If your State has local taxes, the *Other* tab should include the local taxes you must withhold or accrue.

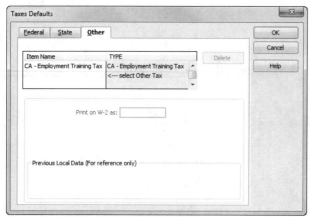

Figure 10-69 Taxes Defaults - Other

> **Note:**
> If your Employees are subject to any of the local taxes that are supported by QuickBooks, you can add those taxes here. If your local tax is not supported directly by QuickBooks, you should set up a *User Defined - Other* tax. See Payroll Taxes (Local) in the QuickBooks onscreen help for more information on these taxes.

Default Settings for Sick/Vacation Time

COMPUTER PRACTICE

Step 1.   On the *Employee Defaults* window, click **Sick/Vacation** (Figure 10-70).

This is where you choose sick and vacation time settings to match your company policies. You can choose *Beginning of year* if your policy is to give each Employee a set number of hours per year. If Employees earn sick or vacation time for each pay period, then choose *Every paycheck*. You can also choose to accrue sick and vacation based on the number of hours worked or just once per year. Select the appropriate option from the *Accrual period* drop-down list.

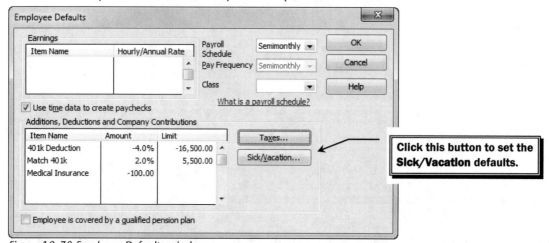

Figure 10-70 Employee Defaults window

Step 2.   Since Academy Photography only offers its Employees vacation time, we will only set up vacation defaults.

Step 3. In the *Vacation* section, select **Every paycheck** from the *Accrual period* drop-down list to indicate how often you want vacation hours accrued.

Step 4. Enter *3:00* in the *Hours accrued per paycheck* field and press **Tab**.

Step 5. Enter *200:00* in the *Maximum number of hours* field.

Step 6. Leave *Reset hours each new year?* unchecked.

Step 7. Leave *Sick and vacation hours paid* unchecked.

Step 8. Check **Overtime hours paid**.

Step 9. Verify your results match Figure 10-71. Click **OK** to save your work on this window, then click **OK** on the *Employee Defaults* window to save your changes.

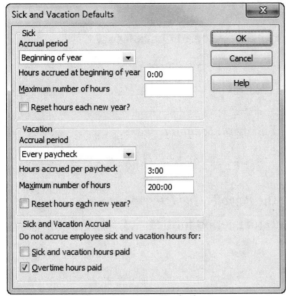

Figure 10-71 Sick and Vacation Defaults

The Employee Contact List report

You can print a list of Employees by following the steps below.

COMPUTER PRACTICE

Step 1. Select the **Reports** menu, select **List**, and then select **Employee Contact List** (see Figure 10-72).

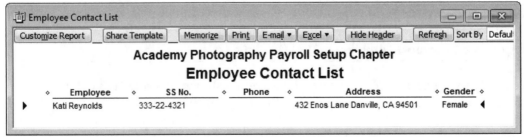

Figure 10-72 Employee Contact List

Step 2. Click **Print** at the top of the report and follow the prompts to print the report. Then, close the *Employee Contact List* report.

Review Questions

Multiple Choice

Select the best answer(s) for each of the following:

1. An easy and convenient way to process Payroll in QuickBooks for Employees on different Payroll schedules would be to:

   a) Move all Employees onto a single schedule
   b) Use the *Payroll Schedule* function in QuickBooks
   c) Outsource Payroll
   d) Make all Employees independent contractors

2. Which of the following Payroll periods is not an option in QuickBooks?

   a) Quarterly
   b) Biweekly
   c) Daily
   d) Semiannually

3. Which Payroll Item cannot be created in the *Payroll Setup Interview*:

   a) Commissions
   b) Bonus
   c) Medical Insurance Deduction
   d) You can create all Items above during the *Payroll Setup Interview*

4. Which is *not* an option when setting the accrual period for sick and vacation time?

   a) Beginning of year
   b) Every month
   c) Every paycheck
   d) Every hour on paycheck

5. The *Payroll Setup Interview* will not allow you to:

   a) Edit the default name for Payroll Items
   b) Associate deduction and withholding Items with Vendors
   c) Set the pay rate for an Employee
   d) Add two Employees with exactly the same name

Payroll Setup Problem 1

APPLYING YOUR KNOWLEDGE

> Restore the **PRSetup-11Problem1.QBM** file.

1. Verify that your *Chart of Accounts* has the accounts shown in Table 10-3 below. These accounts have already been set up for you in the problem template.

◆24000 · Payroll Liabilities	Other Current Liability
◆24010 · Company Payroll Taxes Payable	Other Current Liability
◆24020 · Employee Payroll Taxes Payable	Other Current Liability
◆24030 · Other Payroll Liabilities	Other Current Liability

◆65000 · Payroll Expenses	Expense
◆65010 · Gross Wages	Expense
◆65030 · Payroll Tax Expense	Expense
◆65040 · Employee Benefits	Expense
◆65050 · Officer's Compensation	Expense

Table 10-3 Chart of Accounts for Payroll Setup

2. Using the *Payroll Setup Interview*, add the Payroll Items shown in Table 10-4.

Item Name	Setup Notes
(a) Salary Regular	This Item should point to Gross Wages, a subaccount of the Payroll Expenses account.
(b) Hourly Regular	This Item should point to Gross Wages, a subaccount of the Payroll Expenses account.
(c) Hourly Double-time	This Item should point to Gross Wages, a subaccount of the Payroll Expenses account.
(d) Hourly Time-and-a-half	This Item should point to Gross Wages, a subaccount of the Payroll Expenses account.
(e) Commission	Add a 4% commission Item. This Item should point to Gross Wages, a subaccount of the Payroll Expenses account. Commissions are calculated based upon percentage of sales.
(f) Health Insurance	Use Health Insurance (taxable) Item to set up this Item. Leave the payee and account number fields blank. Use "Payroll Liabilities:Other Payroll Liabilities" to track the withholding. Employee pays for all of it and it is deducted after taxes at a flat rate of $50.00. Select all other defaults.
(g) 401(k) Employee	Payee is Merrill Lynch. Account number with Merrill Lynch is "99-1123456." Liability account is "Payroll Liabilities:Other Payroll Liabilities," Tax Tracking type is "401(k)," and you should use the standard tax settings. The default rate is 4% as a percentage of pay and the default limit is $16,000. This is a traditional 401(k) and not a Roth 401(k).
(h) Match 401(k)	Track this expense by Job. Payee is Merrill Lynch; Account number is "99-1123456." Expense account is "Payroll Expenses: Employee Benefits." Liability account is "Payroll Liabilities:Other Payroll Liabilities." Expense is "Payroll Expenses: Employee Benefits." Tax Tracking type is "None." Use standard tax settings. The default rate is 2% and the default limit is $5,500.00.
(i) Salary Vacation	This Item should point to Gross Wages, a subaccount of the Payroll Expenses account.
(j) Hourly Vacation	This Item should point to Gross Wages, a subaccount of the Payroll Expenses account.
(k) Salary Sick	This Item should point to Gross Wages, a subaccount of the Payroll Expenses account.
(l) Hourly Sick	This Item should point to Gross Wages, a subaccount of the Payroll Expenses account.

Table 10-4 Add these Payroll Items.

3. Set up a new Employee with the following information:

Field	Data
First Name	Casey
M.I.	
Last Name	Miller
Print on check as	Casey Miller
Employee Status	Active
Address	5990 Fog Ave. San Francisco, CA 94555
Employee Tax Type	Regular
SS No.	123-12-3123
Hire Date	7/1/2009
Release Date	
Date of Birth	04/16/1975
Gender	Female
Pay Period	Weekly
Earnings	Hourly Regular – Rate $28 per hour (leave all other fields blank)
Additions, Deductions, and Company Contributions	401(k) Employee (4%), limit $16,000.00 Match 401(k) (2%), limit $5,500.00 Health Insurance ($50)
Sick/Vacation Settings	3 hours sick time per paycheck, maximum 80 hours 3 hours vacation time per paycheck, maximum 200 hours
Employee Works and lives	Works - CA; Lives - CA; Did not live or work in another state
Federal Filing Status	Single, 0 Allowances; Nonresident Alien Withholding: Does not apply; HIRE Act Exemption: Not a qualified employee; Subject to Social Security, Federal Unemployment, Medicare
State Filing Status	CA – Filing Status Single 0 regular withholding allowances; subject to Unemployment, Employment Training tax, and Disability; not subject to any special local taxes
Wage Plan Code	S (State Plan For Both UI and DI)

Table 10-5 New Employee setup information

4. Enter the Unemployment Rate for State Payroll Taxes as shown in Table 10-6.

Item Name	Setup Notes
Payee	EDD
California Tax ID	123-4567-8
Deposit Frequency	Quarterly
State Unemployment Rate	3.4%

Table 10-6 Setup for state Payroll taxes EDD Payments

5. Select **EFTPS** as the *Payee* (Vendor) for United States Treasury Payments. You deposit your taxes quarterly. You use this to pay your liabilities for Federal taxes. Click **Continue** to skip Federal Taxes window.

6. For the State Payroll taxes, setup the *Payee, Employer Acct. No*, and *Payment Frequency* from Table 10-6 above.

7. Do not set up YTD amounts. On the *Payroll History: Do you need to enter?* screen, select **No**. Click **Go to Payroll Center** to complete the *Payroll Setup Interview*.

8. Set up your *Employee Defaults* for the following:

Field Name	Setup Notes
(a) Payroll Schedule	Weekly
(b) Additions, Deductions and Company Contributions	401(k) Employee (-4%), Maximum -16,000.00 Match 401(k) (2%), Maximum $5,500.00 Health Insurance (-$50 per paycheck)
(c) Federal Taxes	Filing Status: Single Subject to: Social Security, FUTA, Medicare
(d) State Taxes	Default State Worked: CA Default State Subject to Withholding: CA
(e) Other Taxes	CA – Employment Training Tax
(f) Sick Hours Accruals	Accrual Period: Beginning of Year Hours Accrued at Beginning of Year: 40 Maximum number of hours: 80 Reset hours each new year
(g) Vacation Hours Accruals	Accrual Period: Beginning of Year Hours Accrued at Beginning of Year: 80 Maximum number of hours: 200 Do not reset hours each new year.

Table 10-7 Employee default settings

9. Create a *Payroll Item Listing Report*. Select the **Reports** menu, then choose **List** and then choose **Payroll Item Listing**. Modify the *Report* to include the *Payable To* column and then print the report. Set the report to print on one page wide.

10. Create an Employee Contact List Report.

Chapter 11
Payroll Processing

Objectives

After completing this chapter, you should be able to:

- Use the Employee Center to view previous Payroll activity (page 334)
- Update your Payroll Tax Tables (page 335)
- Create paychecks and override default calculations (page 335)
- Edit, void, and delete paychecks (page 343)
- Pay Payroll Liabilities (page 346)
- Create Payroll reports (page 349)
- Prepare Payroll tax forms 941, 940, and W-2, as well as reports to help you prepare your state payroll tax returns (page 355)

> **Restore this File**
>
> This chapter uses PRProcessing-12.QBW. To open this file, restore the PRProcessing-12.QBM file to your hard disk. See page 8 for instructions on restoring files. If you are using QuickBooks Premier Accountant, we recommend that you toggle to QuickBooks Premier General Business as described on page x.

In this chapter, you'll learn to process your Payroll smoothly using QuickBooks Payroll.

This chapter presents the use of *QuickBooks Standard Payroll*, which helps you create your paychecks by automatically calculating the Payroll taxes on each paycheck.

The exercise file for this chapter is a sample file, a special file that will allow you to interact with the automated Payroll options without requiring a Payroll subscription. All sample files will set the current date to December 15, 2015 while using the sample file (Figure 11-1). You can identify sample files by a warning on the upper right corner of the Home page (Figure 11-2).

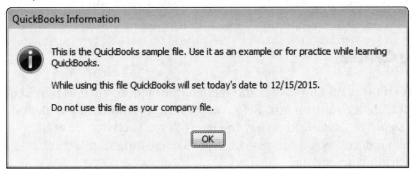

Figure 11-1 Sample File Date Warning

Figure 11-2 Sample File's Home Page

Payroll Processing Checklists

To keep your Payroll running smoothly and to minimize errors, you should complete the following steps at the prescribed intervals:

Every Payday

- Review the previous Payroll activity in the *Employee Center*.
- Verify that your tax tables are current and update them if necessary.
- Create, review, and correct (if necessary) paychecks.
- Print paychecks and pay stubs.

Every Tax Deposit Due Date (monthly or semi-weekly)

- Create, review, and correct (if necessary) liability payments.
- Print liability payment checks.

Every Quarter (after the end of the quarter)

- Verify the accuracy of all Payroll transactions for the previous quarter.
- Create Payroll reports for the previous quarter and year-to-date.
- Create Payroll tax returns (Federal Form 941 and state quarterly returns).

Every January

- Verify the accuracy of all Payroll transactions for the entire previous year.
- Create Payroll reports for the previous quarter and year-to-date.
- Create Payroll tax returns (Federal Form 941, 940, and state quarterly and yearly returns).

Using the Employee Center

The *Employee Center* displays a list of all Employees and related transactions such as paychecks, liability checks, and Payroll Liability adjustments. Before processing Payroll each pay period, it is a good idea to open the *Employee Center* and review the latest Payroll activity for each Employee. Doing so will help reduce Payroll processing errors like creating duplicate checks or processing Payroll checks with incorrect data.

To open the *Employee Center*, click the **Employees** icon on the *Icon Bar*, or the **Employees** button on the *Home* page.

Payroll Center

If you have an active QuickBooks Payroll service subscription, the *Employee Center* will contain an additional *Payroll* tab called the *Payroll Center*. You can use this window to pay Employees, pay taxes and other liabilities, and process Payroll forms (see Figure 11-3).

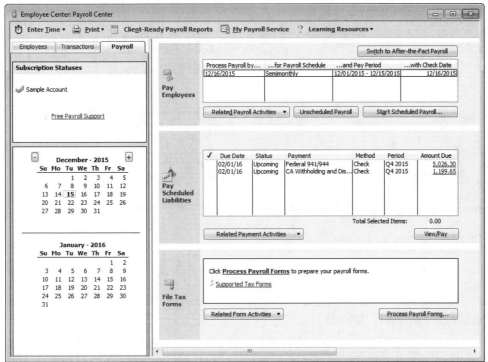

Figure 11-3 Employee Center with active subscription showing Payroll tab

Payroll Tax Tables

> **Key Term:** *Payroll Tax Tables* include the tax rates necessary to calculate an Employee's paycheck. This calculation affects the amounts of taxes that are withheld from an Employee's check (e.g., Federal and state income tax) as well as the amounts of taxes the company must pay for the Employee (e.g., Federal and state unemployment tax). The Payroll Tax Tables also include data that updates the forms that print directly from QuickBooks (i.e., 940, 941, and W-2).

In order for your paychecks to calculate automatically and your forms to print properly, you must have a current Payroll service subscription. Intuit recommends that you connect to their Web site frequently (at least every 45 days) to ensure that you're using the latest tax tables.

Paying Employees

In the previous chapter, you set up Payroll for Academy Photography. Once the Payroll setup is complete, and you have downloaded the latest tax tables (not required in the sample file for this chapter), you are ready to process Payroll.

Selecting the Employees to Pay

COMPUTER PRACTICE

Step 1.   Click **Pay Employees** on the *Home* page. The *Employee Center* opens with the *Payroll* tab selected and the *Pay Employees* section highlighted. (Figure 11-4)

Step 2.   Click the **Start Scheduled Payroll** button.

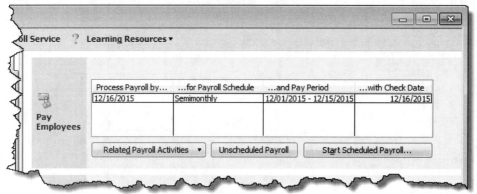

Process Payroll by...	...for Payroll Schedule	...and Pay Period	...with Check Date
12/16/2015	Semimonthly	12/01/2015 - 12/15/2015	12/16/2015

Figure 11-4 Pay Employees Section of Employee Center

Step 3.   The *Enter Payroll Information* window opens (Figure 11-5). Leave the default dates in the *Pay Period Ends* and *Check Date* fields.

The two date fields on this window are very important. The first one indicates the last day of the pay period included on the paychecks, and the second one sets the date of the actual paycheck. Make sure you always verify these dates before creating your paychecks.

> **Important:**
> The check date on paychecks determines when the Payroll expenses show on all reports. For example, if you pay Employees on the 16th of the month for wages earned during the first half of the month, the reports will show the expenses for that Payroll on the 16th.

Figure 11-5 Enter Payroll Information window

Step 4. Click the **Kati Reynolds** link in the list of Employees to open the *Preview Paycheck* window (Figure 11-6). Alternatively you can select **Kati Reynolds** and click **Open Paycheck Detail** button.

The *Preview Paycheck* window displays the automatic deductions that QuickBooks has calculated for the Payroll liabilities based on the tax tables and settings entered in the previous chapter. Kati Reynolds is a salaried Employee and therefore receives *Salary Regular* earnings.

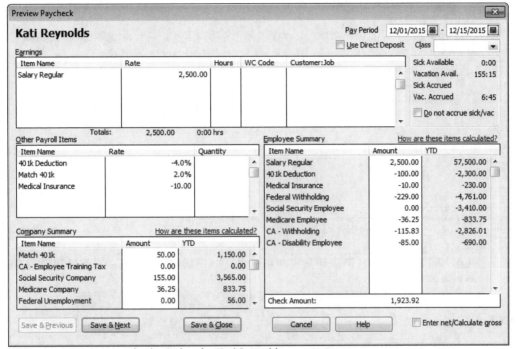

Figure 11-6 Preview paycheck window for Kati Reynolds – your screen may vary

> **Note:**
> The tax withholdings shown in Figure 11-6 may be different than what you see on your screen. Withholdings are calculated using the tax tables loaded on your computer. Some readers with different tax tables will see differences between their exercise file and the screenshots throughout this chapter.

Step 5. In the *Earnings* section, add a second line for **Salary Vacation**. Notice that the salary defaults to automatically split evenly between the two lines.

Step 6. Enter *85* in the *Hours* column for **Salary Regular** on the first line, and *3* in the *Hours* column for **Salary Vacation** on the second line (see Figure 11-7).

With salaried Employees, QuickBooks calculates the total gross pay for the period (annual rate divided by the number of pay periods) and then divides that amount equally into each of the Earnings Items listed in the *Earnings* section. To track sick and vacation hours used, enter the number of hours for each on separate lines in the *Earnings* section. QuickBooks prorates the total salary amount to each line according to the number of hours on that line.

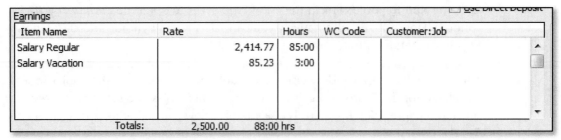

Figure 11-7 Earnings section in Preview Paycheck window

Step 7.   Confirm that **-4%** in the *Rate* column next to *401k Deduction* and **2%** in the *Rate* column next to *Match 401k* in the *Other Payroll Items* section of the *Preview Paychecks* window (Figure 11-8).

Item Name	Rate	Quantity
401k Deduction	-4.0%	
Match 401k	2.0%	
Medical Insurance	-10.00	

Figure 11-8 Other Payroll Items in Preview Paycheck window

Step 8.   Verify that your screen matches Figure 11-9 (tax items may vary). When finished click **Save & Next**.

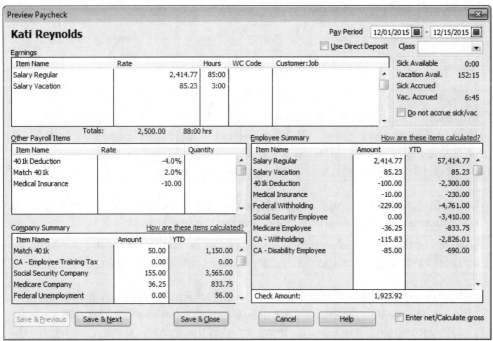

Figure 11-9 Preview Paychecks window after data entry – tax items on your screen may vary

Step 9.   The *Preview Paycheck* window of the other Employee, Mike Mazuki, opens (Figure 11-11).

Step 10.   Notice that *Earnings* section is set to *Hourly Regular* and *80* hours. The number of hours is automatically set from the previous paycheck.

> **Note:**
> If the default setting was set up to *Use Time Data to Create Paychecks* (see page 324), QuickBooks would fill the Earnings section of the paycheck with data entered in the *Weekly Timesheet*. An example is shown in Figure 11-10. You can override any of the information that was automatically copied from the timesheet. However, any changes you make here will not change the original timesheet. If you discover errors at this point, you might want to cancel out of the *Create Paycheck* window, correct the timesheet, and then recreate the paycheck.

Item Name	Rate	Hours	Customer:Job	Class	Service Item
Hourly Regular	24.00	10:00	Garrison, John:Kitchen	San Jose	Design
Hourly Regular	24.00	8:00		San Jose	
Hourly Regular	24.00	36:00	Young, Bill:Window Re...	Walnut Creek	Labor
Hourly Regular	24.00	18:00	Mason, Bob	San Jose	Design
Hourly Regular	24.00	8:00		Walnut Creek	

Figure 11-10 Example Earnings section of the Review Paycheck window including Timesheet data

Step 11.   Verify that your window matches Figure 11-11 (tax items may vary) and press the **Save & Close** button.

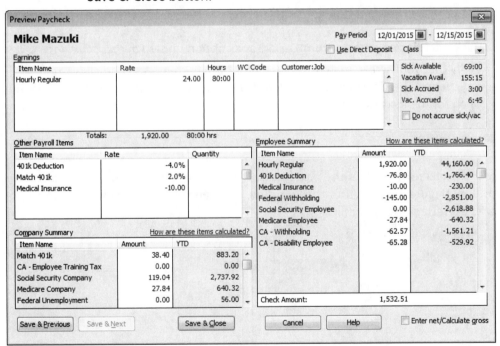

Figure 11-11 Preview Paycheck window – tax items on your screen may vary

Step 12.   Click **Continue** in the *Enter Payroll Information* window. The *Review and Create Paychecks* window appears.

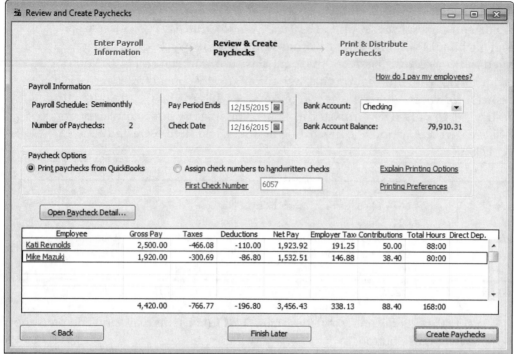

Figure 11-12 Review and Create Paychecks window

Step 13.   Click the **Print paychecks from QuickBooks** option under *Paycheck Options*.

Step 14.   Verify that your screen matches Figure 11-12 (taxes may vary) and click **Create Paychecks**. The *Confirmation and Next Steps* window appears. Leave this window open for the next exercise.

Printing Paychecks

When you're finished creating all of the paychecks, QuickBooks displays the *Confirmation and Next Steps* window (Figure 11-13). From this window, you can print paychecks or print pay stubs. The next exercise prints paychecks.

Figure 11-13 Confirmation and Next Steps window

COMPUTER PRACTICE

Step 1.   Click the Print Paychecks button on the *Confirmation and Next Steps* window.

> **Another Way:**
> If you want to print the checks after you have left the *Confirmation and Next Steps* window, select the **File** menu, select **Print Forms**, and then select **Paychecks**.

Step 2.   Enter **6057** in the *First Check Number* field (see Figure 11-14). Click **OK**.

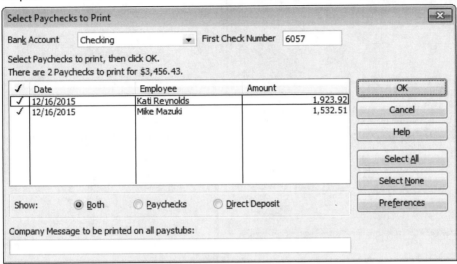

Figure 11-14 Select the paychecks to be printed.

Step 3.   In the *Print Checks* window, QuickBooks lets you know that there are two checks to print and gives the total amount of those checks (see Figure 11-15).

You can also select the check style in the *Print Checks* window. Select **Voucher** as your choice of check style. When you use voucher checks, QuickBooks prints the paystub information on the voucher portion of the checks.

> **Note:**
> For this class you'll print on blank paper instead of real checks. When you're printing on real checks, make sure to load the checks into the printer before you click **Print**.
>
> **Tip:**
> It's best to use voucher checks for Payroll. Make sure your checks are oriented correctly in the printer. With some printers, you feed the top of the page in first, and for others you feed the bottom in first. With some printers, you need to insert the check face up, and with others, you insert it face down.

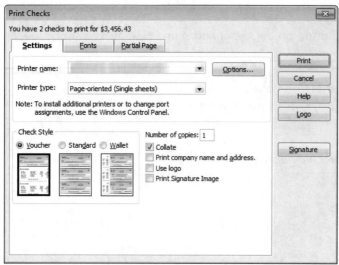

Figure 11-15 Print Checks window

The paycheck and voucher pay stubs for Mike Mazuki are shown as printed on blank paper in Figure 11-16.

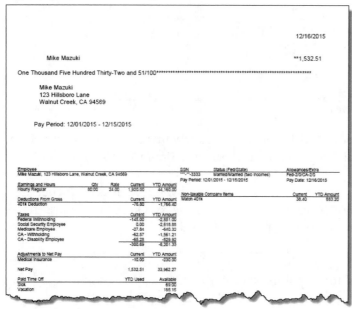

Figure 11-16 Mike Mazuki's paycheck

Step 4.   Verify the printer settings and then click **OK**. Click **OK** on the *Print Checks - Confirmation* message.

Step 5.   Click **Close** on the *Confirmation and Next Steps* window.

Printing Pay Stubs

If you don't print checks from QuickBooks, you can still print pay stubs for your Employees on blank paper.

> **Note:**
> You can print pay stubs at any time, even after you have printed the paychecks.

COMPUTER PRACTICE

Step 1.   Select the **File** menu, then select **Print Forms**, and then select **Pay Stubs** (see Figure 11-17).

Step 2.   Leave the default date of *12/14/2015* for the beginning date and *3/13/16* for the thru date for the pay stubs to print. Paychecks dated in the date range you specify will show in the list.

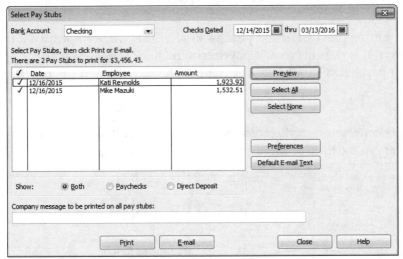

Figure 11-17 Select Pay Stubs window

Step 3.   Click **Preview** to see what the pay stubs look like when they print (see Figure 11-18). QuickBooks prints one pay stub per page.

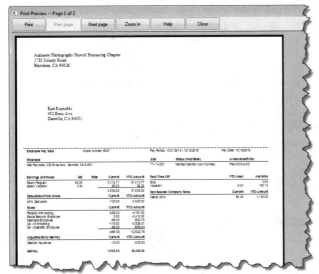

Figure 11-18 Print Preview of a pay stub

Step 4.   After previewing the pay stub, click **Close** to print the pay stubs. If you wished to print, you could print the pay stub from the preview window.

Editing Paychecks

If you find errors on paychecks, you can edit, void, or delete the paychecks. However, be careful when you do any of these actions because changing transactions may adversely affect your records. When in doubt, ask your accountant.

> **Note:**
> If you edit a paycheck that you have already printed, make sure your changes
> don't affect the net pay amount. Also, if this Employee has other paychecks
> dated after this check, the changes you make may invalidate the tax calculations
> on the newer checks. It's best to avoid editing, voiding, or deleting any paycheck
> except the most recent paycheck for each Employee. If you're unsure about any
> adjustments you need to make, check with your accountant.

It's not considered good accounting practice to edit paychecks after they've been printed and
sent to the Employee. However, it is possible to edit paychecks in QuickBooks, even after
they've been printed. Editing paychecks should only be done if you <u>haven't sent the paycheck
to the employee</u>.

COMPUTER PRACTICE

Step 1.   From the *Payroll Center*, select the **Related Payroll Activities** button. Select **Edit or
Void Paychecks** from the drop down menu.

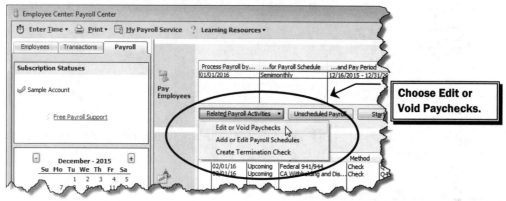

Figure 11-19 Edit Paychecks in the Payroll Center

Step 2.   Set the *Show paychecks dates from* to **12/01/2015** and the *through* date to
12/31/2015. Then press **Tab** (see Figure 11-20).

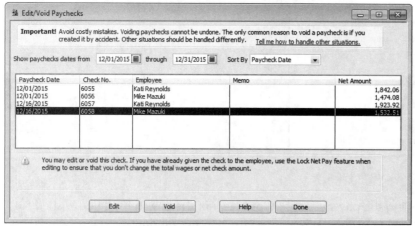

Figure 11-20 Edit/Void Paychecks window

Step 3.   Press **Tab** to leave **Paycheck Date** in the *Sort By* field.

Step 4.   Highlight **Mike Mazuki's** paycheck dated **12/16/2015** and then click **Edit** (see Figure
11-20).

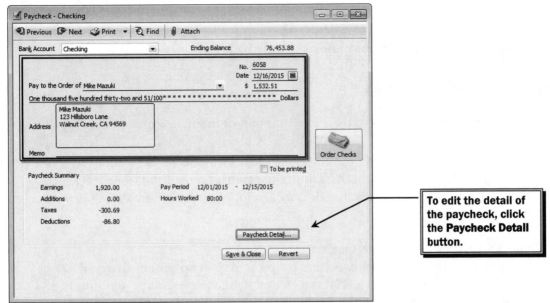

Figure 11-21 Click Paycheck Detail to edit the Items on the paycheck

Step 5.   To edit the Items on the paycheck, click **Paycheck Detail** (see Figure 11-21).

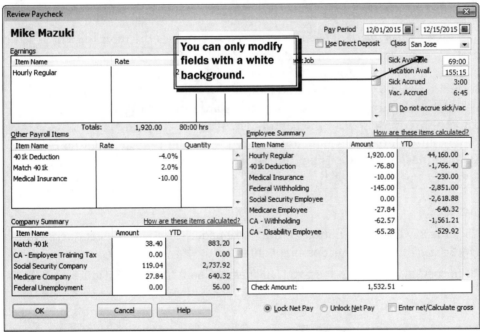

Figure 11-22 Any of the fields with a white background can be edited.

Step 6.   Change the *Class* field in the upper right corner to the **San Jose** class.

> **Note:**
> You can edit only the fields with a white background on the *Review Paycheck* window. To edit the year-to-date amounts, use the *Adjust Liabilities* window, or override the amounts on a future paycheck for this Employee.

Step 7.   Click **Cancel** and then click **Save & Close** to leave the check unchanged. Click **Done** to leave the *Edit/Void Paychecks* window.

> **Another Way:**
> You can also edit a paycheck by double-clicking on the paycheck in the checking account register and then continue from Step 5 above.

Paying Payroll Liabilities

Paying your Payroll liabilities correctly is a critical part of maintaining accurate Payroll information in QuickBooks.

When you pay the liabilities, don't use the *Write Checks* window because doing so won't affect the *Payroll Items*. It also won't show the liability payments on tax forms 940 or 941. To correctly pay your Payroll liabilities, use the *Pay Liabilities* section of the *Payroll Center* window.

> **The accounting behind the scenes:**
> You must use the *Pay Liabilities* feature to record liability payments. Payroll Liability payments decrease (debit) the Payroll liability accounts in addition to reducing the balance due for the Payroll Items. If you don't use the *Pay Liabilities* feature, QuickBooks won't track your payments in the liabilities reports or tax forms such as the 941.
>
> **Note:**
> The IRS publication, *Circular E, Employer's Tax Guide*, specifies the rules for when your Payroll taxes must be paid. Depending on the size of your Payroll, you will be either a "Monthly" depositor or a "Semi-weekly" depositor. Monthly depositors are required to pay all Payroll Liabilities by the 15th of the month following the Payroll date. Semi-weekly depositors are required to pay all Payroll liabilities by the Wednesday after the Payroll date if the Payroll date is Wednesday, Thursday, or Friday, and are required to pay all Payroll liabilities by the Friday after the Payroll date if the Payroll date is Saturday, Sunday, Monday, or Tuesday.

COMPUTER PRACTICE

Step 1.   Click the **Pay Liabilities** button on the *Home* page. The *Payroll Center* opens with the *Pay Scheduled Liabilities* section highlighted.

Step 2.   Place checkmarks next to the two Liabilities due on 02/01/2016 (Figure 11-23).

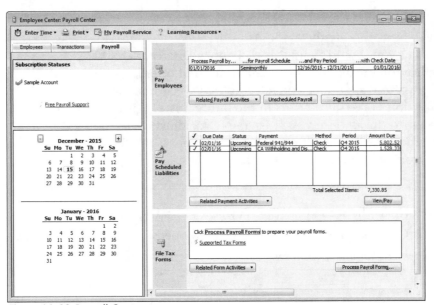

Figure 11-23 Payroll Center

Step 3.   Click the **View/Pay** button.

Step 4.   The first of two *Liability Payment – Checking* windows opens with the fields entered to pay the EFTPS for accumulated Payroll Liabilities (Figure 11-24).

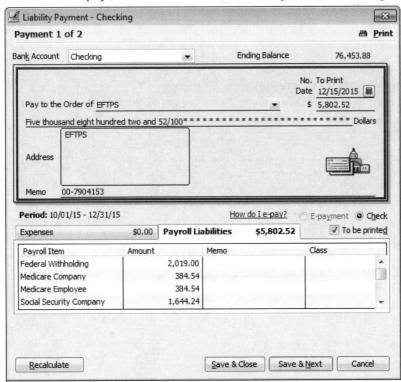

Figure 11-24 Reviewing the liability check before saving

> **Note:**
> QuickBooks allows you to modify the amounts in the *Amount* column of the *Pay Liabilities* window but you should avoid this if possible. Discrepancies here indicate incorrect Payroll calculations or misapplication of prior liability payments. These situations should be corrected at the Payroll Item or transaction level to avoid repetition of the same errors in the future. Instead, if you need to make a small change to the amount you're paying (e.g., adjust for rounding), enter an adjustment on the liability check using the **Expenses** tab. If you consistently have trouble in this area, contact your accountant or QuickBooks Pro Advisor for help.

Step 5.   Click **Save & Next**. The second *Liabilities Payment – Checking* window opens.

Step 6.   Click **Save & Close**. The *Payment Summary* window opens.

Step 7.   Close the *Payment Summary* window.

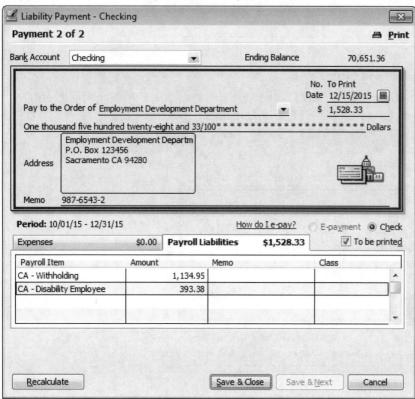

Figure 11-25 Employment Development Department Liability Payment window

> **Tip for correcting Payroll liabilities:**
> If you find an error in the amount that QuickBooks suggests you owe, it could be
> for several reasons. For example, if your state unemployment rate has changed
> in this period, the amount due may still be calculating at the old rate. In this
> case, the Payroll Item needs to be corrected and a *Liability Adjustment* could be
> made to correct the period in question. Another reason *Pay Liabilities* accruals
> may appear wrong is that prior payments were not made through *Pay Liabilities*
> or were dated incorrectly in the *Payment for Payroll liabilities through* field. In this
> case, the payments may need to be created with the improper payments voided.
> Finally, you could check each paycheck to see which one created the error.
> When you find the erroneous paycheck or paychecks, modify the Payroll Items
> on the paycheck. Of course, if you've already printed the paycheck, you should
> never make adjustments affecting net pay. Instead, use the *Adjust Liabilities*
> function, or make an adjustment on the next check for the affected Employees.

Step 8.   Display the **Checking** account register by double-clicking it in the *Chart of Accounts*
               list.

               Notice the transaction type is *LIAB CHK*, as shown in Figure 11-26 (you may have to
               scroll to see it). The *LIAB CHK* transaction is the only type of transaction that properly
               records payment of Payroll liabilities. That's because *LIAB CHK* transactions record the
               details of which Payroll liabilities *and* Payroll Items are paid by that check and the
               date they are relieved. Any other type of payment can't lower the balance due
               shown on the *Payroll Liabilities Report*.

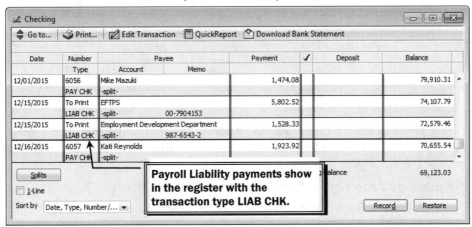

Figure 11-26 A Payroll liability payment in the Check Register

> **Note:**
> If this is the first time you record a liability payment after setting up your data
> file, there will probably be balances due for Federal and State Payroll taxes on
> your start date that do not show in the *Pay Liabilities* window.

Creating Payroll Reports

Payroll Summary Report

There are several reports that you can use to analyze your Payroll. The *Payroll Summary Report*
shows the detail of each Employee's earnings, taxes, and net pay.

COMPUTER PRACTICE

Step 1.   Select the **Reports** menu, then select **Employees & Payroll**, and then select **Payroll Summary**.

Step 2.   Leave the date range *From 10/01/2015 to 12/15/2015* and press **Tab**.

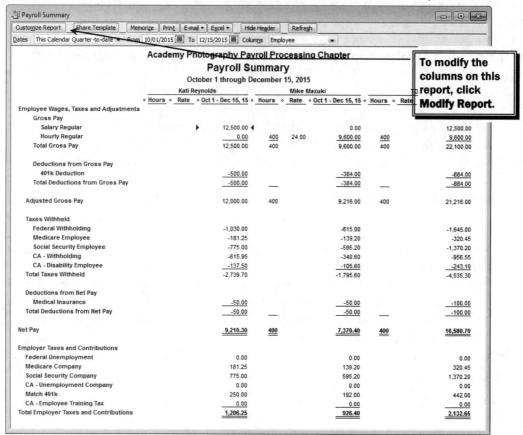

Figure 11-27 Payroll Summary Report

The *Payroll Summary Report* (see Figure 11-27) shows columns for each Employee, along with their hours and rates of pay. If you want to see more Employees on a page, you can customize this report not to show the *Hours* and *Rate* columns.

Step 3.   Click **Customize Report** at the top of the *Payroll Summary* report.

Step 4.   Clear the **Hours** and **Rate** boxes and then click **OK** (see Figure 11-28).

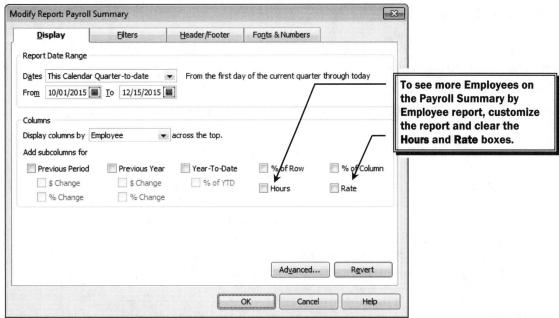

Figure 11-28 The Modify Report window

Step 5.   Your report will now look like Figure 11-29. To print the report, click **Print** (or press **Ctrl+P**).

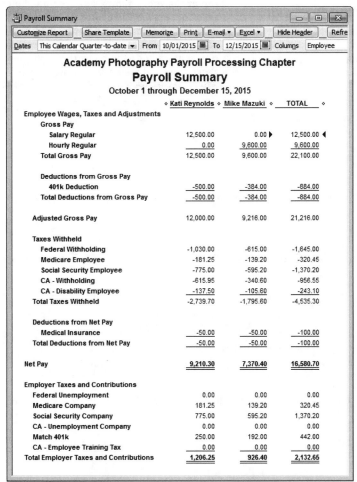

Figure 11-29 Payroll Summary Report without hours and rates

Sales Rep Commissions

If you pay commissions to your Employees, you can create a *Sales by Rep Summary* or *Sales by Rep Detail* report to help calculate the commissions due.

COMPUTER PRACTICE

Step 1.   Select the **Reports** menu, then select **Sales,** and then select **Sales by Rep Summary** (see Figure 11-30).

Step 2.   Leave the date range *From 12/01/2015 To 12/15/2015* and then press TAB.

> **Important:**
> The *Sales by Rep Summary* or *Detail* report requires you to first tag each sale with the Employee who gets credit. To set this up, modify your *Invoice* and *Sales Receipts* template to include the *Rep* field. In the *Rep* field on each sales form, make sure you enter the initials of the Employee who gets credit for the sale. The *Sales by Rep* report will show the total sales for each sales rep.

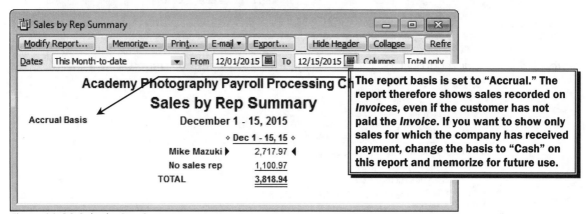

Figure 11-30 Sales by Rep Summary report

Payroll Liabilities Report

The *Payroll Liabilities Report* is used to track the status of your Payroll liabilities by Payroll Item.

COMPUTER PRACTICE

Step 1.   From the **Reports** menu, select **Employees & Payroll**, and then select **Payroll Liability Balances**.

> **Did You Know?**
> QuickBooks Payroll does not offer state forms for its Standard Payroll service. Even with the Enhanced Payroll service, not all state forms are supported. See http://www.quickbooks.com/taxforms for supported state forms.

Step 2.   Leave the *From* date to *01/01/2015* and the *To* date to *11/30/2015*. Then press **Tab** (see Figure 11-31).

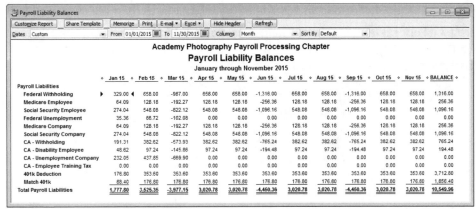

Figure 11-31 Payroll Liabilities report

> **Note:**
> The *To* date field at the top of the Payroll Liabilities report is very important. It tells QuickBooks to report on liabilities for wages paid through that date. Even if liabilities have been paid after the *To* date, the balances in the report reflect the payments. For example, even if you paid February's Federal liabilities in March, the report above would show zero balances for the Federal liabilities in the Feb 15 column (note that the number 15 refers to the year). Therefore, this report really shows your unpaid liabilities for paychecks created before the *To* date.

Step 3.   If you want to see the total unpaid balances only, select **Total only** from the *Columns* drop-down list. See Figure 11-32.

> **Tip:**
> If you are a semi-weekly depositor, select **Week** from the *Columns* drop-down list. The report will then provide a breakdown of your Payroll liabilities by week instead of by month.

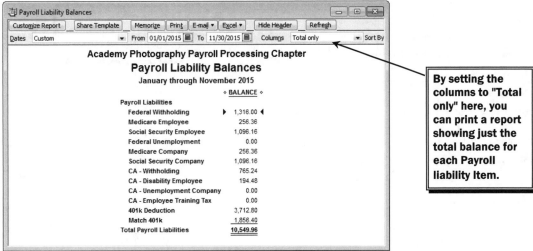

By setting the columns to "Total only" here, you can print a report showing just the total balance for each Payroll liability Item.

Figure 11-32 Payroll Liabilities report showing total unpaid accruals only

COMPUTER PRACTICE

You can filter the report to show only certain liabilities. For example, if you only want to see the Federal liabilities, follow these steps:

Step 1.   Click **Customize Report** and then click the **Filters** tab (see Figure 11-33).

Step 2.   Scroll down the *Filter* list on the left side of the window and then select **Payroll Item**.

Step 3.   Select **All Federal** from the *Payroll Item* drop-down list in the center of the window (see Figure 11-33).

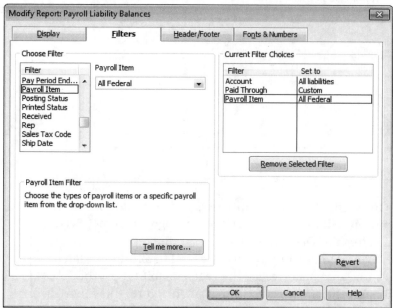

Figure 11-33 Payroll Item filter for all Federal Items

To give the report a new title to match the filtered content of the report, follow these steps:

Step 1.   Click the **Header/Footer** tab.

Step 2.   Enter *Federal Payroll Liability* in the *Report Title* field and then click **OK** (see Figure 11-34).

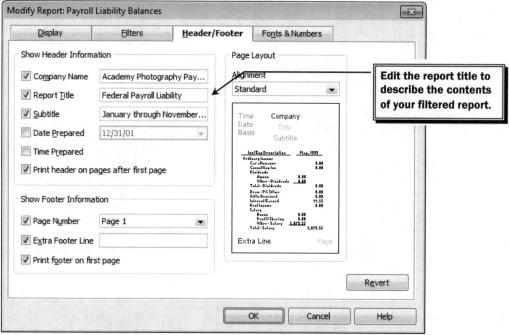

Figure 11-34 The Report Title field allows you to enter a new title

Step 3.   Verify that the *Columns* field shows **Total only**.

Step 4.   Close the report.

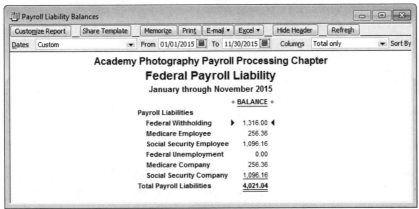

Figure 11-35 Custom Report called "Federal Payroll Liabilities."

Preparing Payroll Taxes

Paying Payroll taxes is an important part of Payroll processing. In the following section, examples are shown for processing Form 941, Form 940, and W-2s as well as local and state Payroll taxes. The following examples use the sample file used in the Payroll Processing chapter.

> **Tip:**
> If you signed up for one of the QuickBooks Payroll Services, upgrade your tax tables before processing Forms 941, 940, or W-2s. Any necessary changes to the forms may be included in the most recent tax tables. You will not need to update your tax tables to complete the exercises in the sample file.
>
> **Tip:**
> Be sure to use the *Pay Liabilities* window to create your tax payments prior to creating your Quarterly and Annual Payroll Forms. The 941 will use these payments for the *Deposits made* calculation. The 940 form computes your Federal Unemployment Tax based on the 940 contributions, your State Unemployment liabilities, and payments made throughout the year (if applicable). All of the Payroll tax forms calculate automatically using the information on paychecks and Payroll Liability payments.

Processing Form 941 and Schedule B

To prepare the Federal quarterly Payroll tax return (Form 941), follow these steps:

> **DON'T PERFORM THESE STEPS NOW. THEY ARE FOR REFERENCE ONLY.**

1. From the *Home* page, select the **Process Payroll Forms** icon.
2. In the *Select Form Type* window, the **Federal form** radio button is already selected. If we were subscribed to the QuickBooks Enhanced Payroll service, the **State form** radio button would be available as well (see Figure 11-36). Click **OK**.

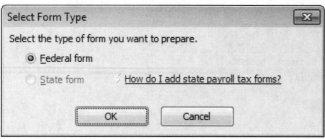

Figure 11-36 Select Form Type window

3.   Select **Quarterly Form 941/Sch. B – Employer's Quarterly Federal Tax Return** in the *Choose a form you want to use:* section of the *Select Payroll Form* window (see Figure 11-37).

4.   Select **Last Calendar Quarter** in the *Select Filing Period* section and set the **Quarter Ending** date to the desired date. Click **OK**.

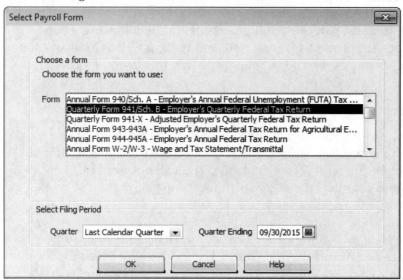

Figure 11-37 Select Payroll Form window

5.   A *Warning* window appears prompting you to download the most recent tax tables. Click **OK**.

6.   QuickBooks opens the *Payroll Tax Form* window titled *Interview for your Form 941/Schedule B* (see Figure 11-38).

7.   Read the entire instructions and check the boxes that refer to your own company. Click **Next** when finished.

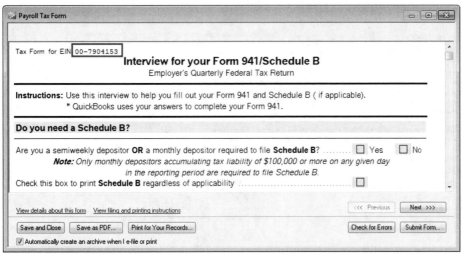

Figure 11-38 Payroll Tax Form

> **Note:**
> Normally companies with large tax obligations use Schedule B to report their tax liability on a more frequent basis. To determine if your company needs to file a Schedule B, consult your accountant or *Circular E, the Employer's Tax Guide*, (available on the IRS website at www.irs.gov).

8. QuickBook displays Form 941 (see Figure 11-39). Most of the data on the form was taken from your QuickBooks file. You can override some fields by right-clicking on them (such as the name and address fields). When finished, click the **Next** button at the bottom of the window.

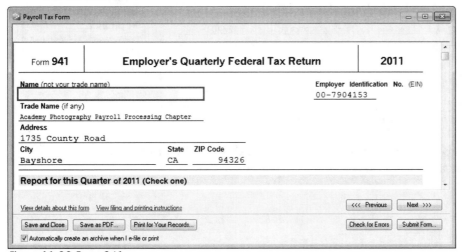

Figure 11-39 Form 941

> **Note:**
> Observant readers will notice that the Form 941 in Figure 11-40 is for the tax year 2011, while the data is from the the tax year 2015. Forms for the tax year 2015 were unavailable at the time of this writing.

9. *Page 2* is displayed (see Figure 11-40). Verify that your information is correct and click **Next** at the bottom of the screen.

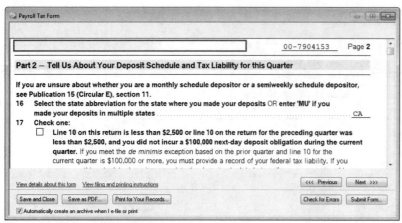

Figure 11-40 Payroll Tax Form, Page 2

10.   Figure 11-41 shows the filing and printing instructions for Form 941. From this screen, you can submit the form, print, or save as a PDF using the buttons at the bottom of the screen. Click **Save and Close**.

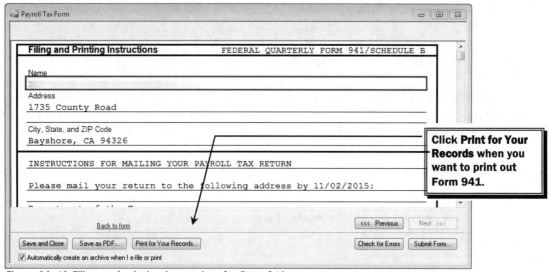

Figure 11-41 Filing and printing instructions for Form 941

11.   The *Next* Steps window appears (see Figure 11-42). Read the information in the *Next Steps* window and click **OK**.

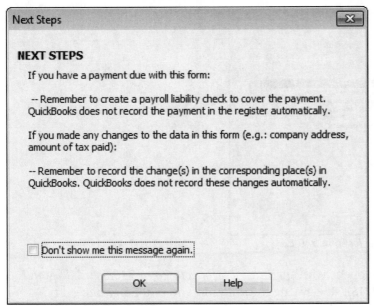

Figure 11-42 Next Steps window

QuickBooks saves your Form 941 and Schedule B as drafts. To review the tax forms again, repeat Steps 1 through 5 and click the **Open Draft** button in the *Saved Draft* window when it appears (see Figure 11-43).

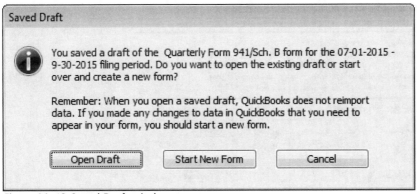

Figure 11-43 Saved Draft window

Processing Form 940

QuickBooks prepares Form 940 which is used to report the annual FUTA tax. The process for creating Form 940 is nearly the same as for Form 941. The IRS requires that you pay Form 940 taxes separately than the Form 941 taxes. You'll also print Form 940 on blank paper suitable for filing with the IRS.

DON'T PERFORM THESE STEPS NOW. THEY ARE FOR REFERENCE ONLY.

1. From the *Home* page select **Process Payroll Forms**.
2. The **Federal form** radio button is already selected. Click **OK**.
3. Select **Annual Form 940/Sch. A – Employer's Annual Federal Unemployment (FUTA) Tax Return** in the *Choose a form you want to use:* section of the *Select Payroll Form* window (see Figure 11-44). Enter the correct year in the *Year* box and click **OK**.

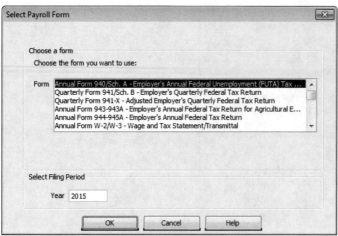

Figure 11-44 Select Payroll Form window for Form 940-EZ

4.   A *Payroll Tax Form* window opens with the *Interview for your Form 940/Schedule A and 940-V* displayed (Figure 11-45). Review the information and enter any necessary changes. Click **Next** to advance through the next screens, reviewing the information entered by QuickBooks.

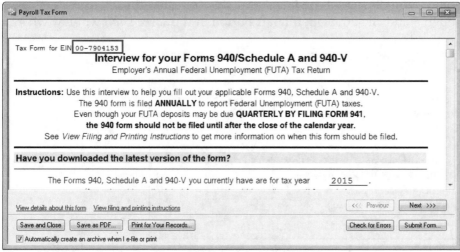

Figure 11-45 Interview for your Form 940/Schedule A and 940-V

5.   After reviewing, you can submit the form, save for PDF or print for your records. Click **Save and Close**. Click **OK** when the *Next Steps* window appears.

Processing W-2s

DON'T PERFORM THESE STEPS NOW. THEY ARE FOR REFERENCE ONLY.

1.   From the *Home* page, select **Process Payroll Forms**.

2.   The **Federal form** radio button is already selected. Click **OK**.

3.   QuickBooks displays the window shown in Figure 11-46. Select **Annual Form W-2/W-3 – Wage Tax Statement**.

4.   Select **All Employees** from the *Process W-2s for* field.

5.   Enter the correct year in the *Year* box and click **OK**.

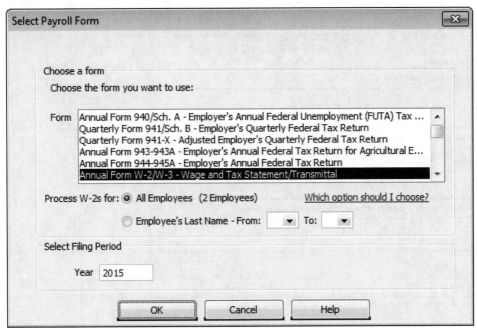

Figure 11-46 Select Payroll Form window

6. QuickBooks displays the *Select Employees for W-2/W-3* window, as shown in Figure 11-47. Select **Review/Edit** to review the W-2s.

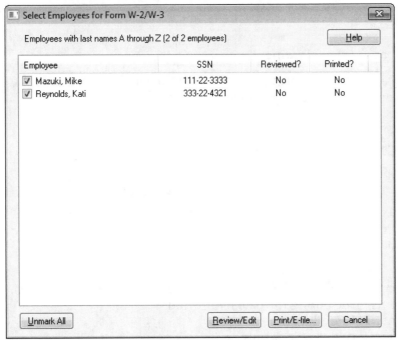

Figure 11-47 Select Employees for Form W-2/W-3 window

> **Note:**
> In order for W-2s to print properly, make sure you've entered the full name and address of each Employee, and that you've properly set up the year-to-date information on your Payroll Setup date. Also, you must enter all paychecks in QuickBooks Payroll in order for the W-2s to be correct.

7. QuickBooks displays *Forms W-2 and W-3 Interview* steps in the *Payroll Tax Form* window (see Figure 11-48). Click **Next** and review the following screens.

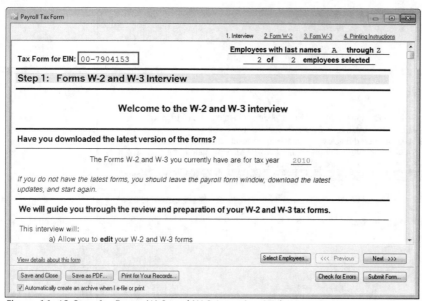

Figure 11-48 Step 1 - Forms W-2 and W-3 Interview Welcome screen

8. In the final screen you are given the option to submit, save as a PDF, or print. Click **Save and Close**.

9. Click **OK** when the *Next Steps* window appears.

Review Questions

Select the best answer(s) for each of the following:

1. To properly affect the Payroll Items, which function (from the *Employee* section of the *Home* page) should you use to pay the Payroll taxes?
    a) *Write Checks*
    b) *Pay Bills*
    c) *Pay Employees*
    d) *Pay Liabilities*

2. Voucher style checks, when used for processing Payroll, may contain:
    a) Earnings and tax withholdings
    b) Adjustments to earnings
    c) Federal filing status
    d) All of the above

3. The Payroll Liability Balances Report identifies:
    a) Liability payments made during the payment period
    b) Liability amounts by Payroll Item
    c) Liabilities for Employee deductions only
    d) Liabilities for employer taxes only

4. The Payroll tax return that reports Social Security, Medicare, and Federal Income Tax is submitted quarterly on:
    a) Form 940
    b) Form 941
    c) Form W-2
    d) *Payroll Liabilities Report*

5. To begin processing your Payroll:

a) Select **Write Checks** from the *Home* page
b) Select the *Employees* menu and then select **Pay Scheduled Liabilities**
c) Select the *Payroll* menu and then select **Process Payroll**
d) Choose **Pay Employees** from the *Employees* section of the *Home* page

Payroll Processing Problem 1

APPLYING YOUR KNOWLEDGE

Restore the **PRProcessing-11Problem1.QBM** file.

1. Process paychecks for both Kati Reynolds and Mike Mazuki with the information shown below. Create printable paychecks, dated 01/01/2016 drawn on the Checking bank account for the Payroll period ending on 12/31/2015.

Kati Reynolds' paycheck

Field	Data
Check Date	*01/01/2016*
Pay Period	*12/16/2015 through 12/31/2015*
Earnings	*Salary Regular, 64 hours*
	Salary Vacation, 16 hours
Other Payroll Items (Deductions)	*401k Employee, -4%*
	Match 401k, 2%
	Medical Insurance,-$10

Table 11-1 Kati Reynolds's paycheck

Mike Mazuki's paycheck

Field	Data
Check Date	*01/01/2016*
Pay Period	*12/16/2015 through 12/31/2015*
Earnings	*72 hours – Hourly Regular*
	8 hours – Hourly Vacation
Other Payroll Items (Deductions)	*401k Employee, -4%*
	Match 401k, 2%
	Medical Insurance,-$10

Table 11-2 Mike Mazuki's paycheck

2. Print both paychecks on blank paper. Use voucher checks for the format of the printed checks. Assign the checks to number 6059 and 6060.

3. On 1/4/2016, pay all liabilities due on 02/01/2016. Print the Payroll liability checks on blank paper, beginning with check number 6061.

4. Print a *Payroll Summary Report* for 10/01/2015 through 01/01/2016. Do not show the *Hours* or *Rate*.

5. Print a *Payroll Liability Balances Report* for 9/1/2015 through 01/01/2016.

Chapter 12 Company File Setup and Maintenance

Objectives

After completing this chapter, you should be able to:
- Perform a complete company file setup using the 12-Step process (page 365)
- Choose a start date (page 365)
- Use the *EasyStep Interview* to set up your company file (page 366)
- Set up accounts in the *Chart of Accounts* List (page 377)
- Gather your information for setting up opening balances (page 388)
- Enter opening balances (page 391)
- Enter year-to-date income and expenses (page 398)
- Adjust the opening balance for Sales Tax Payable (page 399)
- Adjust inventory for physical quantities on hand (page 401)
- Verify your opening balances (page 402)
- Close opening balance equity into retained earnings (page 403)
- Back up the file and set the closing date (page 405)
- Set up Users and Passwords (page 405)

In this chapter, you will learn how to create a new QuickBooks data file, set up the Chart of Accounts, and enter opening balances. You will also learn how to set up user access rights and passwords for each person who will use QuickBooks.

Complete Company File Setup: A 12-Step Process

In this section, you will learn about the 12-Step setup process for completing your QuickBooks file setup.

Choosing a Start Date – Step 1

Before you create your company file, choose a start date for your company file. Your start date is the day before you start using QuickBooks to track your daily transactions. You will need complete information for your opening balances as of this start date.

The 12-Step Setup Checklist

1. Choose a QuickBooks **start date**. See page 365.
2. Create a new QuickBooks **company file**. See page 366.
3. Edit your **Chart of Accounts** and set up other company Lists. See page 377.
4. Enter opening balances for **Balance Sheet** accounts (except Accounts Receivable, Accounts Payable, Inventory, Sales Tax Payable, and Retained Earnings). See page 388.
5. Enter outstanding transactions including **Checks**, **Deposits**, open **Invoices**, and unpaid **Bills** as of the start date. See page 395.
6. If you are setting up in mid-year, enter your **year-to-date income** and **expenses**. See page 398.
7. Adjust **Sales Tax Payable**. See page 399.
8. Adjust **Inventory** to match your physical counts, and set up **Fixed Assets**. See page 401.
9. Set up **Payroll Lists** and **year-to-date** (YTD) **payroll** information. See page 402.
10. Verify that your **Trial Balance** report matches your accountant's trial balance on your **start date**. See page 402.
11. Close the **Opening Bal Equity** account into Retained Earnings. See page 403.
12. Set the **Closing Date** and the **Closing Date Password** to lock the file as of your start date, set up **Users** and **Passwords**, and backup your company file. See page 405.

Table 12-1 The 12-Step Setup Checklist

Assuming you file taxes on a calendar-year basis, the best start date for most companies is December 31. If you file taxes on a fiscal year, choose the last day of your fiscal year as your start date.

Do not use January 1 (or the first day of your fiscal year) for your start date, because doing so would cause the opening balances to affect your first year's *Profit & Loss Report*. This could affect your taxes and distort the picture of the company's financial history.

Keep in mind that you will need to enter all of the transactions (checks, invoices, deposits, etc.) between your start date and the day you perform the QuickBooks setup. Because of this, your start date has a big impact on how much work you will do during setup. If you do not want to go back to the end of last year, choose a more recent date, such as the end of last quarter or the end of last month.

> **Note:**
> In order for your records to be complete and accurate, you should enter every transaction (check, invoice, deposits etc.) that your company performed between the start date and the day you perform the QuickBooks setup. For example, if you are setting up the file on January 5 with a start date of December 31, you will need to enter all transactions that the company performed on January 1 through January 5 for your records to be complete and accurate.

If you are starting a new business, your start date is the day you formed the company.

Creating the File – Step 2

There are two ways to create a file, through the *Express Start* and the *Advanced Setup*. In the following section, we will show you how to create a file using both methods. *Express Setup* creates a file with minimal entries and a default set of *Preferences*. Only users who are familiar with QuickBooks *Preferences* and the impact of creating a QuickBooks file without a start date should use *Express Start*. *Advanced Setup* allows you to set up a number of *Preferences*, as well as set the start date for a company.

Express Start

When you first create a new file, you are given the option of choosing *Express Start* or *Advanced Setup*, as well as several other options such as converting a file from another format, for example Quicken or Peachtree (see Figure 12-1).

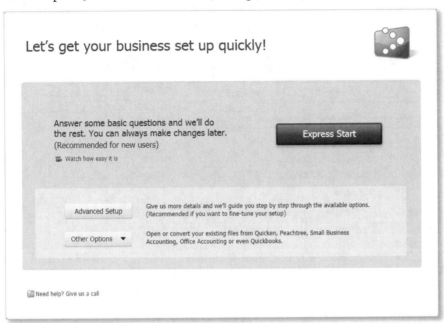

Figure 12-1 New File window

If you choose *Express Start*, you only need to enter your Company and Contact information before creating a file. Once the file is created you can enter *Customers*, *Vendors*, *Employees*, *Items*, and *Bank Accounts*, then start using the file. QuickBooks chooses default *Accounts* and *Preferences* for you based on the *Industry* you select (see Figure 12-2).

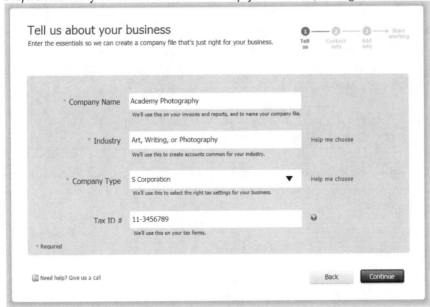

Figure 12-2 Express Start Tell us about your business screen

Advanced Setup

The *Advanced Setup*, also called the *EasyStep Interview*, allows you to enter your Company and Contact information as in the Express Start, however, it also ask you to customize some of the most common preferences and set a start date.

COMPUTER PRACTICE

Step 1.   Select the **File** menu and then select **New Company**.

Step 2.   A new file window appears. Click **Advanced Setup** to launch the *EasyStep Interview* (see Figure 12-1).

Step 3.   The *EasyStep Interview* window appears. Enter the information in the Company information screen as shown in Figure 12-3. Click **Next** when done.

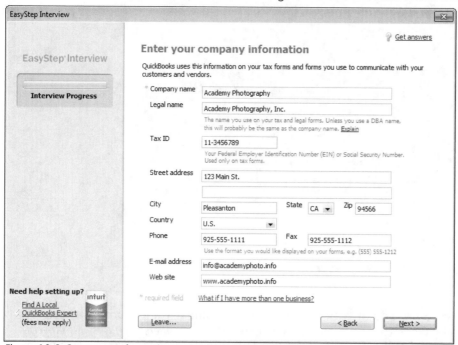

Figure 12-3 Company Information in EasyStep Interview

> **Note:**
> As you answer questions in the *EasyStep Interview*, QuickBooks creates your file, *Lists*, and *Preferences*. To proceed to the next step in the process click **Next**. To go back to a previous window in the interview, click **Back**. To exit the Interview and retain all changes, click **Leave**....
>
> To make changes to the company information after you have completed the *EasyStep Interview*, select **Company Info** from the *Company* menu.

Step 4.   Select **Art, Writing, or Photography** from the list of industry types. QuickBooks uses the industry information to suggest the appropriate income and expense accounts later in the *EasyStep Interview*. Press **Next** when finished.

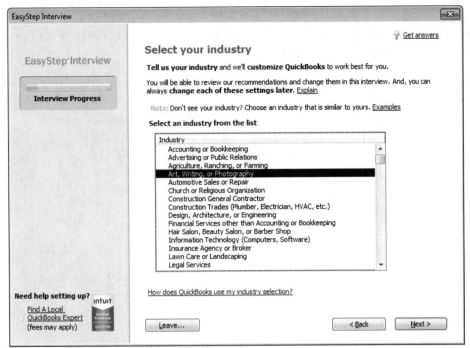

Figure 12-4 Select your industry in EasyStep Interview

> **Tip:**
> *QuickBooks ProAdvisors* are bookkeepers, accountants, software consultants, and CPAs who offer QuickBooks-related consulting services. In addition, *QuickBooks Certified ProAdvisors* are those *ProAdvisors* who have completed a comprehensive training and testing program. For more information on QuickBooks *ProAdvisors* and *Certified ProAdvisors*, refer to QuickBooks in-product Help.

Step 5.   The *How is your company organized?* window appears. Select the **S Corporation** radio button and press **Next**.

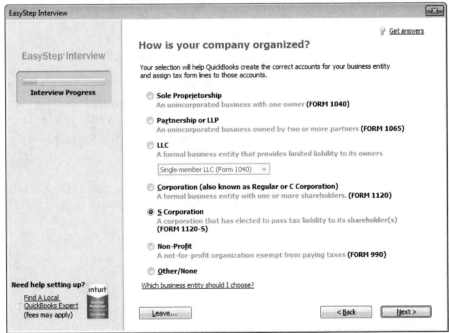

Figure 12-5 How your company is organized window in the EasyStep Interview

Step 6.   The next window prompts the user to select the first month of the company's fiscal year. This should be the first month of the company's tax year. Leave **January** selected and press the **Next** button.

This field indicates the beginning of the year for year-to-date reports, such as the *Profit & Loss* report.

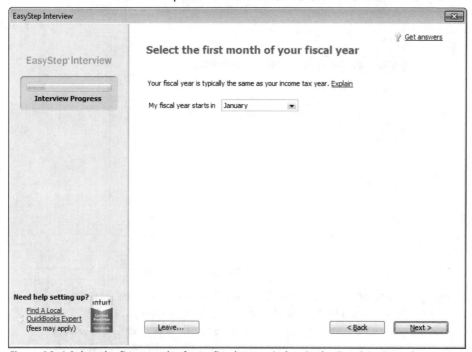

Figure 12-6 Select the first month of your fiscal year window in the EasyStep Interview

> **Note for new businesses:**
> The first month of your fiscal or income tax year is **NOT** necessarily the month you started your business. The first month in your fiscal year specifies the default date range for accounting reports such as the Profit & Loss and Balance Sheet. The first month in your tax year specifies the default date range for **Income Tax Summary** and **Detail** reports.

Step 7.   The Administrator password setup screen will appear (see Figure 12-7). Although it's optional, creating an Administrator password is highly recommended. The Administrator is the only person who has access to all functions within a data file. Establishing an Administrator password restricts other users so that they cannot execute tasks that are normally reserved for the Administrator.

However, since you are just creating a sample data file for this lesson, do not create an Administrator password this time. Click **Next** to move to the next step.

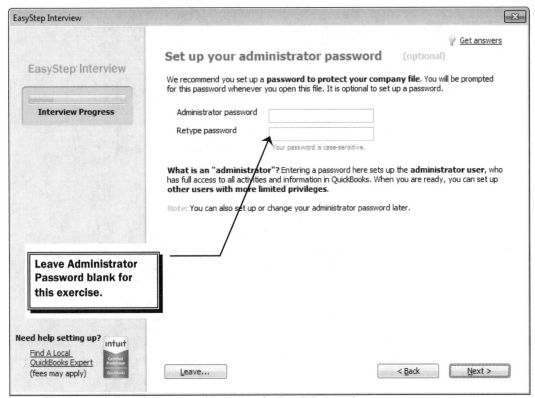

Figure 12-7 The Administrator Password Screen in the EasyStep Interview

> **Tip:**
> If you need help during the interview, click the **Get answers** link at the top of the interview window.

Step 8.   The next window in the *EasyStep Interview* window contains a message about creating your company file (see Figure 12-8). Click **Next** to create the file.

Figure 12-8 Create your company file screen

Step 9.   The *Filename for New Company* window (see Figure 12-9) is where you specify the filename and location for your company file. QuickBooks enters your company name and adds .QBW to the end of your filename.

             In the *Save in* field, select your student data folder. Use the default file name, Academy Photography.QBW.

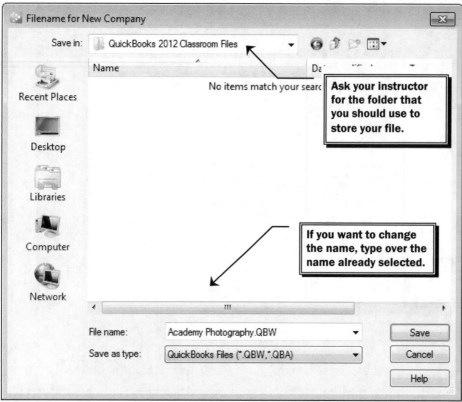

Figure 12-9 Filename for New Company window

Step 10.   Click **Save** to create your company file.

Step 11.   QuickBooks displays the *Customizing QuickBooks for your business* step. Click **Next** to begin the customizing process.

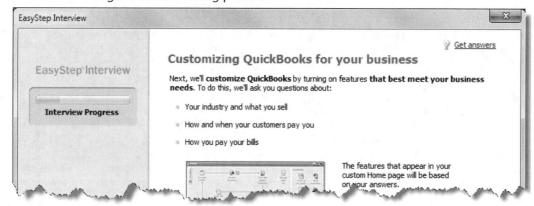

Figure 12-10 Customizing QuickBooks for your business screen

Step 12.   The next several screens of the *EasyStep Interview* will guide you through customizing your company file. Use the data in Table 12-2 to answer initial questions about your business.

EasyStep Interview Data	
Question From EasyStep Interview	Response
What do you sell?	Both services and products

Table 12-2 Your Company's industry type

Step 13.   The next set of questions relate to how QuickBooks sets up *Preferences* in your company file. Use Table 12-3 to complete these questions.

Company Preferences	
Do you charge sales tax?	Yes
Do you want to create estimates in QuickBooks?	Yes
Do you want to track sales orders before you invoice your customers?	Yes (Note: This option is not available in QuickBooks Pro.)
Do you want to use billing statements in QuickBooks?	Yes
Do you want to use progress invoicing?	Yes
Do you want to keep track of bills you owe?	Yes
Do you want to track inventory in QuickBooks?	Yes
Do you want to track time in QuickBooks?	Yes
Do you have employees?	Yes (check the boxes for both W-2 employees and 1099 contractors)

Table 12-3 Data for the Preferences

Step 14.   In the next section of the interview, QuickBooks creates your Chart of Accounts. Click **Next** on the *Using accounts in QuickBooks* screen (see Figure 12-11).

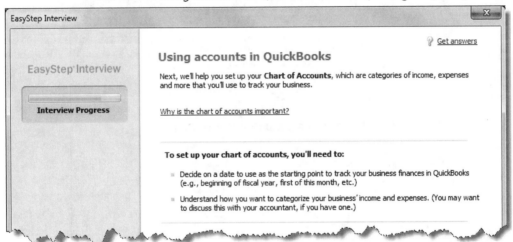

Figure 12-11 Using accounts in QuickBooks section

Step 15.   In the *Select a date to start tracking your finances* screen, select **Use today's date or the first day of the quarter or month.** Then enter *12/31/14* in the date field. Click **Next.**

If you are setting up your file to begin at the start of the fiscal year, it is best to choose the last day of the previous fiscal year as the start date. (see *Choosing a Start Date – Step 1* on page 365).

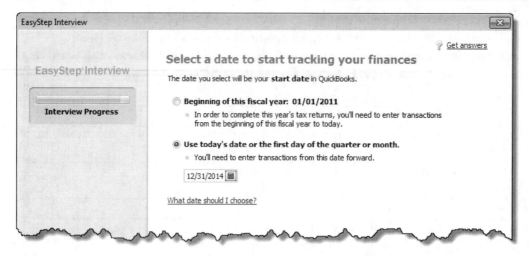

Figure 12-12 Select a date to start tracking your finances window in EasyStep Interview

Step 16.   The following screen contains a list of suggested income and expense accounts based on the industry selected earlier in the *EasyStep Interview*. These accounts can be edited after completing the *EasyStep Interview*.

Leave the default accounts checked and click **Next**.

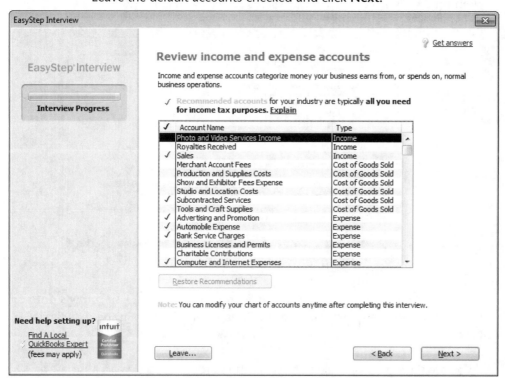

Figure 12-13 Review income and expense accounts window in the EasyStep Interview

Step 17.   Click **Go to Setup** to complete the interview.

Figure 12-14 Final screen in EasyStep interview

Step 18.   The *QuickBooks Setup* window is displayed. The *QuickBooks Setup* window offers a quick way to enter *Customers, Vendors, Employees, Items,* and *Bank Accounts.*

In the remainder of this exercise, you will create a bank account using the *QuickBooks Setup.* Click the **Add** button in the *Add your bank accounts* section in the lower part of the window.

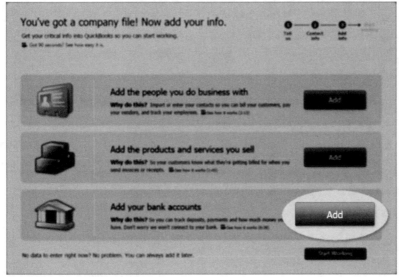

Figure 12-15 QuickBooks Setup

Step 19.   Enter the information in Figure 12-16 to setup the *Checking* account. For now, enter an *Opening Balance* of **0.00**. We will discuss setting up *Opening Balances* on page 391.

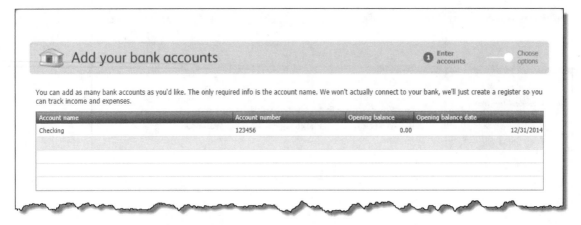

Figure 12-16 QuickBooks Quick Start Add your bank accounts

> Note:
> The *Account number* field in the *Add you bank accounts* window is for the account number assigned from your bank. This is a different number than the five digit QuickBooks Account Number discussed on page 377.

Step 20.   Click **Continue**.

Step 21.   Click **No Thanks** to the offer to purchase checks.

Step 22.   Click **Continue**.

Step 23.   Click the **Start Working** link at the bottom of the *QuickBooks Quick Start* window (see Figure 12-17).

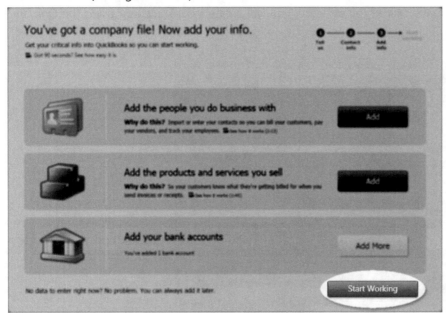

Figure 12-17 Start Working Link in QuickBooks Quick Start

Step 24.   QuickBooks has now created your company file with a default *Chart of Accounts* and a bank account, and has configured your *Company Preferences*.

Step 25.   Close the *Quick Start Center* window.

Step 26.   Close the company file.

Setting Up the Chart of Accounts and Other Lists – Step 3

> Restore the **Setup-12.QBM** file to your hard disk. See page 8 for instructions on restoring files. If you are using QuickBooks Premier Accountant, we recommend that you toggle to QuickBooks Premier General Business as described on page x.

Setting Up the Chart of Accounts

The *Chart of Accounts* is one of the most important lists in QuickBooks. It is a list of all the accounts in the General Ledger. If you are not sure how to design your *Chart of Accounts*, ask your accountant or QuickBooks ProAdvisor for help.

Account Types

There are five basic account *types* in accounting: assets, liabilities, equity, income, and expenses.

QuickBooks breaks these basic account types into subtypes. For example, QuickBooks uses five types of asset accounts: *Bank, Accounts Receivable, Other Current Asset, Fixed Asset,* and *Other Asset.* QuickBooks offers four types of liability accounts: *Accounts Payable, Credit Card, Loan, Other Current Liability,* and *Long Term Liability.* Income accounts can be divided into *Income* or *Other Income* types. Expenses can be classified as *Expense, Other Expense,* or *Cost of Goods Sold. Equity* doesn't have subtypes.

Activating Account Numbers

QuickBooks does not require account numbers. If you prefer, you can use just the account *name* to differentiate between accounts. However, if you prefer to have account numbers, you can activate them in the *Accounting Company Preferences.*

For this section, you will turn on the account numbers, but at the end of *Setting up the Chart of Accounts* section, you will turn them off again.

COMPUTER PRACTICE

Step 1.   Select the **Edit** menu and then select **Preferences** (see Figure 12-18).

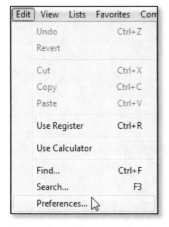

Figure 12-18 Choose Preferences from the Edit menu

Step 2.   On the *Preferences* window, click on the **Accounting** option and select the **Company Preferences** tab.

Step 3.   Check the **Use account numbers** box and click **OK**.

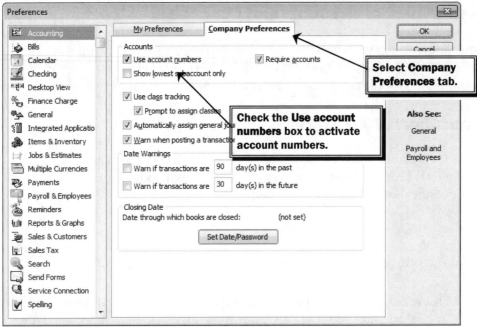

Figure 12-19 The Accounting—Company Preferences window

Did You Know?
All of the *Preferences* in Figure 12-19 are used to configure the way QuickBooks operates. For more information on these and other *Preferences*, see page 205.

Adding Accounts

COMPUTER PRACTICE

Step 1.   Select the **Chart of Accounts** icon on the *Company* section of the *Home page*.

The *Chart of Accounts* list from your sample file is displayed, showing account numbers as well as account names (see Figure 12-20).

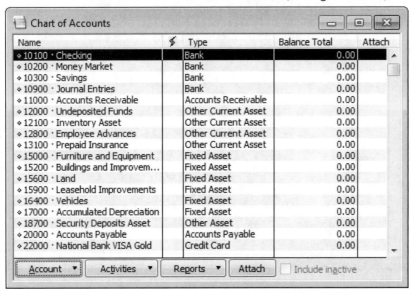

Figure 12-20 Chart of Accounts with account numbers

> **Another way:**
> To open the *Chart of Accounts*, you may also select **Chart of Accounts** from the *List* menu, or press **Ctrl+A**.

Step 2.   Select the **Account** drop-list button at the bottom of the *Chart of Accounts* window and select **New** (see Figure 12-21). Another way to add a new account is to press **Ctrl+N**.

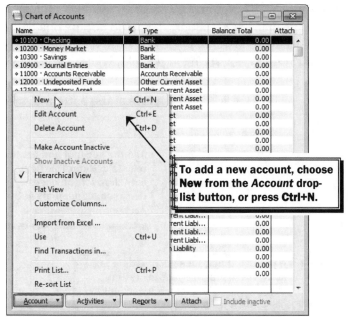

Figure 12-21 Adding an account

Step 3.   Select **Expense** from the choice of account types in the *Add New Account: Choose Account Type* window (see Figure 12-22). Click Continue.

Figure 12-22 Add New Account: Choose Account Type Window

Step 4.   Enter *62600* in the *Number* field and then press **Tab**.

Step 5.   Enter *Entertainment* in the *Name* field and then press **Tab** twice.

Step 6.   Enter *Entertainment Expenses* in the *Description* field and then press **Tab** twice.

The *Description* field is optional. In previous versions, the Description field had a limited length requiring short descriptions. Starting with the QuickBooks 2007, you can enter descriptions with up to 200 characters.

Step 7.   Select **Deductions: Other miscellaneous taxes** from the *Tax-Line Mapping* drop-down list.

If you or your accountant uses TurboTax, ProSeries, Lacerte, or other QuickBooks-compatible tax software to prepare your tax return, specify the line on your tax return that this account will feed. This allows the tax software to fill out your tax return automatically, based on the data in QuickBooks. If you do not use one of the supported tax programs to prepare your taxes, or if you do not wish to otherwise take advantage of any of the income tax reports in QuickBooks, you can leave this field blank.

Step 8.   Your screen should look like Figure 12-23. Click **Save & Close** at the bottom of the window to save the account.

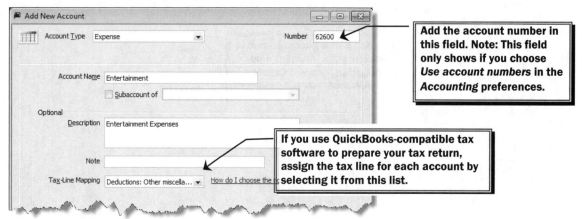

Figure 12-23 Add New Account window

Adding Subaccounts

If you want more detail in your *Chart of Accounts*, you can add *Subaccounts*. Account types for the main account and its subaccounts *must* be same. You can add up to five levels of subaccounts.

> **Did You Know?**
> Clicking the **Collapse** button on *Reports* that include Subaccounts (e.g., *Balance Sheet* and *Profit & Loss Reports*) removes the Subaccount detail from the report. The balance of each primary account on the collapsed report is the total of its subaccount balances.

COMPUTER PRACTICE

Step 1.   Display the **Chart of Accounts** using any method shown previously, if it is not already displayed.

Step 2.   Select the **Account** drop-list button at the bottom of the *Chart of Accounts* window and select **New**.

Step 3.   Select the **Expense** option from *the Add New Account: Choose Account Type* window. Click **Continue**.

Step 4.   Fill out the **New Account** window as shown in Figure 12-24. Notice that the *Subaccount of* field is checked and the main account is selected in its field.

Step 5.   Click **Save & Close** to save the record.

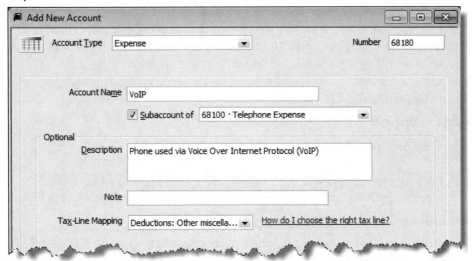

Figure 12-24 Add a Subaccount for more detail in the Chart of Accounts.

Step 6.   Now the *Chart of Accounts* shows your new subaccount slightly indented under its master account (see Figure 12-25).

> **Tip**
> Once subaccounts are set up under a main account, you should only use subaccounts and not the main account in transactions. Using the main account defeats the purpose of getting more detail. Also, in reports, whenever you see an account name with the string "-Other", it means that you used main account instead of a subaccount. To see only subaccounts and not the main account in the drop-down list, select the **Show lowest subaccount only** checkbox in *Accounting Company Preference* (see Figure 12-26).

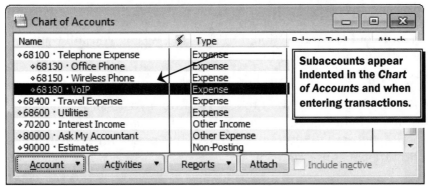

Figure 12-25 Subaccounts appearance in the Chart of Accounts

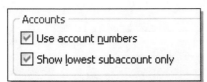

Figure 12-26 Account Numbers Preferences

Removing Accounts from the Chart of Accounts

When you no longer need an account, it is best to remove the account from the *Chart of Accounts* List. Removing unnecessary accounts helps avoid data entry errors by ensuring that no transactions are accidentally posted to these accounts. There are three ways to remove an account from the *Chart of Accounts* List: deleting the account, deactivating the account, or merging the account with another account.

Deleting Accounts – Option 1

To delete an account, follow these steps:

> **DO NOT PERFORM THESE STEPS NOW. THEY ARE FOR REFERENCE ONLY.**

1.   Select the account in the **Chart of Accounts** List.
2.   Select the **Account** menu at the bottom of the *Chart of Accounts* window and select **Delete** or press **Ctrl+D** (see Figure 12-27).

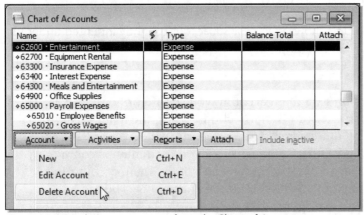

Figure 12-27 Deleting an account from the Chart of Accounts

It is important to note that QuickBooks will not allow you to delete an account if you have used the account in an Item record or a transaction. If this is the case and you still want to remove the account, use either Option 2 or Option 3 below.

Deactivating Accounts – Option 2

If you cannot delete an account but you still want to remove it from your list, you can deactivate it. Deactivating an account causes it to be hidden in the *Chart of Accounts* List. Deactivating an old account reduces the clutter in your Lists while preserving your ability to see the account in historical transactions and reports.

> **Note:**
> Even if an Account (or Item or Name) is inactive, all transactions using that account (or Item or Name) will show on reports.

To make an account inactive, follow these steps:

> **DO NOT PERFORM THESE STEPS NOW. THEY ARE FOR REFERENCE ONLY.**

1.   Select the account in the **Chart of Accounts** list.

2.   Select the **Account** button and then select **Make Inactive** from the menu (see Figure 12-28).

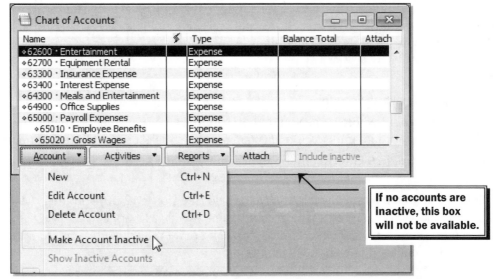

Figure 12-28 Making an account inactive in the Chart of Accounts

To view all accounts in the *Chart of Accounts*, including the inactive accounts, click **Include inactive** at the bottom of the *Chart of Accounts* window (see Figure 12-29). The icon in the far left column indicates that an account is inactive. To reactivate the account, click on the ✖ icon.

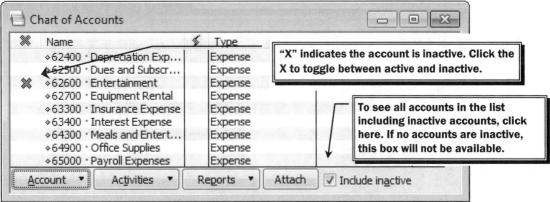

Figure 12-29 When the Show All Field is checked, all accounts appear in the list.

> **Did You Know?**
> You can also deactivate *Customers*, *Vendors*, *Employees*, or *Items* using this same method. Click in the ✖ column to make lines on any list active or inactive.

Merging Accounts – Option 3

When you merge two accounts, QuickBooks edits each transaction from the merging account so that it posts to the merged (combined) account. For example, if you merge the *Entertainment* account into the *Meals and Entertainment* account, QuickBooks will edit each transaction that had been posted to *Entertainment*, making it post to *Meals and Entertainment* instead. Then QuickBooks will remove the *Entertainment* account from the *Chart of Accounts* List.

> **Important:**
> Merging cannot be undone. Once you merge accounts together, there is no way to find out which account the old transactions used (except by reviewing from a backup file). In this example, all transactions that were originally coded to *Entertainment* will post to *Meals and Entertainment*.

COMPUTER PRACTICE

Step 1.   Display the **Chart of Accounts** List.

Step 2.   Select the account whose name you <u>do not</u> want to keep. Here you will merge the *Entertainment* account into *Meals and Entertainment*, so select **62600 Entertainment**.

Step 3.   Right-click on **62600 Entertainment** and then select **Edit Account**. Alternatively, press **Ctrl+E**.

Step 4.   Enter **Meals and Entertainment** in the *Name* field (see Figure 12-30) and then click **Save & Close**. You must enter the account name <u>exactly</u> as it appears in the *Chart of Accounts*. One way of ensuring this is to copy and paste the account name from the merged account to the merging account.

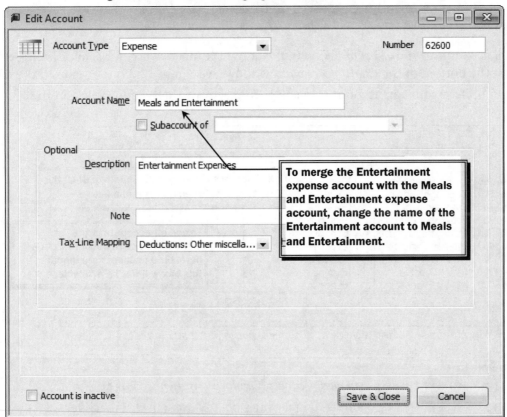

Figure 12-30 Change the name of the account to exactly match the name of another account.

Step 5.   Now that this account has the same name as the other account, QuickBooks asks if you want to merge the two accounts (see Figure 12-31). Click **Yes**.

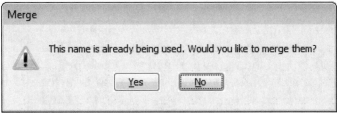

Figure 12-31 Click Yes to merge the accounts.

Did You Know?

If account numbers are in use, another way to merge accounts is to change the account number of one account to match the account number of another. This has the same effect as replacing the account name of the merging account with the account name of the merged account.

Note:

The merge feature is not limited to just the *Chart of Accounts* List; it can be used on most Lists within QuickBooks.

Reordering the Account List

There are several ways to reorder the *Chart of Accounts* list. By default, the Chart of Accounts list sorts first by account type and then alphabetically by account name within the account type (if account numbers are not in use) or numerically by account number within the account type (if account numbers are in use). For example, all of the bank accounts come first, followed by Accounts Receivable, Other Current Assets, and so on. The account types are arranged in the order in which they appear on financial statements.

You can sort the Chart of Accounts list by the account name or number, by the ![online status icon] (online status), or by the balance total column.

DO NOT PERFORM THESE STEPS NOW. THEY ARE FOR REFERENCE ONLY.

---

1.   Display the **Chart of Accounts** (see Figure 12-32).
2.   Click the **Name** column heading to sort the list.

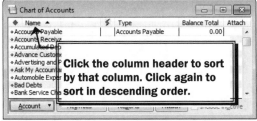

Figure 12-32 Chart of Accounts sorted by name

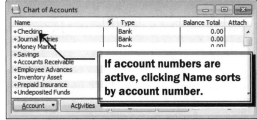

Figure 12-33 Chart of Accounts sorted by number

Note:

When account numbers are inactive and you click the *Name* header, QuickBooks sorts the account list alphabetically by account name.

However, when account numbers are active and you click the *Name* header, QuickBooks sorts the list by account number. Click the other headers to sort by ![online status icon] (*Online status*), *Type,* or *Balance.*

> **Tip:**
> When you assign account numbers, set numbering breaks that correspond to the account types. For example, number all of your asset accounts 10000-19999 and all of your liability accounts 20000-29999, and so forth. When you click the Name header to sort the *Chart of Accounts*, QuickBooks does not also sort the list by account type. Therefore, if you assign an account number of 70000 to a Bank account, QuickBooks will place that account near the bottom of the *Chart of Accounts*, regardless of its type. If you do not use account numbers, it is best not to use the Name header to sort the *Chart of Accounts*. Instead, select the **Account** menu and choose **Re-sort List**. This will sort the list by Account name (or number) while respecting the account types.

You can also use the mouse to drag the accounts up or down within the same account type. Within each account type, the order of the accounts in the Chart of Accounts determines the order of the accounts in financial statements and other reports.

> Tip:
> Once you have manually reordered the *Chart of Accounts*, all new accounts will automatically be added to the top of the list within its type, rather than in alphabetical order.

To reorder the *Chart of Accounts* List using the mouse, follow these steps:

> **DO NOT PERFORM THESE STEPS NOW. THEY ARE FOR REFERENCE ONLY.**

1.   If you have sorted the list by *Name*, *Online Status*, *Type,* or *Balance* by clicking on the column headers, click on the diamond to the left of the **Name** column header. This will remove the sorting (see Figure 12-34).

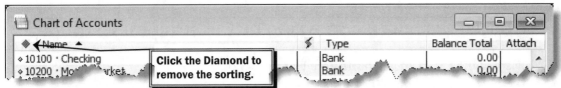

Figure 12-34 Chart of Accounts, sorted by account number

2.   While holding down the mouse button, drag the account up or down (see Figure 12-35).

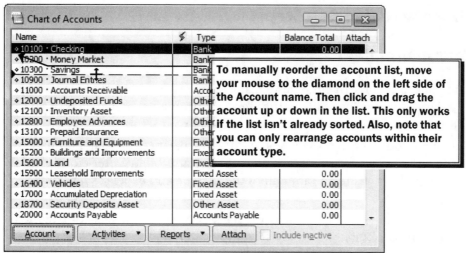

Figure 12-35 Reorder the list by moving an account with the mouse.

> **Tip:**
> To preserve proper financial statement presentation, you can only rearrange accounts within their account type. In addition, QuickBooks treats accounts with subaccounts as a group, so if you want to move your account above or beneath an account with subaccounts, you'll need to drag it above or below the group.
>
> **Tip:**
> If you use account numbers, it may be best to edit the numbers to move accounts up or down in the list. For example, if you want account #10400 to be above account #10300, you can edit its account number so that it is #10200. Then, you may need to select the **Account** menu and then select **Re-sort List**.

Turning Off Account Numbers

For the rest of this chapter, we'll turn off the display of account numbers in the Chart of Accounts.

COMPUTER PRACTICE

Step 1.   Select the **Edit** menu and then select **Preferences**.

Step 2.   In the *Preferences* window, click on the **Accounting** icon and then select the **Company Preferences** tab.

Step 3.   Deselect the *Use account numbers* box and then click **OK**.

Setting Up Other Lists

At this point in the 12-Step process, you would enter additional information in lists, such as *Customers* and *Vendors*. You can use the *QuickBooks Quick Start* (see page 375) to import *Customers, Vendors,* and *Employees* from contact lists in other formats, such as your Outlook contact list. For this exercise, the Setup-12.QBM file you restored earlier already has this data entered. Refer to page 34 and 98 for more information on adding *Customers* and *Vendors*.

Setting Up Opening Balances – Step 4

Gathering Your Information

After you've set up your *Chart of Accounts*, you're ready to enter your opening balances. To set up your opening balances, you will need to gather several documents, prepared as of your start date. The following is a list of items needed to complete your setup:

Trial Balance: Ask your accountant to provide you with a trial balance for your start date. If your start date is the end of your fiscal year, ask your accountant for an "after-closing" trial balance. The term "after-closing" means "after all of the income and expenses have been closed into Retained Earnings."

If a trial balance is not available, use an after-closing Balance Sheet and a year-to-date Income Statement as of your start date. Table 12-4 shows a sample after-closing trial balance for Academy Photography on the start date of 12/31/2014.

Academy Photography		
Trial Balance December 31, 2014		
	Debit	**Credit**
Checking	$17,959.60	
Money Market	12,100.00	
Savings	500.00	
Accounts Receivable	1,253.41	
Inventory	7,158.67	
Furniture and Equipment	13,250.00	
Fixed Assets:Accumulated Depreciation		$1,325.00
Accounts Payable		142.00
National Bank VISA Gold		2,152.00
Payroll Liabilities:Company PR Taxes		368.00
Sales Tax Payable		141.79
Line of Credit		6,700.00
Truck Loan		12,000.00
Common Stock		10,000.00
Retained Earnings		19,392.89
TOTAL	$52,221.68	$52,221.68

Table 12-4 Trial Balance on Academy Photography's start date

Bank Statement (for all bank accounts): You will need the most recent bank statement prior to your start date. For example, if your start date is 12/31/2014 you will need the 12/31/2014 bank statements for all of your accounts.

Business Checking Account			
Statement Date:	**December 31, 2014**		*Page 1 of 1*

Summary:

Previous Balance as of 11/30/14:	$	12,155.10
Total Deposits and Credits: 2	+ $	10,157.28
Total Checks and Debits: 9	- $	7,027.40
Total Interest Earned	+ $	8.62
Total Service Charge:1	- $	10.00
Statement Balance as of 12/31/14:	= $	**15,283.60**

Deposits and Other Credits:

DEPOSITS

Date	Description		Amount
8-Dec	Customer Deposit	$	6,150.00
20-Dec	Customer Deposit	$	4,007.28
	2 Deposits: $		**10,157.28**

INTEREST

Date	Description		Amount
31-Dec	Interest Earned	$	8.62
	Interest: $		**8.62**

Checks and Other Withdrawals:

CHECKS PAID:

Check No.	Date Paid		Amount
316	2-Dec	$	324.00
317	3-Dec	$	128.60
318	5-Dec	$	83.00
319	8-Dec	$	285.00
320	10-Dec	$	1,528.00
321	12-Dec	$	3,000.00
322	13-Dec	$	276.52
323	15-Dec	$	142.00
324	28-Dec	$	1,260.28
	6 Checks Paid: $		**7,027.40**

SERVICE CHARGES

Date	Description		Amount
31-Dec	Service Charge	$	10.00
	1 Service Charge: $		**10.00**

Figure 12-36 Bank Statement for Academy Photography on 12/31/2014

Tip:
If your bank statements are not dated on the end of each month, ask your bank to change your statement date to the end of the month. You may also be able to run a statement on your bank's Web site that ends on the date you choose.

Unpaid Bills: List each vendor bill by date of the bill, amount due, and what items or expenses you purchased on the bill (see Table 12-5).

Bill Number	Bill Date	Vendor	Amt. Due	Account/Item	Job	Class
2342	12/21/14	Wong & Son Video	$142.00	Subcontractors Expense	Mason, Bob	San Jose

Table 12-5 Unpaid bills on Academy Photography's start date

Outstanding Checks and Deposits: You'll need a list of all of your checks and deposits that have not cleared the bank as of the bank statement dated on or prior to your start date.

OUTSTANDING DEPOSTIS AT 12/31/14		
Date	Description	Amount
12/30/14	Customer Deposit	$3,000.00
	1 Deposit:	$3,000.00
OUTSTANDING CHECKS AT 12/31/14		
Check No.	Date Paid	Payee	Amount
325	12/26/14	National Bank	$324.00
		1 Check:	$324.00

Table 12-6 Outstanding deposits and checks on Academy Photography's start date

Open Invoices: List each customer invoice including the date of the invoice, amount due, and the items sold on the invoice (see Table 12-7).

Inv #	Invoice Date	Customer:Job	Class	Terms	Item	Qty	Amt Due
3947	12/18/14	Mason, Bob	San Jose	Net 30	Camera	1	$695.99
					Santa Clara Tax		8.25%
					Total		$753.41
4003	12/21/14	Cruz, Maria: Branch Opening	San Jose	2% 10 Net 30	Photographer 4 Hrs.	125/hr	$500.00
					Total		$500.00

Table 12-7 Open Invoices on Academy Photography's start date

Employee list and W-4 information for each employee: Gather complete name, address, social security number, and withholding information for each employee.

> **Note:**
> The next three payroll-related lists are necessary only if your start date is in the middle of a calendar year and you want to track payroll details with QuickBooks. If your start date is 12/31, skip these lists and enter the opening balances for payroll liabilities in the liability accounts as shown later in this section.
>
> If your start date is 12/31, you need to enter the detail from these lists only if you want to use QuickBooks to create payroll reports, Form 940, Form 941, or W-2s for the previous year.
>
> All payroll setup instructions are covered in the "Payroll Setup" chapter beginning on page 299.

Payroll Liabilities by Item: List the amount due for each of your payroll liabilities as of your start date. For example, list the amounts due for federal withholding tax, social security (employer), social security (employee), and any other payroll liabilities.

Year-to-Date Payroll Detail by Employee: If your start date is not 12/31 and you want QuickBooks to track your payroll, you will need gross earnings, withholdings, employer taxes, and any other deductions for each employee so far this year. For the most detail, this list should include each employee's earnings *for each month* this year.

Year-to-Date Payroll Tax Deposits: If your start date is not 12/31, list each payroll tax deposit during the year by *Payroll Item.*

Physical Inventory by Inventory Part: List the quantity and cost for each product in inventory (see Table 12-8).

> **Tip:**
> If you don't have actual counts and costs for your inventory, you'll need to estimate. However, the accuracy of your reports will be compromised if you don't have accurate setup numbers. If possible, we strongly recommend conducting a physical inventory as of your QuickBooks start date.

Physical Inventory at 12/31/14		
Item	Qty. on Hand	Value
Camera	10	$4,500.00
Case	25	1,125.00
Frame	25	53.75
Lenses	8	1,479.92

Table 12-8 Physical inventory on Academy Photography's start date

Opening Balances for Accounts

To enter opening balances, you can either edit the account in the *New Account* or *Edit Account* window, or create a *General Journal Entry*. Entering the *Opening Balance* in the *New Account* or *Edit Account* window is a good method for setting up a single account. General Journal Entries allow you to set up the Opening Balances for several accounts at once.

When entering opening balances for bank accounts and credit cards, it is very important to use the ending balance from the bank statement dated on (or just prior to) your start date.

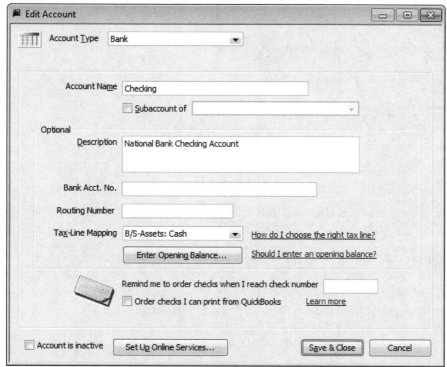

Figure 12-37 Enter an opening balance in the Edit Account window.

Directly Editing the Account

To enter the opening balances, repeat the following steps for each of your Balance Sheet accounts:

COMPUTER PRACTICE

Step 1.   Display the **Chart of Accounts**.

Step 2.   Select the **Checking** bank account by clicking on it.

Step 3.   Select the **Account** button at the bottom of the window and then select **Edit Account**.

Step 4.   Click on the **Enter Opening Balance** Button (see Figure 12-37).

Step 5.   In the *Enter Opening Balance: Bank Account* window (see Figure 12-38), enter *15,283.60* in the *Statement Ending Balance field*.

Step 6.   Enter **12/31/14** in the *Statement Ending Date* field.

Figure 12-38 Enter Opening Balance for a Bank Account window

Step 7.   Click **OK** to finalize the *Enter Opening Balance: Bank Account* window. Then, click **Save & Close** on the *Edit Account Window*. Repeat Steps 2 through 7 for the *Money Market* account. Enter an opening balance of *$12,100.00* as of *12/31/2014* (see Figure 12-39).

Figure 12-39 Edit the Money Market account to enter an opening balance

> **Accounting Behind the Scenes:**
> When you enter an opening balance in an account, a transaction posts to the account and to *Opening Balance Equity*. Also, the opening balance in the account becomes the *Beginning Balance* for the first bank reconciliation.

> **Note:**
> QuickBooks does not allow you to directly enter the opening balance for
> *Accounts Receivable, Undeposited Funds, Accounts Payable, Sales Tax Payable*, or
> *Opening Balance Equity*. To enter opening balances for these accounts, see later in
> this chapter.

Recording Opening Balances Using a General Journal Entry

General Journal Entries allow you to record debits and credits to specific accounts. Other forms in QuickBooks, such as *Invoices* or *Bills*, take care of the credits and debits for you, behind the scenes (See page 2). *General Journal Entries* record transactions that cannot otherwise be recorded using QuickBooks forms.

Because total debits always equal total credits, the total of the debit column and the total of the credit column must be equal or you will not be able to save the *General Journal Entry*. QuickBooks automatically calculates the amount required to make these entries balance as you create each new line in the *General Journal Entry*. On the last line of the *General Journal Entry*, code the amount QuickBooks calculates to the Opening Bal Equity account. This amount may be a debit or a credit, depending on the other figures in the entry.

Although the *Trial Balance* doesn't show any balance in Opening Bal Equity, you use this account during setup to keep everything in balance. At the end of the setup process, you'll transfer the balance from this account into Retained Earnings, as shown later in the setup steps.

You can use a *General Journal Entry* to record some, but not all, of your opening balances. Do not include the following accounts in the *General Journal Entry*: Accounts Receivable, Accounts Payable, Inventory, Sales Tax Payable, *and Retained Earnings*. You will enter the opening balance for these accounts later in the 12-Step setup.

COMPUTER PRACTICE

Use the information from the Trial Balance on page 388 to complete the following steps:

Step 1.   Select the **Company** menu and then select **Make General Journal Entries**. If necessary, click **OK** in the *Assign Numbers to Journal Entries* dialog box. If you are using QuickBooks Premier Accountant, select *Make General Journal Entries* from the *Accountant* menu.

Step 2.   Fill in the **Make General Journal Entries** window as shown in Figure 12-40.

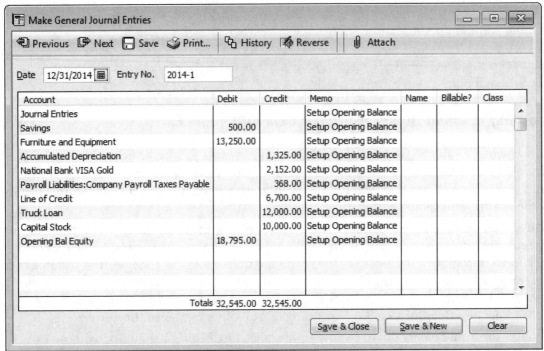

Figure 12-40 Enter opening balances using a General Journal Entry.

> **Note:**
> On the top line of each General Journal Entry, use an account called *Journal Entries*, as shown in Figure 12-40. Use the *Bank* account type when setting up this account in your *Chart of Accounts*. The *Journal Entries* account will never have a balance, so it will never show on financial statements, but it will have a register where you'll be able to look at all of your *General Journal Entries*.

Step 3.   Click **Save & Close** to save the entry.

Step 4.   QuickBooks will warn you that you can set up Fixed Asset Items from the *Fixed Asset Item* List. Click **OK**. If you see the *Items not assigned classes* dialog box, click the **Save Anyway** button.

> **Important Note:**
> In this example, you're setting up the opening balances for Payroll Liabilities directly in the accounts instead of first setting up the Payroll function. This way, you can finalize your opening balances before worrying about the Payroll setup, and you can separate the tasks of Company setup and Payroll setup.
>
> Remember though, because we've set up the liabilities outside of the Payroll system, your first Payroll Liability payment (for last year's liability), must be entered using the *Write Checks* window instead of the *Pay Liabilities* window. Alternatively, you could set up the Payroll Liability Balances using the *Adjust Liabilities* window with the *Do not Affect Accounts* setting. Then, you would use the *Pay Liabilities* window to pay your opening Payroll Liability balances.

The *General Journal Entry* in Figure 12-40 will set up the opening balances in *most* of the asset, liability, and equity accounts. You will not include some of the assets and liabilities in this *General Journal Entry* because you will enter their balances later in the 12-Step setup. For example, you'll exclude Accounts Receivable and Accounts Payable because you will create

Invoices and *Bills* to enter these accounts, respectively. See "Entering Open Bills (Accounts Payable)" on page 396.

If you enter bank accounts through a *General Journal Entry*, the starting balance on your first Bank Reconciliation will be zero. If you want your starting balance to equal your Opening Balance, enter the bank account's Opening Balance in the *Edit Account* window.

Understanding Opening Bal Equity

As you enter the opening balances for your assets and liabilities, QuickBooks automatically adds offsetting amounts in the *Opening Bal Equity* account. This account, which is created automatically by QuickBooks, is very useful if used properly. As you'll see later in this section, each of the opening balance transactions you enter into QuickBooks will affect this account. Then, after you have entered all of the opening balances, you'll "close" *Opening Bal Equity* into *Retained Earnings* (or *Owner's Equity*).

> **Tip:**
> By using the *Opening Bal Equity* account during setup, you will quickly be able to access the detail of your setup transactions by looking at the *Opening Bal Equity* register.

Entering Open Items – Step 5

Entering Outstanding Checks and Deposits

To help with the first reconciliation, you want all of the outstanding checks and deposits to show in QuickBooks so that you can match them with your first bank statement after the start date. If you don't enter the individual transactions, you won't see them in the QuickBooks reconciliation window. In addition, if a transaction never clears the bank, you won't know which transaction it was without going back to your old records.

COMPUTER PRACTICE

For each of your bank accounts and credit cards, enter all outstanding checks (or charges) and deposits (or payments) as additional transactions in the account register. Enter each outstanding check and deposit with the date the check was written or the deposit made, and post each transaction to *Opening Bal Equity*.

Step 1.   With the **Chart of Accounts** open, double-click on the **Checking** account to display its register.

Step 2.   Enter new transactions directly in the register for each outstanding check and deposit (see Figure 12-41). See the list of outstanding checks and deposits in Table 12-6 on page 390.

Step 3.   Close the **Checking** register and the **Chart of Accounts**.

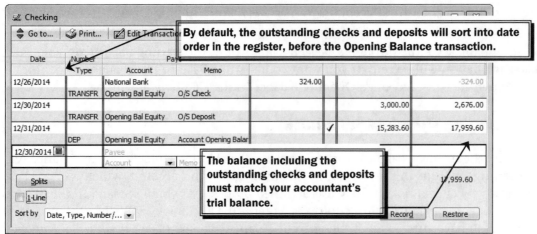

Figure 12-41 Checking account register with outstanding checks and deposits

Entering Open Bills (Accounts Payable)

COMPUTER PRACTICE

Enter your **Unpaid Bills** and **Vendor Credits** as of the start date. Use the original date of the bill (or credit) along with all of the details (terms, vendor, etc.) of the bill. By entering the individual bills, you can preserve detailed job costing and class tracking data if needed.

Step 1.   Click **Enter Bill** on the *Home page*, or select the **Vendors** menu and then select **Enter Bills**.

Step 2.   Enter the **Bill** as shown in Figure 12-42.

Step 3.   Click **Save & Close** to save the transaction.

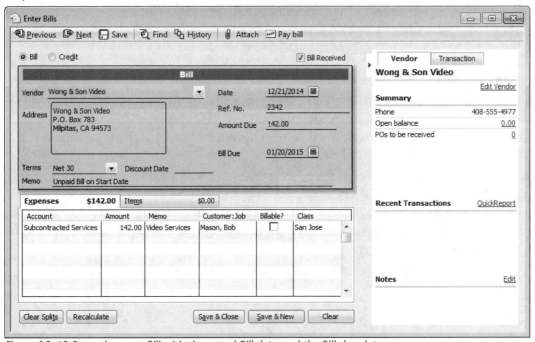

Figure 12-42 Enter the open Bill with the actual Bill date and the Bill due date.

Entering Open Invoices (Accounts Receivable)

Enter each *Invoice* or *Credit Memo* as of the Start Date. Enter each *Invoice* with its original date along with all of the details (terms, customer, etc.) of the original *Invoice*.

COMPUTER PRACTICE

Step 1.   From the *Home page* click **Create Invoices** or select **Create Invoices** from the *Customers* menu. If you see the *Professional Services Form* dialog box, click **OK**.

Step 2.   Enter the **Invoice** as shown in Figure 12-43. When you see the warning about insufficient quantities, click **OK**. If you receive a warning about *Not Enough Quantity and/or Tracking Customer Orders*, click **OK**. Make sure you use the date of the original invoice on this *Invoice,* along with all of the detail from that invoice, exactly as shown in Figure 12-43. Make sure the **Academy Photo Service Invoice** is selected in the *Template* field.

Step 3.   Click **Save & New** to save the transaction and display a new *Invoice.*

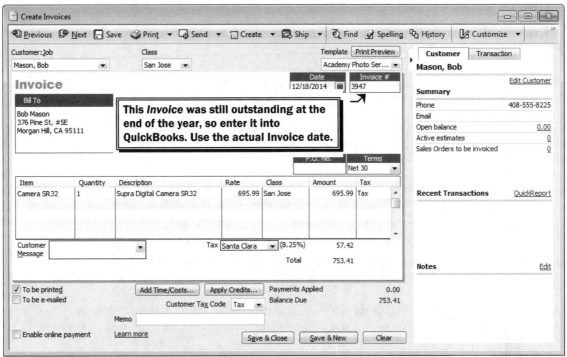

Figure 12-43 Enter the open Invoice with the original Invoice date.

Step 4.   Enter another Invoice as shown in Figure 12-44. Click **Save & Close** to save the *Invoice.*

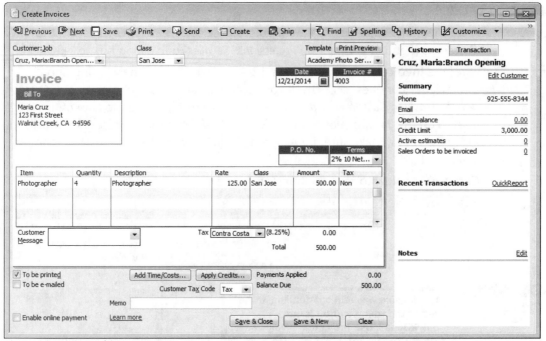

Figure 12-44 Enter this open Invoice.

> **Note:**
> When you set up your company file, it is important that you enter all *Invoices*, *Credit Memos*, *Bills*, and *Bill Credits* separately. QuickBooks needs the details of the transactions, such as the date, terms, and Customer or Vendor information, to prepare accurate aging reports (e.g., *Unpaid Bills Detail* and *A/R Aging Summary*).
>
> In addition, when you receive money against one of your prior year *Invoices* or pay a prior year *Bill*, you will need individual *Invoices* and *Bills* against which to match the receipts and payments.

Entering Open Purchase Orders

If you have open *Purchase Orders*, enter them individually, just as you did with *Bills*, *Bill Credits*, *Invoices*, and *Credit Memos*. Enter each *Purchase Order* with its original date and all of its details. If you have partially received items on the *Purchase Order*, enter only the quantities yet to be received from the Vendor.

Entering Open Estimates and Sales Orders

If you have open *Estimates* and/or *Sales Orders* (for Premier and Enterprise only), enter them individually, just as you did with *Bills*, *Bill Credits*, *Invoices*, and *Credit Memos*. Enter each *Estimate* and/or *Sales Order* with its original date and all of its details. If you have already progress-billed a portion of the *Estimate* or delivered part of the *Sales Order*, enter only the remaining amount to be invoiced.

Entering Year-to-Date Income and Expenses – Step 6

Earlier you learned that Income and Expense accounts are totaled at the end of the fiscal year as the Net Profit (or Loss) and is combined with Retained Earnings (see page 2). In this chapter's exercise the start date is the end of the fiscal year. Later in the 12-Step process you will see the Income and Expense accounts zeroed out and their balances combined with Retained Earnings on the first day of the year (1/1/15). However, when your company file has a start date that is *not* the end of the fiscal year, the year-to-date amounts for the Income and Expense accounts will need to be entered as a *General Journal Entry* (see Figure 12-45).

> THE *GENERAL JOURNAL ENTRY* SHOWN IN FIGURE 12-45 IS FOR REFERENCE ONLY. IT SHOWS A MID-YEAR SETUP ENTRY. DO NOT ENTER IT NOW.

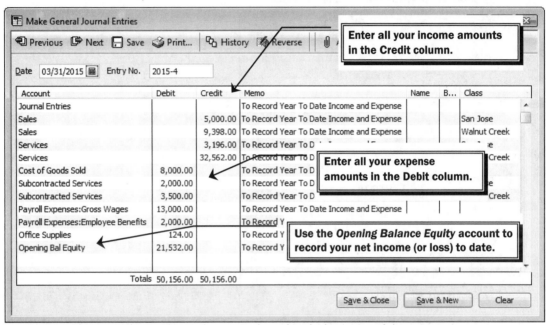

Figure 12-45 The General Journal Entry for a start date after the beginning of the year

Adjusting Opening Balance for Sales Tax Payable – Step 7

To enter the opening balance for *Sales Tax Payable*, begin by opening the *Sales Tax Payable* register to view the activity in the account. Notice that there are entries for each of the *Invoices* you just entered. This is your *uncollected* tax. Since the total Sales Tax Liability is a combination of the *collected* tax and the *uncollected* tax, you will need to subtract the current balance in the account (the *uncollected* tax) from the amount shown on the trial balance from your accountant (or your 12/31/2014 sales tax return) to arrive at the unpaid *collected* tax.

$$TotalTaxDue = CollectedTax + UncollectedTax$$

$$CollectedTax = AmountsAlreadyCollectedButNotPaid$$

$$UncollectedTax = TaxOnOpenInvoices$$

$$...therefore$$

$$AdjustmentAmount = CollectedTax = TotalTaxDue - UncollectedTax$$

Equation 12-1 Calculating the amount of your sales tax adjustment

For example, you know from the trial balance that Academy Photography's Total Tax Due is $141.79. The Uncollected Tax has already been entered with *Invoice* #3947. The sales tax on this *Invoice* was $57.42. By subtracting the Uncollected Sales Tax ($57.42) from the Total Tax Due ($141.79), you can calculate the Collected Tax, $84.37.

Then create a *Sales Tax Adjustment* for this collected tax amount.

COMPUTER PRACTICE

Step 1.   Select the **Vendors** menu, then select **Sales Tax,** and then select **Adjust Sales Tax Due.**

Step 2.   Complete the *Sales Tax Adjustment* window as shown in Figure 12-46 and then click **OK.** If you see the *Items not assigned classes* dialog box, click the **Save Anyway** button.

If you pay sales tax to more than one sales tax agency, you will need to enter a separate adjustment for each agency.

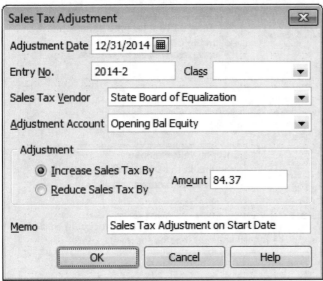

Figure 12-46 The Sales Tax Adjustment window

> **Did You Know?**
> The *Sales Tax Adjustment* window creates a *General Journal Entry* transaction in QuickBooks. Therefore, the Entry No. field will display the next *General Journal Entry* number in sequence. If you prefer, you could instead enter this adjustment using a *General Journal Entry.*

Adjusting Inventory and Setting up Fixed Assets – Step 8

If you have inventory, you will need to create an inventory adjustment to enter the actual quantity and value on hand as of your start date. This is done *after* you enter your outstanding *Bills* and *Invoices,* so that the actual inventory counts and costs will be accurate even if some of the *Bills* and/or *Invoices* include *Inventory Items.*

As with the adjustment to Sales Tax Payable, begin by opening the *Inventory* register to view the activity and the current balance. Also, open the *Item List* to view the current stock status of each Inventory Item. Then adjust the quantity on hand and value of each item so that Inventory will agree with the physical inventory counts and the company's trial balance as of your start date.

Adjusting Inventory for Actual Counts

COMPUTER PRACTICE

Step 1.   Select the **Vendors** menu, then select **Inventory Activities**, and then select **Adjust Quantity/Value on Hand**.

Step 2.   Choose **Quantity and Total Value** from the *Adjustment Type* field (see Figure 12-47).

Step 3.   Enter *12/31/2014* in the *Adjustment Date* field. Press **Tab**.

Step 4.   Select **Opening Bal Equity** in the *Adjustment Account* field.

Step 5.   Click **OK** on the *Income or Expense expected* warning window.

Step 6.   Enter *2014-3* in the *Ref. No.* field. Press **Tab**.

Step 7.   Leave both the *Customer:Job* and *Class* fields blank.

Step 8.   Enter the information in Figure 12-47.

Step 9.   Click **Save & Close** to record the transaction. If you see the *Items not assigned classes* dialog box, click the **Save Anyway** button.

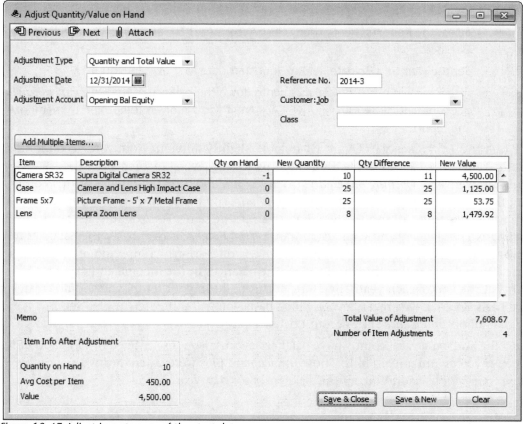

Figure 12-47 Adjust inventory as of the start date

Setting up Fixed Assets

If you have QuickBooks Pro or Premier, you can track detailed information about your company's Fixed Assets. You can set up detailed information about each asset using the *Fixed Asset Item* List. Then, if your accountant uses QuickBooks Premier: Accountant, he or she can use the *Fixed Asset Manager* to individually calculate and track depreciation on each asset.

Setting up Loans

If you have QuickBooks Pro or Premier, you can track detailed information about your loans. You can individually track and amortize each of your loans so that QuickBooks will automatically allocate the principal and interest on each payment.

Setup Payroll and YTD Payroll Information – Step 9

Setting up Payroll in QuickBooks is a lengthy and involved process. Refer to the "Payroll Setup" chapter beginning on page 299 for more information about setting up the Payroll feature.

Verifying your Trial Balance – Step 10

Before you transfer the balance of *Opening Bal Equity* into *Retained Earnings*, make sure the account balances in QuickBooks match your accountant's trial balance.

COMPUTER PRACTICE

Step 1.   Select the **Reports** menu, then select **Accountant & Taxes**, and then select **Trial Balance**.

Step 2.   Set the *From* and *To* date field to your start date as shown in Figure 12-48.

Step 3.   After reviewing the *Trial Balance*, write down the balance of the *Opening Bal Equity* account, and close the window. Click **No** if you are given the option to memorize the report.

Notice that the *Trial Balance* in Figure 12-48 looks slightly different from your accountant's report (in Table 12-4). For example, there are balances in several income and expense accounts, as well as in *Opening Bal Equity*. Do not worry about this difference at this point; you are not finished with the setup yet. Your *Trial Balance* could also differ from your accountant's report if the reporting basis on the two reports is not the same. For example, if you create an accrual basis *Trial Balance* and your accountant's *Trial Balance* is cash basis, the balances in the income and expense accounts may be different. Regardless of which method of accounting you use, QuickBooks will automatically close the balances in the income and expense accounts at the end of each year. Therefore, at this point in your setup, you should create an accrual basis *Trial Balance*, regardless of which basis you will ultimately use on reports. Just verify that all of the *Balance Sheet* account balances are accurate.

The income and expense accounts have balances because you just entered *Invoices* and *Bills* for the open invoices and unpaid bills. Those *Invoices* and *Bills* were dated during the prior year, so those transactions add to income and expenses for that year.

> **Note:**
> To learn more about the cash or accrual basis of accounting see the section beginning on page 164.

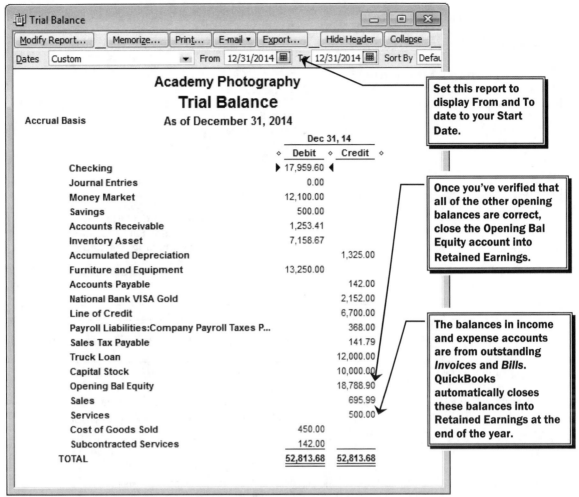

Figure 12-48 Trial Balance for Academy Photography as of the start date

Closing Opening Bal Equity – Step 11

Once you have compared your *Trial Balance* report to your accountant's report, use a *General Journal Entry* to transfer (close) the balance in *Opening Bal Equity* into *Retained Earnings*.

> **Note:**
> If your company is a sole proprietorship, use this same process, but instead of *Retained Earnings*, the account should be called *Owner's Equity*. If your company is a partnership, split the balance of *Opening Bal Equity* between each of the partners' profit accounts.

COMPUTER PRACTICE

Step 1.   Select the **Company** menu and then select **Make General Journal Entry**. If you are using QuickBooks Premier Accountant, use the *Accountant* menu. If necessary, click **OK** in the *Assign Numbers to Journal Entries* dialog box.

Step 2.   Set the **Date** field to your start date.

Step 3.   Enter the **General Journal Entry** as shown in Figure 12-49 and then click **Save & Close**.

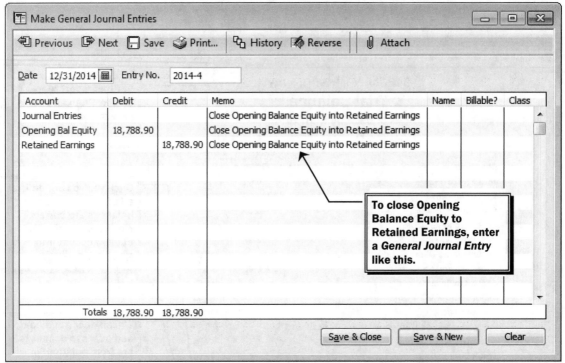

Figure 12-49 General Journal Entry to close Opening Bal Equity into Retained Earnings

Step 4.   The *Retained Earnings* window as shown in Figure 12-50 will appear. Click **OK**. If you see the *Items not assigned classes* dialog box, click the **Save Anyway** button.

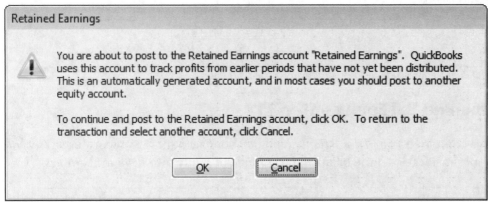

Figure 12-50 Posting to Retained Earnings

When you are finished entering all of the opening balances and you have closed the *Opening Bal Equity* account into *Retained Earnings*, verify your *Balance Sheet*. Create a *Balance Sheet* for *the day after* your start date and verify that the numbers match your accountant's trial balance.

COMPUTER PRACTICE

Step 1.   Select the **Reports** menu, then select **Company & Financial**, and then select **Balance Sheet Standard**.

Step 2.   Set the *As of* field to *01/01/2015*, the day after your start date (see Figure 12-51).

Step 3.   Print the report and then close the window.

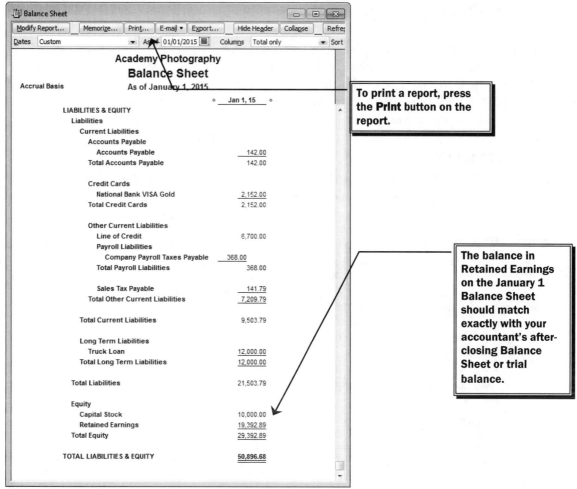

Figure 12-51 Academy Photography Balance Sheet

Setting the Closing Date - Backing up the File – Step 12

Now that you have entered all of your opening balances in the file, create a backup of the file. After you begin entering transactions you should back up your file on a regular basis, but keep the backup you perform in Step 12 of the setup on a separate disk or in a separate folder on your computer's hard drive, so that you always have a clean record of your setup transactions.

Setting the Closing Date to Protect your Setup Balances

For details on setting the *Closing Date* and the *Closing Date password*, see page 435.

Congratulations! You have finished the setup of your company file. You are now ready to set up users of the file, modify your sales forms, and begin entering transactions. The process for setting up users and passwords is in the next section, but the setup of your sales forms is covered on page 224.

Users and Passwords

QuickBooks provides a feature for defining "users" of the file. This feature allows the "administrator" (the owner of the file) to set privileges for each user of the file. This provides security and user tracking when several people have access to the same data file.

Setting Up Users in the Company File

Each user should have a separate user name and password. Once users have been setup, QuickBooks will require a user name and password when a company file is opened. The privileges granted to that user by the administrator determine what functions of QuickBooks they can access. For example, a user might have access to Accounts Receivable, Accounts Payable, and Banking functions, but not Payroll or "sensitive activities" like online banking. For a complete description of each privilege, click the **Help** button on the *User Setup* windows.

COMPUTER PRACTICE

Step 1.   First you will setup the Administrator's password. Select the **Company** menu, select **Set Up Users and Passwords**, and then select **Change Your Password**. The *Change QuickBooks Password* window will appear (Figure 12-52).

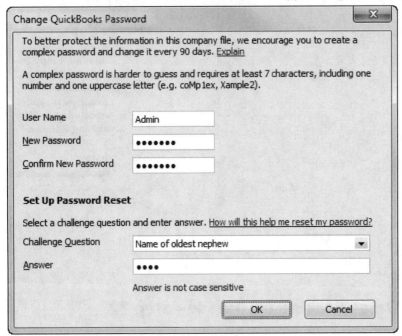

Figure 12-52 Change Administrator's Password

Step 2.   Leave **Admin** in the *User Name* field and then press **Tab** (see Figure 12-52).

You could, of course, change the administrator's *User Name*, but even if you do, you'll always be able to log in (or open the file) as the administrator if you enter **Admin** in the user name field and if you enter the administrator's correct password.

Step 3.   Enter **Abc1234** in the *Administrator's Password* and *Confirm Password* fields. Once you enter this password, you will need to remember this password to open this exercise file in the future.

Several privileges are reserved for the administrator of the file. For example, the administrator is the only one who can view or change the company information (name, address, etc.) for the file. Also, the administrator is the only one who can make any changes to the *Company Preferences* tabs in the *Preferences* section. For more information about the file administrator, see QuickBooks online Help.

> **Note:**
> To protect and secure your QuickBooks data file, always use a complex password. Complex passwords use at least seven characters, including capital and lowercase letters, numbers, and special characters. At least one of the characters should be a number, and another an uppercase letter.

Step 4.   In the *Challenge Question* field, select **Name of oldest nephew**.

Step 5.   Enter **Bill** in the *Answer* field. Click **OK**. After reading the password reminder window, click **OK** again.

Step 6.   Now you will set up the user's privileges. Select **Set Up Users** from the *Set Up Users and Passwords* submenu of the *Company* menu. The *QuickBooks Login* window displays (see Figure 12-53).

Step 7.   Type *Abc1234* in the *Password* field and click **OK**.

Figure 12-53 QuickBooks Login window

Step 8.   The window in Figure 12-54 shows the *User list* for this company file. To create an additional user, click **Add User**.

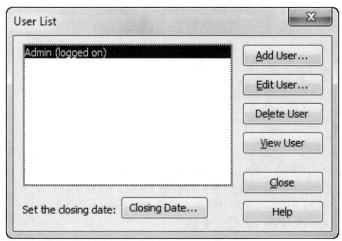

Figure 12-54 The User List for a company file

Step 9.   When you click **Add User**, QuickBooks walks you through a series of windows (a Wizard) where you set privileges for each user (see Figure 12-55). Make your selections as appropriate.

Step 10.   On the *User Name and Password* window, enter **Kathy** in the *User Name* field, and enter *Abc4321* in the *Password* and *Confirm Password* fields. Click **Next**.

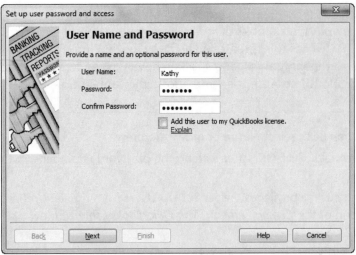

Figure 12-55 The User Name and Password window

Step 11.   On the *Access for user: Kathy* window, select **Selected areas of QuickBooks** (see Figure 12-56). Click **Next**.

As the Administrator, you can give users access to all areas of QuickBooks or you can restrict access to selected areas of the program.

Figure 12-56 You can restrict a user's access

Did you know?
By selecting *Access to All areas of QuickBooks*, you give a user permission to change transactions in closed periods. Choosing *Selected areas* for all users allows you to protect your prior period accounting data without limiting the users' access to any other transactions or reporting (see Figure 12-58).

Step 12.   On the *Sales and Accounts Receivable* window, select **Full Access** and click **Next** (see Figure 12-57).

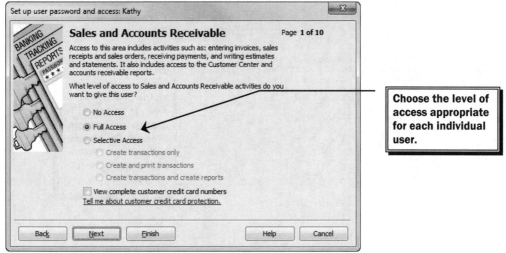

Figure 12-57 The Sales and Accounts Receivable window

Step 13.   Click **Next** on each of the following windows to view the default settings.

When setting up your own file, set access rights for each new user as appropriate. If you are not sure what to select, click **Help**. Online Help will fully explain each privilege.

Each user should be restricted from *Changing or Deleting Transactions recorded before the closing date* (see Figure 12-58). This setting creates additional protection for your accounting data once you have closed the books for a period.

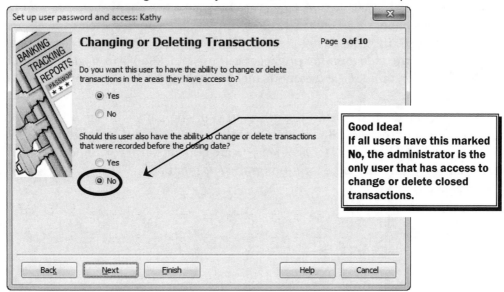

Figure 12-58 Changing or Deleting Transactions window

Step 14.   On the final window, review the privileges that you have set for this user (see Figure 12-59). If you want to make any changes, click **Prev** until you see the window you want to change. To save your new user settings, click **Finish**. If you receive an Intuit Sync Manager warning, click **OK**.

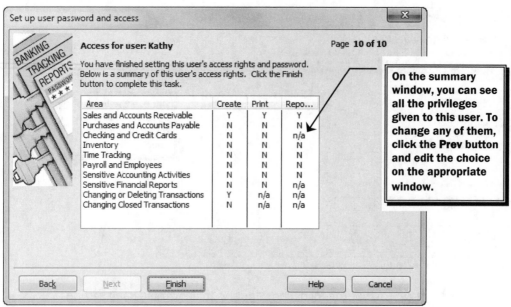

Figure 12-59 .The Summary window

Step 15.   Click **Close** on the *User List* window.

Multi-User and Single-User Modes

QuickBooks is often run in a networked environment, where multiple users access the file at the same time. In such an environment, you will need to have QuickBooks is in *multi-user* mode to allow these users to access the file. However, there are a few changes that cannot be made to a file while QuickBooks is in *multi-user* mode and require you to switch to *single-user* mode. When QuickBooks is in *single-user* mode, only one person can access the file at a time. Any user, not just those with *Administrator* privileges can use QuickBooks in *single-user* mode. Some of the changes that require *single-user* mode include making backups, exporting data, or deleting a list item.

To switch to *single-user* mode, first contact the others in your company who are using your file and ask them to exit out of the QuickBooks file. Once they have exited the file, go to the *File* menu and select *Switch To Single-User Mode*. When you are done in *single-user* mode, you can switch back to *multi-user* from the same location on the *File* menu.

Figure 12-60 Switch to Single-user Mode on File menu

Review Questions

Select the best answer(s) for each of the following:

1. If you're setting up QuickBooks and plan to begin using it at the beginning of the next calendar year, the best start date for your company file setup is:

    a)   The first day of the year (01/01/xx).
    b)   The day you are starting to use QuickBooks, regardless of the fiscal year.
    c)   The last day of the previous year (12/31/xx).
    d)   The first day of the quarter chosen for conversion.

2. This chapter suggests that the best way to set up A/R and A/P balances in QuickBooks is to:

    a)   Enter the total amount of A/R and A/P on a *General Journal Entry* dated on your start date.
    b)   Enter the balance of each account by editing the accounts in the *Chart of Accounts*.
    c)   Use a special account called A/R Setup (or A/P Setup) to record the opening balances.
    d)   Enter a separate *Invoice* for each open invoice and enter a separate *Bill* for each unpaid bill.

3. Setting up a company file does not include:

    a)   Obtaining a business license.
    b)   Selecting the appropriate chart of accounts for your type of business.
    c)   Adding accounts to the chart of accounts.
    d)   Entering *Invoices*.

4. A good example of a liability account is:

    a)   Inventory.
    b)   Accounts Receivable.
    c)   Advertising.
    d)   Accounts Payable.

5. To ensure the accuracy of the information entered during setup, it is important to:

    a)   Know your Retained Earnings.
    b)   Verify that your *Trial Balance* matches the one provided by your accountant.
    c)   Start at the beginning of the fiscal period.
    d)   Know everything there is to know about accounting.

Setup-Problem 1

APPLYING YOUR KNOWLEDGE

Create a *new* QuickBooks company file for Academy Photography. Use the information from the following tables and figures to completely set up the file using 12/31/2014 as your start date. Use the 12-Step setup process discussed in this chapter. Call your file **Setup-12Problem1.QBW**.

Company Info	
Company name	Academy Photography
Legal name	Academy Photography, Inc.
Tax ID	11-1111111
Address	123 Main Street Pleasanton, CA 94588
Country	U.S.
Phone	925-555-1111
Fax	925-555-1112
E-mail Address	info@academyphoto.biz
Web site	http://www.academyphoto.biz
Industry	Art, Writing or Photography
Income tax form	S Corporation
First month of fiscal year	January
Administrator password	*Leave blank*

Table 12-9 Company Information

Advanced Setup Settings	
Products and services	Academy Photography sells both products and services, although they do not sell products online.
Sales	Academy Photography charges sales tax and creates estimates. They want to track sales orders (if using Premier), and use statements and progress invoicing.
Purchases & vendors	Academy Photography will need to create billing statements and track bills. They will be tracking inventory. They will also want to print checks. They do not plan to accept credit or debit cards.
Employees	Academy Photography has both W-2 employees and 1099 contractors. They will want to track time.
Currency	Academy Photography does not need to track multiple currencies.

Table 12-10 EasyStep Interview settings

Additional Accounts for the Chart of Accounts		
Acct #	Account Name	Account Type
10100	Checking	Bank
10200	Money Market	Bank
10900	Journal Entries	Bank
22000	National Bank VISA Gold	Credit Card
24010	Payroll Liabilities:Company Payroll Taxes Payable	Other Current Liability
24020	Payroll Liabilities:Employee Payroll Taxes Payable	Other Current Liability
24030	Payroll Liabilities:Other Payroll Liabilities	Other Current Liability
27000	Truck Loan	Long Term Liability
40000	Services	Income
45000	Sales *(note: change number of existing account)*	Income

Table 12-11 Additional Accounts for the Chart of Accounts

Accounts – In addition to the default *Chart of Accounts*, add the accounts listed in Table 12-1. Since QuickBooks automatically created a Sales Income Account, you will only need to change the account number for this account. It is not necessary to enter descriptions, bank account numbers, or assign tax line items to any of these accounts for this problem. You will also create subaccounts, whose names are separated from the main account by a colon (:). For example, Company Payroll Taxes Payable is a subaccount of Payroll Liabilities. For a full recommended *Chart of Accounts*, see Setup Problem 2.

Items – Table 12-12 is the *Item List* that will be used to track products and services sold by Academy Photography.

Type	Item	Description	Tax Code	Account	Cost	Price
Service	Indoor Photo Session	Indoor Studio Session	Non	Services		$ 95.00
Service	Retouching	Photo retouching services	Non	Services		$ 95.00
Inventory Part	Camera SR32	Supra Digital Camera SR32	Tax	Sales	$ 450.00	$ 695.99
Inventory Part	Case	Camera and Lens High Impact Case	Tax	Sales	$ 45.00	$ 79.99
Non-Inventory Part	Standard Photo Package	Standard Package of Photography from Session	Tax	Sales		$ 55.00
Sales Tax Item	Contra Costa	Contra Costa Sales Tax Vendor: State Board of Equalization (Quick Add)	Non	Sales Tax Payable		8.25%
Sales Tax Item	Out of State (Automatically Created)	Out of State Sales Tax - exempt from sales tax	Non	Sales Tax Payable		0%
Sales Tax Item	Santa Clara	Santa Clara Sales Tax Vendor: State Board of Equalization (Quick Add)	Non	Sales Tax Payable		8.25%

Table 12-12 Item List

Classes – Academy Photography uses *Classes* to separately track revenues and expenses from each of their locations. You will need to turn on class tracking in the *Accounting Company Preferences*.

Class Names	San Jose	Walnut Creek	Overhead

Table 12-13 Class Tracking

Terms – Verify the following terms in the **Terms List**.

Net 30	Net 15	2% 10, Net 30	Due on Receipt

Table 12-14 Terms List

Bank Statements – Figure 12-61 shows the Checking account bank statement for Academy Photography on their Start Date of 12/31/2014. There is no bank statement available for the money market account, but you've been told that there are no outstanding deposits or checks in that account. Enter the **Bank Ending Balance** as the opening balance for Checking account.

Business Checking Account			
Statement Date:	**December 31, 2014**		*Page 1 of 1*

Summary:

Previous Balance as of 11/30/14:		$	32,624.52
Total Deposits and Credits: 2	+	$	10,157.28
Total Checks and Debits: 9	-	$	7,027.40
Total Interest Earned: 1	+	$	8.62
Total Service Charge: 1	-	$	10.00
Statement Balance as of 12/31/14:	=	**$**	**35,753.02**

Deposits and Other Credits:

DEPOSITS

Date	Description		Amount
8-Dec	Customer Deposit	$	6,150.00
20-Dec	Customer Deposit	$	4,007.28
	2 Deposits: $		**10,157.28**

INTEREST

Date	Description		Amount
31-Dec	Interest Earned	$	8.62
	Interest: $		**8.62**

Checks and Other Withdrawals:

CHECKS PAID:

Check No.	Date Paid		Amount
3466	2-Dec	$	324.00
3467	3-Dec	$	128.60
3468	5-Dec	$	83.00
3469	8-Dec	$	285.00
3470	10-Dec	$	1,528.00
3471	12-Dec	$	3,000.00
3472	13-Dec	$	276.52
3473	15-Dec	$	142.00
3474	28-Dec	$	1,260.28
	9 Checks Paid: $		**7,027.40**

SERVICE CHARGES

Date	Description		Amount
31-Dec	Service Charge	$	10.00
	1 Service Charge: $		**10.00**

Figure 12-61 Bank statement for checking account on 12/31/2014

Outstanding Checks and Deposits – Table 12-15 shows a list of outstanding checks and deposits in the Checking account on 12/31/2014. Enter the outstanding check and deposit in the checking account register using the original date and Opening Balance Equity as the offsetting account. Don't worry if payee information is not available.

Outstanding Deposits at 12/31/14		Outstanding Checks at 12/31/14		
Date	**Amount**	**Date**	**Check #**	**Amount**
12/30/2014	$2,000.00	12/26/2014	3475	3,462.85

Table 12-15 Outstanding checks and deposits.

Open Invoices - Table 12-16 shows a list of all open invoices for Academy Photography on 12/31/2014. Enter open **Invoices** using the original information and Intuit Product Invoice template. "Quick Add" each of the customer names when prompted. Save the tax information to be used again.

Inv #	Invoice Date	Customer:Job	Class	Terms	Item/Qty/Amt Due	
2014-955	12/18/2014	Doughboy Donuts	San Jose	Net 30	Indoor Photo Session	
					3 Hours	$ 285.00
					Retouching	
					1 Hour	$ 95.00
					Total:	$ 380.00
2014-942	12/21/2014	Scotts Shoes	San Jose	Net 30	Camera	$695.99
					Santa Clara Sales Tax	
					Total :	$ 753.41

Table 12-16 Open Invoices

Unpaid Bills - Academy Photography had one unpaid bill at 12/31/2014. Enter the **Bill** with original information. "Quick Add" each of the vendor names when prompted. Save the terms information to be used again.

Bill #	Bill Date	Terms	Vendor	Amt Due	Account/Item	Job	Class
52773	12/21/14	Net 15	Boswell Consulting	438.00	Subcontracted Services	Scotts Shoes	San Jose

Table 12-17 Unpaid bills

Physical Inventory– Below are the physical inventory counts and values at 12/31/2014. Enter the Ref. No. as 2014-1 and Opening Balance Equity as Adjusting account. Select **Save Anyway** option when a dialog box appears asking for class information.

Physical Inventory at 12/31/2014		
Item	Quantity on Hand	Value
Camera	20	$9,000.00
Case	20	900.00

Table 12-18 Physical Inventory by Inventory Part

Trial Balance – Table 12-19 shows the ending trial for Academy Photography on 12/31/2014. Enter opening balances for Asset, Liabilities, and Equity accounts to match the trial balance amounts.

Adjust Sales Tax Payable to match trial balance amount, using *Vendor:* State Board of Equalization.

Close the Opening Balance Equity account to Retained Earnings.

You will notice that the Trial Balance does not exactly match the one in Table 12-19. The income and expenses from the open *Invoices* and unpaid *Bills* shows in the income and expense accounts. This is CORRECT! When QuickBooks "closes" the year, those numbers will be posted into Retained Earnings. To see it work, change the date on the *Trial Balance* to 01/01/2015.

Academy Photography		
Trial Balance		
December 31, 2014		
	Debit	Credit
Checking	$34,290.17	
Money Market	$68,100.00	
Accounts Receivable	$1,133.41	
Inventory	$9,900.00	
Furniture and Equipment	$85,365.00	
Accumulated Depreciation		$43,550.00
Accounts Payable		$438.00
National Bank VISA Gold		$2,152.00
Payroll Liabilities: Company Payroll Taxes Payable		$83.00
Payroll Liabilities: Employee Payroll Taxes Payable		$285.00
Sales Tax Payable		$327.03
Truck Loan		$28,625.00
Capital Stock		$10,000.00
Retained Earnings		$113,328.55
TOTAL	$198,788.58	$198,788.58

Table 12-19 Trial balance on 12/31/2014

After completing the setup, print the following reports:

1. Account Listing

2. Item Listing

3. Open Invoices Report at 12/31/2014

4. Unpaid Bills Detail Report at 12/31/2014

5. Inventory Valuation Summary Report at 12/31/2014

6. Trial Balance as of 12/31/2014

7. Trial Balance as of 01/01/15

8. Balance Sheet Standard on 01/01/2015

Notice that Retained Earnings on the 01/01/2015 Balance Sheet has been adjusted for the income and expenses from last year. This shows how QuickBooks automatically calculates Retained Earnings. If you change the date on the Balance Sheet to 12/31/2014, you'll see Net Income on the Balance Sheet and the Retained Earnings number will change back to the "before closing" amounts. Try it.

Optional Setup-Problem 2

In Setup-Problem 1 you used the default *Chart of Accounts* with a few additions. We recommend further customization to the *Chart of Accounts* when you setup a company file. For this problem, create a *Chart of Accounts* using the file you created in Problem 1.

The *Chart of Accounts* is listed in Table 12-11. It is not necessary to enter descriptions, bank account numbers, or assign tax line items to any of these accounts for this problem. Normally, when you create a new data file, QuickBooks will create some accounts on the

Chart of Accounts for you. In this exercise, your goal is to add, delete, or modify the existing chart of accounts (from Setup-Problem 1) as necessary so that it agrees with the list below. As in Problem 1, you will also create subaccounts, whose names are separated from the main account by a colon (:).

After completing the setup, print an Account Listing.

Chart of Accounts		
Acct #	**Account Name**	**Account Type**
10100	Checking	Bank
10200	Money Market	Bank
10300	Savings	Bank
10900	Journal Entries	Bank
11000	Accounts Receivable	Accounts Receivable
12100	Inventory Asset	Other Current Asset
12800	Employee Advances	Other Current Asset
13100	Prepaid Insurance	Other Current Asset
15000	Furniture and Equipment	Fixed Asset
15200	Buildings and Improvements	Fixed Asset
15600	Land	Fixed Asset
15900	Leasehold Improvements	Fixed Asset
16400	Vehicles	Fixed Asset
17000	Accumulated Depreciation	Fixed Asset
18700	Security Deposits Asset	Other Asset
20000	Accounts Payable	Accounts Payable
22000	National Bank VISA Gold	Credit Card
24000	Payroll Liabilities	Other Current Liability
24010	Payroll Liabilities:Company Payroll Taxes Payable	Other Current Liability
24020	Payroll Liabilities:Employee Payroll Taxes Payable	Other Current Liability
24030	Payroll Liabilities:Other Payroll Liabilities	Other Current Liability
24200	Line of Credit	Other Current Liability
24500	Advance Customer Payments	Other Current Liability
25500	Sales Tax Payable	Other Current Liability
27000	Truck Loan	Long Term Liability
30000	Opening Bal Equity	Equity
30100	Capital Stock	Equity
31400	Shareholder Distributions	Equity
32000	Retained Earnings	Equity
40000	Services	Income
45000	Sales	Income
50000	Cost of Goods Sold	Cost of Goods Sold
53000	Purchase Discounts	Cost of Goods Sold
53500	Subcontracted Services	Cost of Goods Sold
54000	Inventory Variance	Cost of Goods Sold
60000	Advertising and Promotion	Expense
60200	Automobile Expense	Expense
60300	Bad Debts	Expense
60400	Bank Service Charges	Expense

61700	Computer and Internet Expenses	Expense
62400	Depreciation Expense	Expense
62500	Dues and Subscriptions	Expense
62600	Equipment Rental	Expense
63300	Insurance Expense	Expense
63400	Interest Expense	Expense
64300	Meals and Entertainment	Expense
64900	Office Supplies	Expense
66000	Payroll Expenses	Expense
66010	Payroll Expenses:Employee Benefits	Expense
66020	Payroll Expenses:Gross Wages	Expense
66040	Payroll Expenses:Officer's Compensation	Expense
66060	Payroll Expenses:Payroll Tax Expense	Expense
66500	Postage and Delivery	Expense
66700	Professional Fees	Expense
67100	Rent Expense	Expense
67200	Repairs and Maintenance	Expense
68100	Telephone Expense	Expense
68130	Telephone Expense:Office Phone	Expense
68150	Telephone Expense:Cell Phone	Expense
68400	Travel Expense	Expense
68600	Utilities	Expense
70200	Interest Income	Other Income
80000	Ask My Accountant	Other Expense
90000	Estimates	Non-Posting

Table 12-20 The Chart of Accounts

Chapter 13
Adjustments and Year-End Procedures

Objectives

After completing this chapter, you should be able to:

- Edit, void, and delete transactions (page 419)
- Make *General Journal Entries* (page 423)
- Memorize and schedule transactions to be automatically entered (page 426)
- Close the year and enter special transactions for sole proprietorships and partnerships (page 430)
- Set the closing date to lock the company file (page 435)

> **Restore this File:**
> This chapter uses Adjustments-12.QBW. To open this file, restore the Adjustments-12.QBM file to your hard disk. See page 8 for instructions on restoring files. If you are using QuickBooks Premier Accountant, we recommend that you toggle to QuickBooks Premier General Business as described on page x.

In this chapter, you will learn how to edit and void transactions in current and closed periods, and you'll learn how to use journal entries and zero-dollar checks to adjust balances and close the year. You will also learn how to memorize transactions and use the closing date in QuickBooks.

Editing, Voiding, and Deleting Transactions

Unlike many other accounting programs, QuickBooks allows you to change any transaction at any time as long as you have sufficient privileges. However, you should almost never change transactions dated in closed accounting periods, or transactions that have been reconciled with a bank statement.

> **Key Term:**
> For the purposes of this discussion, a *Closed Accounting Period* is a period for which you've already issued financial statements and/or filed tax returns.

When you change or delete a transaction, QuickBooks updates the *General Ledger* with your change, as of the date of the modified or deleted transaction. Therefore, if you modify or delete transactions in a closed accounting period, your QuickBooks financial statements will change for that period, causing discrepancies between your QuickBooks reports and your tax return.

In QuickBooks, the *Closing Date* field is used to "lock" your data file to prevent users from making changes on or before a specified date. See page 435 for information about setting the *Closing Date* in QuickBooks.

> **Tip:**
> Using the *Closing Date*, a period can be "closed" even if there is no tax return for the period. For example, you can close the books through January 31, 2015, even though your last tax return was dated December 31, 2014. If management makes decisions based on *printed* financial information dated January 31, 2015, any changes to QuickBooks information dated before January 31, 2015 will cause the reports in QuickBooks to disagree with the printed reports. Also, many companies submit financial information to third parties (e.g., banks) during their tax year on a monthly or quarterly basis.

Some companies close their books monthly, but other companies only close the books quarterly or annually. Make sure you know how often your company closes periods before you make changes to transactions that might affect closed periods.

> **Tip:**
> At the very least, you should lock the file at the end of each fiscal and/or calendar year. You may also choose to lock the file monthly, after you perform bank reconciliations and adjusting entries for the month.

Editing Transactions

From time to time, you may need to modify transactions to correct posting errors. To edit (or modify) a transaction in QuickBooks, change the data directly on the form. For example, if you forgot to add a charge for an Outdoor Photo Shoot to Invoice 2015-106 and *you have not already sent the invoice to your customer or client*, you will need to add a line for the photo session on the previously created invoice.

COMPUTER PRACTICE

To edit an existing transaction, follow these steps:

Step 1.   From the *Customers* menu, select **Create Invoices.** If QuickBooks displays a *Professional Services Forms* dialog box, click **OK.**

Step 2.   Click **Previous** to display Invoice 2015-106 dated 2/28/15 (see Figure 13-1).

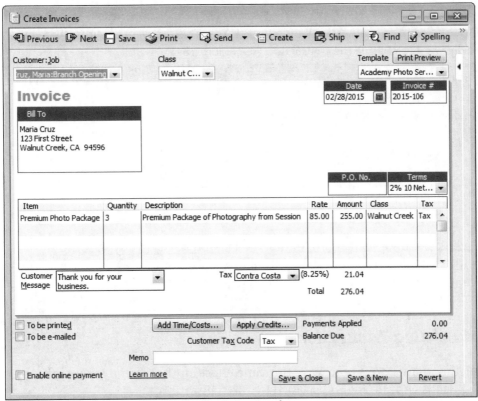

Figure 13-1 Edit the transaction on the Create Invoices form

Step 3.   Click on the second line in the main body of the *Invoice* and enter **Outdoor Photo Session** in the *Item* column. Press **Tab**.

Step 4.   Enter *3* in the *Quantity* column and then press **Tab** (see Figure 13-2).

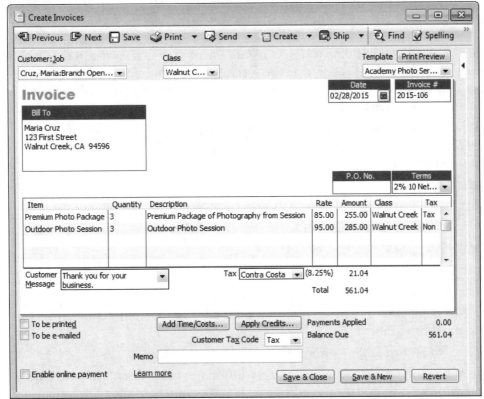

Figure 13-2 Add the labor Item to the Invoice.

Step 5.   Click **Save & Close** to save the *Invoice*.

Step 6.   On the *Recording Transaction* window, click **Yes**. This message confirms that you really want to change the transaction (see Figure 13-3).

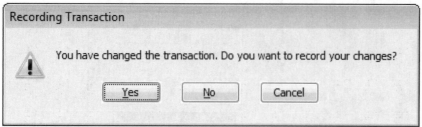

Figure 13-3 Recording Transaction window

> **Note:**
> Do not use this method of changing transactions if you have already sent the *Invoice* to the customer. In that case, you would need to create a new *Invoice* with the separate charge. Also, you should never change transactions dated in a closed accounting period.

Voiding and Deleting Transactions

Voiding and deleting transactions both have the same effect on the *General Ledger* – the effect is to zero out the debits and the credits specified by the transaction.

There is one significant difference between voiding and deleting. When you void a transaction, QuickBooks keeps a record of the date, number, and detail of the transaction. When you delete a transaction, QuickBooks removes it completely from your file.

The *Audit Trail* feature of QuickBooks tracks changes and deletions of transactions. The *Audit Trail Report* lists each accounting transaction and every addition, deletion, or modification that affects that transaction. For more information about the *Audit Trail*, see the QuickBooks Onscreen Help.

In addition to the *Audit Trail*, QuickBooks has a *Voided/Deleted Transactions Report* that lists all voided and deleted transactions. This report is very useful when you have a number of users in a file and transactions seem to "disappear," since the report shows the time, date, and user name of the changes or deletions.

In general, voiding is better than deleting transactions. In either case, make sure you keep a record of voided and deleted transactions. The record should include the date of the voided or deleted transaction and the reason for it.

To **delete** a transaction:

1.   Select the transaction you wish to delete; it may be displayed in a register or form.

2.   Select the **Edit** menu and then select **Delete** (or press **Ctrl+D**).

3.   On the *Delete Transaction* window, click **OK.**

To **void** a transaction:

1.   Select the transaction in a register or display it in the form.

2.   Select the **Edit** menu and then select **Void** (or right-click on the transaction and select **Void** from the shortcut menu).

3.   Click the **Record** button at the bottom of the window.

4.   If you attempt to close the window without recording the transaction, the *Recording Transaction* window displays. If this is the case, click **Yes** to record the transaction.

> **Note:**
> Proper accounting procedures do not allow you to simply delete transactions at will. However, in some cases it is perfectly fine to use the **Delete** command. For example, it is acceptable to delete a check that you have not printed. On the other hand, if you have already printed the check, you should **Void** the check instead of deleting it. That way, you will have a record of the voided check and keep the numbering sequence intact in the register.

Deleting All Transactions

Occasionally, you may wish to delete all transactions from a file, while leaving the *Customers*, *Vendors*, *Employees* and other *List* information as well as the *Preferences* in the file. QuickBooks *Condense Data Utility* allows you to make these changes. You have the option to either delete all transactions, or delete all transactions except for transactions within a specific date range.

You can access the *Condense Data* command from the *Utilities* submenu under the *File* menu. QuickBooks prompts you to select a specific date to delete transactions before, or to delete all transactions. Do not do this now with your exercise file.

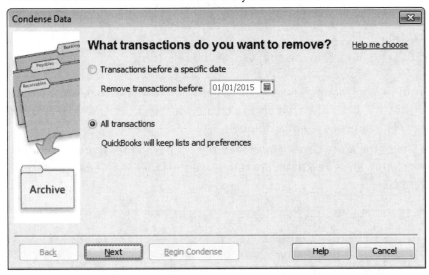

Figure 13-4 Condense Data Utility

General Journal Entries

General Journal Entries are transactions that adjust the balance of two or more accounts.

> **Note:**
> Good accounting practice suggests that you keep a separate record of each *General Journal Entry* you make in QuickBooks. This record will be very helpful if you are ever audited or if you have to research the reasons for the adjustment.

Here are a few examples of adjusting entries in QuickBooks:

- Recategorize a transaction from one Class to another.
- Recategorize a transaction from one account to another.
- Allocate prepaid expenses to each month throughout the year.
- Record non-cash expenses, such as depreciation.
- Close the Owner's Draw account into the Owner's Equity account.

In most cases, you will use a *General Journal Entry* to record adjustments.

Creating a General Journal Entry

> **Note:**
> Depending on your QuickBooks user settings, you may need permission from the QuickBooks administrator to create *General Journal Entries*.

COMPUTER PRACTICE

Step 1.   Select the **Company** menu and then select **Make General Journal Entries**.

Those using QuickBooks Premier Accountant should select the *Accountant* menu and select *Make General Journal Entries*.

Step 2.   If the *Assigning Numbers to Journal Entries* window opens, check the **Do not display this message in the future** box and click **OK**.

Step 3.   Enter *01/31/15* in the **Date** field and then press **Tab** (see Figure 13-5).

If you are using QuickBooks Premier Accountant, your window may look different than Figure 13-5.

Step 4.   Make sure **2015-1** is already in the *Entry No.* field. Press **Tab**.

The very first time you enter a *General Journal Entry*, enter whatever number you want in the *Entry No.* field. Then, when you create your next General Journal Entry, QuickBooks will increment the entry number.

Step 5.   On the top line of the *Make General Journal Entries* window, enter **Journal Entries** in the *Account* column. Press **Tab** three times to leave the *Debit* and *Credit* columns blank for this line.

> **Expert Tip:**
> In these examples, we use a bank account called *Journal Entries* on the top line of each *Journal Entry*. If you create the *Journal Entries* bank account and then enter it on the top line of each *General Journal Entry*, QuickBooks tracks all the *General Journal Entries* in a separate register on the *Chart of Accounts*. This register allows you to quickly look up and view all of your *General Journal Entries*. Though you use this account in every *General Journal Entry*, you will never debit or credit the account and therefore it will never have a balance.

Step 6.   Enter **Recategorize Expense** in the *Memo* column. Press **Tab** three times to leave the *Name* and *Class* columns blank for this line.

Step 7.   Enter the information on the next two lines as shown in Figure 13-5.

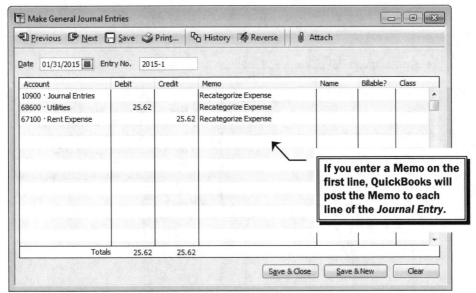

Figure 13-5 General Journal Entry window

> **Note:**
> *General Journal Entries* must balance. The total of the *Debit* column must match the total of the *Credit* column.

Step 8.   Click **Save & Close** to save the transaction.

Adjusting Expense Accounts Associated with Items (Zero-Dollar Checks)

If you use *Items* to track the details of your expenses, you may need to enter adjustments to the *Items* as well as the accounts to which the *Items* are assigned.

However, the *Journal Entry* window in QuickBooks has no provision for entering *Items* as part of the *Journal Entry*.

To solve the problem, use a transaction (such as a *Check*) that allows you to use *Items*. The *Check* will be a "Zero-Dollar Check" in that it will have an equal amount of debits and credits in the splits area of the transaction. You can use the *Journal Entries* bank account so you don't clutter the normal bank account with zero-dollar checks.

> **DO NOT PERFORM THESE STEPS NOW. THEY ARE FOR REFERENCE ONLY.**

Follow these steps to use zero-dollar *Checks* as *Journal Entries*:

1.   Create a *Check* using the *Journal Entries* bank account.

2.   Enter the debits as *Items* with positive amounts and the credits as *Items* with negative amounts as shown in Figure 13-6 below. The total *Check* amount should net to zero.

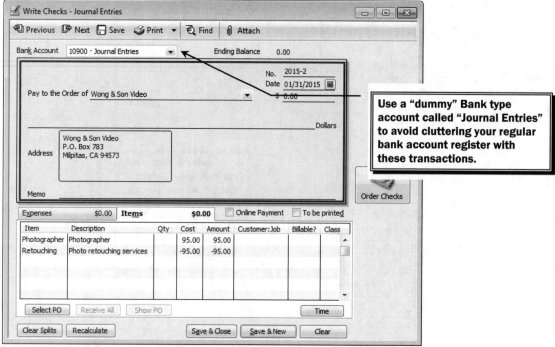

Figure 13-6 Using the Write Checks window to create a Journal Entry affecting job cost.

3.   To review the adjustment to the *General Ledger*, save the zero-dollar *Check*, select the **Reports** menu and then select **Transaction Journal**. QuickBooks displays the report shown in Figure 13-7 below.

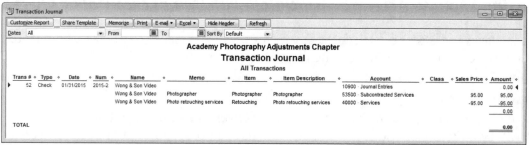

Figure 13-7 Transaction Journal from the Zero Dollar Check

In addition to the example above, zero-dollar *Checks* are very useful for adjustments involving *any combination* of *Items* and expenses. Similarly, you can use zero-dollar *Sales Receipts* to adjust items that affect income accounts.

Memorized Transactions

If you frequently enter the same transaction (or similar ones), you can memorize and schedule the entry of the transaction. For example, if you want QuickBooks to automatically enter the depreciation journal entry each month, you can memorize the transaction and then schedule it to be automatically entered.

> **Note:**
> You can memorize *Journal Entries, Invoices, Sales Receipts, Bills* and other transactions, however, there are some transactions that cannot be memorized, such as *Bill Payment* and *Receive Payment*.

Memorizing a Journal Entry

COMPUTER PRACTICE

To memorize a transaction, follow these steps:

Step 1.	Create a *General Journal Entry* with the data from Figure 13-8

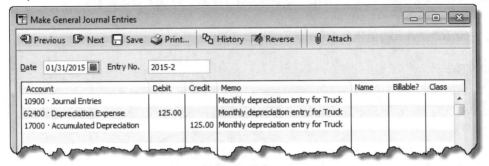

Figure 13-8 Monthly Depreciation for Truck

Step 2.	Before saving the *General Journal Entry*, select **Memorize General Journal** from the *Edit* menu (or press **Ctrl+M**).

Step 3.	Enter ***Vehicle Depreciation*** in the *Name* field.

Use names that you will recognize so that you can easily find this transaction in the *Memorized Transaction* list.

Step 4.	Set the fields as shown in Figure 13-9 to indicate when and how often you want the transaction entered and then click **OK**.

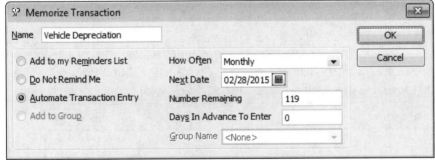

Figure 13-9 Vehicle Depreciation memorized information

Step 5.	Select **Save & Close** to record the *Journal Entry*. If QuickBooks displays a dialog box regarding *Tracking Fixed Assets on Journal Entries*, click **OK**.

Step 6.	If necessary, close all your open windows by clicking the close box (⊠) in the upper right corner.

> **Did You Know?**
> You can memorize *most* transactions in QuickBooks. Just display the transaction, then select **Memorize [Transaction Name]** from the *Edit* menu, or right click on the transaction and select **Memorize [Transaction Name]**. You can also press **Ctrl+M**. The *Memorized Transaction List* contains all the transactions that you have memorized. To display this list, select **Memorized Transaction List** from the *List* menu.

Now, every time you launch QuickBooks, it checks your *Memorized Transaction* list for transactions that need to be entered automatically. If the system date is on or after the date in the *Next Date* field (minus the number in the *Days In Advance To Enter* field), QuickBooks will ask you if you want to enter the memorized transaction.

Deleting, Rescheduling, and Editing Memorized Transactions

Rescheduling or Renaming Memorized Transactions

COMPUTER PRACTICE

To edit the schedule or name of a memorized transaction, follow these steps:

Step 1.   Select the **Memorized Transaction List** from the *Lists* menu, or press **Ctrl+T**.

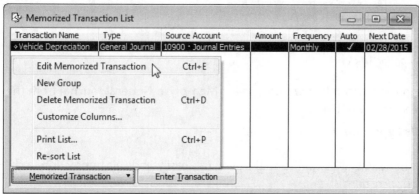

Figure 13-10 Memorized Transaction List

Step 2.   Select the Vehicle Depreciation transaction in the *Memorized Transaction List*. Select **Edit Memorized Transaction** from the *Memorized Transaction* drop-down list or press **Ctrl+E** (see Figure 13-10).

Step 3.   The *Schedule Memorized Transaction* window displays (see Figure 13-11). This window allows you to reschedule or rename the transaction, but it does not allow you to edit the actual transaction. Click **Cancel** and close all open windows.

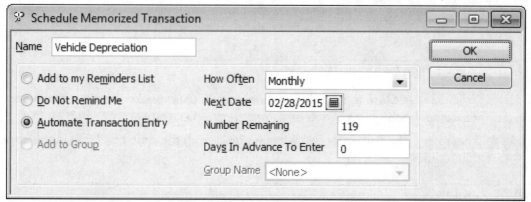

Figure 13-11 Schedule Memorized Transaction window

Editing Memorized Transactions

In addition to editing the schedule or other attributes of a memorized transaction, sometimes it is necessary to edit the actual contents of the transaction such as the *Items*, prices, or coding.

COMPUTER PRACTICE

To edit the contents of a memorized transaction, follow these steps:

Step 1.   Select the **Memorized Transaction List** from the *Lists* menu, or press **Ctrl+T**.

Step 2.   To edit the *Vehicle Depreciation* memorized transaction, double-click it in the **Memorized Transaction List**.

This displays a new transaction (see Figure 13-12) with the contents of the memorized transaction. You can change anything on the transaction and then rememorize it. In this case, we will add the **San Jose** *Class*.

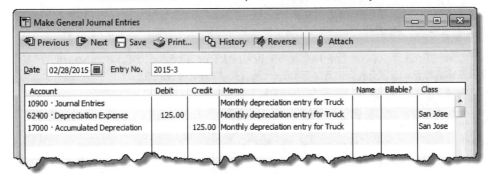

Figure 13-12 Edit the transaction as necessary

Step 3.   To rememorize the transaction, select **Memorize General Journal** from the *Edit* menu (in the program's menu bar), or press **Ctrl+M**.

Step 4.   To save your edited transaction in the *Memorized Transaction* list click **Replace** (see Figure 13-13).

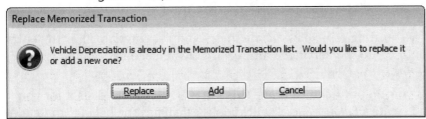

Figure 13-13 Replace Memorized Transaction message

Step 5.   Click **Clear** to erase the contents of the *Journal Entry* and then click **Save & Close**. This will save the changes to the memorized transaction without entering the transaction in the *General Journal*.

Deleting Memorized Transactions

COMPUTER PRACTICE

To delete a memorized transaction, follow these steps:

Step 1.   Select the **Memorized Transaction List** from the *Lists* menu, or press **Ctrl+T**.

Step 2.   The **Vehicle Depreciation** is already selected because it is the first and only memorized transaction on the list.

Step 3.   Select **Delete Memorized Transaction** from the *Memorized Transaction* drop-down list, or press **Ctrl+D** (see Figure 13-14).

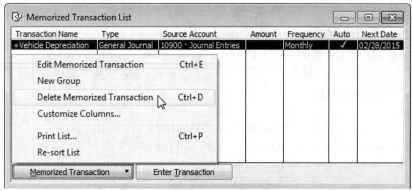

Figure 13-14 Deleting Memorized Transaction option

Step 4.   For now, click **Cancel** on the *Delete Memorized Transaction* dialog box so the
                memorized transaction will not be deleted (see Figure 13-15).

Figure 13-15 Delete Memorized Transaction

Step 5.   Close all open windows.

Closing the Year

At the end of each year, accounting principles dictate that you must enter an adjusting entry
to transfer net income or loss into the Retained Earnings (or Owner's Equity) account. This
entry is known as the *closing entry*.

However, in QuickBooks **you do not need to make this entry**. QuickBooks does it for you,
automatically. When you create a *Balance Sheet*, QuickBooks calculates the balance in Retained
Earnings by adding together the total net income for all prior years. At the end of your
company's fiscal year, QuickBooks automatically transfers the net income into Retained
Earnings.

On the left side of the example in Table 1, notice that the *Balance Sheet* for 12/31/2014 shows
net income for the year is $100,000.00. The right side shows the same *Balance Sheet*, but for
the next day (January 1, 2015). Since January is in a new year, last year's net income has been
automatically transferred to the Retained Earnings account.

Equity on Dec 31, 2014		Equity on Jan 1, 2015	
Opening Bal Equity	0.00	Opening Bal Equity	0.00
Preferred Stock	50,000.00	Preferred Stock	50,000.00
Common Stock	75,000.00	Common Stock	75,000.00
Retained Earnings	100,000.00	Retained Earnings	200,000.00
Net Income	100,000.00	Net Income	0.00
Total Equity	325,000.00	Total Equity	325,000.00

Table 1 Example of QuickBooks closing entry

There are two advantages to QuickBooks automatically closing the year for you. First, you do not have to create the year-end entry, which can be time-consuming. Second, the details of your income and expenses are not erased each year, as some programs require.

Closing the Accounting Period

The following is a list of actions you should take at the end of each accounting period. Perform these steps as often as you close your company's books. Many companies close monthly or quarterly, while some close yearly. No matter when you close, these steps are to help you create proper reports that incorporate year-end transactions. These entries may be non-cash entries such as depreciation, prepaid expense allocations, and adjustments to equity to properly reflect the closing of the year.

At the end of the year (or period), consider doing some or all of the following:

1. Enter depreciation entries.
2. Reconcile cash, credit card, and loan accounts with the period-end statements.
3. If your business has inventory, perform a physical inventory on the last day of the year. Following the inventory count, enter an Inventory Adjustment transaction in QuickBooks if necessary. See the "Inventory" chapter for more information about adjusting inventory.
4. If you are on the accrual basis of accounting, prepare *General Journal Entries* to accrue expenses and revenues. Ask your accountant for help with these entries.
5. If your business is a partnership, enter a *General Journal Entry* to distribute net income for the year to each of the partner's capital accounts. If your business is a sole proprietorship, enter a *General Journal Entry* closing Owner's Draw into Owner's Equity. See the section below for more information.
6. Run reports for the year and verify their accuracy. Enter adjusting entries as necessary and rerun the reports.
7. Print or create a PDF and file the following reports as of your closing date: *General Ledger, Balance Sheet Standard, Statement of Cash Flows, Trial Balance, Inventory Valuation Summary*, and *Profit & Loss Standard* for the year.
8. Back up your data file on a special backup drive or network server, or CD. The year-end backup should be permanent and stored in a safe place.
9. Set the closing date to the last day of the period and set a closing date password to prevent transactions in the closed period from being changed. See page 435 for details on setting the closing date.
10. Consider using the *Clean up Data File* utility. This will "condense" (reduce) the size of your data file, but will probably not be necessary every year. Data file cleanup is an involved process that should be done by your accountant or QuickBooks consultant.

Recording Closing Entries for Sole Proprietorships and Partnerships

> **Note:**
> **Do not enter the transactions in this section.** However, do familiarize yourself with these issues so that you can properly close the year in a sole proprietorship or partnership company.

Sole proprietorships have the following accounts in the Equity section of the *Chart of Accounts* (see Figure 13-16).

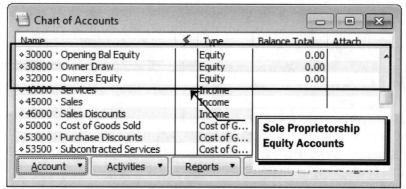

Figure 13-16 Sample Equity Section - Sole Proprietorships

Partnerships have the following accounts (or similar accounts) in the Equity section of the *Chart of Accounts* (see Figure 13-17). Although this list of accounts has a *Retained Earnings* account, it will be cleared out at the end of each year to keep it from accumulating a balance.

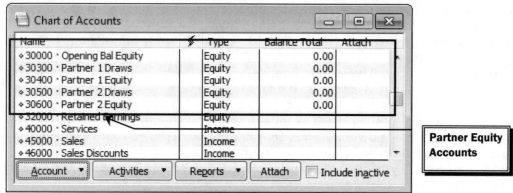

Figure 13-17 Sample Equity section - Partnerships

Throughout the year, as owners put money into and take money out of the business, you will add transactions that increase and decrease the appropriate equity accounts. In a sole proprietorship, you will use the Owner's Equity and Owner's Draw accounts. In a partnership, you will use the Equity and Draws accounts for each partner.

To record owners' investments in the company, enter a deposit transaction in your *Checking* account (or the account to which you make deposits), and enter *Owners Equity* in the *From Account* field (see Figure 13-18).

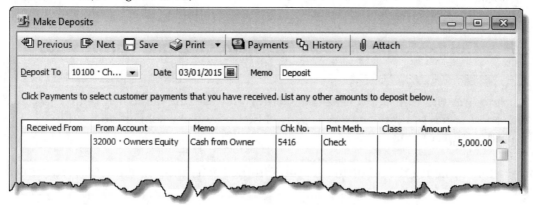

Figure 13-18 Record owner's investments in the Make Deposits window

To record owner's withdrawals from the company, enter a check transaction in the Checking account (or the account from which the owner draws money), and enter **Owners Draw** in the *Account* field (see Figure 13-19).

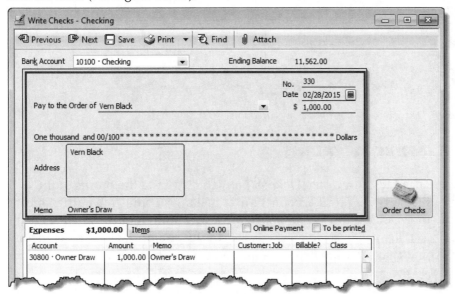

Figure 13-19 Record owner's withdrawals as a check transaction

Closing Sole Proprietorship Draw Accounts

At the end of each year, you will create a *General Journal Entry* to zero out the Owner's Draw account and close it into Owner's Equity (see Figure 13-20).

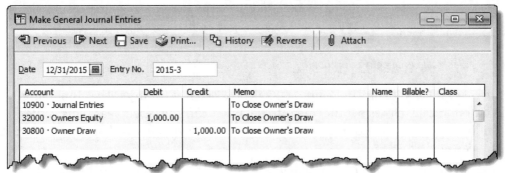

Figure 13-20 General Journal Entry to close Owners Draw

To find the amounts for this *Journal Entry*, create a **Trial Balance Report** for the end of the year. Use the balance in the Owner's Draw account for a *General Journal Entry* to close the account. For example, if your *Trial Balance* shows a *debit* balance of $1,000.00 in Owner's Draw, enter **$1,000.00** in the *credit* column on the Owner's Draw line of this *General Journal Entry*. Then enter a debit to the Owner's Equity account to make the entry balance.

Closing Partnership Draws Accounts

To close the Partners' Draws accounts into each Partner's Equity account, use a *General Journal Entry* like the one shown in Figure 13-21. Use the same process explained above to get the numbers from the year-end *Trial Balance*.

Figure 13-21 General Journal Entry to close partner's draws accounts

Distributing Net Income to Partners

With partnerships, you need to use a *General Journal Entry* to distribute the profits of the company into each of the partner's profit accounts. After making all adjusting entries, create a *Profit & Loss Report* for the year. Use the *Net Income* figure at the bottom of the *Profit & Loss Report* to create the *General Journal Entry*, in Figure 13-22. In this example, assume net income for the year is $50,000 and that there are two equal partners in the business.

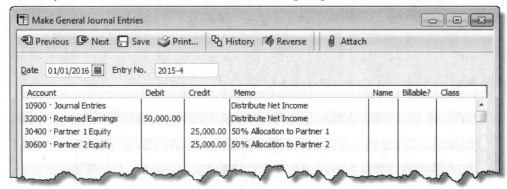

Figure 13-22 Use a General Journal entry to distribute partners' profits

Note that the *General Journal Entry* in Figure 13-22 debits *Retained Earnings*. That is because QuickBooks automatically closes net income into Retained Earnings each year. This is the entry you'll make each year to zero out the balance in *Retained Earnings* and distribute the net income to the partners.

Also, note that the *General Journal Entry* is dated January 1. This is because there is no "after-closing" *Balance Sheet* in QuickBooks. The December 31 *Balance Sheet* should show "undistributed" net income for the year. If the *General Journal Entry* were made on December 31, you would never be able to see a proper (before closing) December 31 *Balance Sheet*. Therefore, to preserve the December 31 before-closing *Balance Sheet*, use January 1 for this closing entry. If you want to see an after-closing *Balance Sheet*, use January 1 for that *Balance Sheet*.

> **Tip:**
> To preserve the after-closing date *Balance Sheet*, it is best to change the date on all normal business transactions that occur on January 1 to January 2. Use January 1 exclusively for the previous year's "closing" entries.

Setting the Closing Date to "Lock" Transactions

QuickBooks allows the administrator to set a closing date that effectively locks the file so that no one can make changes to transactions dated on or before a specified date.

> **Note:**
> Several privileges are reserved for the administrator of the file. For example, the administrator is the only one who can view or change the company information (name, address, etc.) for the file. Also, the administrator is the only one who can make any changes to the *Company Preferences* tabs in the *Preferences* section. For more information about the file administrator, see the QuickBooks onscreen Help.

COMPUTER PRACTICE

To set or modify the closing date and closing date password, follow these steps:

Step 1. Select **Preferences** from the *Edit* menu and then select the **Company Preferences** tab for the *Accounting* preference.

Step 2. Click the **Set Date/Password** button at the bottom of the window (see Figure 13-23).

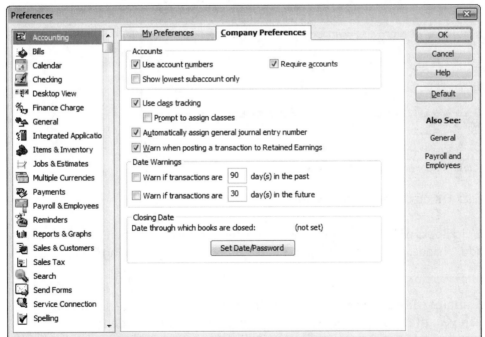

Figure 13-23 The Set/Date Password button in the Accounting Company Preferences

Step 3. The *Set Closing Date and Password* window opens (see Figure 13-24). Enter *12/31/2015* in the *Closing Date* field.

The date you enter specifies that all transactions dated on or before that date are "locked." Depending on each user's access privileges, QuickBooks either prohibits additions, changes, or deletions to any transactions with a date on or before this date; or, warns users before they make additions, changes, or deletions. To further protect transactions in closed periods you can also require all users, including the administrator, to enter a password before they can add, change, or delete transactions dated on or before the closing date.

> **Tip:**
> The user's setup affects the ability to add, change, or delete locked ("closed") transactions. When setting up new users, always choose the setting that prevents them from making additions, changes, or deletions to transactions recorded on or before the closing date. Unless the Closing Date Password is set, the administrator of the file can always bypass the closing date by simply ignoring a warning window. To better protect the closing date in your QuickBooks file, require all users, including the administrator, to enter a Closing Date Password.

Step 4.   Enter Abcd*1234* in the *Closing Date Password* and *Confirm Password* fields and click **Cancel** (see Figure 13-24). For this exercise, you won't save the changes. In reality, you will want to use a strong password.

Figure 13-24 Set Closing Date and Password window

Step 5.   Click **OK** on the *Preferences* window.

QuickBooks will now require all users to enter this password when attempting to add, change, or delete transactions dated on or before the Closing Date.

> **Note:**
> Your accountant will probably recommend that you set the Closing Date at the end of each year (if not more frequently) to prevent users from accidentally changing transactions after your company has filed its tax return.

Review Questions

Select the best answer for each of the following:

1. Which of the following tasks does QuickBooks perform automatically at year-end?

    a)   Creates adjusting journal entries to the income and expense accounts that can be viewed in the *General Ledger* report

    b)   Identifies expenses that are too high in comparison with prior years

    c)   Adjusts the balance in the *Retained Earnings* account to reflect the net income or loss for the year

    d)   Automatically backs up the data file

2. Entering a date in the *Closing Date* field accomplishes which of the following:

    a) Determines which date QuickBooks will use to automatically close the year
    b) Determines which date QuickBooks closes your file
    c) Locks the data file so that no unauthorized users can add, change, or delete transactions dated on or before the *Closing Date*
    d) Prepares a closing entry on that date

3. Voiding and Deleting transactions both do the following:

    a) Keep a record of the date, number, and detail of the transaction
    b) Completely remove all details of the transaction
    c) Zero out the debits and credits specified by the transaction
    d) Both b and c

4. To make an adjustment to *Items* as well as their associated accounts, create a:

    a) *General Journal Entry*
    b) Fixed Asset
    c) Zero-Dollar Check
    d) Memorized Transaction

5. At the end of the year, you should perform the following:

    a) Enter depreciation entries
    b) Perform a physical inventory
    c) If your business is a partnership, enter a *General Journal Entry* to distribute net income for the year to each of the partner's capital accounts. If your business is a sole proprietorship, enter a *General Journal Entry* closing Owner's Draw and Owner's Investments into Owner's Equity
    d) All of the above

Adjustments Problem 1

APPLYING YOUR KNOWLEDGE

> Restore the **Adjustments-11Problem1.QBM** file.

1. Create *General Journal Entry #2015-1* on *01/31/2015* to recategorize *$167.00* from **Office Supplies** Expense to **Postage and Delivery** Expense (*Hint*: Debit **Postage and Delivery**, credit **Office Supplies**). Use the **Journal Entries** account on the top line of the *General Journal Entry* as discussed in the chapter. Enter a descriptive memo *Recategorize Postage* on the top line of the entry. *Class:* **San Jose**.

2. Create a *General Journal Entry* on *01/31/2015*, *#2015-2*, recording *$85.00* in Depreciation for *Fixed Assets* (**Hint**: Debit **Depreciation Expense**, credit **Accumulated Depreciation**). Use the **Journal Entries** account on the top line of the *General Journal Entry* and enter a descriptive memo *Depreciation for Fixed Assets* on the top line of the entry. *Class:* **San Jose**.

3. Memorize the depreciation *Journal Entry* from the previous step using the **Edit/Memorize General Journal** option and schedule it to be automatically entered every month from February through December (11 remaining entries). Name the transaction "Monthly Depreciation." If you see the *Start up* message regarding automatically entering the memorized transactions, select **Later** and *do not* enter the transactions.

4. Create and print a **Balance Sheet** (Standard) as of **01/31/2015**.

5. Create and print a **Journal Report** for *01/01/2015* through *01/31/2015* (The *Journal Report* is in the *Accountant & Taxes* section of the *Reports* menu.) Filter the report to only show *Journal* transactions.

Chapter 14 Horizon Financial Planning Business Scenario

Description of Company – Horizon Financial Planning

After many years with his company, Barry Williams was caught by the entrepreneurial spirit. After carefully saving up enough seed capital and convincing a recently unemployed colleague to join him, he developed a well thought-out business plan and started Horizon Financial Planning (HFP).

Barry saw great opportunities. He lives in a large metropolitan city in Texas, close to several regional colleges and large universities, as well as hundreds of medium to large corporations. He plans to offer financial planning, investment and estate planning seminars, plus related consulting services to individual, corporate and institutional clients. Furthermore, his business plan includes the purchase and promotion of planning kits, along with several popular books and instructional DVDs related to achieving financial stability and success, which he will sell at corporate and collegiate brown-bag lunch seminars. Several times a year he conducts large seminars on financial planning and building wealth. He also offers companion seminars on estate planning and minimizing taxes.

To control his new start-up, he selected QuickBooks software to help manage the business operations while fulfilling fiduciary responsibilities from an accounting, tax and record-keeping perspective. To launch the company, he has hired a full time employee, Shelly James, and a part-time employee, Atasha Williams. He has leased 1,200 square feet of downtown office space.

Using QuickBooks and the sample file (Horizon-12.QBW), you will record initial start-up costs, complete one month of business transactions, including purchases, sales, deposits, accounts receivable, accounts payable, payroll and taxes as well as track inventory and reconcile a bank account. In the end, you will answer several questions about the finances for Horizon Financial Planning.

Company Set Up

> **Restore this File**
>
> This chapter uses Horizon-12.QBW. To open this file, restore the Horizon-12.QBM file to your hard disk.

The company file for this exercise is mostly set up for you, including Accounts, Customers, Vendors, Employees, Payroll, Classes, Items and Fixed Asset Items.

Instructions

1. Restore the Horizon-12.QBM file to Horizon-12.QBW file.

2. Enter the transactions for October 2015 beginning on page 440.

3. Reconcile the bank statement for October for the statement shown on page 448.

4. Prepare the following reports and graphs:

    a) Standard Balance Sheet as of 10/31/2015
    b) Standard Profit and Loss for October 2015
    c) Profit and Loss by Class for October 2015
    d) Statement of Cash Flows for October 2015
    e) Sales by Item Summary for October 2015
    f) Graph – Sales by Month by Customer for October 2015
    g) Inventory Valuation Summary as of 10/31/15

5. Back up your data file to Horizon-12Complete.QBM.

6. Complete the analysis questions on page 447.

Business Transactions

October 2015

Oct	Business Transaction	Transaction Details
1	Deposit owner investment from Barry Williams to provide cash for operations.	Transaction type: **Deposit** Deposit to: **Checking-Texas National Bank** Date: **10/1/2015** Memo: *Deposit Owner's Investment* From Account: **Investments** (Equity Account) Check #401 Class: **Admin/Other** Amount: **$40,000.00**
1	Issued **Purchase Order** to Texas Media and Publications to order Books and DVDs.	Transaction type: **Purchase Order** Vendor: **Texas Media & Publications** Class: **Product Sales** Date: **10/1/2015** PO#: **2015–101** Items: **Books (100 @ $25.00)** **DVDs (100 @ $15.00)** Memo: *Order Books and DVDs* Total purchase order is **$4,000.00**
1	Paid rent plus refundable deposit to Braten Investments.	Transaction type: **Check** Pay to the Order of: **Braten Investments** Check#: **1001** Date: **10/1/15** Memo: *October Rent plus $1,500 Deposit* Expense: **Rent - $1,500.00** Expense: **Refundable Deposits** (Other Current Asset) - **$1500.00** Total Check: **$3,000.00** Class: **Admin/Other**

Oct	Business Transaction	Transaction Details
1	Issued Purchase Order to Office Supply Depot for office equipment.	Transaction type: **Purchase Order** Vendor: **Office Supply Depot** Class: **Admin/Other** Date: **10/1/2015** PO#: **2015–102** Items: **Laptop PC $2,500.00, Copier $1,100.00, Fax Machine $750.00, Projector $2,500.00** Memo: *Purchase office equipment* Total purchase order is **$6,850.00** *Note:* **The items are already added to the Fixed Asset Item list.**
1	Issued Purchase Order to Lone Star Office Supply for office supplies.	Transaction type: **Purchase Order** Vendor: **Lone Star Office Supply** Class: **Admin/Other** Date: **10/1/2015** PO#: **2015–103** Item: **Office Supplies ($360.00)** Memo: *Purchase office supplies* Total purchase order is **$360.00**
4	Received bill from Office Supply Depot.	Transaction type: **Receive Items & Enter Bill** Vendor: **Office Supply Depot** PO #: **2015-102** ⇨ **Items and Class auto fill from PO.** Date: **10/4/2015** Bill Due: **11/3/2015** Amount: **$6,850.00** Terms: **Net 30** Ref No: **68-20** Memo: *Office Equipment*
4	Received bill from Lone Star Office Supply for supply items.	Transaction type: **Receive Items & Enter Bill** Vendor: **Lone Star Office Supply** PO #: **2015-103** ⇨ **Items and Class auto fill from PO.** Date: **10/4/2015** Bill Due: **11/3/2015** Amount: **$360.00** Terms: **Net 30** Ref No: **6433** Memo: *Office Supplies*
4	Issued check to Office Furniture Rentals, Inc. for rental of office furniture for October.	Transaction type: **Check** Pay to the Order of: **Office Furniture Rentals, Inc.** Check#: **1002** Date: **10/4/2015** Memo: *Furniture Rental* Expense: **Equipment Rental ($882.00)** Class: **Admin/Other** Memorize the check, using *Don't Remind me* option.

Oct	Business Transaction	Transaction Details
4	Received bill from Texas Media and Publications.	Transaction type: **Receive Items & Enter Bill** Vendor: **Texas Media & Publications** PO #: **2015-101** ⇨ **Items and Class auto fill from PO.** Date: **10/4/2015** Bill Due: **11/3/2015** Amount: **$4,000.00** Terms: **Net 30** Ref No: **8736** Memo: *Books and DVDs*
8	Enter a Weekly timesheet for Atasha Williams' hours.	Transaction type: **Weekly timesheet** Name: **Atasha Williams** Week of: **Oct 5 to 11, 2015** Payroll Item: **Regular Wages** WC Code: **Leave Blank** Mon: **8 hours** Tues: **4 hours** Wed: **8 hours** Thurs: **4 hours** Fri, Sat, Sun: **0 hours** Billable?: **Not Billable**
14	Received bill from Texas Media & Publications. These non- inventory products were ordered by telephone without issuing a PO.	Transaction type: **Bill** Vendor: **Texas Media and Publications** Date: **10/14/2015** Bill Due: **11/13/2015** Amount: **$1,250.00** Terms: **Net 30** Ref No: **8100** Memo: *Planning Kits* Item: **Planning Kits – 50 Units @ $25** Class: **Product Sales**
15	Enter a Weekly timesheet for Atasha Williams' hours.	Transaction type: **Weekly timesheet** Name: **Atasha Williams** Week of: **October 12 to 18, 2015** Payroll Item: **Regular Wages** Mon: **8 hours** Tues: **4 hours** Wed: **8 hours** Thurs: **4 hours** Fri, Sat, Sun: **0 hours** Billable?: **Not Billable**
17	Pay employees for payroll period 10/01/2015 – 10/15/2015.	Pay Period Ends: **10/15/15** Paycheck Date: **10/16/2015** Bank Account: **Checking – Texas National Bank** Atasha Williams: **48 hours** Shelly James: **Salary** Starting Check Number: **1003**

Oct	Business Transaction	Transaction Details
19	Received bill from Image Contacts, Inc. for printing and mailing of flyers.	Transaction type: **Bill** Vendor: **Image Contacts, Inc.** Date: **10/19/2015** Bill Due: **11/18/2015** Amount: **$1,770.00** Terms: **Net 30** Ref No: **8869** Memo: *Printing and Mailing Flyers* Expense: **Advertising and Promotion** Class: **Consulting/Seminars**
21	Received bill from Rash Productions for consulting fees for an upcoming seminar to be conducted.	Transaction type: **Bill** Vendor: **Rash Productions** Date: **10/21/2015** Bill Due: **11/20/2015** Amount: **$800.00** Terms: **Net 30** Ref No: **8248** Memo: *Consulting Fees* Expense: **Professional Fees** Class: **Consulting/Seminars**
22	Enter a Weekly timesheet for Atasha Williams' hours.	Transaction type: **Weekly timesheet** Name: **Atasha Williams** Week of: **October 19 to 25, 2015** Payroll Item: **Regular Wages** Mon: **8 hours** Tues: **4 hours** Wed: **8 hours** Thurs: **4 hours** Fri, Sat, Sun: **0 hours** Billable?: **Not Billable**

24	Conducted an on-site brown-bag lunch seminar at Computer Manufacturers USA.	Transaction type: **Sales Receipt**
		Customer: **Seminar Sales Summary**
		Class: **Product Sales**
		Date: **10/24/2015**
		Sale No: **2015-101**
		Check No.: Leave Blank
		Payment Method: **Check**
		Items: **Books (22 @ $50.00)**
		       DVDs (16 @ $40.00)
		       Planning Kits (14 @ $100.00)
		Texas sales tax applies.
		Total: **$3,399.05**
		Memo: **Computer Manufacturers USA Seminar Sales**

Oct	Business Transaction	Transaction Details
24	Prepare Invoice to Computer Manufacturers USA for on-site seminar conducted on this date.	Transaction type: **Invoice** Customer: **Computer Manufacturers USA** Class: **Consulting/Seminars** Template: **Horizon Invoice** Date: **10/24/2015** Invoice #: **2015-101** Terms: **Due on Receipt** Items: **Seminar (1 @ $5,000.00)** Total: **$5,000.00** Memo: *Computer Manufacturers USA Onsite Seminar*
25	Received check from Computer Manufacturers.	Transaction type: **Payment** Customer: **Computer Manufacturers USA** Date: **10/25/2015** Amount: **$5,000.00** Check No: **1069** Payment Method: **Check** Memo: *Payment Received – Inv. #2015-101* Apply to: **Invoice #2015-101**
26	Issued check to Education & Medical Fund for contributions.	Transaction type: **Check** Check#: **1005** Date: **10/26/2015** Pay to the Order of: **Education & Medical Fund** Amount: **$500.00** Memo: *Charitable Contribution* Expense: **Charitable Contributions** Class: **Consulting/Seminars**
28	Enter a Sales Receipt to record the product sales at the seminar given at Energy Corporation of Texas	Transaction type: **Sales Receipt** Customer: **Seminar Sales Summary** Class: **Product Sales** Date: **10/28/2015** Sale No: **2015-102** Check No.: **Leave Blank** Payment Method: **Check** Items: **Books (42 @ $50.00)** **DVDs (36 @ $40.00)** **Planning Kits (27 @ $100.00)** Texas sales tax applies. Total: **$6,754.80** Memo: *Energy Corp. of Texas Seminar Sales*
28	Prepare Invoice for Energy Corporation of Texas for on-site seminar conducted on this date.	Transaction type: **Invoice** Customer: **Energy Corporation of Texas** Class: **Consulting/Seminars** Date: **10/28/2015** Invoice #: **2015-102** Terms: **Due on Receipt** Items: **Seminar (1 @ $5,000.00)** Total: **$5,000.00** Memo: *Energy Corp of Texas Onsite Seminar*

Oct	Business Transaction	Transaction Details
28	Received bill from Texas Light & Power.	Transaction type: **Bill** Vendor: **Texas Light & Power** Date: **10/28/2015** Bill Due: **11/27/2015** Amount: **$214.00** Terms: **Net 30** Ref No: **925586** Memo: *Utility Bill* Expense: **Utilities** Class: **Admin/Other**
28	Received bill from South Texas Bell for telephone.	Transaction type: **Bill** Vendor: **South Texas Bell** Date: **10/28/2015** Bill Due: **11/27/2015** Amount: **$129.00** Terms: **Net 30** Ref No: **987543** Memo: *Telephone Bill* Expense: **Telephone Expense:Office Phone** Class: **Admin/Other**
29	Enter a Weekly timesheet for Atasha Williams' hours.	Transaction type: **Weekly timesheet** Name: **Atasha Williams** Week of: **October 26 to November 1, 2015** Payroll Item: **Regular Wages** Mon: **8 hours** Tues: **4 hours** Wed: **8 hours** Thurs: **4 hours** Fri, Sat, Sun: **0 hours** Billable?: **Not Billable**
31	Received check from Energy Corporation of Texas.	Transaction type: **Payment** Customer: **Energy Corporation of Texas** Date: **10/31/2015** Amount: **$5,000.00** Check No: **2021** Payment Method: **Check** Memo: *Payment Received – Inv #2015-102* Apply to: **Invoice #2015-102**
31	Pay employees for time worked during payroll period 10/16/2015 through 10/31/2015.	Pay Period Ends: **10/31/15** Paycheck Date: **11/02/15** Bank Account: **Checking – Texas National Bank** Atasha Williams: **48 hours** Shelly James: **Salary** Starting Check Number: **1006**
31	Deposit funds held in Undeposited Funds account to Texas State Bank.	Transaction type: **Deposit** Deposit to: **Checking-Texas National Bank** Memo: **Deposit** Date: **10/31/2015** Total Deposit Amount: **20,153.85**

Oct	Business Transaction	Transaction Details
31	Pay all bills in a batch sorted by Vendor. Pay from the Checking-Texas National Bank account, and create "To be Printed" checks.	Select **Pay Bills**, and then pay the following bills: Image Contacts, Inc., for $1,770.00 Lone Star Office Supply for $360.00 Office Supply Depot for $6,850.00 Rash Productions, Inc. for $800.00 South Texas Bell for $129.00 Texas Light & Power for $214.00 Texas Media & Publications for $4,000.00 Texas Media & Publications for $1,250.00 Total payments: $15,373.00 Bill Payment Date: **10/31/2015**
31	Print all checks (Chk#1008-1014).	#1008 – Image Contacts, Inc. #1009 – Lone Star Office Supply #1010 – Office Supply Depot #1011 – Rash Productions, Inc. #1012 – South Texas Bell #1013 – Texas Light & Power #1014 – Texas Media & Publications
31	Issued check to Clover Computing for computer repairs.	Transaction type: **Check** Pay to the Order of: **Clover Computing** Check#: **1015** Date: **10/31/2015** Memo: *Computer Repairs* Expense: **Computer & Internet Expenses** Class: **Admin/Other** Total: **$500.00**

Analysis Questions

Use the completed reports and template file to answer the following questions. Write your answer in the space to the left of each question.

1. _____ What is the net income or net loss for October?

2. _____ What is the total Cost of Goods Sold for October?

3. _____ What is the total amount of payroll expenses (gross wages and payroll taxes) for October?

4. _____ What is the gross profit for October?

5. _____ What is the total Product Revenue for October?

6. _____ What is the amount of rent paid for October?

7. _____ What is the Total Income for the Consulting/Seminars Class for October?

8. _____ What is the amount of Fixed Assets on October 31?

9. _____ What is the Total Liabilities on October 31?

10. _____ What is the net cash increase for October?

11. _____ What percentage of October total sales was the Seminar Item?

12. _____ What percentage of October total sales was sold to Energy Corporation of Texas in October?

13. _____ How much does Horizon Financial Planning have in total assets on October 31?

14. _____ How many books does Horizon Financial Planning have on hand as of October 31?

Business Checking Account

Statement Date:		**October 31, 2015**		*Page 1 of 1*

Summary:				**Horizon Financial Planning**

Previous Balance as of 9/30/15		$	-
Total Deposits and Credits: 2	+	$	60,153.85
Total Checks and Debits: 15	-	$	19,755.00
Total Interest Earned	+	$	-
Total Service Charge:1	-	$	10.00
Statement Balance as of 10/31/15:	=	**$**	**40,388.85**

Deposits and Other Credits:

DEPOSITS

Date	Description		Amount
1-Oct	Customer Deposit	$	40,000.00
31-Oct	Customer Deposit	$	20,153.85
	2 Deposits:	**$**	**60,153.85**

INTEREST

Date	Description		Amount
	Interest: $		**-**

Checks and Other Withdrawals:

CHECKS PAID:

Check No.	Date Paid		Amount
1001	1-Oct	$	3,000.00
1002	5-Oct	$	882.00
1005	28-Oct	$	500.00
1008	31-Oct	$	1,770.00
1009	31-Oct	$	360.00
1010	31-Oct	$	6,850.00
1011	31-Oct	$	800.00
1012	31-Oct	$	129.00
1013	31-Oct	$	214.00
1014	31-Oct	$	5,250.00
	15 Checks Paid:	**$**	**19,755.00**

OTHER WITHDRAWALS/PAYMENTS

Date	Description		Amount
0 Other Withdrawals/Payments: $			**-**

SERVICE CHARGES

Date	Description		Amount
31-Oct	Service Charge	$	10.00
	1 Service Charge: $		**10.00**

Figure 14-1 October Bank Statement

Note:
Paychecks are calculated using the tax tables loaded on your computer. In this scenario, we have intentionally not included the paychecks in these bank statements to make the reconciliation consistent for readers using different tax tables.

Index

Intuit Education Program

Every student that graduates in business or accounting will be expected to be proficient in accounting and business management software. We believe a student with in-depth knowledge of QuickBooks, the #1 small business accounting software, will have a significant edge entering the world of accounting. The Intuit Education Program is committed to providing educators and students with the tools and resources needed to integrate QuickBooks into the classroom.

*QuickBooks Software Site Licenses**

QuickBooks software is available for classroom use conveniently and economically via an education site license in 10, 25, and 50 computer packs. To order, call 1-866-570-3843.

*QuickBooks 2012 Academic Version***

QuickBooks instructors have told us that they felt their students could learn QuickBooks more efficiently if they could use it outside the classroom. To facilitate this, we're making it possible for qualifying students to purchase QuickBooks for their individual academic use at a special discounted price. If ordered, the student will receive a full working copy of QuickBooks Accountant software. This software enables the student to work in QuickBooks Pro, Premier or Accountant versions using the toggle feature.

Your school bookstore can order QuickBooks through their preferred reseller or by calling 1-866-570-3843.

(Minimum purchase of four copies and proof of academic status required.)

* Qualifying for QuickBooks 2012 Academic Site License:

- Accredited public or private universities or colleges (including community, junior or vocational colleges) that grant degrees requiring not less than the equivalent of two (2) years of full-time study
- Administrative Offices or Boards of Education of Educational Institutions or Government schools located in United States territories
- Institutions which fit the above criteria must use the software for instructional purposes only.

** Qualifying for QuickBooks 2012 Academic version:

- Full or part time students enrolled at higher education institutions defined as accredited public or private universities or colleges (including community, junior or vocational colleges) that grant degrees requiring not less than the equivalent of two (2) years of full-time study.
- Full or part time faculty and staff employed by accredited K-12 and higher education institutions

PN 502239